Political Women and American Democracy

What do we know about women, politics, and democracy in the United States? The past thirty years have witnessed a dramatic increase in women's participation in American politics and an explosion of research on women, and the transformations effected by them, during the same period. *Political Women and American Democracy* provides a critical synthesis of scholarly research by leading experts in the field. The collected chapters examine women as citizens, voters, participants, movement activists, partisans, candidates, and legislators. They provide frameworks for understanding and organizing existing scholarship; focus on theoretical, methodological, and empirical debates; and map out productive directions for future research. As the only book to focus specifically on women and gender in U.S. politics, *Political Women and American Democracy* will be an invaluable resource for scholars and students studying and conducting women and politics research.

Christina Wolbrecht is Associate Professor in the Department of Political Science and Director of the Program in American Democracy at the University of Notre Dame. Her book *The Politics of Women's Rights: Parties, Positions, and Change* (2000) was recipient of the 2001 Leon Epstein Outstanding Book Award from the American Political Science Association (Political Organizations and Parties Section). She has published articles in many journals, including the *American Journal of Political Science* and the *Journal of Politics*.

Karen Beckwith is Flora Stone Mather Professor of Political Science at Case Western Reserve University. She teaches mass politics, political parties and political movements, and women and politics; her research focuses on comparative women, gender, and politics. She is the founding editor, with Lisa Baldez, of *Politics & Gender*. Her books include *Women's Movements Facing the Reconfigured State* (2003; with Lee Ann Banaszak and Dieter Rucht) and *American Women and Political Participation* (1986). Her work on women's movements and gender has been published in the *European Journal of Political Research*, *Politics & Society*, *Signs*, and *West European Politics*, among other journals. She is a former president of the American Political Science Association's Women and Politics Research Section.

Lisa Baldez is Associate Professor in the Government and Latin American, Latino, and Caribbean Studies departments at Dartmouth College. She is the founding editor, with Karen Beckwith, of *Politics & Gender*. She is the author of *Why Women Protest: Women's Movements in Chile* (2002) and numerous journal articles. She is currently writing a book about gender quotas in Latin America.

Political Women and American Democracy

Edited by

CHRISTINA WOLBRECHT
University of Notre Dame

KAREN BECKWITH
Case Western Reserve University

LISA BALDEZ
Dartmouth College

CAMBRIDGE
UNIVERSITY PRESS

CAMBRIDGE UNIVERSITY PRESS
Cambridge, New York, Melbourne, Madrid, Cape Town, Singapore, São Paulo, Delhi

Cambridge University Press
32 Avenue of the Americas, New York, NY 10013-2473, USA

www.cambridge.org
Information on this title: www.cambridge.org/9780521713849

First published 2008

Printed in the United States of America

A catalog record for this publication is available from the British Library.

Library of Congress Cataloging in Publication Data
Wolbrecht, Christina.
Political women and American democracy / Christina Wolbrecht, Karen
Beckwith, Lisa Baldez.
    p. cm.
Includes bibliographical references and index.
ISBN 978-0-521-88623-9 (hardback) – ISBN 978-0-521-71384-9 (pbk)
1. Women in politics – United States. I. Beckwith, Karen, 1950– II. Baldez, Lisa.
III. Title.
HQ11236.5.U6W628   2008
320.082'0973 – dc22   2007035434

ISBN   978-0-521-88623-9 hardback
ISBN   978-0-521-71384-9 paperback

For Our Children
Ella and Jane Doppke
Fitz Beckwith Collings and Piper Beckwith-Collings
Joe and Sam Carey

Contents

Preface   *page* ix

List of Contributors   xi

1. Introduction: What We Saw at the Revolution: Women in
   American Politics and Political Science   1
   Christina Wolbrecht

2. Gender as a Category of Analysis in American Political
   Development   12
   Gretchen Ritter

3. Gender, Public Opinion, and Political Reasoning   31
   Leonie Huddy, Erin Cassese, and Mary-Kate Lizotte

4. Gender in the Aggregate, Gender in the Individual, Gender
   and Political Action   50
   Nancy Burns

5. What Revolution? Incorporating Intersectionality in Women
   and Politics   64
   Jane Junn and Nadia Brown

6. Women's Movements and Women in Movements: Influencing
   American Democracy from the "Outside"?   79
   Lee Ann Banaszak

7. Representation by Gender and Parties   96
   Kira Sanbonmatsu

8. Women as Candidates in American Politics: The Continuing
   Impact of Sex and Gender   110
   Kathleen Dolan

9. Women as Officeholders: Linking Descriptive and Substantive
   Representation   128
   Beth Reingold

10. Theorizing Women's Representation in the United States   148
    Suzanne Dovi
11. Political Women in Comparative Democracies: A Primer for
    Americanists   167
    Lisa Baldez
12. Conclusion: Between Participation and Representation:
    Political Women and Democracy in the United States   181
    Karen Beckwith

References   199
Index   251

Preface

What do we know about women, politics, and democracy in the United States? The past thirty years have witnessed an explosion of research on women in American politics alongside the dramatic increase in women's political participation and the transformations that women have effected in the American political system during this same period. As women take on new roles and face changing political (and social and economic) climates, their experiences and contributions to American democracy continue to evolve. Our scholarship has evolved as well. Understanding the contributions and experiences of half of the population provides fundamental insight into how American democracy works. Thus each chapter in this volume asks: What does existing research tell us about political women in the United States, and what do we need to understand better? What does and should our scholarship reveal about the opportunities and challenges women face as political actors in the American political system? What do we know, and what more do we need to know, about how American democracy is affected by the presence – and absence – of political women? Overall, this volume provides a critical synthesis of more than three decades of scholarly literature on women, gender, and American politics within political science.

What began as an "ill-formed idea" (the subject heading of the October 2004 e-mail in which Wolbrecht first proposed the idea of a conference to Beckwith and Baldez) has resulted in a collection of critical essays that we hope will make a major contribution to scholarship on political women in American politics. We envision this book as contributing to the production of knowledge in several ways: as a central text in advanced undergraduate and graduate courses on women, gender, and American politics; as a useful, "scope of the field" synthesis of existing studies for scholars conducting research in this field; and as a source of inspiration for future projects for scholars at all levels.

In the spring of 2005, we three editors invited some of the most interesting and expert scholars in the field to write essays that critically engaged the state of the discipline on a particular aspect of political women in American politics and that mapped out their vision for where this research might most productively move in the future. The authors first presented their chapters at a lively and productive three-day conference, "Political Women and American Democracy," which was held on the campus of the University of Notre Dame, May 25–27, 2006. The conference was sponsored by Notre Dame's Program in American Democracy (http://americandemocracy.nd.edu) and supported by a major grant from the Annenberg Foundation. We are most grateful. Lisa Baldez, Kim Fridkin, Jane Junn, Jane Mansbridge, Eileen McDonagh, Suzanne Mettler, and Susan Welch graciously served as discussants at the conference; their insights contributed significantly to the quality of the essays contained in this volume.

A number of people helped us shepherd the essays in this volume from conference papers to polished chapters. We are particularly grateful to Alex Holzman and Ed Parsons. The anonymous reviewers gave our collection a careful and expert reading, which greatly improved the final product. Anne Baker provided exemplary editorial assistance. Most of all, we thank the contributors, whose responses to our invitation far exceeded our expectations, and whose professionalism, friendship, and good humor have made this process a pleasure. Our own collaboration as editors has been characterized by fierce but friendly intellectual debate, constant communication on all matters large and small (some even related to this project), and lots of laughter. We thank each other as well.

In the course of our work and our editorial conversations, we came across abundant evidence that the experiences of both political women and political scientists are gendered in regard to children. Our own children confronted several different kinds of challenges while we were working on this book: mastering how to walk and talk, learning to speak Spanish, getting into college, and starting a business (see www.fitzfiber.com!). At the same time, they dealt with mothers who traveled to meetings, talked endlessly on the phone while wearing headsets, and spent hours at the computer to meet conference and press deadlines. Thus it is only right and appropriate that we dedicate this book to our children: Karen's Fitz and Piper, Lisa's Joe and Sam, and Christina's Ella and Jane, who arrived along with the page proofs.

Christina Wolbrecht
South Bend, Indiana

Karen Beckwith
Hudson, Ohio

Lisa Baldez
Hanover, New Hampshire

30 June 2007

List of Contributors

EDITORS

Christina Wolbrecht (Associate Professor of Political Science and Director of the Program in American Democracy, University of Notre Dame) is the author of *The Politics of Women's Rights: Parties, Positions, and Change* (2000), which received the 2001 Leon Epstein Outstanding Book Award from the American Political Science Association (Political Organizations and Parties Section). She has published articles in many journals, including the *American Journal of Political Science* and the *Journal of Politics*.

Karen Beckwith (Flora Stone Mather Professor of Political Science, Case Western Reserve University) teaches mass politics, political parties and political movements, and women and politics; her research focuses on comparative women, gender, and politics. She is the founding editor, with Lisa Baldez, of *Politics & Gender*. Her books include *Women's Movements Facing the Reconfigured State* (2003; with Lee Ann Banaszak and Dieter Rucht) and *American Women and Political Participation* (1986). Her work on women's movements and gender has been published in the *European Journal of Political Research*, *Politics & Society*, *Signs*, and *West European Politics*, among other journals. She is a former president of the American Political Science Association's Women and Politics Research Section.

Lisa Baldez (Associate Professor of Government and Latin American, Latino, and Caribbean Studies, Dartmouth College) is the founding editor, with Karen Beckwith, of *Politics & Gender*. She is the author of *Why Women Protest: Women's Movements in Chile* (2002) and numerous journal articles. She is currently writing a book about gender quotas in Latin America.

AUTHORS

Lee Ann Banaszak (Associate Professor of Political Science and Women's Studies, Pennsylvania State University) writes on comparative women's movements and the determinants of feminist attitudes among the mass public in the United States and Europe. She is the author of *Why Movements Succeed or Fail: Opportunity, Culture and the Struggle for Woman Suffrage* (1996) and editor of two books, including *Women's Movements Facing the Reconfigured State* with Karen Beckwith and Dieter Rucht (2003). Her current research examines movement activists within government and their effect on the U.S. women's movement.

Nadia Brown (Ph.D. candidate, Department of Political Science, Rutgers University) is writing a dissertation on women and politics, specializing in African American political women.

Nancy Burns's (Warren E. Miller Professor of Political Science, University of Michigan) current work focuses on gender, race, public opinion, and political action and on the relationship between states and cities. Her publications include *The Formation of American Local Governments* (1994) and *The Private Roots of Public Action* (2001). Burns served as Principal Investigator of the National Election Studies from 1999 to 2005. She currently serves as Director of the Center for Political Studies at the University of Michigan. Burns is a Fellow of the American Academy of Arts and Sciences.

Erin Cassese's (Assistant Professor of Political Science, West Virginia University) research interests lie in American politics and political psychology, with an emphasis on political identity, gender identity, and the culture wars. Cassese has collaborated on chapters in volumes such as *Voting the Gender Gap* and *The Affect Effect: Dynamics of Emotion in Political Thinking and Behavior.*

Kathleen Dolan's (Professor of Political Science, University of Wisconsin, Milwaukee) primary research and teaching interests are in the areas of elections, public opinion, and gender politics. She is the author of *Voting for Women: How the Public Evaluates Women Candidates* (2004), as well as numerous book chapters and articles in the *American Journal of Political Science*, *Political Research Quarterly*, and *Political Psychology*, among others. Dolan is currently the coeditor (with Aili Mari Tripp) of *Politics & Gender.*

Suzanne Dovi's (Associate Professor of Political Science and Philosophy, University of Arizona) research interests include democratic theory, representation (especially the representation of historically disadvantaged groups), feminist theory, and normative concepts like hypocrisy and despair. Her work has appeared in the *American Political Science Review*, *Constellations*, *Journal of Politics*, and *Polity*. Her book, *The Good Representative*, has recently been published by Blackwell.

Leonie Huddy (Professor of Political Science and Director of the Center for Survey Research, Stony Brook University) has written extensively on the political psychology of intergroup relations, with a special emphasis on gender, race, and ethnic relations. She is a coauthor of the *Oxford Handbook of Political Psychology*, which received the APSA's Robert Lane Award, and current coeditor of the journal *Political Psychology*. She is the author of numerous scholarly book chapters and articles in journals such as the *American Journal of Political Science, Journal of Politics, Public Opinion Quarterly,* and *Political Psychology,* and her recent work has been funded by the National Science Foundation and the Russell Sage Foundation. Her current research includes work on emotional reactions to war and terrorism and the psychological underpinnings of white racial policy views.

Jane Junn's (Associate Professor of Political Science, Rutgers University) primary interests are political participation and elections in the United States, political behavior and attitudes among American minorities and immigrants, theories of democracy, survey research, and social science methodology. Her research has been supported by the Russell Sage Foundation, the Center for Information and Research on Civil Learning and Engagement (CIRCLE), the National Science Foundation, the Social Science Research Council, the Spencer Foundation, and the Educational Testing Service. She is the author of *New Race Politics: Understanding Minority and Immigrant Politics* (edited with Kerry Haynie, 2008); *Education and Democratic Citizenship in America* (with Norman Nie and Ken Stehlik-Barry, 1996), which won the Woodrow Wilson Foundation Book Award from the American Political Science Association; and *Civic Education: What Makes Students Learn* (with Richard Niemi, 1998), along with articles and chapters on political participation. She is currently at work on a book on race and political participation in the United States, with emphasis on the dynamics of immigration and racial diversity.

Mary-Kate Lizotte's (Ph.D. candidate, Department of Political Science, Stony Brook University) major field of study is political psychology with specific research interests in gender, emotion, and public opinion. Her dissertation addresses the emotional nature of gender differences in support of U.S. foreign policy.

Beth Reingold's (Associate Professor of Political Science and Women's Studies, Emory University) principal research interest is the impact of women, gender, and feminism in American politics. Her book, *Representing Women: Sex, Gender, and Legislative Behavior in Arizona and California* (2000), tests, and often challenges, widespread assumptions that women in public office will "make a difference" for women, as women. She has also written on feminist consciousness and identity politics in such journals as the *Journal of Politics* and *Political Research Quarterly.* Her current collaborative work, supported by the National Science Foundation, examines the impact of racial, ethnic, and gender diversity in the American state legislatures.

Gretchen Ritter (Professor of Government, University of Texas at Austin) specializes in studies of American politics and gender politics from a historical and theoretical perspective. She has published articles, reviews, and essays in numerous peer-reviewed journals in law, political science, sociology, and women studies and is the author of *Goldbugs and Greenbacks: The Antimonopoly Tradition and the Politics of Finance in America* (1997) and of *The Constitution as Social Design: Gender and Civic Membership in the American Constitutional Order* (2006). She is Director of the Center for Women's and Gender Studies at the University of Texas.

Kira Sanbonmatsu (Associate Professor of Political Science and Senior Scholar at the Center for American Women and Politics [CAWP], the Eagleton Institute of Politics at Rutgers University) is the author of *Where Women Run: Gender and Party in the American States* (2006) and *Democrats, Republicans, and the Politics of Women's Place* (2002). Her articles have appeared in such journals as the *American Journal of Political Science*, *Politics & Gender*, and *Party Politics*. Her research interests include gender, race/ethnicity, parties, public opinion, and state politics.

Political Women and American Democracy

Introduction: What We Saw at the Revolution

Women in American Politics and Political Science

Christina Wolbrecht

It is difficult now to imagine: in 1974, when Jeane Kirkpatrick and the Center for American Women and Politics (CAWP) conducted their groundbreaking research on female state legislators, Kirkpatrick (1974, 3) could write: "Half a century after the ratification of the nineteenth amendment, no woman has been nominated to be president or vice president, no woman has served on the Supreme Court. Today, there is no woman in the cabinet, no woman in the Senate, no woman serving as governor of a major state, no woman mayor of a major city, no woman in the top leadership of either major party."

There were a few female political elites in 1974, but only a very few: women comprised about 6 percent of all state legislators (Kirkpatrick 1974) and less than 4 percent of members of the House of Representatives (CAWP 2006). At the mass level, however, the news was more promising: the gender gap in turnout was just 2 percentage points in men's favor in 1972, almost all of which was attributed to older women (Wolfinger and Rosenstone 1980).

Clearly, great strides have been made in the past thirty-some years. In 2007, women hold sixteen percent of seats in both the House and the Senate, and almost a quarter of state legislative seats. U.S. Representative Nancy Pelosi (D-CA) was recently elected madame speaker of the House. Women serve as governors of nine states and are mayors of seven of the fifty largest U.S. cities (CAWP 2007a). Five women currently serve in cabinet-level positions in President George W. Bush's administration, and an additional thirty women – including Kirkpatrick herself! – have held cabinet-level positions since Kirkpatrick wrote her indictment (CAWP 2007b).[1] Indeed, in recent years, two women, including a woman of color, have served as secretary of state, one of the most important and prominent cabinet positions. Sandra

With apologies – and all due credit – to former Reagan speechwriter Peggy Noonan, author of *What I Saw at the Revolution: A Political Life in the Reagan Era* (Random House, 2003), which describes a different (and perhaps, counter) revolution.

Day O'Connor and Ruth Bader Ginsburg sit (or, until recently, were sit-
ting) on the Supreme Court. We have witnessed just one major party vice-
presidential nominee (Geraldine Ferraro in 1984) and none for president,
but at this writing a woman (Hillary Clinton, of course) is a leading con-
tender for the top of a major-party ticket in 2008. Women have been more
likely than men to register and to turn out to vote since the 1980 presidential
election (MacManus 2006).

Kirkpatrick's research was inspired in part by the revolution in gender
norms, expectations, and practices underway by the early 1970s. Among
many other things, the second wave of the women's movement encouraged and facilitated the growing number of women entering politics at both
the mass and elite levels. This was, it is important to emphasize, truly a
revolution: so absurd was the concept of political women at the time of the
nation's founding that most states did not bother formally to disenfranchise
women but simply assumed that only men (albeit, white, propertied men)
would vote (DuBois 1998). Women acted in important political ways before
their enfranchisement in 1920, most notably through various social movements (see Banaszak, this volume), and often by redefining (and benefiting
from redefinitions of) what was understood as political in the process (Baker
1984; Clemens 1997; Cott 1990). Yet the enactment of women's suffrage
required a more-than-seventy-year struggle that achieved equal citizenship
but surely not equal participation or power. Although the past thirty years
have not produced full political equality for women either, they certainly
have been characterized by great strides and fundamental changes to the
expectations and experiences of women as political actors.

Due in large part to the work of female political scientists,[2] political
science has responded to this changing political reality with a significant
increase in scholarly attention to women as political actors, or what we call
in this volume "political women." Women have never been completely absent
from political science; related articles can be found in the flagship *American Political Science Review* (*APSR*) from its first decade, mostly regarding
women's suffrage and social welfare policies directed at women.[3] Yet clearly,
women and gender were not central concerns as the discipline grew and
expanded in the postwar years; from 1926 to 1971, the *APSR* published just
one article related to women or gender, an examination of women in national
party organizations that appeared in 1944. Women gained more prominence
in the *APSR* after 1971, with three articles in the 1970s, eight in the 1980s,
and a whopping nineteen articles in the 1990s, with another fourteen articles appearing through May 2007, including an article on the gender politics
of political science in the centennial issue (Tolleson-Rinehart and Carroll
2006).[4] Other journals have been characterized by similar trends, and often
higher numbers (Kelly and Fisher 1993). In book publishing, Kirkpatrick's
Political Women (1974) was quickly followed by a number of important
books, such as Jo Freeman's *The Politics of Women's Liberation* (1975)

and Irene Diamond's *Sex Roles in the Statehouse* (1977).[5] The trickle soon became a flood, with important works appearing in the 1980s and beyond (e.g., Baxter and Lansing 1983; Carroll 1985; Klein 1984; Mansbridge 1986, to name just a few). By the early 1990s, as many as three-quarters of all political science departments offered regular women and politics courses (Committee on the Status of Women in the Profession 2001).

Although much has changed, both in politics and in political science, the fact that progress is likely less impressive than feminist activists and scholars in 1974 hoped it would be provides important puzzles for political scientists. Although the presence of women in political office has grown, the representation of women still falls far below their 50-plus percent of the population. Women who run for office are as likely as men to win, but women remain far less likely to put themselves forward as candidates (Dolan, this volume). More women serve in legislatures, but their presence has not always been matched by a concomitant increase in power, with parties, committees, and caucuses continuing to constrain and shape women's influence (Reingold, this volume). Women now exceed men in turnout but still lag behind in terms of other forms of political participation, including donating to political campaigns and contacting a public official (Burns, this volume). Clearly, sex and gender still matter in important and consequential ways for political power and influence in the United States.

The aim of this collection, then, is to answer two questions. First, what did we – that is, political scientists – see at the revolution? In other words, what have we learned about the experiences, opportunities, constraints, and contributions of women in various political roles in the wake of the second wave and the transformation of gender roles and opportunities in the United States? And how has the experience and study of political women challenged our understandings of politics and political science? Second, where do we go from here? The quality and quantity of our scholarship on women and politics has grown by leaps and bounds, and yet there is clearly still so much work to do.

To this end, organizers Karen Beckwith, Lisa Baldez, and I asked a number of the most interesting and authoritative scholars in the subfield to provide a critical synthesis of the state of the discipline with regard to political women and American democracy some thirty years after the publication of Kirkpatrick's groundbreaking work. It is worth emphasizing at the start that, for reasons of space and time, we were unable to address a number of issues and kinds of political women, even limiting ourselves (largely) to the American case. Some categories of female political actors, such as those in the executive and judicial branches, are not examined here, although their growing numbers make this an exciting and evolving area of research. More generally, our focus on political women per se means that these essays consider just a slice of the broad, diverse, and expanding subfield focused on women and gender in political science. It is, indeed, one sign of how far women in politics and political science have come in the past thirty years that a volume of this size can only claim to represent a small portion of the subfield.[6]

Nonetheless, the essays in this volume address many of the most productive areas of research on American political women, including work on women as citizens, voters, participants, movement activists, partisans, candidates, and legislators. Other essays place our understanding of those roles into the context of the political theory of representation, American political development, intersectionality, and comparative politics. The contributors provide unique and important insight into both what we know and what we still need to know about how women and gender function in the American political system. The authors of these chapters do not simply recount the findings of the vast literature that has grown up in the past three-plus decades; rather, they provide frameworks for understanding and organizing that scholarship; focus attention on critical theoretical, methodological, and empirical debates; and point us all in valuable and important directions for the future of this subfield. Karen Beckwith's conclusion to the volume takes up the question of future directions directly. Here I introduce this collection by focusing on a few central themes that emerge from a review of the past thirty years of scholarship.

As the word "revolution" suggests, the concept of women as political actors is a fundamentally radical idea. For much of this nation's (and indeed, human) history, politics was – and in many ways still is – synonymous with man. For women to be recognized, permitted, and even welcomed as political actors represents a reordering of politics and a reconceptualizing of what it means to be a woman and a citizen (see Ritter, this volume). Much of this collection considers what we know and how we understand the experiences and contributions of women in traditional political roles, such as citizen, voter, candidate, and officeholder. Yet a common theme that emerges from many of the chapters is that throughout U.S. history, a signal contribution of women has been to redefine the very nature and content of politics (see Sapiro 1991a). This occurs in myriad ways: by bringing issues long considered irrelevant or unimportant to the political agenda. By creating new modes of political action and change through social movements, interest organizations, and civic engagement. By entering into traditional politics in nontraditional ways, through supposedly nonpolitical organizations, volunteer activities, and personal experience. By working within institutions to bring about gender-related change to both public policy and the political institutions themselves. To examine political women, then, requires political scientists to look beyond traditional locales, activities, and issues. In doing so, our understanding of how and why people enter active political life, how citizens shape political outcomes, and how power and influence are exercised (to name just a few subjects) becomes richer, deeper, and more complete.

It also is clear from this literature that politics is different when women are political actors. Female citizens, voters, activists, candidates, and office-holders differ from their male counterparts in important and consequential ways, as each of these chapters details. At the same time, our contributors are appropriately judicious in their claims. As Kathleen Dolan points out in her chapter, for example, female candidates are now substantially similar to men in their ability to raise money, secure nominations, and attract votes. Female legislators behave differently, on average, from male legislators, but the differences, as Beth Reingold reminds us, are not "wide chasms." Other factors, party in particular, are often far more determinative of legislative behavior. The same factors that encourage participation among men have a similar effect on women, and men and women tend to participate in similar ways (see Burns, this volume). The similarity of female and male political actors helps put to rest the long- and widely held assumption that women are inherently apolitical and incapable of effective political action. The persistent lesser influence and power of women thus draws our attention not to deficiencies of women as political actors but to the constraints of the social, economic, and political structures in which they act (see Baldez, this volume; Hawkesworth 2005).

What this means is that although we asked our authors to write about political women, doing so necessarily required them, as it does all students of women and politics, to write about gender. That is, in most cases, our contributors were invited to analyze women per se – what we know and want to know about how women perform and experience various political roles. For the most part, then, our authors were being asked to write about "sex as a political variable" (Seltzer, Newman, and Leighton 1997). Yet understanding the experience and actions of women in politics (and elsewhere) always requires a recognition of the pervasiveness of gender. Although the two terms are often conflated, scholars across the disciplines have long argued and observed that sex and gender are not synonymous. Sex is conventionally treated as a dichotomous variable (Beckwith 2007b), distinguishing men and women on the basis of biological traits. Gender, on the other hand, traditionally has been taken to signify the social meaning given to sexual difference.[7] Rather than dichotomous, gender is multidimensional, specific to time and context, relational, hierarchical, normative, descriptive, and, above all, complex (see Junn and Brown, this volume, on the multidimensionality and variation of gender). Gender is not a stagnant characteristic but actively and continually reproduced, reinforced, and redefined (Scott 1986). Gender attends not only to individuals but to processes, institutions, ideologies, and norms (to name but a few) as well (see, e.g., Acker 1992; Beckwith 2005, 2007; Duerst-Lahti and Kelly 1995a; Hawkesworth 2005; Scott 1986). Much of our existing political science research focuses on sex difference (in part because we are better at measuring sex than gender) but almost always with the (sometimes unstated) goal of understanding gender difference. That is, we are interested in differences between men and women because we recognize and want to understand the consequences of the social construction of gender (see, e.g., Reingold 2000).[8]

Given the close association between socially constructed masculine ideals and dominant constructions of politics and power (see Baker 1984; Brown 1988; Pateman 1994), it should not be surprising that any discussion of political women quickly entails issues of gender. Virtually all of our authors assert that a better understanding of women as political actors requires more attention to the nature, form, and consequences of the gendered expectations, institutions, and processes that shape, constrain, and define the ways in which women perform political roles. This research program is already under way, as exemplified by the important recent work of Joan Acker (1992), Debra Dodson (2006), Georgia Duerst-Lahti and Rita Mae Kelly (1995b), Mary Hawkesworth (2003), and Sally Kenney (1996), among others. Yet clearly we are at the frontier of this research program, and more work should follow the model these authors provide.

For example, both women and men enter the political arena infused with gender identities that shape their political socialization, expectations about political roles, and locations in politically relevant social and economic structures. The different propensity for men and women to work outside of the home, and the different occupational roles and status of men and women who do work, have important consequences for power within families and for the exercise of influence by men and women in the political sphere (see Burns, this volume). Attitudinal and partisan gender gaps have been explained in part by women's greater economic insecurity (a function of, among other things, a gendered division of labor in the workplace and home) and resultant sympathy for those who find themselves in need of a government safety net (see Huddy, Cassese, and Lizotte, this volume). Recent research highlights how unequal family responsibilities and persistent differences in political socialization continue to inhibit women from pursuing elective office (see Dolan, this volume). As Kirkpatrick observed some thirty years ago, "If definitions of femininity, self-conceptions, family and economic role distributions and politics are part of a single social fabric, then major changes in one entail parallel changes in others" (1974, 243).

Women thus enter politics from gendered contexts, and as Gretchen Ritter argues persuasively (this volume), the political system they enter is itself formed by deeply rooted ideas and practices pertaining to gender. For example, many public policies are premised in some way on assumptions about appropriate gender roles, whether it be masculinity with regard to the U.S. military (Katzenstein 1998), motherhood and social welfare policy (Skocpol 1992), or family roles within tax policy (Strach 2007). Women's exclusion from theoretically sex-neutral policies such as the G.I. Bill can have repercussions beyond the denial of specific benefits as these policies encourage and facilitate civic engagement among (mostly male) beneficiaries but not among those excluded from the policy because of their sex (see Mettler 2005).[9] Female legislators seeking to address the needs of women have to do so within an existing policy context shaped by previous assumptions about gender roles and capacities. The liberal democratic ideals on which our political system is premised are infused with expectations about political identity that are inherently masculine. We cannot assume political women experience a level or gender-neutral playing field but must attend to the ways in which political institutions themselves shape and constrain behavior in gendered ways (see, e.g., Acker 1992; Hale and Kelly 1989; Hawkesworth 2003; Stivers 1992). Indeed, we choose to start the collection with Ritter's chapter, which unlike the others, is centrally about gender in the U.S. political system rather than about women per se, in order to provide an appropriate framework for the chapters on women in American politics that follow.

A careful review of the literature on women and politics also reveals that how sex and gender matter has changed over the past thirty years. The experience of female candidates exemplifies this (see Dolan, this volume). Early scholarship emphasized the reluctance of voters to support female candidates, the tendency of parties to nominate women only as "sacrificial lambs," and the bias of interest groups against providing financial support to female candidates who they assumed were unlikely to win. Since the early 1990s, however, the story has been quite different, as summed up by the National Women's Political Caucus' oft-cited 1994 report that concluded "when women run, women win" (Newman 1994). Voters no longer discriminate against women and, in some cases, may prefer them. Parties not only nominate but provide resources and training to female candidates. Interest groups fund women at the same rate as they fund men. Yet the proportion of women serving in elected office remains rather stagnant and far below 50 percent. The changing reality has encouraged political scientists to refocus their attention to issues of candidate mobilization, media effects, and other ways in which gender continues to shape the electoral process. Moreover, the path of change has not always been unidirectional; students of women in the legislature note the important consequences of the Republican House takeover in 1994, most notably the dismantling of the Congressional Caucus for Women's Issues (see Reingold's chapter, this volume). As this example suggests, sex and gender continue to be viewed as a threat to other bases of political solidarity (see Sanbonmatsu, this volume, for a detailed discussion), and women's influence in the political sphere remains fragile and contingent.

As the experiences of women in politics have evolved, so has our scholarship. Many critics have commented on the degree to which political science has maintained dominant approaches, concepts, and methodologies, and simply added sex as a variable or women as a subject (e.g., Bourque and Grossholtz 1974; Ritter and Mellow 2000; Sapiro 1991a). Recent scholarship is more likely to take a more nuanced approach, although all of the authors in this collection call for more research in this vein. At the same time, as Nancy Burns points out in her chapter, we should not dismiss all early scholarship, some of which examined gender with a serious and nuanced eye. In particular, Burns points to some of the classic work on American voting that did not, as is common, assume male behavior is the norm against which female behavior should be judged. This observation highlights what Suzanne Dovi (this volume) calls the "standards problem" – "the difficulty of identifying a proper benchmark for assessing women's political performance in democracies." In a classic example, women have long been described as inadequate and disengaged because their reported political efficacy lags behind that of men. Susan Bourque and Jean Grossholtz (1974) reinterpret these data: given the considerable constraints on the impact of any one citizen on the complex American political process, women may have a more "perceptive assessment" of their place in the political system, whereas men may be expressing "irrationally high rates of efficacy" (231). As this example underscores, scholars of women and politics continue to challenge our assumptions about what we expect from political actors and how we define political engagement.

Nancy Burns also points out the ways in which earlier scholarship used analysis of gender differences to question our theories of politics and political behavior more generally. This, too, has been an important contribution of the literature on women and politics. For example, Kira Sanbonmatsu (this volume) notes that examining descriptive representation challenges liberal theories of republican government by highlighting the degree to which group identity is politically relevant and contesting the assumption that any legislator, regardless of personal characteristics or experiences, can fully represent the interests of every constituent, provided she or he is tied to the electorate through election. In other words, what does the overwhelming evidence that female legislators are more supportive of and active for women's interests (see both Dovi and Reingold, this volume) mean for our understanding of the nature of representation in general? Similar questions arise in other subfields. What do the experiences of female candidates (see Dolan, this volume) tell us about our (gendered) expectations for political leadership? What do women's movements (Banaszak, this volume) teach us about the capacity for effective political influence from the "outside"? What do the specific experiences of women of color (see Junn and Brown, this volume) help us understand about how race and sex/gender shape political engagement in the United States?

As the last example suggests, the study of women and politics has also benefited from, and contributed to, our understanding of other politically less powerful groups. Women face many of the same but also many different constraints as other traditionally underrepresented groups. The most common comparison, of course, is to African Americans, and indeed, the movements for greater racial and gender equality have been interlinked throughout U.S.

history. Scholarship has similarly adopted many concepts and hypotheses from the study of racial minorities in American politics. As useful as those comparisons and adoptions have been, a focus on women also highlights the important ways in which sex and gender are indeed different from other politically relevant divisions. For women, for example, the search for a shared, segregated space in which consciousness and resources can be created has been a crucial challenge for feminist mobilization, whereas segregation was a central problem, and yet also a source of strength and solidarity, for civil rights activists (see Burns, this volume, for a discussion).

At the same time, students of women and politics must avoid the all-too-common assumption that the experiences of one group of women are indicative of the experiences of all women. In particular, we should not conflate "women" with "African American women," "Latinas," and so on. To their credit, many scholars have been sensitive to the intersectionality of race and sex, but as many of the contributors to this volume suggest (see especially the Junn and Brown chapter), much more needs to be done. The growing numbers of African American, Latina, and other minority women in positions of political leadership offer exciting opportunities to expand and deepen our understanding of how race and sex/gender operate in American politics. Similarly, the study of women and politics often has focused on liberal women (feminist activists) and liberal definitions of women's issues (e.g., abortion rights). As Lee Ann Banaszak (this volume) points out, conservative women organize and participate in highly gendered ways and raise issues that are clearly gendered. We need to do more to ensure that our understanding of political women is attentive to the experiences and contributions of all women, regardless of race, ideology, or other characteristics. Moreover, we must avoid the assumption that the experiences of women in the United States are indicative of the experiences of women outside this country, or that women in the United States enjoy a higher level of political equality than women elsewhere. Considering American political women in a comparative context also draws our attention to various types of explanations. As Lisa Baldez (this volume) points out, for example, attention to the cross-national impact of electoral institutions (e.g., majority rule versus proportional representation, presence of gender quotas) shifts our attention away from the dominant candidate-centered explanations for women's underrepresentation in U.S. legislatures that emphasize the failure of individual women to put themselves forward and toward the structural impediments to women's election.

What did we see at the revolution? As the authors in this volume explain, the increasing presence of political women clearly has transformed political life in the United States, but the experiences of women in politics continue to be deeply shaped by gender. Kirkpatrick (1975, 242) ends *Political Woman* by asking, "Must it ever be thus? Is male dominance of power processes written in the stars and underwritten by human biology?" Although Kirkpatrick was hopeful that greater equity is possible, the work reviewed in this volume

highlights how complex the opportunities and constraints faced by political
women truly are.

Notes

1. Two women had served in cabinet-level positions before 1974: Oveta Culp Hobby
held the post of secretary of health, education, and welfare (1953–5) under Eisen-
hower, and Frances Perkins, the first female cabinet member, served as secretary
of labor (1933–45) under Franklin Roosevelt (CAWP 2007b).

2. The percentage of full-time political scientists who are women increased from just
10 percent in 1974 to 22 percent by 2000 (Committee on the Status of Women in
the Profession 2001; Sarkees and McGlen 1999; Tolleson-Rinehart and Carroll
2006).

3. The first article about women or gender to appear in the *APSR* was also authored
(or, more accurately, edited, because it contains items written by other, mostly
male, authors as well) by a woman, Margaret A. Schaffner ("Notes on Current Legislation" 3, no. 3 [1909]:383–428) and includes a short discussion of
the creation of a women's and children's department as part of the Minnesota
Bureau of Labor. Other articles during that first decade (*APSR* began publication
in 1906) examined legislation on the employment of women in Massachusetts,
mother's pensions, and women's suffrage in England (see Kelly and Fisher
1993).

4. The *APSR* figures through 1991 are from Kelly and Fisher (1993). The *APSR*
figures for 1992 through 2007 are data I have collected, based almost entirely
on a review of article titles. This is a slightly different methodology from that
employed by Kelly and Fisher, although I have no reason to expect the results
would differ substantially. Data available on request.

5. As with journal articles, there are a number of important books about women and
politics from the middle of the century (e.g., Duverger 1955). As Nancy Burns
details in Chapter 4 of this collection, a number of the early, classic works of
political science provided a sophisticated treatment of sex and gender, although
most took up the topic in a less insightful way or ignored it altogether (Bourque
and Grossholtz 1974).

6. We note that, even given the restricted coverage of this volume, our combined
references contain more than 800 unique citations.

7. Some scholars disagree with the notion that biological sex difference and the
social meaning of gender are independent of, or distinct from, each other. More
generally, a full explication of the concepts of sex and gender (or the literatures addressing them) requires far more attention than is possible here. Useful
starting places with regard to political science include Acker (1992), Beckwith
(2005, 2007), Burns (2005), Duerst-Lahti and Kelly (1995b), Epstein (1988), and
Hawkesworth (2005), to name just a few.

8. In the chapters of this volume, our authors recognize and highlight the distinction between sex and gender in different ways. Many make a point to use the
word "sex" when discussing simple dichotomous differences between men and
women and employ the term "gender" when considering socially constructed
roles, expectations, processes, and institutions. Others prefer the term "gender"
to encompass the discussion of men and women as social, rather than merely

biological, groups. Because of the association of the term "sex" with other phenomenon – for example, biological distinctions, sexual identity, and sexuality –
the term "gender" has entered into both popular and scholarly usage when discussing differences between men and women, the ubiquitous use of the term
"gender gap" to describe attitudinal and behavioral differences between men
and women being the most obvious example (on the invention of the term, see
Bonk 1988). Regardless of their approach, all of the authors are attentive to the
analytical distinction between sex difference and gender and seek to make those
distinctions evident in their discussion.

9. As Katznelson (2005) and others have shown, American public policy, including
the G.I. Bill, has also been clearly "raced" in ways that have important consequences for the political, social, and economic opportunity and experiences of
African Americans and other racial minorities in the United States.

2

Gender as a Category of Analysis in American Political Development

Gretchen Ritter

According to President George W. Bush, a nation's commitment to liberty and democracy should be gauged by its willingness to extend rights and political recognition to women.[1] As the world's first modern democracy, one might expect that the United States has led the way in granting equal rights to women. Furthermore, champions of political liberalism contend that our government's commitment to legal, individual rights and nondiscrimination has created equal opportunity for all, regardless of race or sex. Yet an examination of American political history reveals the persistence of gender hierarchy in U.S. politics, a stubborn resistance to the idea that gender should not matter to one's political standing, and, at best, an incomplete realization of the liberal ideal of equal rights for all. From a comparative perspective today, the United States is far behind other Western democracies in extending social rights that particularly benefit women and in the proportion of women who hold office in the national government. This has led some scholars to consider whether gender inequality is a deep-seated feature of the American political system and whether liberal political structures will ever provide for equal rights and recognition for women. Scholarship on gender and American political development can move us closer to an analytic framework that clarifies the paradoxical place that women hold in the American system.

What would it mean to think about gender as a category of analysis in American political development? In this chapter I suggest that there are many possible approaches that may be taken in answering this question, some of which have been explored in the research of American political development (APD) scholars and some of which have not. Furthermore, I contend that although the field of American political development has several excellent scholars who take up issues of gender, the subfield as a whole has yet to take gender seriously as a central problematic in the development of American politics. This chapter provides both a review of literature on gender and American political development and suggestions for future research in the field. Finally, the chapter advocates for greater scholarly dialogue – not only among gender scholars within political science but also between political scientists and gender scholars in other fields such as law, history, anthropology, and sociology.

Scholars have, and should, think about the role of gender in American political development in myriad ways. In this chapter I focus on seven particularly central ways that scholars have thought about gender as a category of analysis in American political development. These seven areas are intended to be broad ranging but not exhaustive – they both capture the major contributions made to this field of research and suggest the large range of work being conducted in this area. Across all of the major arenas of politics – from civic engagement, to institutional formation, to the role that international forces play in shaping domestic politics – gender may be identified as a category of analysis for understanding processes of American political development across time. Although all of these approaches to considering gender as a category of analysis increase our understanding of the changing role of gender in American politics over time, it is also worth asking whether there is a more global claim to be made regarding gender as a *central* variable in the large-scale processes of American political development. How significant has gender been to the way politics operates in the United States over time? Is gender not simply a useful category of analysis but also a necessary one for those seeking to understand the nature and development of American political processes and institutions? Could we say about gender, as many have suggested about race in the United States, that it is at the very core of our political system, in that it deeply affects the way that that system has been organized and changed over time? I believe we can make such a claim and sketch my argument about gender as a central problematic in American political development in the last section of this chapter.

Furthermore, by way of preface, let me add two additional notes about where this chapter fits into the broader project of this edited volume, assessing the scholarship on women in American politics. This chapter is explicitly cast as a discussion about "gender" as a category of political analysis rather than a look more specifically at women in politics. One of the key characteristics of how gender operates as a social system is its binary nature, in the tendency for femininity and masculinity to be seen as exclusive and oppositional categories, which are nonetheless interdependent (Rubin 1984). In every society, gender is a dialectical structure that orders social identities, roles, and rights, as well as cultural understandings (Scott 1988). To understand the place of women in American politics, therefore, it is important to understand how gender operates not only in shaping women's political interests and modes of participation but also in defining the rights and roles of both men and women, organizing institutional structures, and assigning political virtue or vice to goals, nations, or actors that are cast as masculine or feminine.

Finally, this chapter is intended as a contribution to scholarship on American political development more specifically. As Karen Orren and Stephen Skowronek (2004) suggest, within the field of American politics, APD scholarship focuses on how politics changes (or remains stable) across time. How do prior political choices and institutional formations affect future political opportunities, governmental commitments, or repertoires for political action? In times of crisis, are there certain political understandings or institutional pathways that appear more available for responding to the problems at hand? Do these pathways or understandings invoke gender as a way to explain the crisis or legitimate the response to it? Moreover, APD scholarship often offers the benefit of a systemwide view of American politics that allows us to see connections not only across time but across political realms as well. The macro perspective of APD scholarship allows us to see how changes in federalism in the 1870s affected the structure of citizenship in the states in the 1910s or how the expansions in social provisioning in the 1930s and 1940s promoted an increased commitment to civic engagement in the 1950s. In considering gender as a category of political analysis, I give particular attention to how the category operates across time and across political realms as an aspect of political development.

GENDER AS POLITICAL IDENTITY

Looking at gender as an aspect of political identity involves exploring how claims to being an American or an American citizen have been gendered over time. Linda Kerber (1980) has elaborated on the emergence of an ideal of republican motherhood in the early national period. This celebration of the importance of maternal virtue coincided with the emergence of a separate sphere ideology and the firm exclusion of women from the public realm. By the latter part of the nineteenth century, some women's rights advocates were building on separate sphere ideology to claim a public political voice for women as the guardians of domestic virtue. Yet around the same time, as Gail Bederman (1995) notes in *Manliness and Civilization*, advocates of American imperialism cast American national identity in masculine terms and represented the identities of colonial subjects in feminine, dependent terms. Or, as Theda Skocpol has suggested in her writings on the origins of the American welfare state, gendered understandings of American citizenship as autonomous and manly thwarted the development of social policies that supported American working men in the Progressive Era (Skocpol 1992; Skocpol and Ritter 1991). Looking across American political history, there seems to be a persistent tension between universalist ideals of equality and individualism and more nationalist understandings of the political virtues affiliated with masculinity and femininity. Under the terms of American national identity, women were celebrated for their feminine role. As many of the feminist studies of nationalism have also noted, gender often plays a central role in nationalist ideology, and when it does, it usually[2] functions to deny women public rights or political voice (Yuval-Davis 1997).

Examining gender as an aspect of political identity illuminates how political projects are motivated and legitimized to the population. Deep-seated understandings about the differences between men and women, differences that are typically combined with understandings about the social meaning of race as well, may be mobilized to help justify a particular political project, such as imperialism. Further, in the process of mobilizing gendered meanings in the interest of political ends, those meanings themselves may be changed or invested with new importance in ways that have consequences for how political roles are imagined and expressed by ordinary citizens. When white masculinity is tied to national identity and social virtue, does it motivate more young Anglo men to join the army? When a military conflict ends, do claims regarding the association among civic virtue, masculinity, and military service create impetus for new social provisioning programs for veterans and their dependents? These are some of the substantive consequences that can be traced to the use of gendered understandings in the evolution of American political identities.

GENDER AND LIBERALISM

Many APD scholars have explored the relationship between American liberalism and the ideologies (and practices) that support social hierarchy, such as white supremacy, nativism, anti-Semitism, anti-Catholicism, and the like.[3] Less attention has been given to the way that American liberalism produces or tolerates ideologies and practices that exclude or disadvantage women. Yet at the intersection between political theory and American political development, important contributions have been made by feminist theorists such as Carole Pateman, Wendy Brown, Iris Marion Young, and Nancy Fraser. In her classic book *The Sexual Contract* (1988), Pateman contends that the modern social contract (which is at the root of liberal philosophy) is premised on a sexual contract in which men are given equal political rights in the public realm and shared authority over women, whereas women are subordinated into the private realm. In a later discussion of this work, Wendy Brown (1995) critiques Pateman for giving too much credence to contracts per se, yet Brown seeks to recuperate Pateman's thesis by suggesting that liberalism as a set of political norms continues to construct a public political identity that is implicitly masculine and, one might add, racialized as well. For Young (1990, 1997), the issue of how public political identities are constructed and what this means for the representation of group interests and social identities in politics is an issue that is particularly fraught in liberal political systems such as our own. Finally, Nancy Fraser, particularly in her contributions with Linda Gordon (1994, 1995), has revisited traditional understandings of the development of liberal citizenship and social welfare through a gendered lens.

American political development scholars can contribute to this literature by providing historical specificity and attention to the way that liberal norms are manifest in political institutions and practices over time. Such an analysis would also clarify the way that liberal political understandings shape or obscure gendered political identities, interests, and aspirations across generations. One question that arises out of the intersection between feminist theory and American political development concerns the way that liberal regimes treat gender difference. This complex issue is elucidated by research that focuses on evolving institutional and legal structures as they address gender directly (e.g., in forbidding women to vote [Baker 1984; Marilley 1996] or mandating that only men must register for the draft [Kerber 1998]) or secondarily by recognizing, rewarding, or regulating specific social roles and relations that attach to gender – including those of husband or wife (Ritter 2002; Siegel 1994), family provider, caregiver, worker (Zeigler 1996a, 1996b), and head of household. By looking across time, APD scholars are well positioned to locate and assess shifts in the treatment of gendered roles and relations – shifts that may signal a reformulation of status hierarchies under such principles as privacy or their alleviation as women gain recognition and standing in the public realm. Finally, at a more abstracted level, we might ask whether the terms of liberal politics and civic membership are conducive to the inclusion of women in politics and the expression of their political interests. Eileen McDonagh's recent work suggests that only when liberal political structures are supplemented by a political tradition that allows for the expression of kinship ties, familial concerns, or gendered social experiences are women likely to become full partners in the life of the polity (McDonagh 2002).

GENDER AND CIVIC MEMBERSHIP

How does gender affect the terms of civic membership in the United States? Civic membership is conceived of here as a broader term than citizenship[4] and allows us to consider the rights, status, and obligations of all those governed under U.S. political authority (Ritter 2006), including those who are not formally counted as citizens, such as immigrants, Native Americans prior to the twentieth century, or residents of the territories taken in the Spanish-American War at the turn of the century. By casting our discussion in terms of civic membership, we also can focus on the differential rights and obligations of various social groups within the American political community. Over time, gendered ideals of civic membership have been invoked to legitimate particular constitutional understandings of the rights and duties of various social groups, as a means of facilitating changes in the terms of civic membership, and as a way to develop new constitutional understandings of the role of government in protecting or restricting the rights of those governed by the American political order.

For instance, in *Constituting Workers, Protecting Women* (2001), Julie Novkov reveals that the Supreme Court's abandonment of the "freedom of contract" doctrine in *West Coast Hotel v. Parrish* (1937) was premised on an elaboration of an earlier understanding developed in the context of women workers. During the Progressive Era, the Court held that labor laws that sought to regulate the conditions of workingmen violated their autonomy and rights as citizens. But for women, the Court recognized (at the behest of various social feminists) that the ideal of social and political autonomy did not apply; therefore it was appropriate for the state to intervene in the contract relationship in support of women workers. Because the Court saw women workers as dependent and vulnerable, it endorsed the government's protective stance toward them. Then, during the Great Depression, the Court came to see that in times of national economic distress, all citizens could be vulnerable to the vagaries of social and economic circumstances. So the standard that had previously been applied only to women workers now came to be applied to all workers, thereby inaugurating a new constitutional understanding in which government could act in support of *positive* rights for all citizens.

Similarly, Nancy Cott's *Public Vows* (2000) reveals that marital status is a central aspect of civic membership in the United States, and the laws governing marriage have been used to regulate the terms of civic membership for different social groups throughout our history. More recent work by both Julie Novkov (forthcoming) and Priscilla Yamin (2005) on miscegenation substantiate Cott's arguments. As the current debate over gay marriage makes clear, marriage remains a constitutional matter that reflects our evolving understandings of who belongs to the American constitutional order and on what terms.

In my own book, *The Constitution as Social Design: Gender and Civic Membership in the American Constitutional Order* (2006), I propose that we consider the way that debates over civic membership propel constitutional development in the United States. My book considers how the changing terms of civic membership shift the polity *institutionally* as well as socially. Such institutional changes may involve new mandates for government action in support of newly recognized rights, shifts in the balance of authority between levels of government or branches of government, or restrictions on the actions of government as interferences with the rights of citizens. Within the American constitutional order, women have undergone a shift from a civic status based on marriage, family relations, and economic dependency to one based on the principles of liberal individualism and legal personhood. Yet women's attainment of a liberal civic status remains partial in the United States – in the struggle to achieve standing as public realm individuals, women still face resistance to the idea that sex does not matter to their civic membership.

Looking across American constitutional history, one can see a shift from the articulation of express social ordering concerns to a more neutral, liberal language that stresses individualism, achievement, and choice. Although we think of the Constitution as being premised on the existence of a community of equal, independent, rights-bearing individuals, there are also less visible ways in which the Constitution recognizes and promotes a particular social structure that is often not especially egalitarian in nature.

GENDER AND DEMOCRATIZATION

In a forthcoming edited volume, a group of scholars led by Desmond King and Robert Lieberman set out to think about the history of American political development from a democratization perspective (King, Lieberman, Ritter, and Whitehead, forthcoming). Going beyond the usual descriptors of the United States as the first democratic nation or as a long-settled democracy, these scholars ask us to consider democratization as an ongoing process that is affected by continuing challenges of inclusion, the development of rights, and evolving standards of political representation. As the recent debate over the renewal of section 5 of the Voting Rights Act suggests, it is easy to see that race poses ongoing challenges to American democracy. Furthermore, in our conflicts abroad, the United States represents itself as the model and purveyor of democratic standards. As President Bush said in a speech before the National Endowment for Democracy in 2003, "The advance of freedom is the calling of our time; it is the calling of our country" (quoted in Mettler, forthcoming). This new scholarship and these contemporary political developments leave open the question of what a gendered analysis might contribute to our understanding of democratization in America.

The work of three scholars illustrates the contribution that a gendered analysis can provide to our understanding of democratization in the United States. First, in her contribution to the King and colleagues volume, Suzanne Mettler (forthcoming) calls for an analysis of gender and democratization that is citizenship-focused and looks at the impact of state policies and practices on the political participation and aspirations of various groups. Mettler notes that much APD scholarship has illuminated historical processes of state building and institutional development in the United States (Orren and Skowronek 2004) while giving less attention to the ongoing operation of states once new policy regimes or state bureaucracies have been built. In this regard, the work of Theda Skocpol (1992, 2003; Skocpol and Fiorina 1999) is instructive, for in her research Skocpol has long been sensitive to the way that institutional arrangements affect patterns of civic engagement. Furthermore, in her work about the New Deal and the impact of the G.I. Bill, Mettler (1998, 2005) shows how social provisioning can either depress or amplify civic engagement and activity for the citizens who receive it. Mettler is also right to call for greater dialogue between APD scholars and political behavior scholars in this regard – for the latter group is particularly attentive to different forms of political engagement by various social groups in the United States.[5] What can be gained from a gendered analysis of democratization of the sort that Mettler proposes is greater awareness of the way that supposed democratic expansions through the addition of new social rights or social provisioning measures, for instance, may inadvertently reinscribe gendered hierarchies by elevating traditionally masculine forms of civic contribution such as family provisioning or military service.

In her article "Rethinking Representation," Jane Mansbridge (2003) contributes to our analysis of gender and democratization by offering a new framework for considering issues of political representation (see also Dovi, this volume, for a discussion of political representation). The Mansbridge article advances our discussion of American democratization in two ways. First, Mansbridge is attentive to issues that are pertinent for a mature democracy such as the United States in which the question is not one of whether citizens have the right to vote but of whether different forms of political representation may be judged as more or less democratic and more or less expressive of the political interests of various groups in the polity. Second, Mansbridge complicates our understanding of democracy and opens up the possibility that there may be different standards of democracy, some of which are favored or seem more favorable over others to certain groups in society.

Mansbridge discusses four forms of representation, which she calls promissory, anticipatory, gyroscopic, and surrogate. Surrogate representation is particularly of interest for scholars interested in a gendered analysis of democratization. Mansbridge suggests that surrogate representation allows for the expression of voices and interests that might not otherwise be heard because they constitute a minority view in most districts. She also contends that this diversity of interests and perspectives is valuable to processes of democratic deliberation because of its ability to deepen political debate by bringing in a range of views. We might add (anticipating McDonagh 2002 discussed in the next paragraph; see also Phillips 1995) that this form of representation can foster political participation and engagement for constituents who see themselves and their experiences being recognized through their surrogate representatives.

Taking yet another angle on the relationship between government institutions and policies on one hand and civic membership and engagement on the other, Eileen McDonagh (2002) challenges long-standing assumptions that liberal democratic political institutions and policies are the most conducive to women's political representation and participation. In a cross-national study of women's officeholding, she concludes that liberal policies and institutions by themselves are not enough to produce a substantial number of women officeholders. Rather, one must move beyond public equality and individualism to both procedures and policies that recognize and value the social experiences and political identities of women *as women* (see Dolan, this volume, for further discussion of the barriers and opportunities for female candidates in the United States). McDonagh's work is instructive in demonstrating that traditional models of democratization do not account for the failure of liberal democratic systems to include and represent fully the interests of their female citizens. Our assumptions about what makes a democracy work may not apply in the same way with regard to gender. Furthermore, McDonagh's research sheds light on the role that gender has played in American processes of democratization. At many points in our nation's history, women's rights activists have followed the lead of civil rights activists in advocating for equality and rights for women. Yet McDonagh's work suggests that the American model of liberal citizenship and individual rights that was developed partly in response to the civil rights movement is not likely to work as well for women, precisely because it makes it more difficult to articulate and make claims about gendered social experiences in political life.

Treating gender as a category of analysis in the study of American democratization will deepen our theoretical understanding of processes of democratization and complicate our substantive views of the state of democratization in the United States.

GENDER AS A FEATURE OF STATE INSTITUTIONS

American political development scholars have long been interested in the way that state institutions shape political opportunities and outcomes over time. From a social politics perspective, we might ask whether state institutions are merely neutral arbiters designed to implement the democratic commitments that result from the political process, or do these institutions express their own set of political commitments and orientations, apart from what the democratic process dictates? In other words, do institutions operate merely as an outcome of politics, or are they also a force in politics? What can a gendered analysis contribute to our understanding of the formation, mission, and practices of state institutions as a force in American politics? Approaching this question from different vantage points, we might begin by exploring the role that gender plays in the formation and continuation of state institutions (Chappell 2002; Lovenduski 1998). Are there occasions when political actors, movements, or government officials offer a gendered rationale for the creation of those institutions? If so, what role did this play in the success of their campaign to create a new state bureaucracy and in the operations of that bureaucracy after it was formed? Furthermore, does the existence of gender-identified institutions within the government have an impact on politics outside the state – by providing sustenance to political interest groups or by providing an alternative avenue to political representation when a group is excluded from more traditional forms of representation

(Muncy 1991; Skocpol and Ritter 1991)? One contribution that APD scholars provide to this analysis is an awareness of the way that institutional
formation influences the development of future political formations, both
within and outside of the state (Skocpol 1992).

Second, in analyzing the operation of state institutions over time, we
may observe the sex of the personnel who inhabit these institutions and
ask whether the gender of those who work in these institutions affects the
mission and practices of the institution (see Reingold, this volume, for a
discussion of women as legislative officeholders). For instance, it has been
observed that the demographic composition of police forces has a considerable impact on how the police understand and operationalize their mission
of law enforcement, as well as how the police are received by the communities they serve (Peek, Lowe, and Alston 1981; Weitzer 2000). Are there
parts of the federal government that have been feminized? If so, does that
affect the mission, prestige, or effectiveness of those institutions? As the military becomes more gender-integrated, does the sex of the military personnel
affect the way that war is conducted? If so, does this have a broader impact
on our understanding of the national interest?

A third approach considers the role that state institutions play in constructing gendered roles in the larger society. How does the work of the military construct standards of masculinity in American society (Rodgers 2005;
Zeiger 2003)? How do social welfare agencies help to construct motherhood for poor women in American society (Boris 2003; Curran 2005; Haney
2004; Mittelstadt 2005)? How is the gendered construction of motherhood
for poor women also racialized? Is there a different construction of motherhood evident in social programs that reward a history of work, such as
Social Security? It is important to recognize the role of state institutions
not only in expressing gendered political interests and norms but also in
constructing gendered roles and sexualities in the larger society (Foucault
1990; Rubin 1984). It may be possible to trace feedback loops between the
state institutions and political actors or social movements in the construction, regulation, and exploitation of gendered roles in politics and society
(Kessler-Harris 2001).

Considering the role that gender has played in institutional development
in the United States sheds considerable light on old questions about the
exceptionalism of the American state. Scholars who look to war (Huntington
1968) or industrialization and the labor movement (Esping-Andersen 1990)
as motive forces in the development of state structures miss the impact that
gender has had on American institutional development.

GENDER AND PUBLIC POLICY

Public policy is intended to advance the public good. An analysis of public
policy, then, can tell us a great deal about how the public good is understood
at different times in our nation's political history. Furthermore, we may draw

a distinction between public policies that aim to regulate or support people (policies that are primarily social in nature) and those for which the primary object is not social – policies that promote economic development or environmental preservation through the building of canals and bridges or the purchase and preservation of new land, for instance.[6] An analysis of how public policies are gendered might focus on three things: first, whether the policies advance the political interests of gendered groups in American society, either implicitly or explicitly; second, whether the clientele served or regulated by a particular policy is gendered, and; third, what the impact of a policy or group of policies is on the civic membership of American men and women. For scholars of American political development, this analysis should also be attentive to historical changes over time, as an indication of how gendered understandings of the public good have evolved over time, and what impact this has had on the gendered terms of civic membership in the United States.

The area of policy that has been most subject to a gendered analysis in American politics is social welfare. Over the past two decades, scholars from history and sociology have joined with scholars from political science in an effort to examine the emergence and evolution of Widows' Pensions, the Aid to Families with Dependent Children program, Social Security, and so forth. A few of the long and prominent list of scholars who have published in this area include Mimi Abramovitz, Eileen Borris, Martha Derthick, Linda Gordon, Alice Kessler-Harris, Suzanne Mettler, Gwendolyn Mink, Barbara J. Nelson, Ann Orloff, Virginia Sapiro, and Theda Skocpol. In the literature on the role of gender in the early formation of American social policy, many of these scholars have stressed the role of the state in recognizing and reinforcing traditional gender norms.

For Mimi Abramovitz (1996), the structure of the Social Security Act both reinforced patriarchal norms and upheld capitalist imperatives for the reproduction of labor. Abramovitz's sentiments are echoed in Gordon's (1994), Kessler-Harris's (1995, 2001), and Mink's (1990, 1995) accounts, although Mink goes further in stressing the linkage between the gender structure and the racial structure of 1930s social provisioning. But if these were the consequences of New Deal social policy, what was the cause? Why were gender (and racial) distinctions reinforced, and perhaps even given new energy, by these social programs? Some scholars have moved beyond the stress on patriarchy and capitalism to a discussion of American political traditions, particularly the republican distinction between independence and dependence.[7]

Nancy Fraser and Linda Gordon (1994, 1995) have written that since the early national period, the relationship of male citizens to the state is premised on a notion of contract or independence, whereas that of female citizens is premised on a notion of charity or dependency. Whereas white men developed the civil and political rights of citizenship in the nineteenth century, women, especially when married, were excluded from these rights.

UNIVERSITY OF MARY WASHINGTON BKST

124 CASH-1   8633 0001 105

978052171384 NEW
WOL RREC/POLITICAL   MDS 1N   24.99
                      TOTAL   24.99

AP : 602663
ACCOUNT NUMBER XXXXXXXXXXXXX7977 XX/XX
    Visa/MasterCard   24.99

NO RETURNS WITHOUT REG. RECEIPT#!

10/21/08 6:23 PM

So while men became possessive, rights-bearing, independent individuals in the eyes of the state, women were cast as family dependents under the authority of men and beyond the public sphere. The legacy of this distinction between contract and dependency in the twentieth century appears clearly in the arena of social policy in which men are covered by social insurance (e.g., old-age retirement benefits) and women are given public assistance (e.g., Aid to Families with Dependent Children). As Barbara Nelson (1990) also notes, men are able to make political claims in their status as workers, while women's political claims (often made for them) revolve around their status as dependent mothers or wives. Thus these overarching ideological traditions helped to give shape to the gendered terms of American social policy in the 1930s.

Other scholars who stress the significance of previously existing policies and institutions thereby take a more historical, developmental view to social policy formation. Ann Shola Orloff (1988), Theda Skocpol (1992), and Suzanne Mettler (1998), in their analyses of 1930s social policy formation, have all stressed the role of prior institutions and policies. Of particular importance, of course, are the mother's pensions that were established through the efforts of social feminists during the Progressive Era.

Yet by the mid-1930s, mother's pensions appeared rather conservative compared with the more generous, nationally based pension schemes being discussed for the elderly. As Mettler (1998) argues, the governance of women under state-based policies ultimately led to the creation of a two-tiered system of social citizenship in the 1930s. Prior policy development affected the structure of social provisioning as it emerged in the 1930s and 1940s. One of the most important influences of prior policy development involved the use of federalism to administer programs in previously developed social welfare areas. This gender and APD literature illuminates how institutional structures intersected with gendered understandings of the public good in the development of social welfare policy and consequently helped to gender American civic membership in the 1930s.

GENDER AND AMERICAN POLITICAL DEVELOPMENT IN A GLOBAL CONTEXT

Over the past few years, several APD scholars have examined the way that the global context affects the terms of domestic politics in the United States, particularly in regard to the federal government's response to the civil rights movement in the 1940s and 1950s (Dudziak 2000; Kryder 2000). In addition, gender scholars in the field of international relations – such as Cynthia Enloe (1989), Joshua Goldstein (2001), Katharine Moon (1997), V. Spike Peterson (1992), Peterson and Anne Sisson Runyon (1999), and J. Ann Tickner (1992, 2001, 2005) – have advanced a significant new agenda for research that includes attention to the following: the way that militarization

promotes a masculine state, the impact of terrorism and warfare on the lives
of women and children, the growth of gender concerns in the field of human
rights, the work of feminist and human rights groups as nongovernmental
organizations, and the impact of economic globalization on women workers
and their families. Feminist international relations scholars have also made
significant contributions to the use of postpositivist methodologies in their
field, as discussed by Ann Tickner (2005) in a recent state-of-the-field essay
in *Signs*. Drawing on the insights of this fine scholarship, it is now an oppor-
tune moment to consider how the global context has had an impact on the
role that gender plays in American political development.

One example of the interplay between international and domestic gender politics in American political development involves the simultaneous
1940s debates over equal rights for women in the United States and human
rights for all internationally.[8] In 1945, the full Senate debated and narrowly
defeated the Equal Rights Amendment (ERA). Women's contributions to the
war effort had galvanized support for the amendment. The debate over constitutional equality was not a new issue in the 1940s. Since the early 1920s,
the National Women's Party had promoted the ERA in its campaign to have
women treated as equal, autonomous individuals in the public realm and to
prevent legal discrimination on the basis of sex. Yet among the leading opponents of the ERA in the 1940s was another group of activist women – social
feminists and labor progressives associated with the Democratic Party – who
believed that women ought to be protected by the state and shielded from
the rigors of a competitive labor market. Eleanor Roosevelt counted herself
among the social feminists who opposed the ERA because it threatened to
overturn protective labor laws for women. At the time, Roosevelt was also
known as an advocate for international human rights. Indeed, in 1948, the
Commission for Human Rights, with Eleanor Roosevelt as its chair, produced the Universal Declaration of Human Rights, which was adopted by
the United Nations (UN).

Prior campaigns for gender equality shaped the debate that occurred in the
1940s. American equality feminists made few gains in their *domestic* campaigns for equal rights for women in the 1920s and 1930s. In frustration, they
began to look beyond the United States and joined with feminists from other
nations in pursuit of international rights accords. There was an earlier tradition of transnational cooperation among women's rights organizations that
dated back to the nineteenth-century suffrage campaigns in Europe and the
United States and expanded to include Latin American feminists in the early
twentieth century. These transnational ties were revitalized in the interwar
years, with ongoing efforts to secure suffrage for women in various countries, as well as international campaigns against militarism in which so many
feminist groups participated and the international gender-equality campaign
led by the National Women's Party in the 1920s and 1930s. The venues in
which the equality activists pursued such accords included the League of

Nations, international tribunals in Geneva, and the gatherings of the Pan American Union.

At the founding convention for the UN, Latin American women delegates "were the authors of the amendment giving women equality in the Charter of the United Nations" (Bernardino 1947). These feminists had worked with American equality feminists in the 1920s and 1930s on international rights accords for the Pan American Union. In contrast, at the UN convention, the United States and Great Britain were "the greatest opponents of the inclusion of women in the Charter." One observer at the time suggested that the reason that the United States opposed gender equality at the UN founding conference was because of the domestic debate over the ERA. Within the New Deal coalition, social feminists and labor activists remained opposed to this vision of gender equality. Nonetheless the inclusion of women in the charter had a positive effect internationally. It inspired several nations in Latin America to grant political rights to women in the late 1940s. It also gave impetus to further efforts within the UN to analyze and address problems of gender inequality worldwide (Ritter 2003).

The history of the simultaneous efforts to forward human rights and women's rights through both the U.S. federal government and the UN in the middle and latter 1940s demonstrates several things that are of interest for scholars seeking to understand the impact of the intersection between global and domestic politics on women. First, institutional and political legacies mattered. In particular, the effort to forward women's rights through the Pan American Union in the 1920s and 1930s (an effort that was pursued by U.S. feminists after they were shut out of the domestic political arena) created an institutional legacy for gender equality in international governance that was immediately felt through the efforts of Latin American women's representatives at the founding convention of the UN in 1945. Second, social movement activists may have found it easier to influence political outcomes in the context of the more open, less formed political environments of the international governance organizations. Given the importance of small working groups such as the Commission on the Status of Women and the Commission on Human Rights, organizational representatives who were able to be present at the meetings and to lobby the members of these groups were sometimes quite influential. Third, broader international currents – including the increasingly hostile Cold War competition between the United States and the Soviet Union – shaped debates over rights in international forums such that the American UN representatives were extremely conscious of the efforts of the Soviet Union and its allies to use political inequality in the United States as propaganda in their campaign for the political allegiances of other nations and populations. Yet their reaction to these efforts in the realms of race inequality and gender inequality were quite different.

Few scholars of gender and American political development have begun working in this area yet (but see Mathews-Gardner 2006). However, gender scholars in international relations, as well as scholars of gender and American history (e.g., Bederman 1995; Boris 2005; Kessler-Harris 2004), have begun to produce fine scholarship in this area. Further, gender scholars in sociology (e.g., Adams and Orloff 2005) are bringing together an awareness of historical specificities to their analyses of the intersections between domestic and global politics on the political status and engagement of women. There is a great deal of interesting work to be done in this area, and the current global context makes clear how important it is for American gender scholars to develop a deeper understanding of the intersection between domestic and international politics in the past so that we might have more perspective on current events as well.

GENDER AS A CORE PROBLEMATIC IN AMERICAN POLITICAL DEVELOPMENT

So far, this chapter has demonstrated how gender as a category of analysis in American political development illuminates our understanding of key processes and outcomes in American politics. This final section seeks to go further and suggests not only the usefulness but also the *necessity* of taking gender into account for scholars who seek to understand processes of democratization, the role of liberalism and illiberalism in our nation's political development, or the way that international security concerns and political forces shape the domestic political landscape in the United States. A gendered analysis is necessary to addressing these fundamental questions about the nature and development of American politics because gender has operated as a core problematic in American politics throughout our nation's history.

Others have argued that race is a core problematic in the development of the American political system (Brown, Carnoy, Currie, et al. 2003; Horton 2005; King and Smith 2005; Klinker and Smith 1999; Nieman 1991). Can such claims also be made about gender as a central problematic in the development of American politics? Let me sketch what such an account would include.[9] Developmentally, it would imply that gender issues have been a key topic of repeated debate (explicitly or implicitly) at crucial junctures in American political history and that gendered understandings have been available for use in advancing political agendas or in legitimating political change. Institutionally, it would mean demonstrating that gendered concerns or understandings have been instrumental in shaping governmental structures as they emerge and change over time. Ideologically or normatively, it means showing that gender has given important meaning to our core governing ideologies – the norms that ground our constitutional order, the ideals that animate our democratic aspirations, and the beliefs that shape our understanding of the national interest and the general welfare. Finally, claiming that gender has been a core problematic in American political development does *not* mean that we must demonstrate that gender somehow trumps race (or ethnicity, class, or religion) in shaping American politics. Rather, the expectation here is that gender concerns are strongly intertwined with both race- and class-based political ideologies and practices.

Development

At crucial moments in our nation's history, gender has played a central role in shaping the terms of political debate and in advancing and consolidating political change. For instance, the consolidation of American mass politics in the early nineteenth century was cast in terms that were both racialized and gendered. Civic membership in the early national period was expressed most strongly in the arena of partisan mobilization and electoral politics, a realm that was associated with manly independence. In this instance, gender provided a logic of political legitimation, which had an impact on the terms of civic membership for all Americans.

Andrew Jackson is often credited with the development of American mass politics. Jackson expanded electoral politics beyond the elite or nobility to the mass citizenry. In the 1820s and 1830s, voting eligibility was extended to all white males regardless of their economic status. This made the United States the most democratic nation in the modern world. It also gave rise to an electoral system in which partisan identity became closely aligned with civic membership. Being a voter and a loyal partisan became nearly synonymous with citizenship in the United States. At the same time, electoral citizenship in the United States became highly gendered and racialized. Prior to the rise of mass politics, social class remained an important marker of civic membership, and propertied women who were active in petition drives and the like during the Revolutionary Era were regarded as members of the political community (Kerber 1980). In New Jersey until 1807, some women were even permitted to vote. However, the expansion of electoral politics to all white men drove women out of the political sphere and placed them more firmly in the domestic sphere, where "republican mothers" were expected to cultivate civic virtue in their sons (Kann 1991). Electoral politics became a masculine domain – campaigning and voting occurred in barbershops and bars (McGerr 1990; Ritter 2000; Ryan 1990, 1997). Eventually women did find their own feminized place within the domain of electoral politics, but as Baker (1984) has argued, for many Americans in the nineteenth century, the value of electoral citizenship was partly based on its identification as a manly activity.

Institutions

Regarding the impact of gender on the emergence and endurance of our government's institutional structures, there is now an excellent body of literature documenting the role that gender played in the formation of the welfare state in the United States. Most theories of the development of social welfare states focus on the role of class and political structures in these developments. The history of American social welfare development makes apparent the importance of gender to the creation of social provisioning for poor families in the early twentieth century (Skocpol 1992), the elaboration of a dual welfare structure in the 1930s (Mettler 1998), and the dismantling of social provisioning for poor families in the 1990s (Handler and White 1999). Much of this literature was reviewed in my earlier discussion of policy formation and state structures as the focus of a gendered analysis of American political development.

In considering gender as a core problematic of American political analysis, the history of social welfare development is instructive in two ways. First, this history suggests that in a nation that has historically had a very limited understanding of class as a source of political identity and mobilization, gender may serve as an alternative form of political mobilization and institutional development. Second, to the degree that this is the case, it is almost certain that these gendered roles and understandings are also connected to racial understandings in politics. To the degree that we have analyzed gender as a matter of the political activism of white women in American history, we may be missing a great deal of the larger story regarding the political and constitutional governance of social relations in the United States. Similarly, Barbara Welke's (2001) book on the rise of segregation on American rail carriers in the late nineteenth and early twentieth centuries demonstrates that the issues of gender and racial governance were inextricably linked in the emergence of the institutions of segregation.

Ideology

Finally, gender also gives substantial and sustained meaning to our governing norms and ideologies. In her fine book *Belated Feudalism* (1991), Karen Orren contends that liberal constitutional governance in the United States only emerged after a struggle to overcome embedded common-law norms of personal relations. The common-law relation that Orren is particularly concerned with is the master-servant tradition in labor law, but her insight about the existence of embedded common-law norms and their impact on our system of governance may be explored in other arenas as well, including the realm of husband-wife relations. Reva Siegel (1994) has written that status hierarchies connected to marriage were modernized within the modern constitutional order, but they have not been eradicated. I agree and believe that we need to look at the way that liberal constitutional structures not only tolerate but also perpetuate status hierarchies connected to race and gender. Liberal feminism in the 1960s and 1970s never succeeded in its campaign to erase gender difference as a matter of constitutional and political relevance.

We should consider both why ungendered legal individualism was the goal and why that goal was never obtained. What that inquiry reveals, I suggest, is the unfinished transition from a political order in which status hierarchies related to race and gender were explicit matters of constitutional governance to a political order in which the social regulation of race and gender still plays an important role but in ways that are less explicit (Ritter 2006).

Although this analysis is only meant to be suggestive, it underscores the insights that would be gained by researchers in American political development (and American politics more generally) by treating gender as a core problematic and category of analysis. It would enrich our understanding of many of the enduring questions in American politics, and it would shed light on a substantial issue of political inclusion and democratization. It would also benefit scholars who consider the role of political women in American democracy to understand the various ways in which our political institutions, culture, and modes of behavior have been gendered, as demonstrated by the other contributors to this volume.

Notes

1. See the president's January 29, 2002, State of the Union address. http://www. whitehouse.gov/news/releases/2002/01/20020129-11.html. Accessed May 10, 2007.
2. But not always; see Aretxaga 1997.
3. In addition to the seminal work of Rogers Smith and Karen Orren, other scholars who have made thoughtful contributions in this area include Desmond King and Anne Norton.
4. Citizenship is a legal status that is governed for Americans under the terms of the Fourteenth Amendment. It is awarded automatically to all of those born on U.S. soil and under U.S. authority. Yet there have been many people who are not formally counted as citizens, whose political rights and membership are nonetheless governed by the federal government. Examples include Native Americans for much of U.S. history, particularly in the period prior to the Indian Citizenship Act; African American slaves (and sometimes free African Americans as well) in the Antebellum era; immigrants of all types, including the undocumented (who may nonetheless be taxed and given social services), those in the process of naturalizing, and permanent residents (including those deemed ineligible for citizenship); residents of territories governed by the United States following military conquests, including, for instance, Filipinos and Puerto Ricans following the Spanish-American War; and American women who were stripped of their citizenship for marrying a foreign national between 1877 and 1922 (Ritter 2006).
5. I might add here that I think there are several especially thoughtful and nuanced political behavior scholars who focus on issues of race and gender and whose scholarship would be of particular interest to gender APD scholars, such as Nancy Burns, Tali Mendelberg, and Lynn Sanders.
6. Of course, even these "nonsocial" policies can have important social effects. The development of the interstate highway system, for instance, had an enormous

demographic impact on the United States because it facilitated the growth of suburbs and the departure of many white middle- and working-class Americans from the cities.

7. On the importance of notions of independence and dependence to political traditions of citizenship in the United States, see Shklar 1991 and Kann 1991.
8. What follows is drawn from an unpublished paper of mine (Ritter 2003).
9. This sketch is meant only to be suggestive. None of the points in the developmental account offered here are fully elaborated and would require much more evidence to be sustained.

3

Gender, Public Opinion, and Political Reasoning

Leonie Huddy, Erin Cassese, and Mary-Kate Lizotte

Men and women differ in their political attitudes and behavior, but these differences are modest and inconsistent (Sapiro 2003). The much-discussed gender gap in voting choice and partisan preference in which women identify more strongly with the Democratic Party and give greater electoral support to Democratic candidates is real, persistent, and consequential. However, it is also modest in size, with women and men differing in their support for Democratic presidential and congressional candidates by 8 to 10 percentage points on average. This difference is small compared with other political differences across demographic groups such as race, in which the gap in vote choice between blacks and whites is closer to 40 percentage points (Tate 1994). There are also small or inconsistent differences between men and women in many areas of public opinion, leaving researchers to analyze various "gender gaps" of differing origins, in addition to many areas of public opinion in which there are simply no such differences (Schlesinger and Heldman 2001). In reality, men and women both differ and converge politically in interesting ways that deserve the scrutiny of empirical researchers (for a similar point about differences between male and female politicians, see Reingold, this volume).

Differences between men and women are slight, but that does not necessarily neutralize their political power. A difference of even 8 to 10 percentage points can determine the outcome of elections because women represent a larger segment of the voting population than do men. Similar logic applies to small gender differences in various aspects of public opinion that can have large political effects through their impact on vote choice. The gender gap in electoral choice, partisanship, and issue preferences has thus drawn the deserved attention of researchers, political pundits, campaign strategists, and political candidates. In this chapter, we review evidence on the existence of gender differences in various areas of public opinion and voting behavior, underscoring throughout the need for a deeper theoretical and empirical investigation of such differences. Our overarching goal is to encourage researchers to more carefully trace the origins of broad gender differences to particular sociopolitical beliefs, personality traits, and social roles that are associated, however loosely, with being male or female. Our focus is more psychological than sociological, with an emphasis on internalized psychological aspects of gender as proximate causes of differences in men and women's political views. This rectifies an intellectual imbalance noted by Burns (this volume) in which insufficient attention has been paid to the psychological causes of gender differences.

Before proceeding further, we need to clarify our use of terminology. Karen Beckwith (2005) has argued that "sex" is the appropriate term to use for men and women, whereas "gender" should be reserved for culturally embedded notions of masculine and feminine. We use gender differently, however, to refer more broadly to men and women and assume that political gender effects (which are far from homogeneous) stem from the psychological and sociological factors linked to being male or female in a given context. Our use of gender to refer to men and women should not be seen as an attempt to essentialize women. Our current project is fully consistent with the goals of many gender researchers who argue for a movement away from the simple assessment of male-female to an investigation of "the paths, the experiences, and the mechanism through which gender formations operate" (Burns 2005, 140).

We begin with an overview of the major theoretical explanations advanced for gender differences in political attitudes and behavior, move on to attitudinal differences in specific policy areas, and then evaluate what is known about the origins of such differences in different domains of public opinion. This is followed by a discussion of gender differences in vote choice and partisanship. We concentrate on findings from the United States, noting evidence from other countries where possible, and focus exclusively on published reports of public opinion. There is a voluminous social science literature on gender differences to which we cannot do justice. As a consequence, we confine our discussion to key findings on the existence of gender differences in public opinion and their more proximate origins in broader political beliefs, psychological factors, and, to a lesser extent, sociological roles and status.

BROAD THEORETICAL APPROACHES TO GENDER DIFFERENCES

It is deeply unsatisfying to examine political differences between men and women without exploring their origins, as noted by several other contributors to this volume (see Wolbrecht, this volume). Indeed, in many respects, the most interesting question about gender differences is their origins, because the answer holds the key to the future dynamics of the gender gap in voting and public opinion. Are political gender differences stable? Long-lived? Consistent? Observed across diverse nations? The answers hinge on whether political differences emerge from elemental differences between men and women that cross political context, fleeting and more ephemeral factors embedded within specific cultures and polities, or some mixture of the two.

We examine here three broad theoretical explanations for gender political differences that are not necessarily mutually exclusive. The three approaches hold differing implications for the development of political differences between men and women and are discussed separately to understand better their political consequences.

Socialization and Personality

Political differences are often traced back to differences between men and women in basic personality characteristics and behavioral tendencies. Paul T. Costa, Antonio Terracciano, and Robert R. McCrae (2001) recently examined the existence of differences in self-rated personality traits across numerous diverse cultures. They found robust but small differences in four of the Big Five personality factors, with women scoring more highly on neuroticism (e.g., anxious, depressed, vulnerable), agreeableness (e.g., trusting, tenderminded, altruistic), the warmth component of extraversion, and openness to feelings (a subscale of openness to experience). Men scored more highly on the assertiveness subcomponent of extraversion and openness to ideas (a subscale of openness to experience). Similar differences have been widely reported in other studies (Eagly 1987). Of course, it is important to note that as for political differences, such personality differences are small, on average, and swamped by differences among men and women.

Self-rated differences in personality observed by Costa and colleagues (2001) are consistent with gender stereotypes that portray women as more caring, emotional, and vulnerable than men, and men as more assertive and rational than women (Best and Williams 1982). When taken together, these small differences in personality could account for similarly modest differences in basic values such as egalitarianism, government activism, and antimilitarism on which women score more highly than men (Eagly, Diekman, Johannesen-Schmidt, and Koenig 2004; Howell and Day 2000; Schwartz and Rubel 2005). Differences in the endorsement of these values could, in turn, drive modest differences in attitudes toward specific government policies concerning poverty, education, the use of force, and ultimately vote choice.

Different theoretical explanations have been advanced to account for observed differences in men's and women's personalities. They could arise from either innate tendencies associated with women's biological role as mothers or from childhood socialization in which girls are taught to be more nurturing than boys and boys are taught to be more assertive and self-reliant than girls. The relatively small magnitude of personality differences and the existence of considerable within-gender diversity suggests, however, that

observed personality differences do not simply arise from basic physical differences that distinguish men and women (Fausto-Sterling 1985).

Alice Eagly has advanced a theory of gender differences grounded in men
and women's differing social roles and socialization (Eagly 1987). Eagly has
argued that gender differences in attitudes originate in gender-role socialization, which conveys expectations about the attributes of men and women
regardless of their adoption of specific gender-typed roles such as mother or
family breadwinner. Gender-role expectations arise from the reality of men
and women's differing social roles. Women's continued role as family caregiver helps to explain why gender stereotypes depict women as more caring
and nurturing than men (Bianchi, Milkie, Sayer, and Robinson 2000). The
greater preponderance of male family providers likewise produces expectations that men will be more assertive and hardheaded than women (Eagly
1987; Eagly and Steffen 1984). Gender-role expectations are further reinforced in the workplace. Men are more likely than women to hold leadership positions at work and to work in technical fields. In contrast, women
populate lower-level clerical positions and tend to be more numerous in the
"caring" professions (Reskin, McBrier, and Kmec 1999). Role expectations
also influence the formation of public policy (Ritter, this volume).

In a variant on Eagly's approach, Sandra L. Bem (1981; Frable and Bem
1985) argues that men and women differ in how thoroughly they internalize
specific gender types or identity and developed the Bem Sex Role Inventory to measure gender identities with a sixty-item checklist of gender-typed
personality adjectives. Some women and men diverge in terms of their self-
concept, holding strongly sex-typed and differentiated self-schemas. Others
converge and see themselves as having both typical male and female qualities,
a group Bem labels "androgynous." Still others score low on both masculine
and feminine traits, exhibiting few gender-linked characteristics. Moreover,
gender identity appears to have real political consequences with a "female"
sex-typed identity leading to support of values linked to a communal outlook and a "male" identity linked to instrumental values (Feather 1984).
Differences among men and women in the extent to which they hold gender-
typed identities may play an important role in conveying political gender
differences. Unfortunately, there is little public opinion research on this to
date, a point to which we return as we consider empirical evidence for the
origins of gender differences in various domains of public opinion.

One obvious problem for a personality explanation of political gender
differences is evidence of a recent emergence of the gender gap in vote
choice in the United States and Europe at a time when gender roles and
identities have become less, not more, distinct. Eagly and colleagues (2004)
argue that women's growing political awareness explains the gap, suggesting that potential differences existed in the past but were not translated
into political attitudes and behaviors because women remained uninterested
and uninvolved in politics. This is an intriguing but untested possibility that

is consistent with political theorists' contention that the women's movement empowered women to develop a distinctive political outlook (Conover 1988).

Gender and Feminist Consciousness

Group interest or group consciousness theories provide an alternative explanation for political gender differences. From this vantage point, differences arise from beliefs concerning women's and men's positions within society. The specific form taken by group consciousness varies, as does its measurement. In one common approach developed by Arthur H. Miller and colleagues (1981), group consciousness depends on three interrelated beliefs: a sense of subjective group identification, a belief that one's group is relatively deprived, and a sense that the system is to blame for group disparities. Building on this approach, gender consciousness has typically been measured as support for equal gender roles and perceived gender inequality (Banaszak and Plutzer 1993; Kalmuss, Gurin, and Townsend 1981; Plutzer 1988). Other researchers have focused on a more explicitly political version of gender consciousness, labeled "feminist consciousness," that has been measured in several ways: as combined support for feminists or the women's movement and equal gender roles (Cook 1989; Cook and Wilcox 1991; Howell and Day 2000; Sapiro and Conover 1997), positive attitudes toward feminists (Rhodebeck 1996), or some mix of feminist identity, support for egalitarian gender roles, and an emotional bond with other women (Conover 1988; Conover and Sapiro 1993).

Overall, women tend to exhibit higher levels of feminist consciousness than men in the United States and Western Europe (Hayes, McAllister, and Studlar 2000; Howell and Day 2000; Huddy, Neely, and LaFay 2000; Sapiro and Conover 1997). But men and women do not differ on all aspects of gender or feminist consciousness. They largely agree in their positive assessment of the women's movement and women's organizations (Huddy et al. 2000). They also generally support equal pay scales and egalitarian roles for women outside the home (Simon and Landis 1989). Ronald Inglehart and Pippa Norris (2003) document a recent similar convergence in men's and women's support of equal gender roles in a large number of countries throughout the world.

There are no differences in attitudes reported by men and women on a slew of other policy questions that touch on support for efforts to strengthen women's status, what the women's movement means, or its general and specific effects (Huddy et al. 2000), although findings are not entirely uniform. For example, Nancy J. Davis and Robert V. Robinson (1991) found that women were more likely than men to perceive gender inequities and support efforts to reduce it in the United States, Great Britain, and West Germany in the mid-1980s. Overall, however, meager gender differences on attitudes toward the women's movement parallel past reports of few differences in public support for the Equal Rights Amendment, gender equality, and related public policy issues (Sapiro 1991b; Sears and Huddy 1990; Simon and Landis 1989).

Even if differences in gender or feminist consciousness are small or inconsistent, such views could have greater political impact among women than men, producing differences in policy views and values. Women are more committed movement supporters than men; they are more likely to identify as feminists, more supportive of collective action, and more likely to have participated in movement-related events (Huddy et al. 2000). Gender or feminist consciousness could thus have greater political impact for women than men. This explanation seems to have little empirical traction, however, a point to which we return in greater detail as we review the origins of the gender gap in vote choice and partisanship.

Gender or feminist consciousness may not directly explain political differences between men and women, but it might work via resultant differences in political outlook. Pamela Johnston Conover (1988) reports that feminist identity among women is linked to a liberal political outlook, stronger egalitarianism, less traditional morality, more sympathy toward the disadvantaged, and more support for increased spending on social programs. She concludes that these political differences may ultimately come down to divergence between men and feminist women, finding little difference between men and nonfeminist women on basic values and political policy positions. Elizabeth Adell Cook and Clyde Wilcox (1991) counter that feminist identity leads to a distinct liberal, egalitarian outlook among both feminist women and men.

Self-Interest: Work and Family

Self-interest provides a third way to explain political differences between men and women, grounded in their differing material circumstances. From a self-interest perspective, political decisions are made on the basis of one's own personal concerns rather than those of women or men as distinct groups. Several different self-interest explanations have been advanced to account for gender differences in public opinion and political behavior. One possibility is that the gender gap is concentrated among economically vulnerable women. Low-income women have typically been more dependent than men on government assistance, relying on government child-care assistance to obtain employment and undertake job retraining in the aftermath of the 1996 passage of welfare reform and depending more heavily on direct government assistance through Aid to Families with Dependent Children prior to 1996. Women may also have a greater investment in programs directed at low-income children such as Head Start (Piven 1985). Janet Box-Steffensmeier, Suzanna De Boef, and Tse-Min Lin (2004) found that, in the aggregate, the gender gap in Democratic identification has grown over time with an increase in the number of single women in American society, a potentially vulnerable group economically. As a result of the special concerns and circumstances of economically disadvantaged women, their political attitudes and behavior may strongly diverge from those of other women and men.

There is some overlap between the economic vulnerability hypothesis and notions of intersectionality, discussed at some length by Jane Junn and Nadia Brown (this volume). Within public opinion research, self-interest effects have been typically viewed as nongendered. A dependence on social welfare benefits, for example, is thought to produce support for an expanded social welfare state among both men and women. This type of self-interest is typically tested through mediational analyses in which economic vulnerability conveys the political effects of gender. The intersectionality hypothesis obviously predicts something different that is best captured by looking at the coincidence of gender and economic vulnerability. This involves conducting various empirical analyses, testing for the distinct political effects of economic vulnerability among men and women. Relatively little empirical research has seriously tested the notion of intersectionality to date.

Alternatively, the gender gap might originate among women who are economically autonomous from men but not necessarily economically vulnerable, as suggested by Susan J. Carroll (1988, 2006). Single or well-educated women who are in professional employment are more likely to be employed in the public sector (education, health care, etc.) and thus have more to gain from the success of the Democratic Party (Erie and Rein 1988; Manza and Brooks 1998). Indeed, working women may generally have more to gain than nonemployed women from Democratic administrations, which are more inclined than their Republican counterparts to support assistance to working parents and promote affirmative action programs that help women's advancement in the workforce. Furthermore, women employed in higher-status, male-dominated occupations may benefit the most from specific legislation concerning job discrimination and affirmative action, as well as court decisions mandating redress of pay inequities. These considerations suggest that professional or well-educated working women may have the most to gain from the election of Democratic candidates and may be responsible for the gender gap in policy attitudes and voting behavior.

Other noneconomic tangible interests could also fuel distinct political views among men and women. For example, mothers with adult sons or sons in the military may be especially opposed to belligerent foreign actions that might involve their child in overseas military service (Conover and Sapiro 1993). The presence of male children may also have a specific impact on support of policies that crack down on violent crime domestically, because men are more likely than women to be the victims of violent crime. From this perspective, mothers are more likely than fathers to support government policies that protect their children from violent crime or direct involvement in military action. Finally, for similar reasons mothers of young children may be more supportive of expanded child-care policies, greater education spending, and government programs aimed at children very generally. However, there is limited empirical support that self-interest or other tangible interests account for differences in public opinion or electoral behavior, a point to which we return on closer examination of specific political differences between women and men.

GENDER DIFFERENCES IN PUBLIC OPINION

Social Welfare Policies and Compassion

There are consistent differences between American men and women on support for social welfare policies (Shapiro and Mahajan 1986). Women are more likely than men to support policies that provide for the disadvantaged including policies on health care, housing, education, child care, and poverty; they are also more likely to support government spending on Social Security, the homeless, welfare, food stamps, child care, schools, government-provided health insurance, government-guaranteed jobs, support for expanded government services, and government spending on the poor (Clark and Clark 1993, 1996; Howell and Day 2000; Schlesinger and Heldman 2001; Shapiro and Mahajan 1986).

These differences in support of social welfare policy issues are modest in size, however, averaging roughly 3 to 4 percentage points on typical poll questions and vary in magnitude and consistency across policy areas (Shapiro and Mahajan 1986). In the 1988 and 1992 American National Election Studies (ANES), women were more supportive than men of government spending on Social Security, child care, and the homeless by somewhere between 10 and 15 percentage points (Clark and Clark 1993, 1996). The gap is somewhat smaller in other areas, including government aid to minorities, government-funded health insurance, government-guaranteed jobs, spending on the poor, food stamps, and programs targeted at the working poor. An overall gender difference in support of social welfare policies persists even after controlling for partisanship and demographic factors (Cook and Wilcox 1995; Eagly et al. 2004; Howell and Day 2000).

There are also modest differences between women and men on racial policy positions, with roughly 3 to 4 percent more women than men in support of government action (Clark and Clark 1993, 1996; Howell and Day 2000; Hughes and Tuch 2003). Michael Hughes and Steven A. Tuch (2003) examine data from several ANES and General Social Survey national surveys and find that women are more supportive than men of government assistance to blacks, increased government spending to improve the position of blacks, a greater government role in school integration, and affirmative action in college admissions. Differences are less common for other racial attitudes, including racial stereotypes and social distance measures, although women are more willing than men to live in an integrated neighborhood (Hughes and Tuch 2003).

Origins of Gender Differences in Support of Social Welfare Policies

Compassion and Empathy. Differences in support of social welfare policies might arise from women's slightly greater tendency to rate themselves as more compassionate, caring, and expressive than men (Costa et al., 2001). It is important to note, however, that although these personality differences are robust in self-report data, they are less apparent in studies of actual behavior. For example, women report higher levels of empathy and concern for others than do men but do not exhibit more supportive nonverbal responses to those in distress in observational studies and are less likely to help those in distress because of the physical dangers involved in real-world helping situations (Beutel and Marini 1995; Eagly and Crowley 1986; Eisenberg and Lennon 1983).

Developmental psychologist Carol Gilligan developed a widely cited and popular account of differences in this realm that rests on distinct patterns of moral reasoning. According to Gilligan (1982), men resolve moral dilemmas through a reliance on the ethic of justice whereas women rely on an ethic of care. But there has been a persistent lack of empirical support for Gilligan's position. A careful review of findings in research on children fails to find the expected differences in moral reasoning (L. J. Walker 1984). Furthermore, a recent meta-analysis of numerous empirical studies finds weak support, at best, for Gilligan's predictions (Jaffee and Hyde 2000). These findings raise questions about the extent to which compassion drives gender differences in support of social welfare politics.

Egalitarianism, Activist Government, Humanitarianism. Specific gender-related traits may influence political attitudes through their impact on basic social and political values. Consistent evidence reveals that women are more supportive than men of a strong, activist government (Clark and Clark 1996; Howell and Day 2000; Seltzer, Newman, and Leighton 1997). Moreover, this difference extends beyond the United States to Europe, Africa, Latin American, and Asia (Inglehart and Norris 2003). Such differences in support of an active government are linked to men and women's different ideological affiliations (Clark and Clark 1996; Inglehart and Norris 2003). There is also a moderately reliable gap in egalitarianism, with women tending toward stronger support than men of general societal equality. This difference has been observed in many (Eagly et al. 2004; Feldman and Steenbergen 2001; Howell and Day 2000; Sapiro and Conover 1997) but not all studies (Christensen and Dunlap 1984; Conover 1988; Cook and Wilcox 1991). The gap between women and men in endorsement of egalitarianism is also consistent with men's greater social dominance orientation and stronger support for the maintenance of social hierarchies (Sidanius and Pratto 1999).

In addition, there is evidence that women and men hold somewhat different political values. Stanley Feldman and Marco R. Steenbergen (2001) found women scored more highly on an empathy scale, fueling increased scores on a scale of humanitarianism. Shalom H. Schwartz and Tammy Rubel (2005) found that women in seventy countries place a consistently higher value than men on benevolence (enhancing the welfare of those with whom one is in close contact) and universalism (protecting the welfare of all people), whereas men rank instrumental values (e.g., achievement, self-direction) more highly than do women. These value differences are modest in size and not observed uniformly in all countries (Prince-Gibson and Schwarz 1998).

Such divergence in the endorsement of basic values is politically consequential. The gap between women and men in support of social welfare policies can be traced, in part, to differences in basic values, especially egalitarianism. Susan E. Howell and Christine L. Day (2000) report that women's greater egalitarianism mediated the effects of gender on social welfare policies in their research, and humanitarianism moderated the impact of gender such that it played a greater role in shaping policy support among women than men. Both values together accounted for fully half of the observed difference in social welfare attitudes in this study. In a similar vein, Eagly and colleagues (2004) report that women's greater egalitarianism and liberal ideology mediated the effects of gender on social compassion issues.[1] It is thus tempting to conclude that women's greater compassion drives at least some of the gender gap in support of social welfare policies. However, as noted earlier, women's stronger endorsement of egalitarianism could derive from either basic personality characteristics such as compassion or ideological beliefs reflected in support of gender and feminist consciousness (Conover 1988).

Self-interest plays a more modest role in accounting for differences in social welfare attitudes. In Howell and Day's research (2000), women with children under age eighteen years were more likely to support social welfare policies than men with similarly aged children; furthermore, the greater preponderance of women in occupations described as "redistributive" (e.g., health, education, social welfare) mediated the effects of gender on social welfare attitudes.

There are still too few studies that rigorously tackle explanations for women's greater support of social welfare attitudes. On the basis of the research reviewed here, some of the difference in social welfare support can be traced to gender differences in egalitarian outlook and some to possible self-interest. Unfortunately, the role of gender or feminist consciousness and self-rated personality traits remains unclear. Future research should examine the origins of the gender gap in social welfare attitudes and consider the extent to which framing an issue in terms of interests, compassion, or feminism increases or decreases the gap.

Attitudes toward Governmental Use of Force

The largest gender difference in policy preferences emerges on issues linked to violence and the use of force. A number of studies point to pronounced differences between men and women in support of military intervention in overseas conflicts, punitive crime policy, and gun control. On these issues, women are less likely to endorse the government's use of force and express greater fear of its consequences. Broadly construed, differences between men and women in support of government use of force average around 8 percent and are twice the size of differences on nonforce issues including social welfare (Shapiro and Mahajan 1986). Of course, it is important to point out that gender differences in support of the use of force are small and overshadowed by differences among women and men.

The gap between women and men in support of overseas military action ranges from 7 to 9 percentage points for World War II, Korea, and Vietnam (Shapiro and Mahajan 1986). Significant differences are also evident in support of the Gulf War (Bendyna et al. 1996; Conover and Sapiro 1993), the military campaign in Afghanistan (Huddy, Feldman, Taber, and Lahav 2005) and the Iraq War (Huddy, Feldman, and Cassese 2007; Huddy, Feldman, and Cassese, in press). There is some evidence that the size of this difference in support for overseas military action varies with the stage of the conflict. In the initial stages of conflict, women are consistently less supportive than men of military action. These differences are most pronounced prior to the commitment of troops. As a conflict persists, the gap narrows but does not disappear (Bendyna et al. 1996; Conover and Shapiro 1993).

Women are also more inclined than men to favor peaceful and less militaristic solutions to international disputes (Fite, Genest, and Wilcox 1990). Looking at ANES data on midconflict attitudes toward the Korean War, Vietnam, Operation Desert Shield, and Operation Desert Storm, Miroslav Nincic and Donna J. Nincic (2002) found that women endorse goals of peace and reconciliation at greater rates than men, whereas men are more likely to favor alternatives that escalate conflict. Findings on this point are not completely uniform, however (Wilcox, Hewitt, and Allsop 1996).

Women's reluctance to endorse the governmental use of force extends to domestic contexts, including the criminal justice system. They are much less likely to support capital punishment than men, although majorities of both men and women support it (Stack 2000; Whitehead and Blankenship 2000). Women are also less likely to condone the use of police violence in a variety of scenarios (Halim and Stiles 2001). They are more likely than men to oppose harsh punishment for criminals, although this difference depends on the nature of the crime and disappears for crimes such as rape and the sale of drugs to children (Hurwitz and Smithey 1998; Smith 1984). Women are also more likely than men to favor government restrictions on access to firearms, expressing greater support of gun-control measures, including assault-weapon bans, seven-day waiting periods, and door-to-door searches for illegal weapons (Wolpert and Gimpel 1998).

Origins of Gender Differences on Force and Violence

A variety of theoretical explanations have been offered to explain differences between men and women in support of the government's use of force. We once again consider evidence for the origins of political gender differences in personality, including psychological vulnerability and gender or feminist consciousness.

Personality – Compassion, Aggression, and Psychological Vulnerability.
Some researchers argue that men's greater willingness to use force arises from basic gender differences in personality, including differences in compassion and empathy. This notion is linked to Gilligan's (1982) work on moral reasoning, which documents women's greater use of an "ethic of care." Ruddick (1989) suggests women's social roles as wives and mothers shape their personality and lead to ways of thinking and acting that provide a foundation for pacifism. Maternal practices involve nonviolent conflict management, compromise, and reconciliation, consistent with a pacifist orientation. Empirical support for this "maternal" perspective has not materialized, however (Bendyna et al. 1996; Conover and Sapiro 1993).

Common male and female stereotypes portray men as more aggressive than women, and men are far more likely than women to carry out violent crimes, leading to the notion that men may be more supportive of violence in all realms of life, including the governmental use of force (Eagly and Steffen 1986). However, differences in aggressive attitudes and behavior are complex, with greater aggression observed among men than women only when an action causes physical harm or is likely to lead to retaliation, anxiety, or guilt. Costa and colleagues (2001) report higher levels of hostility among men in some studies, higher levels of anger among women in others, and find no difference in other instances. Moreover, such differences in aggression are eradicated under conditions of strong provocation (Bettencourt and Miller 1996). More research is thus necessary to examine whether men and women's different orientations toward anger and aggression fuel related differences in foreign policy attitudes.

As noted earlier, there are small differences linked to the personality trait of neuroticism in which women report feeling more vulnerable, worried, and anxious than men report. The link between these personality characteristics and attitudes toward foreign policy has rarely been explored directly, but a number of studies hint at their possible importance. Women are more pessimistic about the costly outcome of war, including casualties; report more depressive symptoms such as difficulty sleeping and concentrating at work in response to military conflict; and are more worried about retaliation or an escalation of conflict and the possibility of nuclear war (Bendyna et al. 1996; Conover and Sapiro 1993; Gwartney-Gibbs and Lach 1991).

Recently there has been increased interest in gender differences in response to terrorism, which seem to preoccupy and disproportionately concern women. Women have reported higher levels of threat, personal vulnerability, and anxiety in response to recent terrorist acts (Goodwin, Willson, and Gaines 2005; Huddy et al. 2005). A series of studies suggest that women were more likely to experience posttraumatic distress than men and exhibit more severe symptoms following the September 11 terrorist attacks (Silver et al. 2002). Furthermore, these differences can be consequential. In a survey of Israelis following the terror attacks of the Al-Aqsa Intifada, Zahava Solomon, Marc Gelkopf, and Avraham Bleich (2005) found that women reported greater personal threat than men, which was linked, in turn, to a significantly heightened susceptibility to posttraumatic stress.

Women's stronger emotional reactions to war and terrorism are intriguing. Our analysis of American responses to the Iraq War in October 2002 reveals that roughly half the gender gap in support of military intervention in Iraq (which men supported by roughly 8 percentage points more than women) was due to women's greater anxiety about the war (Huddy, Feldman, and Cassese, in press). Overall, further study is needed to understand the impact of personality, especially characteristics that produce a heightened sense of psychological vulnerability, on support for the governmental use of force.

Leaving aside basic personality differences that may make women feel more vulnerable, self-interest alone may drive women's greater opposition to the use of force. Although women are statistically much less likely than men to be victims of both violent and nonviolent crime, they are more likely to be victims of sexual assault. Women are more concerned than men about the prospect of sexual assault in any crime situation, heightening their general fear of crime (Ferraro 1996). Women's greater fear of crime is linked to a lower sense of personal security and self-efficacy and is greater among older and lower socioeconomic status individuals (Schafer, Huebner, and Bynum 2006). Such anxieties over sexual victimization may explain women's greater support for gun-control laws as a measure to control crime. They also raise an interesting but unanswered question about whether women's fear of sexual assault is linked to their greater sense of anxiety about all forms of violence, including war.

Feminist Consciousness. Historically, the women's movement has endorsed principles of nonviolence (Beckwith 2002; Costain 2000) and many have pointed to a link between feminist consciousness and pacifism (see, e.g.,

Brock-Utne 1985). Conover (1988) found pronounced differences between feminists, nonfeminist women, and men on foreign policy issues. Feminist women (and men) are consistently less supportive of conventional and nuclear war, intervention in Central America, and defense spending (Cook and Wilcox 1991). Conover and Virginia Sapiro (1993) offer additional evidence of the link between feminism and pacifism, reporting a feminist gap among men and women in attention to the Gulf War, and a feminist gap among women in opposition to civilian bombing and emotional distress in response to the war, but not overall war support. Feminist consciousness thus provides a partial explanation for gender differences in support of the use of force, and more work is needed to understand what basic values or beliefs mediate this effect.

Morality Issues

On average, women report higher levels of religiosity and religious fundamentalism than men (Kelley and DeGraaf 1997; Walter and Davie 1998) and stronger commitment to religion and religious institutions (Batson, Schoenrade, and Ventis 1993; Tolleson-Rinehart and Perkins 1989). Moreover, religiosity is associated with moral traditionalism, which can translate into support for government policies that promote traditional values. Eagly and colleagues (2004) find women are less supportive of behaviors and policies that violate conventional moral norms, such as casual sex, drug use, and suicide. Women are also more supportive than men of school prayer and greater governmental restrictions on access to pornography and are more opposed to the legalization of marijuana. Such differences are moderate in size, ranging from 7 percent on school prayer to 18 percent on pornography (Clark and Clark 1993).

Differences between men and women on moral issues are not fully consistent, however, because women are also more supportive than men of gay rights. On average, women report higher levels of tolerance toward homosexuals than men, more positive affect, and fewer negative feelings. This difference is associated with stronger support of gays in the military among women and greater support for gay civil rights (Herek 2002; LaMar and Kite 1998), although findings are not fully consistent (Davies 2004). In the end, it may be heterosexual men's intolerance toward gay men that drives this difference in attitudes toward gays overall, although women's greater egalitarianism may also play a role (Kite and Whitely 1996).

Some scholars attribute gender differences in religiosity and traditional morality to gender-role socialization that promotes traits such as passivity and obedience in women (Thompson 1991). Others argue for a social-role explanation in which women have the primary responsibility for the moral development of children (Iannocone 1991). Eagly and colleagues (2004) find that gender differences on morality issues are slightly moderated by demographic factors such as having children in the home, but these effects are slight, and the large gap between men and women occurs even when variables are controlled statistically. More research is needed to understand the degree to which differences on moral issues derive from personality traits, such as obedience, women's roles as caregivers, or associated beliefs about the protection of vulnerable individuals.

Women's Issues

An explanation of political differences between men and women grounded in heightened gender and feminist consciousness among women goes hand in hand with the notion that women are more supportive than men of women's issues. In reality, however, men and women equally support governmental action on most women's issues – policies that are either explicitly concerned with women's rights or have a disproportionate impact on women (Sapiro 2003). Negligible differences were observed in the late 1970s and early 1980s on the Equal Rights Amendment, which explicitly promoted women's collective interests. There are also few differences on other women's issues as well, including abortion (Chaney, Alvarez, and Nagler 1998; Clark and Clark 1996; Cook and Wilcox 1995; Shapiro and Mahajan 1986; Strickler and Danigelis 2002).

ELECTORAL POLITICS

Vote Choice and Partisanship

We turn finally to consider the gender gap in vote choice and partisanship, which has elicited considerable research interest. Since the early 1980s, American women have consistently voted in greater numbers than men for Democratic presidential and congressional candidates (Carroll 2006; Manza and Brooks 1998). They have also expressed stronger identification with the Democratic Party over the same time period (Box-Steffensmeier et al. 2004; Chaney et al. 1998; Cook and Wilcox 1995). Data from the pooled 1980 to 2004 ANES demonstrate these trends, as seen in Figure 3.1. In most election years, women demonstrate greater support than men for the Democratic presidential candidate. A majority of women preferred Ronald Reagan to his Democratic opponent in 1980 and 1984. In all other presidential elections, however, a majority of women in the ANES sample voted for the Democratic over the Republican candidate. In contrast, a majority of men supported only one Democratic presidential candidate – Bill Clinton in 1992 and 1996 – expressing a preference for the Republican candidate in all other elections.[2]

Overall, the gap in vote choice between men and women is relatively modest, with somewhere between 6 and 12 percent more women than men

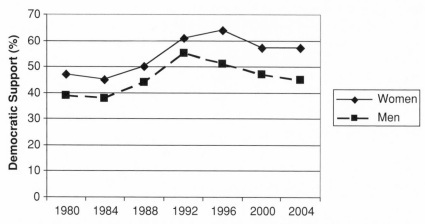

FIGURE 3.1. Gender Differences in Support of Democratic Presidential Candidates. *Note:* Data are unweighted. Entries are the percent who supported the Democratic candidate in each year and are confined to those who voted for one of the two major-party candidates. Missing values are excluded. *Source:* ANES pooled data set.

voting for the Democratic than Republican presidential candidate in the past seven elections. Moreover, the difference persists even with the inclusion of multivariate controls and is found within similar demographic groupings based on age, race, education, religiosity, and marital status (Huddy, Cassese, and Lizotte 2008). This finding points strongly toward a psychological rather than a sociological explanation for the gender gap.

The gender gap in Democratic partisanship is similar in magnitude to the gender gap in support of Democratic presidential candidates. Excluding partisan leaners (independents who lean toward one of the parties), women were more likely than men to identify as Democrats in all presidential election years between 1980 and 2004. This partisan gap is modest in size, ranging from 12 percentage points in 2004 to 7 points in 1980, 1983, and 1992 and can be traced to an aggregate decline in Democratic identification among men coupled with an increase in their Republican identification (Huddy, Cassese, and Lizotte 2008; Norrander 1997). Once again, differences persist with multivariate controls and are observed within a variety of demographic subgroups of women and men, including the highly religious, parents, low-income households, and professionals (Huddy, Cassese, and Lizotte 2008).

Explanations for the Gender Gap in Vote Choice

The electoral and partisan gender gap is fueled by women's and men's somewhat different positions on several political issues (Chaney et al. 1998). Women's stronger (or men's weaker) support of government social welfare spending is the most consistent explanation for the existence of these differences over time (Gilens 1988; Kaufmann and Petrocik 1999; Manza and Brooks 1998). As noted earlier, egalitarianism explains some of the gender gap in support of social welfare issues. However, more work is needed to understand this. Can we trace these differences back to stable differences in men and women's self-rated compassion? Does the impact of compassion have limits so that is it more focused on the protection of the young and elderly than on poverty more generally? And do women translate compassion into greater support of specific types of candidates and policies? The compassion hypothesis would gain stronger support from evidence that the gender gap is fueled by women who score highly on empathy scales, rate themselves as compassionate, or express sympathy with the plight of disadvantaged people.

Other theoretical explanations for the gender gap in vote choice garner little empirical support. There is no support for an explanation based on women's gender consciousness (Chaney et al. 1998; Cook and Wilcox 1991; Klein 1984; Mansbridge 1985; Manza and Brooks 1998). The gender gap in support of Democratic candidates may reflect a growing difference between men and women in their reactions to the economy. In recent elections, women have been more pessimistic than men about the state of the economy and their personal finances (Chaney et al. 1998). This finding exists for retrospective (Kaufmann and Petrocik 1999) and prospective (Clark and Clark 1993, 1996; Cook and Wilcox 1995) economic evaluations. Moreover, women vote on the basis of national economic assessment (compared with men, who rely more on their personal finances), translating their greater pessimism into greater opposition to an incumbent president or his party (Chaney et al. 1998; Welch and Hibbing 1992). This should not necessarily benefit Democratic candidates but is likely to do so when a Republican president presides over a weak national economy. It remains unclear, however, whether gender differences in economic outlook reflect women and men's differing economic self-interests, egalitarianism, or concern for the less fortunate.

In a test of the intersectionality hypothesis, we find no evidence that the effects of gender differ by race, education, occupation, or income (Huddy, Cassese, and Lizotte, 2008). Of course, blacks are much more likely than whites to support the Democratic Party and candidates. Likewise, union members and individuals living in low-income households are more supportive of the Democratic Party than are members of nonunion and higher-income households. However, there is no evidence that the gender gap in partisanship and vote choice is greater among blacks than whites or members of low-income than high-income households. These findings raise questions about the empirical basis of intersectionality that demand further research.

Defense and military issues can elicit a gender gap in support of political candidates, as was observed for presidential elections in the early 1980s (Frankovic 1982; Gilens 1988). Men's stronger support of the use of military force resulted in greater support for Ronald Reagan among men than women in 1980 and 1984. The political focus on terrorism during the 2000s alters this dynamic somewhat. As noted earlier, women are more anxious about terrorism, and, as a general rule, anxiety increases opposition to risky military interventions. However, anxious people must also weigh the risks of inaction, and this may outweigh the effects of action in some political environments. Some women may have seen military action as the least risky course in Iraq, providing a potential boost to George Bush in 2004, who received a slightly higher percentage of votes from secular women in 2004 than 2000 (Huddy, Feldman, and Dutton 2005).

Finally, it is important to underscore the powerful political effects of race, religion, and economic status, which have typically overwhelmed the effects of gender in recent elections (Huddy, Cassese, and Lizotte, 2008; Sapiro and Conover 1997). Black women (and men) are vastly more supportive than white women of the Democratic Party; both black and Jewish women are more likely to identify as Democrats than other women; and women in union households are more supportive than others of Democratic candidates and more inclined to identify with the Democratic Party. A more recent Republican coalition of high-income and religious individuals is also apparent, producing further cleavages among women. Differences among women based on race, religion, and economic status are much larger, on average, than the gap between men and women and place it in needed perspective.

CONCLUSION

Differences in men's and women's political outlooks are small, moderately consistent, and politically consequential. There is an average gender difference of roughly 10 percentage points in support of Democratic candidates and the Democratic Party and comparable or somewhat smaller differences within specific policy domains. Consistent differences between men and women emerge in support of social welfare issues, the governmental use of force, and issues linked to traditional morality. However, the link between these issue positions and electoral choice is likely to vary by election, lending a dynamic quality to the electoral gender gap. Opposition to the use of force was a factor in women's greater opposition to Ronald Reagan in the early 1980s but has played little role in driving opposition to other recent presidential candidates. A gender gap in support of social welfare issues has played a more consistent and prominent role in driving electoral behavior more recently. Nonetheless, women's preferences could easily shift in future elections in tandem with a change in salient campaign issues. For example, women are unlikely to provide greater support than men for Democratic candidates in an election dominated by concerns over pornography, drug usage, and morality. Indeed, in such a climate women may be more inclined to support Republican candidates on average. Far more research is needed on how temporal fluctuations in issue salience influence the emergence and size of the gender gap in partisanship and vote choice.

Consistency in the size of the gender gap across partisanship, vote choice, and various issues does not mean that such gaps have common origins. Consider the differences between men and women in social welfare support, one of the strongest influences on the electoral gender gap to date. It is fueled in part by women's greater support for egalitarianism and possibly humanitarianism, which could arise, in turn, from differences in basic personality traits, such as compassion. But women's greater self-rated compassion is unlikely to account for their greater opposition to the governmental use of force, which is more likely rooted in women's stronger sense of psychological vulnerability or feminist consciousness. Finally, women's greater support for traditional morality issues has more to do with religiosity and family roles than compassion or vulnerability. These differences highlight the diverse origins of political differences between men and women.

We have stressed throughout this review the need for more comprehensive and theoretically grounded research on the origins of political differences between men and women. To some extent, explanations based on self-interest and group consciousness have received more thorough examination than psychological explanations based on differences in basic personality orientations, including self-rated traits, feelings, and basic values. Research on political differences between men and women has moved increasingly beyond the description or documentation of gender differences toward an examination of their origins. Yet pressing questions on all sides remain. What beliefs account for feminists' greater opposition to the use of force? Why are women more egalitarian than men? What role does women's greater self-rated compassion play in accounting for differences in electoral choice? How is women's greater support for traditional morality compatible with stronger support of Democratic candidates at a time when politics is characterized by increasing cultural conflict over these issues? These are a few of the many unanswered questions concerning differences between men's and women's political thinking and behavior. We look forward to a surfeit of satisfying empirical answers in the near future.

Notes

1. The clarity of their findings is reduced, however, by the inclusion of police brutality, gun control, and the death penalty in the combined measure of social welfare attitudes

2. This support among men for Clinton is inflated in Figure 3.1 because voters who supported third-party candidate Ross Perot were omitted. In exit poll data, somewhat more men than women voted for Perot in both 1992 and 1996 (Pomper 2001).

4

Gender in the Aggregate, Gender in the Individual, Gender and Political Action

Nancy Burns

The literature on gender and political action comes in two forms – one that is aggregate, sometimes institutional, and often centered historically, and one that is individual and largely focused on the here and now. We care about both, of course – about the social organization and deployment of gender and about what gender means in individual lives. In this chapter, I argue that we should encourage these two kinds of analysis to engage each other more intimately. This engagement would give political scientists the tools to say more about when, for whom, and for which outcomes gender matters. The conversation would give us better ways to understand how context makes gender relevant.

I believe gender is a property of collections of people and social systems. We care about it because it is about systematic disadvantage and advantage. In this chapter, I am especially interested in thinking about tools for identifying the political contexts in which this disadvantage and advantage come to matter in individual lives.

If Iris Young is right in saying that gender is not much about a "self-consciously, mutually acknowledging collective with a self-conscious purpose," that instead gender is a "less organized and unself-conscious collective unity" (Young 1994, 724), then part of our task as social scientists interested in gender is to come to understand when social and political contexts can make gender relevant, sometimes in a way that people notice and call "gender," and sometimes not. Of course, doing that well requires a research design centered on comparison across contexts – different states, different years, different electoral campaigns.

I have two ideas about where to turn to develop tools to use to think about when political context makes gender matter. I've already mentioned the first: a conversation between macro- and individual-level analyses of gender. The second is the literature on other properties of collections of people, and here I especially mean the literature on race and politics. I focus in this chapter – for reasons of space – almost exclusively on the first strategy.

WHAT COULD COME OF A SERIOUS, CONTINUOUS CONVERSATION BETWEEN AGGREGATE AND INDIVIDUAL ANALYSIS?

Aggregate analyses can help individual-level scholars with political context – with the political conditions under which gender matters in individual lives – because such aggregate analyses offer smoother data, data with which it is easier to see broad structural trends. If gender is a property of groups and systems, then aggregate and systemic analyses put it easily on display.[1] These more macro, aggregate, or institutional analyses also have the (often underused) potential to keep the context of politics and policy in front of us. They can offer ideas about ways to theorize context.

Individual-level analyses have things to offer aggregate scholars as well. Aggregate analysis almost always runs at the elite level or with archival data, and so, like archaeological work in general, it runs the risk of missing systemic features of the lives of ordinary people because the remains of the activities of ordinary people have often been discarded. With aggregate or macro analysis, it is next to impossible to see individual-level mechanisms in action, and so psychological and some sociological mechanisms can only be distantly inferred. Individual-level analysis can provide access to psychological and sociological mechanisms. However, analyses at this level can have trouble putting gender on display, partly because of the aggregate construction of gender, partly because of the explicit work one has to do to incorporate context and history, and partly because analyses at this level have to incorporate theory and measures that tie these individual-level data to the social phenomenon of gender.

Thus we need both levels of analysis. We need the tools and results that would come from serious engagement of one with the other. Aggregate work can provide insights into aspects of political context that might make gender matter in individual lives; individual work can show whether and how these aspects of context actually do matter. Paired with systematic data from more than one year, more than one campaign, more than one location, this understanding could generate a raft of new ideas about gender.

It is not only the gender and politics literature that faces the problem of locating a social construction in individual lives, of linking aggregate and individual analyses, and that takes me to my second idea about how to put gender on display in our work. The literature on race in black and white faces an identical problem (see, e.g., the discussion on race and identity in Brubaker and Cooper 2000). There are, however, ways the parts of the race and politics literature dealing with race in black and white have moved faster than the gender literature to allow linkages between aggregate and individual-level analyses. Scholars in this literature moved early to build connections between campaigns and discourse of political elites and ordinary citizens in their work on race and framing (Gamson and Modigliani 1987; Kinder and Sanders 1990, 1996). In addition, scholars have incorporated social repertoires of race – that is, tools ordinary Americans use to think about race – into their analyses, especially into their analyses of public opinion, building the link between the toolkit of ideas available from politics and ordinary action (Swidler 1986). I mean here racism, black nationalism, and the like (Dawson 2001; Kinder and Sanders 1996). Furthermore, researchers have begun to work through the consequences of segregation with the lenses through which some blacks see politics (see Dawson 1994).

Of course, gender scholars cannot borrow wholesale from the race literature because of the crucial differences between race in black and white and gender at the aggregate level. First off, race has been a key feature, a key driving force, of the American political tradition. This does not mean that gender has been absent from American political history. It has just often been offstage, not taken up explicitly by politics; instead, gender has appeared in action in everyday life – in the understanding of women's fitness for political roles, in the ways institutions outside of politics allocate advantages to men. Politics has built assumptions about women's place into policy.

Second, gender is organized largely through integration, whereas race in black and white is organized through separation (Goffman 1977; Jackman 1994). This means that gender often works more subtly, and it means that studying gender policy and studying women's action are pretty different activities because women are systematically on different sides of political battles about gender. By contrast, race in America works blatantly, and African Americans are a more unified force in politics.

Such integration and intimacy make gender invisible in a number of ways. Because it often works through psychological intimidation, coercion, love, and acquiescence, gender hierarchies are recipes for the morselization of experience. In other words, gender hierarchies enable people – both scholars and the individuals they study – to explain any individual outcome as the product of individual and idiosyncratic circumstance and not as a consequence of large-scale structural forces such as discrimination.[2] To be visible, these cumulated wrongs must be added up – either over institutions or over time. A single snapshot can miss these inequalities unless the snapshot is viewed through a structural account of disadvantage. Otherwise, disadvantage may be hard to see and easy to explain away. Without one of these two approaches – adding up what seem like small potatoes or setting the small inequalities within a structural account – disadvantage, even disadvantage that is perpetrated with violence, can seem like a consequence of choice.

Of course, the implications of morselization extend far beyond research design. They also shape the questions we ask about gender in the first place. Can context – elites, parties, policy, events, and the like – enable people to overcome morselization? What are the conditions under which gender becomes obvious and openly acknowledged? When and how do contexts make gender salient? Are there conditions that enable people to use ideas about gender to shape their political thinking? To shape their political mobilization? When and what about politics encourages or discourages individuals from making gender operate to advantage some groups and disadvantage others? When and what about politics encourages a collectivity to become a self-conscious group?

Of course, context could affect the benefits of participation or the costs. It could shape benefits by priming identification with women, people's investments in or understanding of policy, their sense of obligation as a member of a group (Burns and Kinder 2002; Miller and Rahn 2002). It could shape costs by undercutting or adding to their efficacy, interest, or information; by providing an obvious framework for mobilization (Burns, Schlozman, and Verba 2001; Rosenstone and Hansen 1993; Zaller 1992). Furthermore, following Riker and Ordeshook's (1968) classic formulation, it could shape individuals' sense of the likelihood of getting benefits in the first place. It could work by differentially doing these things for women and men.

A conversation between macro and micro can help us ask – and answer – these questions. Aggregate approaches can provide ideas about relevant dimensions of context and about contours of gender inequality. Individual-level approaches can offer ideas about the mechanisms through which context could come to matter in individual lives.

BEFORE THERE WAS A LITERATURE: THE EARLY HISTORY OF THE STUDY OF GENDER AND PARTICIPATION

Of course, scholars noticed sex differences in political action early on, before scholars viewed themselves as contributing to a literature on the topic and before scholars thought to cite one another on the subject of gender and political action.[3] By the 1940s, scholars were already conceptualizing gender in political and social context, despite the fact that they still were not self-conscious of creating a literature.

One research team in particular, Paul Lazarsfeld, Bernard Berelson, and Hazel Gaudet, used puzzles that emerged when thinking about differences between men and women to shape a general approach to understanding the relationship between political interest and political action. In their 1944 book, *The People's Choice*, Lazarsfeld, Berelson, and Gaudet examined the relationship between sex and political interest and found that women were somewhat less interested in the 1940 presidential campaign than were men. Lack of interest in politics translated into nonvoting for all respondents and identical patterns emerged among those with different levels of education, different economic resources, different ages, and different religions. The one exception was men and women. As Lazarsfeld, Berelson, and Gaudet pointed out, "the result is startlingly different for the sex of the respondents" (1944, 48). They continued: "Sex is the only personal characteristic which affects non-voting, even if interest is held constant. Men are better citizens but women are more reasoned: if they are not interested, they do not vote.... If a woman is not interested, she just feels that there is no reason why she should vote. A man, however, is under more social pressure and will therefore go to the polls even if he is not 'interested' in the events of the campaign" (1944, 48–9). Bernard Berelson, Paul Lazarsfeld, and William McPhee (1954) took this idea, developed to think about differences between women and men, and applied it more broadly in their study of the 1948 election. By this point, they had become interested in the contrast between the social forces and the political forces that create expectations for people to be interested in politics (1954, 25–7). The expectations that grow out of social factors – such as sex or education – were constant, they found, but these expectations were often overshadowed by the ways politics itself made some people want to be interested. There were strong differences between men's and women's levels of interest before the campaign. By the end of the campaign, those differences collapsed (28).

Other scholars also took up the question of sex differences in political action with individual-level data and aggregate-level lenses. Maurice Duverger (1955) framed his comparative examination of sex differences and political action with Simone de Beauvoir (in French, and that matters) in mind.[4] He thought about individual-level and elite-level differences between women and men and found greater differences at the elite than at the mass level. He used de Beauvoir's analysis to think about why this was and how it might change. He said, "the small part played by women in politics merely reflects and results from the secondary place to which they are still assigned by the customs and attitudes of our society and which their education and training tend to make them accept as the natural order of things" (1955, 130). He thought real change would come after people succeeded in discursive work that would destroy the "deeply-rooted belief in the natural inferiority of women" (130).

In 1960, using data from the Michigan Election Studies, Angus Campbell, Philip Converse, Warren Miller, and Donald Stokes continued the focus on the social expectations for political interest and action for men and women to work through a dynamic account of gender and political action. They worried that "social roles are deeply ingrained in day-to-day assumptions about behavior in any culture, and these assumptions are not rapidly uprooted" (484). They imagined a good deal of variation in the definition of these social roles. They expected that social change might start among those with the most education.

They wondered about the future and argued that there were countervailing possibilities. Higher education would erode differences between women and men, they thought. Nevertheless, small children might continue to keep women from political action (488–9). They worried about what they saw as the weaker political efficacy, political engagement, and political sophistication of women and imagined the roots of this to rest in social expectations about women's and men's roles.

These early analyses, especially those of Lazarsfeld, Berelson, and Gaudet, are, to my mind, an underappreciated model for later work in the way they pay attention to political context – both within a single year and across years – and use context to build specific observable implications, in the way they resist assuming men are the norm, in the way they use gender to build analyses that incorporate women and men, and in the way they use results generated with a gendered theoretical lens to shape their thinking about other social factors. Their research designs – centered as they were on collecting data from more than one election cycle – laid the framework for dynamic thinking. For these scholars, context involved the ways campaigns mobilized individuals, and it involved the climate of gendered expectations in which ordinary individuals live.

A SELF-CONSCIOUS LITERATURE

More recently, scholarly analyses of gender and political activity have continued to report small but persistent sex differences in overall levels of political activity. This small gender gap in participation is, it seems, narrower in the United States than in other countries (Christy 1987; Verba, Nie, Kim, and Shabad 1978). Scholars have been developing a mostly structural story of constraint, located in institutions outside of politics.

Scholars have offered four major explanations for women's slightly lower levels of political participation in the United States – explanations centered largely outside of political contexts. One explanation is squarely sociological. The other three move between sociology and psychology in their focus on why women might have lower levels of political interest than men. All four are foreshadowed in the early thinking on gender and participation. First, scholars have suggested that the difference is a consequence of resource disparities between women and men. Earlier work focused on income and education (Welch 1977); later work looked at a wider array of resources, ranging from institutionally acquired skills to free time to the control of money at home (Burns, Schlozman, and Verba 1997, 2001). Second, scholars thought that women might participate at lower levels than men because marriage, motherhood, and homemaking socialize women out of politics and lead them to lower levels of political interest (Andersen 1975; Jennings and Niemi 1981; Sapiro 1983; Welch 1977). Third, scholars have asked whether childhood socialization depresses women's political interest (Welch 1977). Finally, scholars have examined the role of perspectives on gender roles as a cause of political activity – the idea is that women's political interest might be depressed by ideologies of motherhood, that politics is simply not a proper arena for women; this explanation is often linked to adult or childhood socialization (Clark and Clark 1986; Sapiro 1983; Tolleson-Rinehart 1992). In the first explanation, gender exists outside of individuals, in social structures that govern the distribution of resources. In the next two, gender exists in social expectations and women's responses to them. In the last one, gender exists in women's own ideologies.

Scholars have been keen to understand the nonpolitical roots of women's political disadvantage. Early scholars (that is, scholars in the 1970s and 1980s) yearned for data on the details of institutional experiences, especially for details about the workplace to move toward a differentiated view of the social processes that come to make sex matter (Andersen and Cook 1985, 622). These scholars built a field by creatively and opportunistically making due with the data available on employment, housewife status, parenthood, marriage, education, beliefs about women's place, and gender consciousness to test complex theoretical ideas about the relationship between gender and political participation.

With the advent of data sets containing much more detail on experiences in the workplace and in the family, scholars have been able to broaden their investigations to examine more fully the sociological, structural mechanisms that link gender with political involvement (Burns et al. 2001). They have been able to ask, in more detail, whether and how inequality at home shapes political participation. They found that division of labor does not seem to matter directly. For women, what does seem to matter is participating in the process of decision making within the family, and for men, what matters, alas, is being in control at home (Burns et al. 1997, 2001). In the end, the current account on the table is one of small cumulative differences in resources growing out of a host of institutions, in childhood and in adulthood. Women have access to lower levels of education and income. They are also tremendously disadvantaged, however – and men are tremendously advantaged – by the ways gender links the home and the workplace, putting men in and keeping more than a few women out of the workplace. The workplace goes farther than that to disadvantage women; in particular, workplaces allocate their benefits – money, politically relevant skills, and mobilization – on the basis of gender. Marital status and children do not have a direct impact on political participation in the cross-section, but they do have an indirect effect. For women, the indirect effect comes largely from the ways large-scale division of labor at home keeps some women with small children out of the workforce. For men, the indirect effects come from advantages to men, advantages that come from the ways children encourage men's workforce *and* religious participation. The story has come to center on the way gender links institutions and on the centrality of gender to institutions outside of politics.

Women have, of course, been involved in nonpolitical civic life for a long time, and their presence in these institutions – institutions that are often sex-segregated, that have often enabled women to take on serious leadership roles in a way that less segregated institutions have not – has given them access to resources. Their movement between civic spaces – between religious institutions, social reform groups, and partisan organizations – has been well documented in the literature (Cott 1977; Davis 1981; Giddings 1984; Greenberg 2001; Harris 1999; Lerner 1979; Scott 1984). These nonpolitical civic spaces have often provided the skills and mobilization to bring women and men to politics (Harris 1994, 1999; Tate 1991, 1994; Walton 1985).

Work on the political roots of inequality has been less common, but there are striking exceptions to this claim. Kristi Andersen's earliest work on political action does exactly this kind of work. In her early, exemplary analysis, Andersen uses systematic data collected in the Michigan Election Studies' repeated cross-sections to understand the ways in which feminism was unusually salient in the 1972 presidential race – mobilized to be so by George McGovern's campaign and by the women's movement. Her analyses of repeated cross-sections gave her the foundation for a dynamic account of the power of gender to serve as a mobilizing tool. She said then: "[I]t is hard to imagine this unity persisting. Women are probably too cross-pressured ever to constitute a lasting political movement. In fact, unless the women's movement is accepted as a structural critique of American society – unlikely, to say the least – the achievements of the movement's own social goals will produce increasing political fragmentation among women" (1975, 452). Later work by Karen Beckwith (1986) on gender differences in participation over time, Virginia Sapiro with Pamela Johnston Conover (1997) on the 1992 Year of the Woman, and Sue Tolleson-Rinehart and Jeanie Stanley (1994) on Ann Richards's race in Texas builds on this understanding of gender in political context.

Scholars studying gender differences in psychological engagement in politics have turned to political context as well and have begun to put the power of repeated cross-sections and state comparisons to work. Evidence of gender differences in psychological involvement with politics is abundant (Andersen 1975; Baxter and Lansing 1983; Beckwith 1986; Bennett and Bennett 1989; Delli Carpini and Keeter 1993, 1996; Rapoport 1982, 1985; Sapiro 1983; Soule and McGrath 1977; Tolleson-Rinehart 1992). The most successful recent efforts to understand women's lower levels of political engagement have turned to look at political context, at the paucity of elite women in politics, especially. Through both longitudinal and cross-sectional analyses, these efforts have suggested that the presence of women in visible political positions engages women citizens (Burns et al. 2001; Campbell and Wolbrecht 2006; Hansen 1997; Sapiro and Conover 1997; Verba, Burns, and Schlozman 1997; Wolbrecht and Campbell 2007). Monika McDermott (1997) makes a compelling case for the role candidate gender plays in low-information elections, demonstrating the power candidate gender has in shaping vote choice when citizens know little about a candidate. Leonie Huddy and Nayda Terkildsen (1993a) explore the traits and issue competencies that women and men have in mind when faced with cues from candidate gender; their work suggests that traits, such as compassion and trustworthiness, might be at the center of people's interpretation of gender in the electoral context (see, too, Kahn 1992). Karen Stenner (2001) goes farther than this to show that women faced with strong female candidates gain self-esteem and self-confidence, and these in turn lead to an increase in their political knowledge and interest. In Stenner's experiments, men experience exactly the opposite outcome when faced with strong women candidates: they tune out. Work by Kim Kahn suggests that the media has historically covered women candidates less well than men candidates (Kahn 1994a) and that this difference in coverage may make women candidates seem less viable (Kahn 1992, 1994b).[5] Suzanne Mettler (2005) investigates the ways the G.I. Bill fostered men's engagement with politics but had little effect on women's political engagement. This line of work offers increasingly tight linkages to the psychological literatures that can help sort through the mechanisms that might enable women candidates to engage women (and possibly disengage men) with the political system.[6] The puzzle pushes us, I think, to theorize political contexts more thoroughly, noticing how aggregate opportunities for interest and disinterest are created politically and how those opportunities change over time and space (see Ritter, this volume, for more ideas on this point). For now, context is the presence or absence of women elites and their ability to spark or discourage political interest (see, too, Dolan, this volume). More could be done, however, much more. Taking a cue from the literature on racism, scholars could look at the incentives elites – movement and establishment elites – face to use ideas about gender politically. Scholars could build on the work of Steven Rosenstone and Mark Hansen (1993) and Corrine McConnaughy (2005) to think about the strategic mobilization of women. What, to borrow Donald Kinder and Lynn Sander's (1996) language, are the "electoral temptations" of gender? Are there "electoral temptations"? This puzzle is a perfect opportunity to draw insights from the macro literature I'll talk about next into individual-level analyses.

The literature on gender consciousness offers another obvious place for building a connection between aggregate and individual. Although scholars have fine-tuned their measures of gender consciousness over time from Patricia Gurin's seminal work on gender consciousness (Gurin 1985) through Sue Tolleson-Rinehart's important effort to tease ideology out of the measure of gender consciousness (Tolleson-Rinehart 1992) and Cara Wong's efforts to compare measures of closeness to a range of different groups (Wong 1998), scholars have had trouble demonstrating the impact of consciousness.[7] In recent years especially, they have had an easier time demonstrating that consciousness relates to policy preferences than it does to political action (Conover 1988; Conover and Sapiro 1993). Although consciousness may channel political action (Burns et al. 2001), it has been unreliably connected to political participation since the early 1980s. Many scholars – using a range of different measures – have found that the power of gender consciousness to generate action has waned over the past thirty years. In the 1970s, women's consciousness seemed to encourage political participation among women (Conway, Steuernagel, and Ahern 1997, 88–91; Hansen, Franz, and

Netemeyer-Mays 1976; Miller, Gurin, Gurin, and Malanchuk 1981; Klein 1984, 136; Tolleson-Rinehart 1992, 134–9). Since then, no. Furthermore, when scholars have compared the power of black consciousness with the power of gender consciousness to generate activism, they have gotten different results, sometimes finding that black consciousness is especially important (Wilcox 1997, who found that gender consciousness did not make a difference) and sometimes not (Ardrey 1994). Roberta Sigel (1996, 127) offers hope that scholars will pay more attention to the priority that members of a disadvantaged group give to their group membership. She argues that when scholars move to incorporate priority into their traditional measures of group consciousness, they will see much more clearly the role of group consciousness in shaping a range of outcomes.

The existing work on consciousness and the changing results over time – changes that seem more connected with the year the data were collected than with the method employed by the researcher – suggest a dynamic account of consciousness, one that links elite mobilization to mass participation and that draws more heavily on notions of political opportunity (Andersen 1975; see Banaszak, this volume; see Sapiro and Conover 1997; Tarrow 1994). We have important beginnings of this argument in the work of Costain (1992), Conover and Gray (1983), Klein (1984), and Katzenstein and Mueller (1987). One could go even farther to develop a rich account of the incentives and actions of elites and their consequences for citizen behavior, perhaps along the lines of Rosenstone and Hansen (1993) or Kollman (1998). Anna Harvey (1998) does some of this, but, although she alludes to citizen behavior, her work and her evidence are concentrated at the elite level. McConnaughy (2005) builds an account of the woman's suffrage movement with one version of this goal in mind. She worries that the literature on women's social movements has rested in the demand side of politics and has paid much less attention to the ways institutions do and do not supply outcomes activists demand. And so she embeds movement activism in states with parties and state legislatures and develops a powerful new way to understand when and why activists succeeded in some states and not others (see, as well, McCammon et al. 2001).

The most successful work combining context and gender has done two things simultaneously. It has employed theories and measures placing gender in context, and it has deployed theories and measures of individual-level mechanisms, usually from psychology. In the end, that has not just helped us understand that context enables gender to matter but also has allowed us to begin to specify why and exactly how.

WHAT COULD INDIVIDUAL-LEVEL ANALYSES LEARN FROM THE AGGREGATE LITERATURE ABOUT POLITICAL CONTEXT?

I am going to provide examples of the kinds of tools that could be powerfully integrated into the individual-level literature from just one aggregate literature, the social movement literature. Other aggregate literatures would prove equally valuable conversation partners. In fact, there are the beginnings of an important conversation between the literatures on policy development and political action (A. Campbell 2003; Mettler and Soss 2004; Ritter, this volume; Soss 1999, 2000; Mettler 2005, offers the clearest example using gender). With the social movement literature in mind, what kinds of conversations emerge?

How Do Preexisting Organizations Shape Political Action?

Social movement scholars have shown that women's movements, like most social movements, depend heavily on indigenous – preexisting, sex-segregated – organizations and networks. We have seen this over and over again: in Jo Freeman's (1975) pathbreaking work on the networks that enabled the modern women's movement; in Nancy Cott's (1977) book on the ways in which women used the skills and arguments they developed within religious institutions to move to public work on social reform; in Jane Mansbridge's (1986) arguments about the mobilizing advantages of anti–Equal Rights Amendment (ERA) forces compared with pro-ERA activists; in Donald Mathews and Jane Sherron De Hart's (1992) engrossing account of the whole range of networks on which anti-ERA activists could draw. Of course, this reliance on indigenous organizations is a general result about social movements (McAdam 1982). What is perhaps especially interesting is the repeated reliance on an institutional space in which women have been especially active (although not always especially honored): religious institutions. Organizers have been quite creative: they have drawn on religious institutions to craft a wide range of women's movements. Women seem to have only fleeting opportunities – like those Freeman (1975) outlines – to draw on other kinds of indigenous institutions. Women's movements that have not been able to rely, for the long term, on the grassroots support provided through indigenous institutions have sometimes ended up relying on a small group of activists, for good or ill (Mansbridge 1986). Of course, other social movements – movements not focused on gender – that rely on indigenous organizations often end up reproducing the gender hierarchies within those organizations (see, e.g., Cohen's [1999] discussion of gay and lesbian activists' efforts to be heard in modern black politics and Payne's [1995] investigation of women's activism within the early, rural civil rights movement). There are hints in this literature about what might be special about women's indigenous institutions, about the difficulty – striking in comparison with race – of finding a segregated space in which to build consciousness and resources.[8] I take this part of the field to be a demonstration of the good that can come from a conversation between the aggregate and individual analyses of gender. The macro-level literature offers accounts of the ways these institutions construct gender, accounts that have been put to good use in the micro-level literature.

What Are the Consequences for Ordinary People of Activists' Bureaucratic and Electoral Strategies?

Scholars believe that the sometimes surprising places where feminists find themselves make for a diffuse and potentially resilient movement (Boles 1994; Costain 1992; Katzenstein 1998). This has been true even inside American political parties, where women were active and influential well before women had the right to vote (Andersen 1996; Cott 1990; Edwards 1997; Freeman 2000; Harrison 1988; Harvey 1998; Higginbotham 1990). Their insider strategies often changed the relationship of the parties to political issues (such as the ERA; see Freeman 1987; Harrison 1988; Sanbonmatsu 2004; Wolbrecht 2000), and these strategies almost always increased the representation of women in federal bureaucracies. What are the consequences of these strategies for ordinary citizens? Do these strategies offer different kinds of education for ordinary citizens about the relevance of politics?

Are There "Electoral Temptations" of Gender, as There Are for Race?

Politicians and political parties in the United States have faced tremendous "electoral temptations" when it comes to using race to win elections (Kinder and Sanders 1996). When it comes to gender, elites have been able to exploit gender identity for their own ends, in the ways Harvey (1998) suggests, as a kind of campaign slogan parties learned how to use, or in the ways Kathy Bonk (1988) points to in which women are seen by politicians as a kind of infinitely redescribable, recombinable, redividable group. Scholars have examined the ways gender issues have been incorporated into the party system (Sanbonmatsu 2004; Wolbrecht 2000). I could imagine using this literature to build an explicitly political model of citizen mobilization and demobilization around gender.

Do Social Movements Offer Up New Discursive Tools for Ordinary People?

Mary Katzenstein (1998) arrives at an account of discursive strategies of women in the Catholic Church. Kenneth Kollman (1998, 108) discusses the ways groups like the National Organization for Women (NOW) have tried to shape public opinion, hoping that "[p]ublic legitimacy for policies [NOW proposes]...will follow the group's activities rather than precede them." Paul Freedman (1999) analyzes the consequences of the campaigns that pro-choice and pro-life groups wage, in Freedman's words, to "manipulate ambivalence," that is, to build legitimacy for their side among those who do not yet know their own minds. And Michael Dawson (2001) provides evidence of the emerging payoffs to the discursive strategies black feminists are pursuing within the academy. Given these aggregate analyses, do the ideas that movements offer have individual-level consequences? Does it matter that we have more ways gender inequality is "storied" now than it was in the past?[9] Do people have new tools to use to think and unthink gender hierarchy? How does framing work at the individual level?

CONCLUSION

I am excited about the good that can come from the discussion I just outlined. The conversation will give us tools to build an even richer understanding of gender and political action, one with dynamic moving parts. I am excited especially about work that draws on the power of repeated cross-sections, cross-sections connected to and representing different political worlds. Now classic works took advantage of ideas about political context wed to the power of repeated cross-sections to set high standards for the field (Andersen 1975). We can learn a lot from revisiting these studies.

As Rogers Brubaker and Frederick Cooper (2000, 27) point out, "A strongly institutionalized ethnonational classificatory system makes certain categories readily and legitimately available for the representation of social reality, the framing of political claims, and the organization of political action." However, as they also make clear, just because a system is available does not mean it is used. Part of our job is to understand when and among whom this system becomes salient. Brubaker and Cooper (2000, 4–5) argue:

These are categories of everyday social experience, developed and deployed by ordinary social actors . . . used by "lay" actors in some (not all!) everyday settings to make sense of themselves, of their activities, of what they share with, and how they differ from, others. [They are] also used by political entrepreneurs to persuade people to understand themselves, their interests, and their predicaments in a certain way, to persuade certain people that they are (for certain purposes) "identical" with one another and at the same time different from others, and to organize and justify collective action along certain lines.

Understanding when and how this happens – understanding how politics enables gender to shape individuals' political actions and public opinions – is, I think, one of our next big jobs as political scientists interested in gender.

Notes

1. We might make gender up as we go, but that idiosyncratic sort of gender would not offer the same sort of systematic disadvantage that coordinated answers to what gender is offer, and so we would not care as much.
2. For a review of literature on such morselization, see Stewart and McDermott 2004, 532.
3. For an early critical review of the literature on women's voting, see Breckinridge 1933.

4. On the serious problems with the English version of *The Second Sex*, see Moi 2002a and Glazer 2004.
5. Scholars have also grown concerned about the measurement of political engagement, worrying especially that measures of political information designed to encourage people not to guess actually only discourage women (but not men) from guessing (Mondak and Davis 2001).
6. In addition, because the gap in engagement appears to open well before women and men are settled into adulthood, scholars will want to turn back to consider childhood. We are in a position now, I think, to develop a contingent account of gender and childhood socialization to politics.
7. Of course, consciousness has a long history in the study of race and class (for a discussion, see, for example, Elster 1985; Schlozman and Verba 1979; Verba and Nie 1972).
8. As Goffman (1977, 308) put it, women are "cut off ecologically from congress with their kind."
9. On "storied" identities, see Somers 1994.

5

What Revolution?

Incorporating Intersectionality in Women and Politics

Jane Junn and Nadia Brown

Right around the time Jeane Kirkpatrick's *Political Woman* (1974) appeared in print, a different uprising was taking shape. That very year, a group of radical black feminists began to meet, later calling themselves the Combahee River Collective. The group's name was inspired by the actions of Harriet Tubman, the former slave who freed nearly 800 slaves during the Civil War at the Combahee River in South Carolina. Black feminism or womanism[1] grew out of black women's dissatisfaction with the women's movement and the black nationalist movement. In 1977, the Combahee River Collective issued a historic and powerful call to recognize the intersectional position of women of color:

We are actively committed to struggling against racial, sexual, heterosexual, and class oppression and see as our particular task the development of integrated analysis and practice based upon the fact that major systems of oppression are interlocking. The synthesis of these oppressions creates the condition of our lives. As Black women we see Black feminism as the logical political movement to combat the manifold and simultaneous oppressions that all women of color face. . . . We believe that sexual politics under patriarchy is as pervasive in black women's lives as are the politics of class and race. We also often find it difficult to separate race from class from sex oppression because in our lives they are most often experienced simultaneously. (The Combahee River Collective Statement, April 1977)[2]

"Revolution" is a heady term, and one that should be applied cautiously particularly when implicating a category of people as broad and varied as that of women in the United States. The publication of Kirkpatrick's book is certainly an important turning point for political science inasmuch as it signaled new direction in the recognition of women in politics. From various vantage points, however, the change in women's roles as political actors has been far less radical than revolutionary. The everyday realities of the lives of women of color provide testimony to the sentiment that the revolution has reached only so far into the diversity of American women. With the recent surge in foreign migration to the United States, more than one in five people is either an immigrant or the child of immigrants, and fully a third of the U.S. population considers itself to be a race other than white. American women of color are on the rise, not only in number but also in terms of the degree of racial and ethnic diversity.

Nevertheless, and despite important increases in political participation and representation, women of color are disproportionately worse off economically and more likely to be victims of crime than are white women. Equally as important, the field of women and politics in political science has remained stubborn in its treatment of gender as the single and primary category of analysis in its observation and interpretation of women's political activity. Gender is not a unitary category of analysis, and interpretations and inferences that follow from this assumption remain suspect. Instead, gender is a dynamic category intersecting at multiple locations with other characteristics that are most often ordered hierarchically. The analytical payoffs to taking a dynamic and intersectional approach to studying gender in women and politics include the production of interpretations that more accurately reflect the complex reality of women's lives and, equally as important, the expansion of the theoretical reach of the study of gender and politics. Although scholars of women and politics recognize the importance of secondary categories of race, class, and sexuality within gender, entreaties for closer examination of these dynamics are frequently left to concluding remarks about "future topics to consider."

That future can wait no longer, and we argue the time is now for the field of women and politics to take an intersectional and dynamic theoretical approach to the construction of research questions and analysis of data. If we are to move gender, as Karen Beckwith suggests, "into the core of political science and democratic theory" (Beckwith, this volume), we should attempt to do so while utilizing all of the methodological and theoretical sophistication that can be mustered. It is simply not enough to add African American women, Latinas, or Asian American women to what is now the default category of white women. Rather, the dominant approach of static and unitary categories must be wrestled down and left behind in favor of a strategy of inquiry that treats political beings as dynamic subjects with a multiplicity of categorical homes. In so doing, the wide varieties of political contexts in which women engage in political action can provide critical leverage to identify the mechanisms by which power is manifested in the creation of categories such as gender, race, class, and sexuality. Observing and analyzing particular intersectional contexts in which women engage the political sphere can help illuminate categories that are at turns intractable, and at others transitory. These insights are critical, for discriminatory practices not only emanate from biased structural frameworks and political institutions but also have important origins in the categorical imperative of defining difference.

The U.S. political system not only has developed by practices deeply rooted in an ideology of gender inequality (see Ritter, this volume) but also is fundamentally grounded in beliefs of white racial superiority. It is a fallacy to argue that American women, writ large, gained suffrage in 1920 with the ratification of the Nineteenth Amendment to the U.S. Constitution. For of course the right to vote was not enjoyed equally by all women. Asian Americans were denied even the right to become naturalized citizens until 1952, and African Americans gained more uniform access to voting only after the 1965 Voting Rights Act. This simple but often overlooked example of unequal enfranchisement of women of color highlights the notion that experiences of marginalization and discrimination are contingent on the patterns and history of migration, as well as government policies directed at controlling population growth and movement. As a result, Americans categorized by race and ethnicity develop distinct strategies of adaptation, expression, and political mobilization. In this regard, African Americans, Latinos, Asian Americans, American Indians, and, most recently, Arab Americans experience the process of racialization in the United States in ways unique to the group in which they have been classified. For some, group membership runs far deeper than the color of one's skin; for others, the grouping is ersatz, the result of government imperatives to place race into four neat categories.

Yet studying women of color alone – grouped either by racial and ethnic identification or together as "minority women" – separate from white women is also analytically unsatisfying. Viewing the politics of gender from a different vantage point can be illuminating in myriad important ways, not the least of which is to give voice to previously marginalized and silent groups of women. At the same time, however, we need to leapfrog over this categorical imperative and extend beyond the classic identity politics model that itself often produces other hierarchies and exclusions. Instead, political interests exist at the intersection of multiple and dynamic identities, and treating categories as static only constrains our analytical reach. "Identity cannot... provide an adequate political basis for last social change. Identity-based movements, while effective for short term political or material gains, end up with restricted constituencies and visions of social justice" (Fernandes 2004, 25).

Mapping this complex territory is an enormous task not only for women and politics but for all contemporary social scientists in the United States who struggle to interpret the intentions and actions of an increasingly diverse polity. As Wendy Smooth has argued, intersectional analysis is costly and complicated, but it is "a mess worth making" (Smooth 2006). In this chapter, we lay some conceptual groundwork for a foray into this muddled terrain by identifying two problems with the standard approach to the study of women's political activity. In particular, we highlight the reasons it is so tricky for scholars to accommodate the study of political context and diversity within the default category of white women. The difficulty emanates from a set of methodological presuppositions about the individual as the unit of analysis, combined with a normative position on political action that assumes equality of agency among individuals. In searching for a way out of this thicket, we suggest scholars take careful account of theories of intersectionality when analyzing women's political activism. We focus on black feminism because black feminists were the first to articulate the need to recognize interlocking systems of oppression. Exemplary works in this tradition underscore the impossibility of separating individual-level characteristics into discrete categories and instead provide a model for analyzing the complex interaction of race, gender, class, and sexuality. By taking culture seriously, work in black feminism provides a window into how categories are at once stubbornly stable – easily observed at "face value" – while simultaneously socially constructed and fleeting. The promise of intersectional and dynamic analytical strategies remain to be fully recognized, yet we argue that the future of research in women's political activism in U.S. politics is one that can no longer ignore the multiplicity of diversity in the American polity and one that must embrace intersectional perspectives for the study of women and politics.

BANISH THE DUMMY VARIABLE: THE TROUBLE WITH CATEGORIES IN STUDYING WOMEN IN ACTION

Since its inception, the field of women and politics has been concerned with how to define and analyze women's political participation. Critiques of narrow definitions of the political and of traditional public activities are well articulated and accepted, as are a diverse array of observational strategies utilizing qualitative and quantitative measurement (Bourque and Grosholtz 1971). More recently, scholars have struggled with how to explain women's political participation and, in particular, how to distinguish it as unique from the political behavior of men. What makes women's political activity different? Are there a different set of motivations or costs to political action for women? Does a political voice for women carry less, the same, or more weight than that of men when it comes to elected officials? Predicated on the notion of group-based differences, the existence of the gender gap has taken the field of women and politics a long way in documenting the divergence in vote choice and policy preferences by sex. Nancy Burns (this volume) lays out an ambitious proposal to develop a politicized context of gender to speed development of theory, as well as to aid in the interpretation of data comparing political activity of men and women.

Exploiting variation over time and across groups to gain inferential leverage is promising in theory but fraught with difficulty in practice because categories are treated in static rather than dynamic terms. A theory of politicized context of gender is up against an imposing set of current analytical practices common in individual-level analyses of political behavior. In its most common form, analysis of political action in the mass public is accomplished by aggregating empirical observations taken from individuals. These data are typically quantitative responses to closed-ended questions in surveys from large N samples. Among nationally representative data, the American National Election Studies (ANES), spanning presidential and midterm election years between 1948 and the present, are the most widely utilized data to study voting behavior, candidate choice, and public opinion. Among the many virtues of ANES data is the ability to examine changes and continuities in behavior and attitudes over time, in large part due to the consistency of content and question wording in the survey instruments across time. Similarly, the sample sizes are large enough to analyze important groups of voters categorized by gender, region, partisanship, and race.[3]

At the same time, gender and race at the individual level are taken as given – as exogenously determined – and then aggregated into static and unidimensional categories. Typical analyses of the effect of gender on political action begin by observing the different rates at which women and men participate. Studies utilizing data over time show the divergence in political engagement by gender has narrowed dramatically, and there are now only small differences in the level of political activity between men and women. Despite the diminution in unequal rates of participation, the differences that do remain add up collectively to many fewer women's voices in politics (see Burns, Schlozman, and Verba 2001). Nevertheless, in synchronic cross-sectional studies, just as Burns argues, these small differences make it difficult to put gender on display and to see inequalities by gender at the individual level.

The analytical strategy of static categories in individuals as the unit of analysis not only impedes our ability to disentangle the roots of political inequality embedded in gender, but it also creates other undesirable and unintended consequences. Regarding unforeseen outcomes, adherence to the perspective consistent with most individual-level behavioral accounts results in what has been described as the "puzzle of participation," the observation of stagnant rates of political activity despite substantial increases in formal educational attainment in the mass public over time The most important explanatory variable for political action at the individual level is some mix of the socioeconomic status (SES) duet of education and income. Anybody who analyzes survey data knows educational attainment is the 800-pound gorilla in results of model estimation; depending on your version of the analogy, the gorilla sits on or eats up much of the explained variance. The problem with this most venerable of social scientific models is its application to explain change over time. If indicators of SES, particularly education, are critical antecedents to participation, and if formal education has risen dramatically and monotonically over time, why hasn't political activity increased at a commensurate rate?[4] Conventional explanations are unable to explain away this phenomenon.

Similarly, and of particular relevance to the issue of gender and political action, is the development of a sea change in patterns of educational attainment by sex that has taken place slowly but surely over the past twenty years in the United States. The gender gap in college attendance has now reached a level considered newsworthy; 57 percent of college students today are female, and for African Americans, the difference is even more substantial, with black women making up 63 percent of African Americans enrolled in higher education (Slater 1994). Should we expect the gender gap in political action to favor women in politics as a function of this now unequal gender distribution in the critical resource behind individual-level activity? Although there have been improvements in women's participation in terms of voter turnout, as well as running for office and winning, most observers and analysts would agree that despite higher levels of education among women compared with men, inequality in the political sphere will likely persist for the same reasons that income inequality remains between men and women of identical educational attainment and credentials. Analyses structured around static categories and driven by aggregated individual-level data form the foundation for explanatory models, and result in specific forms of substantive knowledge. Yet some of that knowledge is contrary to observed phenomena – no increase in political participation despite rising education levels in the mass public, and no greater political activity among women in the face of higher college attendance, creating at best a puzzle and at worst an embarrassment for scholarship in this tradition.

Further complicating the picture of marrying individual-level analysis with a politicized context of gender is the issue of overlapping categories. For example, Michele Wallace (1990, 60) argues that analyses based in the dominant culture erase black female subjectivity by placing people into one of two mutually exclusive categories, the universalized subject, usually claimed by white men, or the "other," typically encompassing white women or men of color. Deviations from these categories, black and a woman, or lesbian and poor, disqualify people who do not readily fit into the standard categories from participation (Wallace 1990). When categories are constructed from static accounts – woman, African American, poor – analyses most often look for the independent effect of one category against another. Race may be a more important predictor than sex for one dependent variable, whereas class might overwhelm the effects of race for a different outcome. Results, indeed substantive knowledge structured by this analytical perspective, are meaningful when the default categories are assumed to be male, white, middle class. But why continue to assume this? What is the inferential utility of arguing, for example, that race is more visible or more important than gender? How would this generalization apply to women of color? These questions underscore the notion that categories are fluid and porous, overlapping multiplicities at times and stubbornly stable in other contexts. The complexity of categories must be acknowledged and embraced and then integrated into the methodology of studying gender and political action rather than perpetuated as mutually exclusive dummy variables.

NEUTRALITY AND INDIVIDUAL AGENCY

Beyond acknowledging the complexity of categories and fashioning analytical strategies to accommodate this shift, individual-level approaches need to reevaluate in a radical way another assumption driving the design of research questions and the interpretation of empirical results addressing women and political action. The current state of knowledge in the participation literature based in individual-level approaches has been built substantially on an analytical triumvirate of individual-level synchronic data, the SES model, and a mainstream definition of political participation as voluntary legal acts directed at government officials toward policy outcomes. Undergirding this perspective is the assumption that individuals have equal agency. Inferential models estimated with the data belie this bias: one more year of education or one more mobilization request will increase political participation among people regardless of the particularities of their social and political context. The starting position that makes this assumption defensible is that the system itself – whether political, social, or economic – is neutral, not favoring one or another for any particular characteristic. Put more concretely, if communication to a member of the U.S. Congress from a middle-class black man receives the same attention as one from a wealthy white contributor, then there may be good reason to proceed without examining further the assumption of equal agency. However, if we are suspicious that political responsiveness varies systematically by race, class, gender, or some other category in which individuals exist, we must scrutinize the assumption and devise strategies to test the validity of the starting claim. As Melissa Harris-Lacewell (2003, 244) argues, "The particular racial history of this country requires that researchers be more careful in their assumptions of neutrality. At a minimum, these researchers must engage the historical evidence and offer an alternative account. Ignoring the history of Black people and racialized political ideologies is insufficient."

There is ample evidence within political science and other disciplines to document pervasive inequalities inside the political, economic, and social systems of the United States (see Frymer 1999; Marable 1983; Oliver and Shapiro 2006; Sidanius and Pratto 1999; Tilly 1999; Walton and Smith 2000; Wilson 1980). Yet there is surprisingly little sustained empirical and theoretical effort to illuminate more precisely when and how power and hierarchy structure opportunities and incentives to act in politics. There are certainly exceptions, chief among them John Gaventa's (1982) brilliant study of powerlessness and quiescence in Appalachia. Similarly, important work in comparative politics such as James Scott's *Weapons of the Weak* (1979) serves as a stark reminder to political scientists that one cannot assume all individuals have equal ability and desire to influence the political system, and further that the return on that investment in time and resources will be the same for all who take part.

Instead, agency or individual rights in the liberal democratic vernacular operate in both a social context of power relations and a structural context of democratic political institutions where actors deploy accumulated capital in pursuing their interests. Mary Hawkesworth makes a compelling argument identifying the roots of the "voluntarist" conception of politics within social contract theory. "Initially conceived by Hobbes, the voluntarist conception ties power to the voluntary intentions and strategies of individuals who seek to promote their interests. Within this frame, power is nothing other than 'the present means to some future apparent good'" (Hawkesworth 2005, 147–8). However, the context of democratic politics itself is not neutral, not level, not fair. It matters who got there first and set up the rules of the game, and it matters that they were men. In this regard, a theorized political context must account for power that is manifested in the political state as institutional structure and practice. Civil society is inextricably linked to the state and political society, both as an extension of state hegemony as well as an arena of potential counterhegemony. Thus political action is a double-edged sword; it has potential for liberation and transformation, but it is also a uniquely powerful tool for the development of false consciousness. In this regard, and as the literature in women and politics amply attests, more women in government does not always mean better government for women. As long as government – replete with gendered and discriminatory institutions – remains intact rather than transformed, populating it with diversity can at best alter outcomes incrementally. Is small change better than no change? Perhaps, but let us at least acknowledge it is small change.

Women of color operate in a political sphere guided by laws and social policy rooted firmly in an order that is anything but neutral. Rather, it is a system designed to maintain the continued monopoly of power and wealth that is primarily based on racial, gender, and class oppression. This political context is one that goes well beyond the domain of a single demographic variable and, rather, strikes to the heart of oppression of multiple varieties. The situation for women of color is dire in that they disproportionately occupy more of the space of oppression. Interpreting political action – or inaction in the face of tremendous power and low odds for success – must therefore take place within the context of this political framework. Thus the task for scholars interested in gender and political action is to fashion innovative strategies both to account for complexities in categories populated by individuals and to discern how power and hierarchy structure the opportunities and rewards for political action among individuals.

THE ORIGINS OF INTERSECTIONAL THEORY IN BLACK FEMINISM

The idea of intersectionality has its most significant roots in U.S. black feminist thought, which began its scholarly presence with seminal works such as

Women, Race and Class by Angela Davis (1981), "A Black Feminist Statement" drafted by the Combahee River Collective (1977), and *Sister Outsider*
by Audre Lorde (1984). In many ways, this early work was a critical response
to the additive models of oppression faced by women of color, emphasizing
how multiple forms of oppression affect black women in a "matrix of domination" (Lorde 1984). Black feminist scholars such as Cheryl Clarke (1983),
Barbara Smith (1985), bell hooks (1984), Audre Lorde (1984), Deborah King
(1988), Jacquelyn Grant (1979), Patricia Hill Collins (1990), Paula Giddings
(1984), Darlene Clark Hine (1988), June Jordan (1992), Barbara Omolade
(1983), Michelle Wallace (1978), and Angela Davis (1982) pushed academia
to include black women. These writers theorized that black women's lives
are colored by interlocking oppressions that are bound by patriarchy, racism,
capitalism, and heterosexism. However, these intellectuals did not use the
term "intersectionality" to describe black women's oppression, using instead
"black feminism" and "womanism" to describe what Kimberle Crenshaw
(2000) would later term "intersectionality." From Sojourner Truth to Anna
Julia Cooper to Fannie Lou Hamer to Angela Davis, black women have
spoken about how their unique position has oppressed them or forced them
into a place of subordination. The wellspring of black feminist theory is
developed through the experiences of black women's subordination and triumph. Black feminism was "actively committed to struggling against racial,
sexual, heterosexual, and class oppression... [that requires] the development of integrated analysis and practice based upon the fact that the major
systems of oppression are interlocking" (Guy-Sheftall 1995, 232). Since its
inception, black feminism has always been concerned with multiple systems
of oppression.

   In addition to traditional models of intersectionality that focus on race,
class, and gender, black feminists such as June Jordan, Cheryl Clarke,
Barbara Smith, Audre Lorde, and Hawley Fogg-Davis add heterosexism or
homophobia to the traditional model. These scholars argue that coerced
heterosexuality denies black women sexual identity and expression. Cheryl
Clarke and Barbara Smith are particularly critical of black feminist writers who refuse to acknowledge the plight of black lesbians, specifically how
heterosexism is reinforced by patriarchal domination. "The Black lesbian
is coerced into the experience of institutional racism – like every other nig-
ger in America – and must suffer as well the homophobic sexism of the
Black political community, some of whom seem to have forgotten so soon
the pain and rejection, denial, and repression sanctioned by racist America"
(Guy-Sheftall 1995, 244). Like Clarke, Barbara Smith calls into question
homophobia within African American culture. She urges black heterosex-
uals to understand their own heterosexuality by defining it as other than
attacking anyone who is not heterosexual. Moreover, she argues "the notion
that struggling against or eliminating racism will completely alleviate Black
women's problems does not take into account the way that sexual oppression cuts across all racial, nationality, age, religious, ethnic, and class groups"

(Guy-Sheftall 1995, 256). Both Clarke and Smith add sexuality to intersectionality by challenging the notion that racism is the only oppression black women have to confront, reminding scholars that other categorical imperatives that continue to mark and oppress women deserve scrutiny.

Intersectionality involves an acute sense of awareness that black women "don't have the luxury of choosing to fight only one battle" because they must contend with multiple, interlocking systems of oppression and the actuality of layered experiences of multiplicative as opposed to additive" (T. Jones 2000, 56). "Third wave" black feminism brings a distinctive generational perspective to the traditional intersectionality framework. Writers such as Joan Morgan (1999), Dream Hampton (1999), Tara Roberts (2006), Angela Ards (1991), Kristal Brent-Zook (2006), Ayana Byrd and Lori Tharps (2001), Gwendolyn Pough (2003), Shani Jamila O'Neal (2000), and Lisa Jones (1994) have produced reader-friendly, hip-hop-oriented work as a hybrid of academic writing mixed with popular culture and journalistic style. Unfamiliar to many outside of black or youth culture, the hip-hop culture originated on the East Coast in the late 1960s, although it has its roots in the Caribbean, paricularly Jamaica, as well as Africa. Rap music is the popular music form of hip-hop music that began commercially in the late 1970s. These authors confront the complexities of being "black girls now – sistas of the post–Civil Rights, post-feminist, post-soul, hip hop generation" (Morgan 1999, 56–7). Third wave black feminism adds a generational component to the analysis of intersectionality within the context of black feminism more generally, emphasizing the significance of cultural forms and the interaction of class, sexual oppression, race, and gender.

Third wave black feminism is critical to a generation of young women of color who have internalized negative self-images, suffer from a lack of self-esteem, and are victims to materialism that glorifies rap music. Hip-hop feminism attempts to avoid the scholar-activist dichotomy present in the earlier waves of feminism, arguing instead for a worldview that offers an "epistemology grounded in the experiences of communities of color under advanced capitalism, as a cultural site for rearticulating identity and sexual politics" (Pough 2003, 242). Pough notes a need for a "feminism that would allow us to continue loving ourselves and the brothers who hurt us without letting race loyalty buy us early tombstones" (Pough 2003, 243). Third wave black feminism tackles questions of particular interest to the hip-hop generation by analyzing hip-hop culture, music, and visual arts through a black feminist lens. Specifically, the "Baby Mama/Chickenhead" identity within popular black culture often times denotes the intersection of race, gender, and class and is significant because it highlights the importance of class to contemporary analysis of black feminism. These black women are the modern-day Jezebel character of the hip-hop generation, with the added emphasis on "gold digging."[5] On the flip side, there are artists such as Lil' Kim who use this modern Jezebel stereotype to empower black women. Although many third wave black feminists take issue with Lil' Kim's distorted vision of sexual and monetary empowerment, they note that she is a powerful force of discussion in the black feminist hip-hop community. Indeed, she uniquely challenges the typical forms of ideological control about black women. But again, because Lil' Kim falls into a lower-class image of black women that the black middle class wants to shun, a distinction is made between "us" and "them" in a division between upper-class and lower-class black women.

Gwendolyn D. Pough (2003) argues that Erykah Badu's "Bag Lady" is a remix of Ntozake Shange's *For Colored Girls Who Have Considered Suicide/When the Rainbow Is Enuf* (1975). Shange encouraged black women to find "God in themselves and love 'her fiercely' in an attempt to circumvent the negative responses that most Black women internalize when faced with the multiple oppressions they encounter" (Pough 2003, 236). Badu similarly encourages hip-hoppers to let go of their baggage, which consequently weighs them down. Hip-hop feminists are engaged in the work of bell hooks and Cheo Coker by offering a culturally based critique of rap music. Consistent with Collins's black feminist theory, third wave black feminism and hip-hop feminism draw from the lived experiences of black women by producing theory that is accessible to nonintellectual and everyday black women. Furthermore, third wave black feminism adds a generational component to the intersectionality framework by considering systematically the stereotypes faced by women of the hip-hop generation. The interlocking oppressions of race, gender, class, and sexuality are seamlessly integrated in the work of third wave black feminists. The explicit intersections inherent here emphasize the importance of analyzing simultaneously and, in dynamic fashion, these overlapping categories of oppression.

INTERSECTIONALITY IN ACTION

In addition to the groundbreaking work of black feminists – first wave and beyond – there are a number of examples of intersectional analyses in action that navigate the difficult terrain inherent in studies that allow subjects to exist in multiple locations of identity. We have argued that an intersectional imperative requires analysts to consider the multiple locations of identity, oppression, and political context in which women are situated. This derives from the impulse to leave behind a static categorical imperative in favor of a dynamic set of shifting identities. Engaging in dynamic intersectional analysis, however, is much more difficult in practice than in theory.

Approaching intersectionality through the theory of marginalization, Cathy Cohen critiques the response of black leaders to the AIDS epidemic. In *The Boundaries of Blackness*, Cohen uses race as an analytic category to evaluate traditional black politics' failure to respond to secondary marginalized groups within the black subgroup (e.g., homosexuals, drug addicts, and the poor). Using media content analysis, legislative assessment tools, and interviews with black gay activists, Cohen finds that mainstream black politics reinforces middle-class norms that exclude secondary marginalized groups who have a "legitimate" claim to AIDS because of immoral or sexually deviant (or both) lifestyles. Cohen's work offers valuable insight in researching the multiple identities of subjects. She is concerned with the characteristics that interact with racial identity such as "sexual orientation, geographical location, education, and one's relationship with welfare" (Cohen 1999, 346–7). Furthermore, Cohen's framework provides a highly effective tool that can broaden the way researchers understand identity and the way subjects view the world through their unique lived experiences. Understanding the complexities between the multiplicity and fluidity of identity through studying Chicano and Chicana genealogy parallels black feminists' theory of intersectionality. As developed by Gloria Anzaldúa (1987), mestiza identity is located within the intersection of identity-based discourses that combines inclusion-exclusion, conqueror-conquered, Spanish-Indian identities by encompassing the psychological, sexual, linguistic, and spiritual borders between the Texas–U.S. Southwest–Mexico border. The mestiza hybrid subject "challenges existing categories by her refusal/inability to fit within them" (Beltrán 2004, 596). This hybrid subject uniquely challenges the essentialist approach to identity by combining experience, multiplicity, and fluidity rather than stability and singularity.

In critiquing the binaries of traditional second wave feminist theory, Cherríe Moraga warns against ranking oppressions in a hierarchical manner. Similar to Anzaldúa, Moraga challenges the oppositional dialectic of identity. She argues that to confront the "isms" of oppression, feminist theory must not isolate or insulate experience by silencing difference. "Without an emotional, heartfelt grappling with the source of our own oppression, without naming the enemy within ourselves and outside of us, no authentic, non-hierarchical connection among oppressed groups can take place" (Moraga 1981, 29). A hybrid or Chicana identity that recognizes the fluidity of identities threatens the long-established norm of suppressing difference within second wave feminism. Acknowledging the borders or shifting and multiple identity and integrity creates a site of evolution in identity politics by developing a mestizaje consciousness. Cristina Beltrán (2004) cautions theorists of mestizaje against reproducing the current narratives of identification and exclusion by privileging experience as a precondition for political agency. Subjectivity must be called into question when theorizing hybridity. Existing categories do not adequately challenge the production of knowledge that is inherent in standpoint theory. Chicano hybridity naturalizes experience by privileging the mestiza role of "bridge maker" devoid of subjectivity. Stability must be called into question. Anzaldúa's vision of the mestiza identity of multiculturalism as a bridge builder, universal citizen, tutor, and occupant of the space between marginalization creates a false sense of commonality between those who claim the mestiza identity.

Beyond these two exemplary analyses of intersectionality in action are a series of more general theoretical approaches, emphasizing the methodology of intersectional analysis. A 2007 issue of *Politics & Gender* includes five extremely valuable works on the concept and use of intersectionality by Lisa Garcia Bedolla, Ange-Marie Hancock, Julia Jordan-Zachery, Evelyn Simien, and Julie Anne White. Following two important articles published in 2006 by Laurel Weldon and Wendy Smooth in *Politics & Gender*, these articles provide distinctive angles on the question of how to operationalize intersectionality in academic research and political activism. In addition to this recent published work is scholarship by Leslie McCall, who builds on the work of scholars who advocate a relational perspective. McCall's work on inequality is exemplary as an approach to feminist intercategorical complexity that "requires that scholars provisionally adopt existing analytical categories to document relationships of inequality among social groups and changing configurations of inequality among multiple and conflicting dimensions" (2005, 1773). McCall's model of intercategorical complexity allows for scholars to investigate the differences within categories of intersectional analysis. This cutting-edge model forwards the notion that identity vectors are not monolithic, and traditional categories such as race and gender must instead be explored internally rather than treated as homogeneous categories.

The combination of McCall's, Cohen's, and Beltrán's perspectives provides a useful theoretical construct for modeling the complex and intersectional relationship between race, gender, class, sexuality, and ethnicity. Their combined theories allow for fluidity within groups, pay attention to secondary marginalized groups, give consideration to inequalities within groups, and analyze under which conditions group stability can be dismantled. These insights reinforce the notion that categories are not monolithic assemblages but instead unstable and dynamic groupings. Fashioning research design and interpretation of data with these perspectives is hard work. But treating categories as static and unidimensional misrepresents circumstances of everyday life and produces substantive knowledge about political action of a particular kind. This knowledge can be used to identify erroneously causes for political outcomes, as well as be utilized in the development of public policies based in these inferential stories. To develop and utilize a theory of a politicized context of gender, scholarship must treat categories dynamically, remaining suspicious of the homogenizing generalizations that go along with classification while examining specific intersections of categories at particular points in time. This is precisely the project of intersectional approaches to political analysis.

Although empirical work in intersectionality remains rare in the women and politics scholarship, it represents an area of strong growth and innovation. In studying marginalized populations, most often women in intersecting political contexts of oppression, scholars are faced with the dilemma of documenting and giving voice to the experiences of people occupying these categories, and the competing imperative to go beyond the constraint of the categories themselves. There is no easy way out of this predicament, and intersectional scholarship in women and politics must continue to finesse the empirical analysis, leaving room for dynamic accounts of identity while forging ahead conceptually.

TRANSFORMING WOMEN AND POLITICS THROUGH
INTERSECTIONAL PERSPECTIVES

We have argued that the field of women and politics in political science must take greater account of the diversity of the locations in which women engage in politics, paying particular attention to the categories of race, class, and sexuality. Theoretical and empirical developments of intersectional perspectives are appealing as approaches to identifying the dynamics of the political mechanisms at work in overlapping oppressions. We emphasize that holding the categories constant, however, is a strategy that cannot take intersectional approaches any farther, for categories conceived as homogeneous entities may themselves act to enhance oppression. Our perspective is based in a critique of the dominant approach in the field of studying women as a static unitary category. When race, class, sexuality, or any other set of characteristics is taken into consideration, it is most often – although not always – analyzed by the introduction of dummy variables that serve to control for what are by definition independent effects of race or class, for example. We advocate for the banishment of the dummy variable, favoring instead a strategy of inquiry that treats political beings as dynamic subjects with a multiplicity of categorical homes. This is no easy fix, however, although the imperative in supporting this approach is to take account of the variation in political contexts in which women engage in political action. Viewing women's political activism from a variety of vantage points provides critical leverage in identifying the mechanisms by which power is manifested in the creation of the categories we often take for granted. In this regard, observing, giving voice, and interpreting the constraints and opportunity structures for people in specific intersectional contexts aids in revealing the dynamics of discriminatory practices in U.S. politics, and in identifying their location in structural frameworks and political institutions, as well as the categories themselves.

To do this, we borrow from feminist theorists of intersectional approaches and argue that we must begin by accepting in a provisional way existing categories of sex, race, class, and sexuality. Studying specific intersectional locations allows scholars to observe and document relationships of parity and inequality, configurations of power relations, and distinct political, economic, and social contexts that produce these outcomes. Scholarship in women and politics must work hard to link the theoretical imperatives of intersectional feminist theory to the everyday lives of women of all colors by facing the interlocking oppressions that confront them daily. Learning from allied fields in the social sciences and humanities, particularly women and gender studies, sociology, and legal and cultural studies, can help to transform the study of women and politics in the United States, for at its core intersectionality is an interdisciplinary approach to understanding the complexities of identity. In this regard, black feminist thought, third wave black feminism, mestiza, and hybridity perspectives, along with gay and lesbian critiques of politics, offer useful insight into how to approach the study of intersectionality.

To foment a revolution may be too much to ask of an academic field constrained by disciplinary structures and long-standing epistemological frameworks. To transform the study of women in action, however, is a task for which intersectional perspectives will be critical. Although we may never be able to leave categories behind, we must always remain suspicious of them and their potential to reinscribe and exacerbate existing structural inequalities. Transformation in scholarship in the field of women and politics can best begin by acknowledging the lived experiences of intersectional subjects, situating appropriate research strategies to capture these dynamics, and providing voice and agency to the women occupying multiple locations.

Notes

1. Alice Walker used the term "Womanist" to describe a woman who "appreciates and prefers women's culture, women's emotional flexibility (values tears as natural counterbalance of laughter), and women's strength. Sometimes loves individual men, sexually and/or non-sexually. Committed to survival and wholeness of entire people, male and female. Not a separatist, except periodically, for health. Traditionally universalist. . . . Loves music. Loves dance. Loves the moon. Loves the Spirit. Loves love and food and roundness. Loves struggle. Loves the Folk. Loves herself. Regardless" (Walker 1984, xi).
2. Consistent with the writing of the Combahee River Collective, we prefer to capitalize "Black," but we accede to editorial consistency in this volume.
3. Analysis by racial categories has until recently been viable only for whites and African Americans.
4. See Nie, Junn, and Stehlik-Barry (1996) for a review of the research and an elaboration of why it is not a puzzle.
5. The black Jezebel stereotype began in slavery, defining black women as breeders, prostitutes, and the exotic "other." This stereotype depicted black women as lascivious by nature, seductive, alluring, worldly, beguiling, tempting, and lewd. The black Jezebel lacked modesty and sexual restraint; therefore, her rape by white men (especially during slavery, Reconstruction, and Jim Crow) was seen as provoked. The term "Jezebel" has biblical roots, specifically the story of Jezebel, a Phoenician princess whose reign was marked by persecution and guile. The name "Jezebel" denotes a deceitful and immoral woman in First Kings chapters 18 and 19 and in Second Kings chapter 9.

6

Women's Movements and Women in Movements

Influencing American Democracy from the "Outside"?

Lee Ann Banaszak

In the United States, social movements represent a major means by which unrepresented or underrepresented groups gain access to decision making or achieve social change. Women are among the many groups that have stood outside politics, needing social movements to acquire change. Although women face the same problems as all outsiders, the gendered nature of politics and women's oppression also creates problems unique to women. In this chapter, I examine what we know about the role of U.S. women's movements in American democracy. How have women's movements contributed to women's representation and shaped American democracy? What factors influence their mobilization, actions, and outcomes? These questions are central to our understanding of women and American politics and to the larger field of social movements, which seeks to understand the causes of movements and their effects on the political process. My discussion addresses both literatures.

I begin by critically analyzing the definition of women's movements, showing the problems and inherent contradictions in the conceptualization of these movements within the wider field. I then provide a short description of the major concepts in the study of social movements as background for the discussion to follow. Third, I focus on the political development of women's movements, examining both the conditions that foster women's movements and the factors that have shaped their evolution over time. A fourth section discusses the complexity of the concept of activism, which occurs at multiple levels and in a variety of arenas. I then examine how U.S. women's movements have shaped social change. Finally, I conclude with suggestions for further research.

DEFINING WOMEN'S MOVEMENTS

Social movements are usually defined as a mixture of informal networks and organizations that make "claims" for fundamental changes in the political,

79

economic, or social system, *and* are "outside" conventional politics, *and* utilize unconventional or protest tactics (Diani 1992). Women's movements are therefore not clearly defined groups but a diffuse and complex set of individuals, organizations, and informal groups. Studies of women's movements focus on multiple levels: (1) micro-level explorations of individual activists and their interactions, (2) meso-level examinations of groups and institutions and their interactions, and (3) macro-level analyses of this eclectic mix of challengers as a coherent whole dynamically or comparatively across movements.[1] The diffuse nature of movements makes defining their boundaries difficult, and increasingly scholars are critically examining these boundaries (see, e.g., Beckwith 1996; Katzenstein 1998; Raeburn 2004).

In the United States, we typically use the term "women's movement" to mean feminist movement. Yet the true meaning of "women's movement" is much wider (Beckwith 2000; Ferree and Mueller 2004).[2] The feminist movement seeks the elimination of women's inequality with and subordination to men; for many feminists, this entails eradicating hidden forms of oppression built into existing institutions and norms in addition to formal legal equality. The larger category of women's movements includes other movements that mobilize women as a group and articulate women's interests, however defined. Conservative women's groups, such as Concerned Women for America, which oppose feminist goals, are part of a women's movement because they organize women as women around women's interests as they see them (see Klatch 1987; Schreiber 2002a, 2002b). I distinguish between the women's movement and feminist movement here, preserving "women's movement" for discussions relevant to the wider set of movements.

A focus on *the* women's movement (or *the* feminist movement) presents a different problem, downplaying the multiple intersecting movements incorporated under this label. Specific issues stimulate movements of their own, developing out of the feminist movement but taking on unique characteristics (see Elman 1996 and Weldon 2002a on battered women's movements; see Staggenborg 1991 on the pro-choice movement; see Taylor 1996 and Morgen 2002 on women's health movements). Increasingly scholars have also recognized that movements exist at different geopolitical levels. Thus although most works focus on the U.S. women's movement at the national level (Costain 1992; Ferree and Hess 1985; Freeman 1975; Ryan 1992), there are also analyses of U.S. women's movements' role in transnational movements (Keck and Sikkink 1998; Rupp 1997) and studies of local movements, which act separately (but not completely independently) from their national counterparts (Naples 1998; Staggenborg 2001).

The number of feminist movements also multiplies as we recognize that feminist movements exist at the intersection of other movements (Ferree and Mueller 2004, 578). For example, the specific character of gender oppression (and its connection to race oppression) for black and Chicana women requires that they organize their feminist movements separately from their white counterparts (Roth 2004; see also Springer 2005). Indeed, the gender discrimination these women experience is inseparable from their racial and class background (Crenshaw 1991; see Junn and Brown, this volume; King 1988; Smith 1985, among others). Because white feminist organizations commonly identified with the movement did not address their needs, African American and Latina women organized independently, addressing the sexism they experienced while also critically engaging the white feminist movement. The existence of multiple women's movements (and feminist movements) reflects the varied nature of gender – that is, the social construction of women and men – at different intersections of race, class, sexual orientation, and sex oppression, as well as the gendered nature of American politics (see Ritter, this volume).

Equally important has been recent recognition that women's movement activism occurs within institutions as well as in opposition to institutions (Banaszak 2004, 2005; Fonow 2003; Katzenstein 1998; Raeburn 2004; Staggenborg 2001). Women's movements scholarship, inspired by feminist theory, has been exceedingly good at recognizing both private-sphere activism and public-sphere activism focused against the state (see Van Dyke, Soule, and Taylor 2004). Yet to the extent that the feminist movement opposes patriarchal institutions, some scholars have ignored activism within institutions, overlooking the contributions of feminist activists who are institutional members.

The "women's movement" is not unique in incorporating multiple movements and intersecting with other movements and institutions. Similar analyses could be made of the environmental movement or African American movements for racial equality. However, women's movement scholars have been quicker to investigate these boundary issues and to utilize a wider view of movements to provide new insights into the nature of women's struggles and into old questions and central theoretical concepts in the social movement literature (see, e.g., Banaszak 2007; Beckwith 1996; Robnett 2006; Roth 2004).

SOCIAL MOVEMENT CONCEPTS

Three theoretical perspectives dominate social movement research: *mobilizing structures, political opportunities,* and *ideational aspects. Mobilizing structures* refer to the forms that social movements acquire as they develop (McAdam, McCarthy, and Zald 1996, 3). Formal mobilizing structures include the rules, norms and organizational forms adopted within the movement; informal structures include a movement's networks and action repertoires (i.e., the array of tactical choices movements have at their disposal). Social movement scholars have long realized that group structure, as well as other concrete resources such as money and membership, influence whether and how movements mobilize, develop, and act as well as what they can achieve (Cress and Snow 1998; McCarthy and Zald 1977; Oberschall 1973).

Political opportunities consist of the larger political environment that provides spaces for women to mobilize, targets that encourage specific types of movement action, or specific historical periods[3] when movements can achieve certain goals.[4] Political opportunities also constrain women's movements. Although the political environment has limitless characteristics, social movement scholars tend to focus on political rules and institutions, elite characteristics, political alliances or coalitions, and police brutality and repression. These characteristics change over time but also differ by local or national political system, leading to both dynamic and comparative analyses.

Ideational elements (or what Ferree and Mueller [2004, 597] call "meaning work") are those aspects of ideology, values, norms, and beliefs that influence social movements or their actions. Within movements, ideational elements influence two related processes. First, movement mobilization and action requires the creation and maintenance of a *collective identity* by developing common ideas, norms, and values that define the movement (Bernstein 1997); this process includes demarking the goals and underlying movement ideology, delineating the source of the problems, and defining the difference between the movement and "the other." The second ideological process is the strategic *framing* of public arguments and events by movements and their opponents (Ferree 2003; Snow and Benford 1988, 1992; Snow et al. 1986). These two processes occur within national or localized *cultures*[5] – sets of beliefs, rituals, and language, which may limit social movements' abilities to frame or create collective identities (Banaszak 1996b; Ferree 2003; Ferree et al. 2002; Swidler 1986).

U.S. women's movement scholars have contributed to the development of these concepts in two ways: (1) by empirically and theoretically enumerating how these concepts intersect in causing women's mobilization and in influencing the (often unexpected) outcomes of movements and (2) by highlighting the gendered aspects of these social movement concepts and their implications for understanding U.S. women's movements, and, indeed, all social movements.

AMERICAN POLITICAL DEVELOPMENT AND WOMEN'S MOVEMENTS

Meso-level analyses examining the ebb and flow of the feminist movement often use the terminology of waves. The feminist movement is defined as starting in the 1960s, and as analytically distinct from the "first wave" suffrage movement. Different waves are often essentially considered to be separate movements defined by increased contention and mobilization. Yet longer views of the feminist movement provide better leverage for analyzing its development and its influence on American political development.

Continuity between Waves

Studies of second wave feminism have been supplemented by recent studies examining both the causes and consequences of the first wave (Banaszak 1996b; Clemens 1993; Harvey 1998; Jeydel 2004; King, Cornwall, and Dahlin 2005; McCammon 2001, 2003; McCammon, Campbell, Granberg, and Mowery 2001; McConnaughy 2005; Szymanski 2003). One conclusion of this literature was that the feminist movement continued from the first wave to present, even during apparently dormant periods. Because movement scholars focus on mobilization, studies of the feminist movement in "abeyance" help us understand the long-term dynamics of women's movements as they show the feminist movement existing and acting long after its presumed death (see Banaszak 1996a; Harrison 1988; Rupp and Taylor 1987; Ware 1981). Recently, Suzanne Staggenborg and Verta Taylor (2005) have argued that rather than examining rises and declines in women's movements as evidenced by mobilization, we should focus on dynamic changes in organization, culture, and tactics.

Dynamic Changes in the First Wave

Indeed, in the study of early women's movements, scholars have concentrated on how political opportunities, resource mobilization and framing affect changes in organizations, tactics, and cultures (Buechler 1986; Jeydel 2004; McCammon 2001). Here the most interesting work has examined the intersections and gendered nature of the core concepts in social movement theory, thereby improving our understanding of the development (and outcomes) of first wave women's movements.

Early women's movements underwent significant tactical innovation over time, adopting very different strategies and organizational forms in later years. Traditionally this innovation is seen as a response to political opportunities – movements react to new opportunities with appropriate tactics. Yet such interpretations beg the question of where such tactical innovations come from. Elisabeth Clemens (1993) argues that innovation in the organizational form of the Women's Trade Union League (WTUL) developed from particular opportunity structures. Working women, searching for an effective model of activism, exchanged the trade union model for one based on middle-class women's clubs. Although this alienated the WTUL from trade unions, it improved cooperation with middle-class women, leading to adoption of their tactical strategies as well.

Others argue the large-scale tactical changes in first wave movements resulted from the intersection of culture and political opportunities. A major

innovation in the woman suffrage movement was the introduction of suffrage parades – large-scale protest marches of suffrage activists demanding
the vote (Banaszak 1996b; McCammon 2003). How did large-scale protest
enter women's movements' repertoire when it had not been used before? In
previous work, I argue that the women's movements' culture, with organizational structures that encouraged innovation, provided the impetus for
movements to adopt such tactics from their allies (Banaszak 1996b; see also
Clemens 1993).[6] Here tactical change is driven by the political environment,
which creates movement subcultures, which in turn allow movements to take
advantage of other political opportunities.

Analyses of the first wave have also reconceptualized political opportunities to include gender. Holly McCammon and colleagues (2001) argue
that societal gender roles and norms themselves represent opportunities that
influence the success of the woman suffrage movement. First wave women's
movements succeeded in part because gender roles shifted as women entered
institutions of higher education, professions, and politics. They conclude
that other types of social movements need to recognize their specific cultural opportunities. Yet gendered opportunities – although class-, race-, and
movement-specific – influence women's participation in *every* movement
(Beckwith 1996, 1998; Ritter, this volume; Robnett 1996, 2000), suggesting
the need to incorporate gender into studies of political opportunities' effect
on other social movements as well.

Even as scholars recognize the continued existence of women's movements after 1920, surprisingly little research focuses on periods of decline
and abeyance.[7] The ostensible decline in the early women's rights movement
in the late 1920s represents a continuing puzzle given that other women's
movements of the period continued to be highly mobilized (Skocpol 1992).
Much of the work on this period focuses on the women's rights movement (an exception here is Skocpol 1992) without attempting to examine the "waves" of other women's movements or to compare various U.S.
women's movements to study the timing and causes of demobilization. Thus
although we know much about the rise and success of early women's movements, we remain in the infant stages of understanding these movements
after maturity.[8]

Analyses of the decline of women's movements, although sparse, differ greatly in their explanations for demobilization. Theda Skocpol (1992)
argues that the lack of a woman's voting bloc after enfranchisement elim-
inated the lobbying power that women's organizations had developed in
the pre-suffrage era. Although women's movements mobilized well into the
late 1920s, elected officials were simply less receptive and opponents grew
more vocal. Others argue that divisions within the movement – particularly between those seeking protective legislation for women and those seeking an Equal Rights Amendment – led to demobilization (Banaszak 1998;
Rupp and Taylor 1987). Research that might reconcile or test these differing

explanations has yet to be conducted, although such an analysis might go far in helping to develop our understanding of the demobilization of women's movements more generally.

Movement Consequences

If gendered and nuanced theoretical concepts have helped us better understand the development of early U.S. women's movements, other work demonstrates that these movements altered American parties and politics in fundamental ways.

First wave women's movements were major innovators of interest group politics in the modern era (Clemens 1993). Although previously lobbying was associated with backroom party politics, women's groups developed the public interest lobby (characterized by the idea of the "Front Door Lobby"), changing the locus of lobbying from personalistic partisan connections to the pursuit of legislation through petitions and citizen mobilization. As such they helped to herald a new era of American politics (Andersen 1996; see also Cott 1987; Ritter, this volume).

Early women's movements' effects on policy especially after 1920 have been more hotly debated. Beyond well-documented effects on women's enfranchisement (Banaszak 1996b; King, Cornwall, and Dahlin 2005; McCammon et al. 2001), women's movements sought a wide array of legislation including social policy, health legislation, education laws, and government reform (Andersen 1996, 154). However, while Skocpol (1992) emphasizes the inability of women's movements to maintain benefits for mothers in the Shepard-Towner Act, Kristi Andersen (1996) claims women's mobilization after suffrage resulted in a wide range of legislation, even though many policies, such as the Child Labor Amendment, failed along the arduous route to passage.[9] Women's movements' greatest effects were their ability to create social change outside the formal political arena, away from courthouses and legislatures. Andersen (1996) chronicles many such changes resulting from first wave women's movements, from our understandings of women's citizenship to the regendering of the electoral process that occurred as voting and campaigning moved away from male-dominated spaces. These social changes set the stage for the second wave of the women's movement, regendering the second wave's political opportunities as well.

U.S. women's movements in this early period also operated at multiple geographical levels, the transnational in particular. U.S. activists saw themselves as part of a global movement, and many famous activists were devoted to this early transnational feminist movement. For example, Elizabeth Cady Stanton and Susan B. Anthony helped to found the International Council of Women and the International Woman Suffrage Alliance (later the International Alliance of Women), and Carrie Chapman Catt and Alice Paul – more often opponents than allies – spent years building international women's organizations (Rupp 1997; Rupp and Taylor 1987). Feminist scholars have traced the historical legacies of their international feminism, particularly on the League of Nations and United Nations (Daley and Nolan 1995; Keck and Sikkink 1998, 51–8; Rupp 1997), arguing that even in these early years transnational feminists influenced the international community.

Yet several important issues have only begun to be addressed. We know little about how the ideas and tactics employed at different levels (i.e., local, national, and international) cross-fertilize women's movements. Activists working at both the national and international level also develop collective identities within both women's movements, raising issues of how activists negotiate different levels of identity (Rupp 1997).

As we move to the second (and perhaps the third) wave, scholars have observed that the upturn in movement activism begun in the 1960s continues in a wide array of locations, even as others observe a decline in political participation (Putnam 2000; Skocpol 2004). These contradictory findings may result from the hidden nature of recent feminist activism, occurring as it does in multiple venues – at different geographic levels and inside institutions. Wider views of activism adopted by women's movement scholars contradict these negative forecasts of decreasing participation, showing little or no decline in women's movement activism since the 1960s, although the form of activism and the specific actors changed dramatically (Barakso 2005; Reger 2005; Whittier 2005).

MULTIPLE ACTIVISMS/IDENTITIES AND INTERSECTING CAUSES

The literature on recent women's movements has helped to redefine movements by examining women's movement activism in multiple locations and movement identity at the intersection of gender, race, class, and sexual orientation. It has also expanded our understanding of social movement concepts by exploring their overlapping effects on women's movements' development.

Multiple Activisms

Studies of second wave women's movements focus not only on national developments but also on transnational (e.g., Keck and Sikkink 1998; Moghadam 2005) and local (e.g., Cohen, Jones, and Tronto 1997; Naples 1998) levels. Individuals do not solely work at a single level nor does activism follow a continuum from local to national and then to transnational; local groups may bypass the national level to work directly within transnational movements (Naples and Desai 2002). Although many focus on a single level, increasingly scholars are examining how levels of activism intersect with each other, raising a range of interesting questions. One such question is how national movements influence grassroots activism. For example, Maryann Barakso (2004) and Jo Reger and Suzanne Staggenborg (2005) find that the national-level National Organization for Women (NOW) influenced local sections' grassroots activism, even as national NOW was the product of local activism.

Moreover, individual activists often engage in activism at multiple levels simultaneously. How do activists negotiate this, particularly when action on one level conflicts with another level? In their analysis of pro- and antiabortion rights groups, Deana Rohlinger and David S. Meyer (2005) find that transnational framing often conflicts with the way activists in national groups frame the issue. Activists engaged on both levels must decide how to deal with conflict between activism on the national and transnational level.

A different issue arises in studying activists within institutions, where scholars tend to presuppose a "linkage of location, form, and content" (Katzenstein 1998, 195). Here scholars assume a lack of multiple activisms of women in institutions, focusing largely on how these women are co-opted by their institutions. The form their activism takes is thus predetermined by the institution within which these women are located. Mary Katzenstein's (1998) work questions these assumptions by identifying the Catholic Church as an institution open to feminist activism and by chronicling activism within the military. Here we need more and better theory about how and when institutions determine the form and content of activism.

Multiple Identities

How women view themselves and their movements and how movements frame themselves also influence women's organizational efforts (see, e.g., Freeman 1975), as does women's gender consciousness generally (see Burns, this volume), but there has been little attempt to incorporate this work in the movement literature. Recent studies advance our understanding of women's movements' collective identities by examining their diversity. Activists may belong to multiple women's movements and women in a particular women's movement may also belong to other (non-women's) movements. Even within a single movement (however narrowly defined), different collective identities may exist (Bernstein 2002; Reger 2002a).

Initial discussions of collective identity found that differing identities within a movement (or movement group) led to discord, factionalism, and eventually decline (see, e.g., Freeman 1975; Ryan 1992). However, in recent years authors have noted the benefits of diversity in collective identity. Nancy Whittier (1995) found that feminist activists from different time periods differ significantly in their collective identity, allowing the movement's identity to shift over time. Very different collective identities among activists in the lesbian movement in Vermont (Bernstein 2002) and within New York City's NOW (Reger 2002a) strengthened these local movements by mobilizing a wider population and providing multiple faces to outsiders.

Recent scholars also focus on the relationship of organizational structures to multiple collective identities. Studies of black feminist organizations (Springer 2005) and New York's NOW (Reger 2002a) note that organizational structures permitting multiple identities facilitate the maintenance of these groups. Barakso (2004) also shows that organizing structures can adapt to changing circumstances over time, even as they continue to maintain continuity in values, taking on new purposes and allowing multiple identities to exist. In the case of NOW, statutes emphasizing its grassroots base and a federalized organizational form allow diversity in local activism even when it differs from the national organization's focus.

Other women's movement scholars focus on how movements define collective identity in which activists are also members in other movements (see Beckwith [1998] on mining unions; see Klatch [1987, 2002] and Schreiber [2002b] on conservative movements; see Roth [2004] and Springer [2005] on African American and Hispanic movements; and see Faderman [1991], Bernstein [1997, 2002], Cavin [1990], and Taylor and Whittier [1992] on lesbians in gay rights movements). Here U.S. women's movement scholars have sought to understand the effect of activism in other, non-sex-specific movements on women's collective identity. Although we know that in such cases collective identity is defined at the intersection of multiple movements, more recent work develops in two countervailing trends. The first identifies the role that strategic choice plays in creating collective identity (Bernstein 1997). According to this approach, activists choose particular identities to help them make a political statement or to counter specific oppositional forces. The second approach maintains that collective identity is limited by the political and gender context (Beckwith 1998; Katzenstein 1998).

These two processes are not necessarily contradictory; rather, they reflect differences in emphasis, where the former focuses on the opportunities for conscious choice, and the latter concentrates on societal limitations of such choices. Mary Bernstein's (2002) analysis of Vermont lesbian-gay movements shows that activists consciously define collective identity in response to opponents, political experiences, and the diversity within the movement itself. Yet much more remains to be done. As in the case of political opportunities, analyses of identity require, as Bernstein (2002) shows, nuanced understandings of gender to supplement the standard bag of tools of social movement theory, as well as careful analyses of the intersection of these standard social movement concepts.

Intersecting Causes

Women's movement scholars have made a distinct contribution to social movement theory by defining and elaborating the intersection of what had been separate theoretical concepts, especially in showing how organizations and political opportunities are imbued with culture and how gender permeates organizations, opportunities, and ideational elements.

Although scholars of the U.S. feminist movement have long discussed culture (see, e.g., Ferree and Hess 1985; Ryan 1992), its rise as a core concept (separate from mobilizing structures or political opportunities) in social movement theory occurred relatively recently (e.g., Johnston and Klandermans 1995). Newer work has begun to tie culture to organizations. Staggenborg (2001) sees women's movements as engaging in the creation of culture – a necessary activity for women's movement mobilization – alongside more typical political actions. Periods of "cultural feminism" in the history of the feminist movement, she argues, occur when political opportunities discourage other forms of political action.[10] Thus groups are tied to culture through their activism. Alternatively, Barakso (2004) sees cultural values, particularly founding values and norms, embodied in the organizational structures of feminist groups. Therefore when we study mobilizing structures, we are by definition also studying culture. Both studies change culture's definition from a contextual phenomenon to something generated by movements or movement groups in opposition to established cultures (see also Banaszak 1996b). Indeed, as Suzanne Staggenborg (2002) notes, understanding culture at the group or movement level strengthens our ability to theorize across levels – from individual perceptions of activists, to organizations and their collective identity, to society.

Others have focused on the intersection of political opportunities and culture. Culture has long been recognized as a societal-level phenomenon that influences the actions of movements (Ferree 2003; Gamson and Meyer 1996; Jenson 1987). The recognition that movements and movement groups create culture has led to the realization that cultural opportunities may be wielded by specific groups for or against movements. Myra Marx Ferree (2004), for example, argues that cultural repression, through ridicule, stigma, and silencing, is utilized to silence the U.S. women's movement. In this sense, cultural opportunities (or constraints) are not just contextual but result from other political actors' activities (if not volition).

Movement groups can and do act outside of the available opportunities, although such behavior and discourse is less likely to be recorded (Ferree 2004). Women's movement groups are free to ignore political opportunities and, Ferree notes, there are good reasons to do so. Framing issues in ways that lack cultural resonance allows groups to maintain a vision of the possible that would otherwise not exist. Such groups trade the risk of remaining unnoticed and being on the outskirts of society for maintaining radical ideas. Such work suggests both the framing and opportunity literature overemphasize the goal of reaching society over important internal goals of the movement.

The previous discussion of culture in organizations and opportunities makes no specific mention of gender. Yet gender culture permeates all facets of women's movements and, indeed, all movements. Beyond McCammon and colleagues' (2001) study of the suffrage era, others observe gendered opportunities affecting second wave feminism as well. In a study of second wave feminism in the United States and Chile, Lisa Baldez and Celeste Montoya Kirk (2005) argue the exclusion of women and women's issues from newly formed partisan coalitions sustains the vision of women as political outsiders and provides women with an opportunity to mobilize on the basis of that exclusion. Yet gender is also a characteristic of ideational elements such as framing and culture (Beckwith 2001; Ferree 2003), and studies of women in the civil rights movement also show these organizations are gendered (Robnett 1996, 2000). Much of the work on gendered organizations and framing studies women in other movements rather than women's movements (Beckwith 2001; Fonow 2003; Robnett 2000). Yet gender may explain differences between women's movements – even different feminist movements. Diverse gender roles exist for women of different class, race, and sexual orientation, not to mention men and women in different women's movements. For example, women garment workers and women miners may both participate in the women's trade union movement, although the gender roles associated with each may lead to widely differing organizational structures, framing, and opportunities. Groups may also adopt different gender roles and framing, leading to differentiation within the community of women's movements. Thus gender's incorporation into social movement concepts might provide important leverage on understanding difference within the U.S. women's movement.

AFFECTING THE DEMOCRATIC PROCESS

Work examining movement outcomes tends to focus on specific policy outcomes that reflect women's movements' goals.[11] However, women's movements seek large-scale social change as well as state policy, and strive to build and maintain their movements. Thus, the results of intense mobilization may be both internal and external to women's movements and include more than the achievement of state policies.

External Effects

One of the primary questions that remains unanswered in this field is the relationship of women's movements to large-scale social change. Women's movements developed in part in reaction to the large-scale social and demographic changes, such as women's increasing education levels, migration into the labor force, and decreasing fertility rates (Klein 1984; Ryan 1992). These movements also affected changes in these very factors: feminist mobilization changed gender-role attitudes as feminists shaped policy changes that altered the character of society. Because social change was occurring as the movement arose, distinguishing the effects of women's movements is difficult. Attitudinal change cannot easily be documented because most measures of gender attitudes follow the rise of the women's movement (but see Ondercin 2007). Kira Sanbonmatsu (2004), looking at party change, notes that the public is still ambivalent about feminist policies, laying open the question of how much attitudinal change the feminist movement wrought. This remains one of the unanswered questions in the area of women's movements.

Much more work has been done analyzing the effect of women's movements on the political agenda (Costain 1992; Sanbonmatsu 2004; Wolbrecht 2000; L. Young 2000). Attention to women's rights issues increased substantially after the feminist movement mobilized and was accompanied by a rise in the number and types of issues comprising the political agenda (Wolbrecht 2000). Changes in the policy agenda in turn influenced the women's movement, diversifying and expanding the number of women's groups (Wolbrecht 2000, 126).

Changes wrought by the feminist movement also altered political parties, although scholars disagree on the strength of this effect and its root causes. Many scholars maintain that the women's rights agenda divided and polarized political parties (Freeman 1987; Wolbrecht 2000; L. Young 2000). Yet Sanbonmatsu (2004) argues that there is less polarization because feminist issues are still marginalized by both parties, the implication being that the feminist movement had less impact on the political process. Even those scholars that find the women's movements caused parties to shift position (however slightly) disagree on why this occurred. For Jo Freeman (1987, 1993) the basic structure of the Democratic Party (as opposed to the Republican Party) gave organized interests (such as the feminist movement) greater influence. Alternatively, Lisa Young (2000) argues that the feminist movement's intervention into electoral politics was central to parties' position changes, whereas Christina Wolbrecht (2000) finds party elites and changes in the nature of women's issues to be responsible.

Inadvertently, the feminist movement contributed to polarized political parties by inspiring antifeminists to mobilize as well. Phyllis Schlafly's Stop ERA and Concerned Women of America arose in opposition to the ERA ratification campaign (Mansbridge 1986; Sanbonmatsu 2004; Schreiber 2002a). Similarly, antiabortion groups developed in the wake of victories by the feminist movement (Staggenborg 1991), which in turn further mobilized feminists responding to threats to policy gains. Although Staggenborg (1989, 1991) and Staggenborg and Meyer (1996) explore the interaction between the pro-choice and pro-life movement and provide empirical evidence for the widely held claim that oppositional movements are intricately linked, we do not yet fully understand the nature of those connections.

Despite these partisan realignments, women's movements have increasingly engaged in both nonpartisan and partisan efforts to increase women's representation in elected office, to the point where women's movements' funding has become one of the most significant sources of money for Democratic women candidates (Day, Hadley, and Brown 2001; L. Young 2000). During the first years of the second wave, women's movement activists pushed for greater representation of women in appointed positions as well (Harrison 1988); over time, however, mobilization to demand political appointments has lessened, reflecting differential success in influencing elected versus appointed office, and reduced opportunities for affecting appointments in the 1980s and since 2000. Although equal opportunity of women and increased women's representation continues to be heralded by both parties, since 1980 they have been less willing to adopt feminist policies, and existing policies are under attack (L. Young 2000).

The existing literature on women's movements in the United States has addressed many of the ways in which movements have affected changes in social characteristics, the political agenda, political parties, countermovements, and public policy. We understand less well how these changes in turn influence future movement activity and outcomes. In short, missing from the literature on women's movements are explorations of *dynamic* interactions between movements and the political opportunities movements themselves have shaped.

Internal Effects

The choices that activists in U.S. women's movements make about organizational structure and agenda directly shape their own future. Decisions that women's movement groups make early on affect the future development of those movements in both positive and negative ways. One debate occurs around advocating for radical system change versus stepwise change in politics without large changes in existing institutions. Considered in comparison to women's movements in other countries, U.S. women's movements tend to be overwhelmingly liberal feminist in their ideology, advocating incremental change, although they also have radical elements.[12] Some U.S. women's movement scholars argue that focusing on radical change may be important for long-term movement maintenance. For example, building alternative communities and visions of the future were crucial to second wave black feminist organizations (Springer 2005; see also Minkoff 1997). Similarly, movement organizations' decisions not to focus on advocacy may reflect the need to focus on movement maintenance instead. The National Women's Party's emphasis on community building during the 1940s and 1950s, for example, enabled the group's survival during years of movement abeyance (Rupp and Taylor 1987; see also Minkoff 1995). Strategies that focus primarily on organization building may limit movement influence in the short term but nonetheless enable groups to survive hostile political contexts, thus allowing them to contribute to greater institutional change in the long term.

A second debate revolves around the degree to which women's movements "institutionalize" over time. In its earliest manifestations, institutionalization involved deradicalization of movement goals, bureaucratization and formalization of movement groups, and cooperative, insider strategies (e.g., Zald and Ash 1966). However, several women's movement scholars have debunked institutionalization as a universal process, arguing that these characteristics do not go hand in hand (Banaszak 2004; Katzenstein 1998). Debra Minkoff (1999, 1681), for example, argues that formal organizations move from insider to outsider tactics with more flexibility than less formal groups, although large tactical shifts increase the probability that the organization disbands.

These works suggest that considerable path dependency exists within U.S. women's movements. Earlier decisions create internal contexts that define future mobilization, although not always in the conservative ways assumed by early social movement scholars. Similarly, the external effects that U.S. women's movements have on the political agenda, public policy, and the character and strength of allies and opponents influence the future ability of the movement to mobilize and influence the political process.

CONCLUSION: TOMORROW'S AGENDA

I have argued throughout this chapter that a recognition of the diverse women's movements in the United States and of the complex and gendered nature of the analytical concepts used to analyze these movements characterize the frontiers of women's movement research. In addition to the extensive work on U.S. women's movements reviewed here and the suggestions for further research raised throughout, what questions remain to be answered?

One remaining avenue of research is to explore the sequence of and interconnection between different U.S. women's movements in systematic detail. Some work has already been done on women of color movement organizations, lesbian organizations, and movement-countermovement relations. Yet if women's movements are nested within one another and operating at multiple geographic levels, we need to understand their interconnection more systematically. For example, the feminist movement has many submovements, such as those for abortion rights and against violence against women, that share activists and organizations and occasionally agendas or events. The internal dynamics and political opportunities of these submovements differ, so we need to analyze the relationships among these submovements to understand the general trend in "the U.S. women's movement." We should also examine U.S. women's movements in comparison to other U.S. movements. Do these movements have similar nested qualities or is this specific to women's movements?

We also need to focus on the less studied U.S. women's movements. Scholars have studied some women's movements extensively, but movements inside institutions, conservative movements, and women's movements that fall outside of the traditional feminist definition remain understudied, limiting our understanding of U.S. women's movements as a whole.

Another missing link has been a focus on the long-term dynamics of collective identity, particularly for activists on the intersection of U.S. women's movements and other movements. We have a sense of how collective identity develops in such cases, influencing both tactics and outcomes, but these have largely been single-movement studies over short time periods. These methods limit our ability to analyze how history constrains collective identity and how much freedom movements have to define their own identity. Even if identities are strategically crafted within particular contexts, long-term studies will help us to understand how earlier identities constrain later ones.

More work is also needed on the gendered nature of culture and institutions, which compose the context for women's movements. Although all movements are outsiders to the political process, studying gendered processes helps us to understand the continued impenetrability of political institutions to U.S. women's movements. Because gender varies by race, class, and sexual orientation, we need to examine how gendered opportunity structures or culture vary for different women's movements. The work on the gendered nature of organizations, opportunities, framing, collective identity, and culture also may help explain the specific role of women (and men) in other movements (see, e.g., Beckwith 1996, 1998, 2001; Robnett 1996, 2000).

Finally, the field of U.S. women's movements needs creative quantitative work that can test alternative theories and provide wider analyses of new concepts. Recent work recognizing the overlapping nature of culture, political opportunities, collective identity, and organizational structures or delineating the multiple activisms and identities of U.S. women's movements relies heavily on qualitative case studies in part because developing these new theoretical ideas requires such methodology and in part because quantitative work is more difficult here. Yet the study of U.S. women's movements has always benefited from both close qualitative case studies and quantitative statistical work. We need more comparative studies both across countries and within the United States across different movements or across time. Here new statistical methods such as those that allow for nested cases, such as hierarchical linear models, or for the analysis of political rhetoric may be particularly helpful. Time series methods such as Granger causality that allow us to disentangle causal relationships may also help to sort out how much social change results from women's movements mobilization and how much women's movements are affected by social change. Similarly, alternative measures of public opinion (see Lee 2002) might provide better or longer time series data on a range of attitudes toward women, allowing us to examine the relationship between public opinion and movement mobilization. All of these may offer new means of analyzing women's movements in the years to come.

Notes

1. See Gerhards and Rucht (1992) and Staggenborg (2002) for more extensive explanations of the micro, meso, and macro distinction.
2. While I focus here on the multiple movements that exist within the definition of "women's movement," equally important are the role of women in movements.

Women also participate in other movements as women; while the goals of these movements do not incorporate women's interests, women's movement scholarship also helps to explain how women act and organize within other movements (Beckwith 2000).

3. For example, periods of punctuated equilibrium mentioned by Beckwith (this volume) may serve as particular historical eras when movements have additional opportunities to influence the policy-making process. See also Baumgartner and Jones (1993).

4. For elaborations of the political opportunities concept, see Meyer and Minkoff (2004).

5. Scholars have examined national culture's influence on movement development, but cultures may also be localized by ethnic, racial, class, or geographic location. In any one arena, there is a national culture and multiple subcultures operating, within which movements create collective identity and frames.

6. For a slightly different viewpoint, see McCammon (2003), who argues that tactical innovation arose from the diverse set of organizations within the movement

7. Such studies are also lacking in the literature on later women's movements.

8. Some exceptions that examine religious women's movements or the women's club movements between the first and second wave include Barnett (1995), Cott (1987), Lynn (1992), Mathews-Gardner (2003), and White (1999).

9. See also Harvey 1998. King and colleagues (2005) provide one explanation for these differing assessments. Looking at states' adoption of woman suffrage, they argue women's movements influenced policy largely by introducing legislation, but their effect on policy weakened as bills advanced through the legislative process.

10. Cultural feminism occurred in the late 1970s when many local feminist groups, advocating radical change in society and politics, focused on creating autonomous communities that would allow radical individual transformation.

11. For empirical studies of movement policy changes, see Costain (1992) and L. Young (2000); for discussions of the failure of the Equal Rights Amendment, see Berry (1988), Boles (1979), and Mansbridge (1986).

12. Working for incremental change is often seen as synonymous with inside strategies, but these elements must be separated because some activists using insider tactics have more radical views (Banaszak 2004).

7

Representation by Gender and Parties

Kira Sanbonmatsu

Modern democracy is arguably unthinkable save political parties (Schatt-schneider 1942). What about democracy for women? Does democracy for women depend on political parties? At first glance, the answer might appear to be no. Women's representation is potentially at odds with representation by parties. The U.S. party system has often been unwelcoming and unrespon-sive to women. The two major parties were a barrier to women's suffrage. Indeed, after suffrage was won, the leading women's suffrage organization chose to become a nonpartisan organization. The modern women's move-ment, which emerged decades later, initially eschewed the political parties. Yet because parties organize government and field candidates for office, the political representation of women in American politics is likely to necessitate representation by parties.

One form of women's political representation is descriptive representa-tion, or the presence of women in political office. Descriptive representation poses a fundamental challenge to liberal theories of representation. Whereas district-based representation assumes that political interests are geographi-cally based, descriptive representation posits that interests arise from group identities that transcend geographic boundaries (e.g., Guinier 1994; Williams 1998). Indeed, a descriptive representative may act as a surrogate for group members beyond the district (Mansbridge 2003). Scholars have given more consideration to the relationship between descriptive and geographic rep-resentation than to that between descriptive and party representation, and many theories about descriptive representation barely mention parties (e.g., Mansbridge 1999, 2003; Williams 1998).

I am grateful for the important comments of Christina Wolbrecht, Karen Beckwith, Lisa Baldez, Suzanne Dovi, Eileen McDonagh, Denise Baer, Timothy Frye, and participants of the 2006 "Political Women and American Democracy" conference at the University of Notre Dame. I thank Amanda King for research assistance.

Representation by parties also can transcend district boundaries and the traditional dyadic notion of representation. For example, Democratic voters may not feel represented if their representative is a Republican, but the presence of Democratic legislators in the chamber can provide adequate representation. Thus partisan representation can produce collective representation (Hurley 1989). Yet attention to the numerical presence of under-represented groups reflects dissatisfaction with prevailing forms of representation – including party representation.

This chapter focuses on how women's political representation – both descriptive and substantive – is related to the role of parties as representative institutions. Does the political representation of women inherently conflict with party representation? When does women's representation coincide with representation by party? What are the implications of theories about women's descriptive representation for theories of parties?

Most scholarship concerning gender and parties can be divided into two types of works depending on how the relationship between gender and party representation is conceptualized.[1] In the first, gender and party are believed to be in competition and women's representation achieved at the expense of party. For example, many scholars regard party as an institutional constraint on the ability of women legislators to substantively represent women. Meanwhile, mass-behavior scholars ask whether voters defect from their party in order to support (or oppose) a woman candidate. Thus scholars frequently pit gender against party.[2]

In the second approach, scholars investigate women's influence within the party and the presence of women's interests on the party agenda. Here, representation is believed to occur by gender *and* party. Women's descriptive representation depends on parties because most candidates run on a party label. In addition, because women within the party are more likely than men to press women's interests, party representation of women's issues depends on the efforts of women within the party. Thus gender and party are not necessarily in conflict and women can achieve representation by working through the party. Meanwhile, the party stands to benefit by representing women.

In the following sections, I review scholarship in these two areas in more detail. I then discuss ways to integrate these two strands of research. I argue that scholars should seek to unite party theory with theories about descriptive representation and focus on the conditions under which women's representation coincides with party goals.

REPRESENTATION BY GENDER OR PARTY

Although the U.S. Constitution does not mention parties and the nation's founders opposed parties, most party scholars view strong parties as central to American democracy.[3] Theoretically, responsible parties in a two-party system enhance democracy by providing voters with a clear choice; such parties have strong organizations, pursue a coherent agenda within government, and are accountable to the public (Committee on Political Parties 1950). Nearly two decades ago, Anne N. Costain and W. Douglas Costain (1987) observed that women were gaining influence within the parties at a time when parties were declining in importance. Evidence of the renewed health of political parties abounds, however, including increased party unity in government and greater organizational strength of the state and national parties (e.g., Gibson et al. 1983; Herrnson 1988; Rohde 1991).

Despite the contention that strong parties are fundamental to U.S. democracy, most party scholarship is silent on the consequences of strong parties for women. Yet strong parties may be at odds with women's representation. Research related to gender and U.S. parties has typically examined either women's descriptive or substantive representation, but both forms of women's representation pose similar dilemmas for parties.[4] Both forms of women's representation threaten to undermine the role of parties in organizing American politics. And both have the potential to be electorally costly.

Party theorists such as E. E. Schattschneider (1942) posit a zero-sum game between interest groups and parties: where parties are weaker, interest groups are expected to play a greater role. Indeed, because of their exclusion from partisan politics before suffrage, women turned to nonpartisan activities and interest group politics (Clemens 1997; Cott 1987; Skocpol 1992). The utility of partisanship and the relative merits of working through the major parties – compared with adopting an independent or nonpartisan stance – generated much debate among suffragists (Andersen 1996; Edwards 1997). After suffrage was won, party women faced many obstacles in their recruitment efforts, including the reluctance of many women to participate in partisan politics (Andersen 1990; Rymph 2006). As Kristi Andersen (1990, 187) explains: "The problem, from the point of view of women who wanted to have an impact on the political system, was that parties, by their nature, served the selfish interests of those who supported them; they were not serving the *public* interest." Meanwhile, male party leaders feared that newly enfranchised women would align with independent women's groups rather than the parties and resisted their presence in leadership roles (Harvey 1998).

Many scholars have described a zero-sum dynamic between women's political influence and the strength of parties over time. The development of interest group politics in the late nineteenth and early twentieth century – which women helped to pioneer – arguably led to the decline of parties (Andersen 1996; Clemens 1997). Anna L. Harvey (1998) sees 1960s party decline as leading to an opening for women's interest groups. Similarly, Lisa Young (2000) argues that a decrease in the role of parties in candidate selection in the 1980s led to an increase in opportunities for women's organizations and political action committees (PACs) and the pursuit of women's descriptive representation.

Women have long weighed the costs and benefits of organizing as women within the party (Freeman 2000). Many women value their independence from party (Rymph 2006). Yet women also have sought equal representation within the party on a gender basis, including equal representation on party committees. Historically, women who achieved leadership posts within the party organization were not necessarily sympathetic to the collective interests of women – especially if their lack of loyalty to women as a group was the very reason for their advancement (Freeman 2000). Male party leaders belittled the notion of women's common interests. Parties may be ill-equipped, and even unwilling, to address women's concerns.[5] Third parties were the key supporters of women's suffrage, suggesting the inherent limitations of working with the two major parties. Yet forming a third party – which the National Organization for Women (NOW) contemplated in the early 1990s – seems impractical (Barakso 2004, 106–7).

The Democratic Party adopted reforms after the 1968 party conventions to provide greater internal democracy and equal representation for delegates on the basis of gender – reforms that, according to critics, weakened the parties. Women may even seem threatening to the party as individuals: women party activists appear to be more amateur, more ideological, and less party-oriented than men – suggesting a trade-off between women's commitment to feminism and their commitment to the party (e.g., Baer and Bositis 1988; Baer and Jackson 1985; Paddock and Paddock 1997; Shafer 1983). In sum, women's allegiance is often suspect.

Today 157 parties in seventy-three countries have candidate quotas, achieving women's descriptive representation through party representation (see Baldez, this volume, for a discussion of comparative research on quotas).[6] In the United States, however, gender quotas for candidates are not on the agendas of the major parties – in part because of the prevalence of single-member rather than multiple-member districts and proportional representation. Thus there is no direct correspondence between women's descriptive representation and party representation in the United States.

If women candidates are perceived to be electorally costly, then party representation may conflict with women's descriptive representation (Norris 1993). From a rational choice perspective, the primary goal of the party is to win office (Downs 1957; Schlesinger 1975). Despite much research arguing that women and men fare about the same when they run for office (e.g., Burrell 1994; Darcy, Welch, and Clark 1994; Seltzer, Newman, and Leighton 1997), party leaders are not agreed on women's electability (Sanbonmatsu 2006).[7] Indeed, the parties have arguably failed to recruit and support women (Carroll 1994).

Voters subscribe to both gender and party stereotypes about politicians (Kahn 1996; Rahn 1993). When voters' gender stereotypes about candidate ideology intersect with partisan stereotypes, Republican women appear to be disadvantaged: Republican voters may not regard Republican women candidates as typical Republicans because they perceive women as liberal (King and Matland 2003). If Republican women candidates perform worse than men (Cooperman and Oppenheimer 2001; King and Matland 2003), there is little incentive for the party to recruit them.

The substantive representation of women also may pose an electoral risk. For example, the parties have arguably been relatively unresponsive to most gender equality issues because they are controversial (Sanbonmatsu 2002a). The parties' centrist positions on many gender issues are unsurprising given the tendency of the parties to pursue the median voter (Downs 1957).[8] Because changes in gender roles have been so widespread, gender issues pose considerable uncertainty for strategic politicians looking for winning issues (Sanbonmatsu 2002a).

A growing body of scholarship finds evidence of responsible party government and identifies the mechanisms by which the majority party pursues its goals (e.g., Cox and McCubbins 2005). Meanwhile, gender has the potential to threaten party cohesion (Dodson 2006; Osborn 2003; Swers 2002). For example, women legislators in Colorado decided to form a legislative caucus in the 1980s, having found common cause on some women's policies. But the idea was short-lived: because of the house speaker's vehement opposition, no women's caucus formed; any type of loyalty that might disrupt the speaker's power as party leader was strictly forbidden, and no caucus (save the party caucus) permitted.[9]

Party leaders may fear that women candidates, once elected, will act for women rather than the party. Gender scholars have investigated whether – controlling for party – women are more likely than men to represent women's interests. Thus party is typically regarded as an institutional constraint on women's ability to legislate for women (e.g., Evans 2005; Reingold 2000; see Reingold, this volume).[10]

Within Congress, women's issues are fragmented across committees (Norton 1995). Therefore gender scholars have had to assiduously identify those committees that are more likely to handle women's issue bills (Norton 1995; Swers 2002). Yet scholars have not addressed the larger question of why committees are not organized around women's interests. If committees are organized to benefit the majority party (Cox and McCubbins 1993), then the lack of correspondence between committee organization and women's interests may indicate yet another disjuncture between party and gender.

Voters may defect from their party to pursue descriptive representation by gender instead of party representation (e.g., Brians 2005; Dolan 1998; Plutzer and Zipp 1996). The movement to elect more women to office may take precedence over supporting the party. In general, though, candidate gender is believed to have a greater influence in settings without a party cue: in primaries, nonpartisan elections, or among independent voters (Cook 1994;

Seltzer et al. 1997; Zipp and Plutzer 1985). Absent parties, one would expect a greater role for identity-group politics (Goodin 2005).

If gender and party conflict, women's representation would seemingly be enhanced by weak political parties and women's representation best pursued through interest groups or social movements. However, parties remain central to American politics. Unlike interest groups, parties seek to control government; they are "mobilizers of majorities," whereas interest groups "mobilize minorities" (Schattschneider 1942, 193). Indeed, Leon D. Epstein (1986) characterizes parties as "public utilities" because of their unique role in conducting elections.

REPRESENTATION BY GENDER AND PARTY

Much research regards gender and party to be in competition. But as Denise L. Baer (2006a, 1) notes, "political parties are at once gendered institutions *and* institutions permeable to women's political power and representation." Women may need parties in order to achieve descriptive and substantive representation. Meanwhile, women, women's groups, and women's movements arguably strengthen parties, and attention to gender contributes to party theory itself.

Jo Freeman (2000) argues that "party women" emerged as a distinct set of political activists in the early twentieth century. Male party leaders opposed gender solidarity and insisted on party – rather than gender – loyalty in the first half of the twentieth century (Freeman 2000). Women infiltrated the party organization although they wielded little influence. Yet their party loyalty led to success in garnering women's appointments to the bureaucracy; in turn, these women were positioned to play a critical role in policy making during the modern women's movement (Freeman 1975).

Thus rather than seeing an inherent conflict between gender and party, scholars have studied women's activities within the party – an important site of political participation (e.g., Clark, Hadley, and Darcy 1989; Fowlkes 1984; Freeman 2000; Gustafson 2001; Gustafson, Miller, and Perry 1999; Jennings and Farah 1981). In recent years, women have achieved leadership posts within the legislative party, such as Nancy Pelosi's election to be speaker of the U.S. House of Representatives.[11] Women and men may participate in the party for different reasons (Fowlkes, Perkins, and Tolleson-Rinehart 1979) and often have different issue positions and ties to different types of organizations (Clawson and Clark 2003; Day and Hadley 1997; Jennings 1990; van Assendelft and O'Connor 1994). Therefore the presence of women's issues on the party agenda is likely to depend on women's influence within the party. This is particularly true of gender equality issues, which are relatively new issues and have the potential to crosscut the existing line of cleavage between the two parties concerning the role of government (Sanbonmatsu 2002a).

For the Democratic Party, representing women's policy preferences may not conflict with the pursuit of the party's policy goals. The primary issue divide between the two parties on the role of government is a gendered cleavage, and gender itself is becoming a more defining feature of the party system (Box-Steffensmeier, De Boef, and Lin 2004; Carroll 1988; Kaufmann and Petrocik 1999; Kenski 1988). Indeed, women voters are less likely to identify as independents and more likely to identify with the parties than men (Norrander 1997). Thus women's substantive representation coincides with party representation automatically because women's support for a larger role for government makes them a natural ally of the Democratic Party. Not only do women today have a stronger preference for a more activist government than men, but women helped to create U.S. social policies in the first place (Baker 1984; Skocpol 1992; Ware 1981).

The parties have arguably absorbed women's rights issues (Adams 1997; Wolbrecht 2000, 2002a). Freeman argues that differences in the political cultures of the parties made the Democratic Party more receptive to feminist claims because influence is established by group clout, whereas influence within the Republican Party emerges from networks and "whom you know" (1986, 333). Although the parties took similar positions in response to the modern women's movement initially, they are now responding differently – and to different groups of women (Freeman 1987, 1989, 1993, 1999, 2000). Feminist activists wield influence within the Democratic Party and antifeminists within the Republican Party. Women's movements throughout the world have tended to ally with leftist parties (Katzenstein 1987). Thus the greater responsiveness of the Democratic Party to women's interests may not be surprising (Freeman 2000; Wolbrecht 2000).

The women's movement has arguably strengthened the parties as representative institutions. Denise L. Baer and David A. Bositis (1988) argue that because parties tend toward oligarchy, social movements are needed to ensure that party elites are more inclusive and representative of the mass base. They help to unite the three aspects of party – electorate, organization, and government – within one model. Moreover, women, as descriptive representatives, can strengthen the parties. In this view, reform critics are mistaken to believe that the inclusion of women as party elites weakens the party. Baer and Bositis focus on convention delegates rather than elected officials, but their theory has implications for women's descriptive representation more broadly. Because descriptive officeholders can enhance communication between representatives and constituents (Mansbridge 1999; but see Lawless 2004), women's descriptive representation has the potential to strengthen parties.

Women's descriptive representation may not be at odds with party success – especially if women are more competitive candidates than men. Because women run on the party label, it may be necessary to disaggregate women by party to analyze women's descriptive representation

(Sanbonmatsu 2002b). Women are often tapped to speak for the party and help close the gender gap because they are viewed as particularly credible and expert on women's issues (Dodson 2006; Swers 2002). They are also perceived by voters as more trustworthy and honest than men (Kahn 1994b). Furthermore, strong party organizations, which provide needed resources and networks, may facilitate women's election (Burrell 1993, 1994; Caul and Tate 2002; Darcy et al. 1994). The parties appear to recruit women and fund men and women equally (Burrell 1994).

FUTURE DIRECTIONS FOR RESEARCH

Men and women can be found in both parties, suggesting an uneasy fit between gender and party. Yet the lack of alignment between gender and party and the status of women as a majority group grant American women opportunities for leverage. Better integration of studies that regard gender and party in conflict with studies that link party and women's representation can enrich our understanding of both gender and political parties. Indeed, party theories that fail to take into account the interaction of parties with interest groups and social movements are likely to misunderstand the dynamics of party politics. In this section, I propose that future research focus on the conditions under which (1) women achieve substantive representation in the party, (2) women's descriptive representation coincides with the party's electoral goals, and (3) women's descriptive representation coincides with the party's electoral goals *and* furthers women's substantive representation.

Substantive Representation

The modern women's movement initially opted to exploit its contacts and work directly with members of Congress, the president, and agencies rather than working through the parties (Costain and Costain 1987; Freeman 1987). Scholars have pointed to a range of important factors to account for the parties' receptivity to women's interests. Party representation of women's interests also may emerge inadvertently: party polarization on women's rights issues may be driven by the parties' positions on race or general ideological divergence rather than by women's rights issues per se (Wolbrecht 2000).

Party competition is one way to achieve responsiveness. Women's commitment to social reform and threat posed to party machines in the late 1800s and early 1900s helps explain Democratic and Republican opposition to women's suffrage. However, the electoral threat of third parties induced greater support for suffrage among the major parties (Banaszak 1996b; McConnaughy 2004). Corrine M. McConnaughy (2004) argues that "programmatic enfranchisement" better explains the success of suffrage than does "strategic enfranchisement." Working within partisan politics to build coalitions and pressure the major parties was more effective, she argues, than the elusive promise of a women's vote. Thus strategic enfranchisement, whereby parties would support suffrage to expand the electorate for strategic purposes, finds less support than an account that emphasizes coalitions and third-party support.

Interest in women's votes can be a driving force in securing women's substantive representation (Costain 1992). However, such a focus can also lead to a narrow issue agenda (Carroll 1999). In addition, Sanbonmatsu (2002a) observes that party interest in representing women may not lead to responsiveness across gender equality issues. The existence of a gender gap can also create more concern about men's votes than women's votes, reducing the party's interest in representing gender equality issues. Moreover, if the decline of the Democratic Party was caused by its success among women and a female-dominated party is viewed as a liability (Stark 1996), then it is unclear whether women's interests are well served by a gender gap in party identification. In general, the gender gap has not been large enough to give women significant leverage within the parties (L. Young 2000, 205).

Harvey (1998) sees the threat by independent women's groups to organize women's votes as the key to increasing party responsiveness to women's issues. However, the mechanism may not be threat so much as promise. Perhaps women's groups win representation from the party by promising to deliver women voters to the party rather than by threatening to lead women away. Lisa Young (2000, 204–5) observes: "When women's movement organizations have appeared to be able to offer political parties what they most desire – electoral success – parties have welcomed these organizations into the partisan fold and have adopted the movement's issues as their own."

Thus pursuing representation via the avenues of parties, interest groups, or social movements are not necessarily mutually exclusive choices. Parties and interest groups are arguably complementary institutions; party activists are tied to interest groups, without weakening the party (Baer and Dolan 1994). Indeed, the interaction of interest groups and social movements with parties may give women the most leverage. The women's movement increased the influence of women within the parties because of party concern about possible shifts in women's voting behavior (L. Young 2000, 89–90). Women's organizations also provided an interpretation of the gender gap, using the gap to enhance women's substantive representation (Mueller 1988a). Thus the influence of women's organizations in the party system seems to depend on the status of women voters and the extent of cohesion among women voters as a group – cohesion that may be induced by the women's movement itself. Yet women's organizations risk co-optation by being associated too closely with the parties (Freeman 1987). An electoral politics strategy and party alliance can be controversial within women's organizations (Barakso 2004) and may come with costs to the movement, as well as the party

(L. Young 2000). For example, gay and lesbian groups could be considered a captured electoral group of the Democratic Party, leaving them marginalized and without leverage (Frymer 1999).

Freeman (1999) links social movements and parties explicitly, identifying social movements as a cause of elite party realignment. She explains that since 1980, "the parties have polarized sharply on all issues touching on women, sex, and the family. Instead of seeking the center, the national parties are staking out distinct ideological territories" (Freeman 1999, 180). Thus feminist and antifeminist party activists have transformed the parties (Freeman 1999). Ideological groups and activists in general have pulled the parties apart since the 1960s (Aldrich 1995).

As the parties have become more responsive to activists and absorbed divisive social issues such as abortion, politics has arguably become less relevant to average citizens, dampening mass participation (Fiorina 2002, 2005).[12] Morris P. Fiorina (2005) observes that responsible party theorists of the 1950s assumed that the dominant issues would continue to be foreign policy, the economy, and the welfare state – issues on which there was a general level of consensus. However, today's politics are dominated by social issues and identity politics, with gender equality issues playing a central role. Ironically, abortion is arguably one of the only gender issues on which the parties have been responsive – precisely because of the campaign contributions and votes that abortion groups bring to the parties (Sanbonmatsu 2002a). It is unclear how women's group interests would fare were parties more moderate and less responsive to their allied interest groups – including women's groups.

Perhaps women's group interests would be better represented in a less polarized party system. The single most successful period of congressional enactment of women's rights legislation occurred in the early 1970s with bipartisan support and less cohesive legislative parties (Costain 1992; Freeman 1975). Partisan polarization has made the bipartisan efforts of congresswomen much more difficult (Gertzog 2004). Indeed, Costain and Costain (1987, 210) questioned the wisdom of a close alliance of feminist groups with the Democratic Party as opposed to a bipartisan interest group strategy. In a very polarized setting, the threat of exit by feminist (or antifeminist) groups may not be credible. Yet the early 1970s was characterized by the absence of an organized opposition to the women's movement, which is not the case today. The parties' responsiveness to women's groups is also likely to depend on whether the parties view those groups as an electoral liability (Freeman 1987).

Meanwhile, incorporation into the parties' agendas does not necessarily mean policy enactment: it may be precisely because the parties have incorporated women's rights issues, and polarized on them, that those issues are stalled in Congress today (Wolbrecht 2000). Thus many questions remain about the comparative wisdom of achieving women's substantive

representation through bipartisan versus partisan approaches, the consequences of the parties' alliances with feminist and antifeminist organizations,
and whether women should work with parties or interest groups allied with
the parties to achieve influence.

Descriptive Representation

A second area for additional research is to specify the conditions under which
women's descriptive representation is believed to further the party's electoral
goals. A number of scholars argue that party strength is positively related
to women's descriptive representation (Burrell 1994; Caul and Tate 2002;
Darcy et al. 1994;). Yet party organizational strength is negatively related to
the presence of women state legislators (Sanbonmatsu 2006). Thus the trend
of stronger party organizations may not bode well for enhancing democracy
for women. And parties are not the only institutions that can recruit women
candidates: because women's interest groups and PACs can recruit and help
elect women candidates, it is not self-evident that strong parties are necessary
to improve women's representation (Sanbonmatsu 2006). For example, the
pro-choice Democratic PAC EMILY's List (EMILY is an acronym for "early
money is like yeast," i.e., it helps the dough rise) has been criticized for
taking sides in primaries when the party might be better served by consensus
on the party nominee. More research is needed on how primary elections
and party endorsements affect women's representation (Caul and Tate 2002;
Welch 1989).

Concern about the gender gap can spur party interest in women candidates (Andersen 1996; Burrell 1994) – particularly if party leaders believe
that women candidates will attract women's votes (Kittilson 2006) or if the
other party is fielding women (Caul 2001; Matland and Studlar 1996). Yet
recruiting women candidates may be a costly electoral strategy if the party
is looking to attract older, less educated, or conservative voters, who are
less likely to support women candidates (Dolan 2004). Skepticism about
women's chances is likely to reduce party recruitment of women (Sanbonmatsu 2006). In general, more research on internal party politics can shed
light on women's underrepresentation (Baer 1993) – particularly because the
representation of women is likely to depend on beliefs about women candidates and the gender of party leaders (Niven 1998a; Sanbonmatsu 2006).

Descriptive, Substantive, and Party Representation

A third area for research is investigation of the conditions under which
women's candidacies and office holding can further both party goals and
women's substantive representation. The next generation of gender and party
scholarship will need to unify work on parties with work on the ability of
women legislators to act for women.

Lisa Young (2000, 203) observes an inverse relationship between representational responsiveness and policy responsiveness – or women's descriptive and substantive representation. When the women's movement failed to help elect the Democratic presidential nominee in 1972 and 1984, the party became less responsive to its policy demands (L. Young 2000, 192). Feminist activists have subsequently focused on descriptive instead of substantive representation.

Meanwhile, women's organizations and PACs face strategic dilemmas about whether to support women candidates – making women's descriptive representation the priority – or friendly Democratic candidates – men or women – in order to pursue women's substantive representation (e.g., Barakso 2004; L. Young 2000). Yet EMILY's List demonstrates the possibility of simultaneous pursuit of party goals (e.g., election of a Democratic candidate), women's descriptive representation, and the advancement of women's interests (e.g., EMILY's List pro-choice issue criteria). Indeed, most EMILY's List contributors consider themselves to be strong Democrats (Day and Hadley 2005, 51).

Electing more women to office in order to increase women's substantive representation is attractive because legislators can pursue their own initiatives outside the confines of party discipline (L. Young 2000, 185). Swers (2002) found the greatest gender differences in congressional behavior on bill sponsorship – the stage of the policy process where members are least constrained by party loyalty. Meanwhile, fewer gender differences in legislative behavior were expected on social welfare issues than feminist issues because social welfare issues are the primary line of cleavage between the parties and are well integrated into congressional organization (Swers 2002, 14–15). Thus whether gender and party representation conflict depends on which of women's interests are under consideration.

Factors such as majority party status and electoral vulnerability also have implications for the ability of women to act for women. For example, Jocelyn Evans (2005) finds that whereas Democratic women tend to represent safe Democratic congressional districts, Republican women tend to be elected from more marginal districts. The greater electoral vulnerability of Republican women, and differences between the two parties' cultures, constrains Republican women's participation within the legislature to a greater extent than Democratic women's participation. Democratic women have played a unique role in Congress in promoting women's interests (Wolbrecht 2002b). The Democrats' minority status in the 104th Congress meant that Republican women had more institutional power to advocate for women, but gender cohesion seemed more difficult to achieve when Republicans were in the majority (Swers 2002).

Party leader perceptions about women's ideology may reduce women's descriptive representation (Young 2006). Potential women candidates may be perceived to be (and may in fact be) more liberal than the party median.

If parties only recruit candidates who are close to the party median, then women – who may be expected to defect from the party once in the legislature – may not reach the legislature in the first place (Young 2006).

As Baer (2003) argues, more research is needed on women's access to party leadership. The dearth of women in leadership has implications for the presence of women's interests on the party's agenda. Yet advancing within the legislative party may mean forgoing women's interests. At the same time, the strength of the women's movement and the status of women's groups within the parties have implications for women's descriptive representation because party leaders may be recruited from those venues (Baer 2006b).

Our theories about parties in the legislature would be strengthened were more party scholars to grapple with the challenges raised by thinking about gender. Differences in methodological approach may partially account for the seeming disconnect between the literatures on women's representation and legislative parties. For example, formal theory is rarely used to study gender politics. Yet past work suggests the fruitful ways that rational choice can be used to study gender (e.g., Frechette, Maniquet, and Morelli 2006; Harvey 1998).

Additional research should also be conducted to compare gender and party to race and party (e.g., Htun 2004) and to integrate the study of race, gender, and parties. The parties' conflict on race has shaped the parties' response to gender (Freeman 2000; Wolbrecht 2000), and race and gender intersect within the parties (e.g., Crawford 2001; Rymph 2006). Although women are an underrepresented and historically disadvantaged group, women's majority status provides them greater opportunities for leverage than are available to racial and ethnic minorities.

CONCLUSION

Representing women – acting on behalf of women's interests and incorporating women descriptively – poses a series of challenges to political parties that are primarily interested in winning office. Pitting gender against party appears to capture the relationship between the two. At the same time, however, working within the parties is an inevitable part of furthering democracy for women.

As scholars continue to investigate the complex ways in which gender intersects with party, opportunities abound to more closely link scholarship on parties to debates about descriptive representation. Political parties may be critical to understanding when women legislators can act as the substantive representatives of women. Because women are relative newcomers to electoral politics and remain underrepresented in party leadership, the extent to which they are incorporated into parties is likely to depend on the status of the women's movement. And if parties are central to American democracy, then American democracy itself depends on women's representation in political parties.

Notes

1. By gender, I mean the social categories of "men" and "women." "Gender" is a contested term and has been used by scholars in a wide variety of ways (see Beckwith 2005; Hawkesworth 1997; Nicholson 1994). I use "gender" to signal my interest in men and women as social groups rather than biological groups. As Roberta S. Sigel (1996, 14) explains, "By referring to gender rather than sex, scholars aim to signify that the alleged or observed differences between men and women are not ordained by nature"; rather, gender is a social construction. "The gender perspective holds that, with the exception of physiological and reproductive differences, sex-based behavioral differences observable in men and women, especially in their overt public behaviors, are not biologically ordained but are the results of long-standing and complex socially ordained arrangements which, through a division of labor, assign different roles and different spheres of activities to men and women" (Sigel 1996, 14).

2. Racial representation and party representation may also conflict. Race-conscious districting, which increases minority descriptive representation, may yield a cost in terms of the substantive representation of black interests in Congress if fewer Democrats are elected (Lublin 1997; Swain 1995).

3. Coleman (1996, 373) observes: "When party organization students contend that 'parties matter,' they are making both an empirical and normative statement."

4. I recognize that descriptive representation is arguably substantive representation. I distinguish between the two types of representation for presentation purposes.

5. On the question of women's interests, see the debate between Sapiro (1981) and Diamond and Hartsock (1981). Women's concerns may necessitate a reconsideration of what constitutes politics and may not be easily absorbed in an interest framework. See Dovi, this volume, for further discussion of the meaning of women's political representation.

6. Statistics are from the IDEA (International Institute for Democracy and Electoral Assistance) quota database (http://www.quotaproject.org/system.cfm#political).

7. Frechette and colleagues (2006) posit that gender quotas in France can be explained by the belief that women are more likely to lose their races: male incumbent politicians may support equal gender representation on party lists because it will increase their chances of being reelected.

8. The two-party system poses a structural barrier to representing African American interests: strategic elites are likely to push racial issues outside of party competition in their attempts to attract the median voter (Frymer 1999, 2005).

9. Personal interviews with former women state legislators conducted in Denver and Boulder, Colorado, 2001.

10. For further discussion on gender within legislatures, see Reingold, this volume.

11. See Center for American Women and Politics (2005) for data on women's leadership roles in Congress.

12. However, women's groups have created new opportunities for political participation (Barakso 2005), which suggests that the interest group explosion of the 1970s and 1980s may not have harmed participation.

8

Women as Candidates in American Politics

The Continuing Impact of Sex and Gender

Kathleen Dolan

Taking the long view of women candidates in the United States, the contemporary time is one of unbelievable success and promise. Gone are the days of public rejection of the idea of a political life for women, of political parties only supporting women in hopeless situations, when campaign money was reserved for serious candidates (read: men) with a chance of winning. Instead we routinely see thousands of women running for, and winning, office at every level all over the country. Each election year brings more women candidates than the year before. In 2007, 86 women serve in Congress, 1,734 women hold seats in state legislatures, 77 women are statewide elected officials, and hundreds, if not thousands, of women serve in local elected office (Center for American Women and Politics [CAWP] 2007a). However, at the same time, we know that the people we still refer to as "women candidates" make up a much smaller percentage of the candidate population than they do of the general population, that these women are viewed by the public through the lens of stereotypes, and that sex and gender considerations, although not necessarily disabling, are ever-present on the campaign trail. For all of the success of women candidates, women in office only represent between 15 and 25 percent of the offices at any level of government. So today we are presented with the classic "half empty–half full" scenario. Women candidates have made enormous strides but still have a long way to go on the road to parity.

Taking the long view of scholarship on women candidates in the United States, the contemporary time is also one of significant achievement and promise. Over the past thirty years or so, political science has produced a voluminous literature on all aspects of the situations facing women candidates. We know more today about the challenges and opportunities facing women candidates than ever before. Nonetheless, many unanswered questions about the role that sex and gender considerations play in shaping these challenges and opportunities still remain.

The fundamental issue in understanding the present state of women's candidacies is this: a significant body of work demonstrates that women candidates are just as successful as similarly situated men – they raise the same amounts of money (Burrell 2005; Fox 2006), get the same share of the vote (Seltzer, Newman, and Leighton 1997), and face a public largely free of bias toward them on account of their sex (Dolan 2004). This work, summarized best by the phrase "when women run, women win," led many scholars to conclude that sex and gender are much less a factor in contemporary elections than in the past (Newman 1994). Yet, at the same time, the marginal rate of growth in the number of women in office, the slow growth in the number of women candidates, and the uneven geographic pattern of women's success all signal that sex and gender still matter in very real ways. So the question for scholars today is not whether sex and gender still matter but instead when and how they matter. How do sex and gender considerations continue to shape the opportunities for women candidates?

The goal of this chapter is to take stock of what we know about women candidates and think about directions for future research. In doing so, I identify some broad theme questions motivated by the current literature. These questions do not propose explicit research directions (that will come later) but instead seek to provide a framework in which to consider the specific inquiries we still need to make.

- Are sex and gender considerations "universal," a permanent part of all women's candidacies in the United States? Are women candidates seen through the lens of sex and gender from the moment they emerge as candidates or is there a point in a campaign when these issues come into play? Is it even possible for a woman to contest for office in a campaign that is not significantly shaped by sex and gender?
- What is the impact of the context of an individual election on sex and gender considerations? Any of the elements of an election – the unique mix of candidates, resources, issues, local and national political influences at play in that specific race – can contribute to whether sex and gender considerations assume a major or more minor role in the election. For example, in the political world since September 11, are women's candidacies shaped by stereotypes about their abilities to handle the war on terror? Do sex and gender considerations play a different role depending on the party of the woman candidate? Does the amount of media attention given to the woman candidate shape whether sex and gender concerns are "activated" in the minds of voters? Is sex and gender important the first time a woman candidate seeks a particular office or runs in a particular district or state? How do gendered concerns take shape in a race with two women candidates? All of these questions serve to remind us that sex and

gender are not necessarily constant forces that influence all elections in the same way.

- How much of what we know about women candidates is a function of the data we have, which tends to focus on congressional elections and state legislatures? To some (unknown) degree, what we know about the situations facing women candidates is shaped by the offices we examine. So we should take care in assuming that our understanding of how sex and gender shape elections involving women candidates for Congress or statewide office translates to those seeking office of other types and at other levels.

- How much of what we know is a function of the current party imbalance among women candidates? If more than two-thirds of women candidates run as Democrats, what we know about sex/gender considerations in elections has been accumulated in a particular framework. Because recent works find evidence that party matters to women candidates, we need to recognize that our understanding of how sex and gender shape elections may change if the party imbalance among women candidates changes.

- What are the experiences of minority women? The small number of women candidates of color has limited our ability to understand whether race and sex interact to shape the reality of these women candidates. This is exacerbated by the fact that our data on women who run for local offices, where there may be more women candidates of color, is the most limited. As we examine the present situations of women candidates, we have to consider whether what we have learned from studying mostly white women candidates can be applied to the situations of women of color.

- How do we account for the interconnectedness of sex and gender effects? We need to consider several elements in determining whether and when women candidates are successful – women's presence in the eligibility pool, the uneven burden of family responsibilities, party recruitment patterns, public evaluations. Each can contribute to the context in which women candidates exist. Yet each is itself gendered. This leads to situations in which gendered institutions and processes combine or overlap to shape the situations of women candidates. For example, structural elements of elections such as incumbency or the types of offices women candidates are most likely to seek, both of which are gendered processes, can shape the (gendered) media frames employed to report on women and men candidates. This can, in turn, influence the responses of a public that is more likely than not to evaluate women candidates through a gendered lens. Disentangling all of the gendered elements of an electoral situation is a complex exercise that we have not yet perfected.

Although the literature on women candidates in the United States deals with a wide range of topics, this chapter focuses on reviewing the state of our knowledge in seven specific areas: (1) ambition and candidate emergence, (2) public stereotypes, (3) campaigning, (4) media coverage, (5) structural aspects of the electoral system, (6) vote choice, and (7) the impact of women candidates on the public. In each area, I review our current knowledge and identify some paths for future researchers to consider.

AMBITION AND CANDIDATE EMERGENCE

After the National Women's Political Caucus' groundbreaking report on patterns of success among women candidates demonstrated that women do as well as similarly situated men (Newman 1994), the phrase "when women run, women win" came into popular usage. The evidence accumulated since has borne this out. Yet "when women run" implicitly points us to another part of the process that, until recently, had not received adequate attention from scholars of women candidates – the process of candidate emergence. Once it was clear that women candidates suffer few party, financial, or vote share disadvantages, it became obvious that candidate pool issues helped explain the relatively small number of women in elected office.

Whether sex is related to ambition is a question that has motivated research for quite a while, although the findings of this work are somewhat ambiguous. Early work indicated that women tended to be less ambitious than men, particularly among those active in the parties (Constantini 1990; Fowlkes, Perkins, and Tolleson-Rinehart 1979; Kirkpatrick 1974; Sapiro 1982). However, other research that focused on women officeholders found no real differences in political ambition among women and men (Carroll 1985; Diamond 1977). Barbara Palmer and Dennis Simon (2003) suggest that the inconsistent findings of past work are explained in part by the lack of a common concept of political ambition among gender scholars.

In more recent years, the focus of research has shifted to candidate emergence – the conditions under which candidates for elected office come forward. Here, the evidence suggests that highly gendered patterns in American cultural and political life shape the political opportunities for women. In recent work, Jennifer Lawless and Richard Fox (2005) conceive of candidate emergence as a two-stage process: first, people must consider a candidacy, and second, they must make a decision to enter a specific race. Their work focuses on the first stage, on how and whether the consideration of political candidacy is shaped by sex and gender. Drawing on data from more than 3,500 men and women in education, business, political activism, and law, they describe the realities of the "eligibility pool" for women: women are less likely than men to (1) consider running for office, (2) run for elective office, and (3) be interested in running for office in the future. The explanations for this reality are varied and help us identify gendered elements of political socialization, individual psychology, and institutional settings that can inhibit women's ability to run for office. Women are less likely than men to be socialized to think about politics as a vocation, women bear greater responsibility for family and children, and women are less likely to be encouraged to think about running for office by those in their immediate personal and professional lives. However, this work also identifies other individual and institutional roadblocks: both women and men perceive electoral bias against women, women are less likely to be recruited to run by parties and interest groups, and women in this sample were less likely than equally credentialed men to believe they were qualified to run for office, more likely to doubt their qualifications, and less likely to think they would win if they ran. Lawless and Fox conclude that increasing the number of women candidates will require significant social and systemic changes.

In a different approach to emergence, Barbara Burrell and Brian Frederick (2006) focus on the "recruitment pool" – the intermediate stage between the eligibility stage and actual candidacy. By examining whether equally viable women are more or less likely than men to be mentioned as potential candidates and whether, once mentioned, they are more likely or less likely than men to actually run, they account for reputational evaluations, actions of party and group leaders, and individual attributes that can shape the recruitment process. The authors find that women are no less likely than men to be mentioned as potential candidates for open House seats in 2004 and no less likely to become candidates than men, supporting the notion that there is relatively little bias against those women who have entered the political process.

Related to candidate emergence is the role of political parties in recruiting candidates to office. Some work suggests that party organizations are less supportive of women candidates (Lawless and Fox 2005; Niven 1998b), whether through sins of omission or commission, such as some party organizations being significantly less likely to encourage women or, as David Niven (1998b) suggests, sometimes actively discouraging women from running for office. Kira Sanbonmatsu (2005) has also found evidence that party leaders may misperceive women's electability, which could serve to limit their activities to recruit women candidates.

On the other hand, research on the national parties suggests that parties may act to bring more women into the process by recruiting and funding women candidates for Congress (Burrell 2006). These findings are supported by other research that demonstrates that parties, at the least, do not disadvantage women in the candidate recruitment process (Maestas, Maisel, and Stone 2005), and, at best, actively seek them out (Biersack and Herrnson 1994; Burrell 1994).

This work on party activities is important on its own, but is particularly important in light of findings about women's psychological attitudes about running. If women are less likely to see themselves as qualified to run for office and are less likely to receive encouragement to run from personal and professional networks, external recognition of their credentials by parties may be worth more to women. Further examination of the benefits of active recruitment and encouragement to run as a way of mediating women's gendered psyche could prove valuable.

The body of work on ambition and candidate emergence does a fine job of demonstrating why women in the pool of potential candidates are less likely to emerge as candidates than are men. But what would also be valuable is a greater understanding of what moves those women who do seek office forward. If family, cultural, and professional forces still make running for office more challenging for women, what provides the motivation for those women who do overcome the barriers and run? Are there characteristics, experiences, or attitudes that set these women apart from the women who do not become candidates?

The evidence of the persistence of gendered family and political socialization patterns points us to another underdeveloped research area. The study of political socialization still has much to contribute to our understanding of differences in the political lives of women and men. Work by Kim Fridkin and Patrick Kenney (2004) traces the roots of the partisan gender gap back to a gender gap in political positions among eighth-grade boys and girls. This suggests that, despite the advancement of women in society, patterns of political socialization may still conform to traditional mores with regard to the roles of the sexes. More work on the experiences and influences that shape how boys and girls think and feel about the world of government and politics would be important.

Finally, we need to examine more closely how family responsibilities shape women's and men's decisions about entering political life. Many of the women in Lawless and Fox's (2005) sample mentioned having children and taking care of them as one of the major barriers to women's running for office, an assumption the conventional wisdom makes about the factors that hold women back. More work on how family issues shape the political decisions of women and men, particularly at the local and state levels, would help identify whether and how traditional family patterns continue to influence politics.

STEREOTYPES

The extensive literature on women candidates for elective office has demonstrated that the public looks at women and men in politics in predictably stereotypic ways. These stereotyped assessments of political leaders and candidates focus on three major areas: ideology, personality characteristics, and issue specialization.

One of the more enduring stereotypes of women politicians and candidates is that they are more liberal than men, a finding repeatedly confirmed among various populations (Alexander and Anderson 1993; Huddy and Terkildsen 1993a; King and Matland 2003; McDermott 1998). The impact of these stereotypes is complicated by the fact that sex stereotypes can interact with, and perhaps moderate, partisan stereotypes and that women candidates *are* in fact often more liberal than men (Dodson 2001; Frankovic 1977; Welch 1985), yet recent research (Koch 2002) demonstrates that not only are women candidates of both parties seen as more liberal than their male counterparts but also they are perceived as more liberal than they actually are. Because most voters consider themselves to be moderates, the perceived liberalism of Democratic women candidates moves them farther away from the average voter, while the exaggerated liberalism of Republican women candidates actually moves them closer to the average voter.

Voters also see women candidates as having certain character traits: women candidates are warm, compassionate, kind, and passive; men are perceived as strong, knowledgeable, tough, direct, and assertive (Huddy and Terkildsen 1993a; Kahn 1996; Leeper 1991). The importance of stereotypes is demonstrated by research that indicates people often value masculine traits more highly when considering what the "good politician" should be like. They also consider these masculine qualities to be more important as the level of office they are considering rises from local to national (Huddy and Terkildsen 1993b).

The final major stereotype that voters connect with women candidates is a set of beliefs about their policy interest and expertise. Voters most commonly associate women candidates with the "compassion" issues – poverty, health care, the elderly, education, children and family issues, the environment–whereas men are seen as more concerned with economics, defense, business, crime, and agriculture (Alexander and Andersen 1993; Huddy and Terkildsen 1993a; Leeper 1991). As with trait stereotypes, some express concern that voters may actively use these judgments about women's and men's perceived policy differences against women candidates. This concern, although potentially valid, raises the question of whether the opposite might also be true. If stereotypes about ideology or traits or issue competency can work against women candidates, are there not also times when they might work in their favor, such as when voters value candidates who are perceived as more honest and as "outsiders" to politics (Alexander and Andersen 1993; Kahn 1996; Koch 1999)? Women candidates are also perceived to be much better than men at addressing issues like sexual harassment, abortion, and women's rights (Huddy and Terkildsen 1993a; Kahn 1996). When women's issues are particularly salient, such as in 1992, this focus on candidate sex and gender issues can brighten the election prospects of women candidates, particularly among women voters (Dolan 1998; Paolino 1995; Plutzer and Zipp 1996).

An additional thing to consider when discussing voter stereotypes of women candidates is the role of political party. Given the primacy of partisanship, our understanding of stereotypes should consider whether candidate sex loses some of its impact when it is measured against other important political variables. Recent work concludes that partisan cues often overwhelm all other sources of information about candidate beliefs and positions, even a candidate's sex (Huddy and Capelos 2002).

We also need to consider whether the possible interaction of sex and party stereotypes causes people to evaluate women differently on the basis of their political party. Because people's party and sex stereotypes often correspond – Democrats and women are assumed to be better able to address social issues and poverty, whereas Republicans and men are seen as better suited for economic and military policies – this could create situations in which sex and party stereotypes can work to reinforce or offset each other. For example, we know that candidate sex is significantly related to people's evaluation of Democratic House candidates (with women being seen as more liberal than men), but not to people's evaluations of Republican candidates (with women being seen as no more or less conservative than men) (Dolan 2004). This is counter to what the stereotypes literature would suggest, and it does support the notion that partisan stereotypes may attenuate the influence of sex stereotypes. It may also be that the overlap between stereotypes of women and Democrats makes the evaluation task "easier" for respondents than when they are faced with the more contradictory nature of stereotypes of women and Republicans.

Finally, it might be fruitful to shift our focus on stereotypes away from a comparison of women to men and instead look more closely at public stereotypes across women candidates. It would not be unreasonable to assume that sex and gender stereotypes could be shaped by a woman's image, name, marital and family status, or age, but we have relatively little empirical evidence that examines stereotypes among women candidates. We should also more closely examine the ways in which minority women candidates are subject to race and sex stereotyping. Just as party and sex stereotypes can interact, racial stereotypes may act to shape the ways in which people evaluate women candidates. Comparing minority women and men would also be fruitful in helping us understand this potential interaction.

CAMPAIGNING AND "PRESENTING"

Campaign decisions are crucial ones for any political candidate, because campaign advertising and information are the primary vehicles candidates use to present a particular image to the public and to send a particular message about their experiences, strengths, and interests. Although former Representative Pat Schroeder (D-CO) once famously asked, "Do I have an option?" when asked if she was considering running for president as a woman, women candidates do indeed have choices to make with regard to how they present themselves: from hair and dress, to how to present their spouses and children (if relevant), from the issues they showcase to their personal speaking and presentation style (Witt, Paget, and Matthews 1994, 12). Generally, the major consideration is whether to embrace public stereotypes about women or to work to challenge them by presenting an image that counters these stereotypes. This can take the form of campaigning "as a woman" and making women's issues a centerpiece in the campaign, or it can mean consciously choosing to burnish more "masculine" credentials by emphasizing male issues and a masculine leadership style.

For much of the recent past, women and men candidates behaved in ways that largely conformed to the public's gender stereotypes about women and men (Bystrom 2006; Dabelko and Herrnson 1997; Witt et al. 1994). However, even since the 1990s, there seems to be a change in the trend, with recent research finding relatively few differences in how women and men campaign. Dianne Bystrom (2006) finds that women's campaigns appear to be similar to those of men, presenting a balance of masculine and feminine issues and emphasizing traditionally masculine traits such as "toughness" and "strength." Virginia Sapiro and Katherine Cramer Walsh (2002) have found that women and men generally campaign on the same issues, emphasize the same character traits (with women showing a bit more interest in demonstrating their "toughness"), and appear in similar campaign settings. Other studies confirm a lack of sex differences in campaigning by examining candidate Web sites, a new and increasingly utilized campaign tool (Dolan 2005; Niven and Zilber 2001). In most venues over which candidates have control, women candidates do not appear to be playing to stereotypes but instead are attempting to present themselves as candidates concerned with a wide range of issues and demonstrating more "male" personality attributes.

Although a general similarity of approach to campaigning among women and men may be the order of the day, we see that women can accrue an electoral benefit from running "as women." Paul Herrnson, J. Celeste Lay, and Atiya Brown Stokes (2003) find that women candidates who campaign on women's issues and target women's groups received an electoral bonus over other candidates, whereas Eric Plutzer and John Zipp (1996) found that women in 1992 who ran as feminists drew more votes from women than those who did not highlight women's concerns in their campaigns. So it may be the case that, in some circumstances, women candidates could lose an advantage by failing to capitalize on their distinctiveness, personality attributes, or perceived strengths.

The evidence from research on women's campaign styles suggests that women candidates shape personal and policy images that are more free of excess sex and gender baggage than in the past. However, we still know relatively little about how women candidates make decisions about the image they will cultivate. Because sex and gender considerations are not the same in every campaign, we should ask whether they matter more or less in cultivating public images for candidates at different levels (local, state, national) or for different offices (executive, legislative, judicial). We should also consider the ways in which men create their images when faced with a woman opponent. In light of evidence that the increasing number of women candidates has an impact on men's behavior (Fox 1997), we should examine whether and how men adjust their images or the issues on which they campaign to counter the gendered aspects of running against a woman.

Finally, more work that examines whether women candidates gain an electoral benefit from campaigning on a certain set of issues would be important. The evidence that women candidates benefit from campaigning "as women," is limited (Herrnson et al. 2003). However, that is, in part, because of a lack of research. Of course, the effectiveness of a strategy to run a gendered campaign will be shaped by the context of a particular election – the party of the candidate, the issues at play in the election, the level of office sought – but there may be patterns that can help us determine whether gendered campaign appeals help or hurt women candidates.

MEDIA COVERAGE

The literature on media coverage of women candidates demonstrates an evolution in the ways that women candidates are framed, from a time when the influence of stereotypes was strong to the present day when women are presented in a more balanced light. First, several studies find evidence that women candidates for statewide office such as governor or U.S. senator receive less media coverage than do men candidates; the coverage they do receive tends to focus on their viability and also tends to distort the message that women candidates seek to send (Bystrom 2006; Kahn 1996, 2003). The media also tend to focus on casting women candidates in gender stereotypical frames, talking about their interest and abilities on "feminine issues" and focusing on their appearance (Bystrom 2006; Witt et al. 1994). Besides perpetuating gendered stereotypes, this pattern of media coverage is problematic for women candidates if it negatively affects public perceptions of them (Kropf and Boiney 2001).

More recent research suggest that, since the late 1990s, the quantity of television and print coverage of women and men is evening out and that the tone of coverage is equally positive for women and men (Bystrom et al. 2004). Other work finds that in some races, women candidates receive more media attention than men do, that the general tone of articles on both women and men is neutral, and that there is no real viability bias against women (Bystrom, Robertson, and Banwart 2001; Smith 1997). In all of these studies, the evidence of a change in the coverage of appearance and personality issues of women candidates, however, is more of a mixed bag. Although the media rely less on personal and appearance issues since 2000 when covering women candidates, women still receive more of this kind of coverage than do men. Additionally, they found evidence that the media still rely on a "novelty" frame in discussing women candidates, focusing on their sex and the relative uniqueness of their candidacies (Bystrom et al. 2001).

One place where there still seems to be stereotyped coverage of women candidates is at the level of the presidency. Several recent studies of Elizabeth Dole's run for the 2000 Republican nomination for president find consistent patterns of her receiving less coverage than some of her male opponents and more coverage focused on her appearance, sex, and viability (Aday and Devitt 2001; Bystrom 2006; Heldman, Carroll, and Olson 2005).

Although recent research suggests that the stereotyped coverage of women candidates may be changing, these new data are somewhat at odds with previous findings. Clearly, more work is needed to continue the examination into this trend. At the same time, Kim Kahn (2003) argues for more research into the coverage of women officeholders, because this media coverage can have an important impact into their success in office and future mobility. Researchers should tie these streams together, treating the transition from candidate to officeholder more fully, with an eye toward determining whether and how media treatment changes as a woman's status changes. This could be accomplished in comparison to men but could also be done to make comparisons among women, perhaps by party or area of issue specialization chosen for attention (masculine or feminine) or region of the country represented.

STRUCTURAL AND ELECTORAL

Regardless of their level of ambition, support from the public, or the media attention they receive, women candidates, like men, have to function in an electoral system, the rules and realities of which can significantly shape important aspects of candidacy. These structural mechanisms are gendered, making them an important consideration when evaluating the status of women candidates in American politics.

Of all of the elements of the electoral system that can influence the prospects for and success of candidates, candidate status may be primary. Because those already in office are largely male, women tend to have to compete for access to the system through open-seat races for office. It is important to point out that incumbency does benefit women in the same general ways that it benefits men (Dolan 2004; Fox 2006), but recent work suggests that women incumbent members of Congress attract stronger and better financed opponents than do male incumbents (Berch 2004; Palmer and Simon 2005). Women candidates, then, are most likely to be successful (as are nonincumbent men) when they run for open seats. Women candidates are also strategic enough to focus on open seats and are about as likely as men to win those seats (Fiber 2004; Fox 2006; Palmer and Simon 2001). However, some research finds that women's success in open-seat races has declined a bit since the mid- to late 1990s, which observers assume relates to the fact that women tend to run as Democrats, and Republicans have won more congressional races during that period (Hoffman, Palmer, and Gaddie 2001; King and Matland 2003).

Primaries are another important point of access to candidacy. We know that, at least in the past twenty years or so, Democrats have had more women candidates running in primaries than the Republicans have and that Democratic women tend to be more successful in primaries than Republican women (Gaddie and Bullock 1995; Palmer and Simon 2001). Kathleen Bratton's (2004) research confirms this trend and demonstrates that Republican women candidates, even incumbents, are more likely to face opposition in their primaries than Democratic women. Interestingly, she also finds that an increasing number of women candidates in a primary decreases the vote share for each woman candidate to a greater degree than the reduction for men candidates. However, we need much more research on when and how women candidates run in primaries to determine whether this access point has additional gendered elements.

Focusing on the structure of elections raises the issue of political parties. Parties are a significant influence on elections involving women candidates in a couple of different ways. First, we need to recognize the current imbalance in the party identification of women candidates for office: about 60 percent of women candidates run as Democrats (CAWP 2006). This may be a reflection of patterns of women's personal identification, or of the relative openness of the two parties to women's candidacies, or of the formal attempts by party leaders to recruit more women candidates to office, or of each of these things simultaneously. Regardless of reason, the pattern is clear – more Democratic women than Republican women seek office, Democratic women are more successful than Republican women in primaries and general elections, and Democratic women make up a greater proportion of the Democratic members of Congress than Republican women make up of their party's total (Bratton 2004; Fox 2006; Ondercin and Welch 2005).

Alongside party support, financial backing is crucial. The historical concern that contributors and parties would not support women candidates seems to be a thing of the past. Since the 1970s, women candidates have reached parity with men in terms of campaign financing and have, in some situations, shown a clear advantage, raising money from a range of PACs and attracting large donations (Burrell 1994, 2005; Fox 1997; Werner 1998). With the advent of women-centered PACs such as EMILY's List (EMILY is an acronym for "early money is like yeast," i.e., it helps the dough rise), women are able to tap into a network of early money, one that is funded largely by women donors. However, some researchers warn that this seeming financial parity does not necessarily translate into equality of impact because, in some circumstances, women candidates may need more campaign resources to achieve the same effects those resources provide men (Green 2003). Moreover, the lingering perception that women have more difficulty raising money than men may contribute to the reticence of women to broach candidacies. Also, we need to know more about the funding of women candidates below the congressional and statewide level and about the impact of public financing systems on the emergence and success of women candidates.

Besides a party imbalance in the representation of women candidates, it is also clear that successful women candidates are not equally distributed across the country. Palmer and Simon (2006) recently introduced the concept of the "woman friendly" district, from which women are more likely to be elected to Congress. These districts are more urban, more ethnically and racially diverse, and have income and education levels above the national average. Zoe Oxley and Richard Fox (2004) find that women candidates for statewide office are more likely to emerge in states with higher percentages of women lawyers and are less likely to emerge in states with traditional political cultures. The power of political culture is also evidenced by work that demonstrates that women in the South are less likely to seek and win election to more "masculine" offices (Lublin and Brewer 2003).

Another structural aspect of determining where women run involves the type of offices they seek. Recent work suggests that gendered considerations shape the choices women make when deciding which office to pursue: women are more likely to run for statewide office in states that have more executive offices that specialize in "feminine" policy areas, yet women are no more or less likely than men to win either "masculine" or "feminine" offices (Fox and Oxley 2003). Other research indicates that women in the South are more likely to run for and hold less "desirable" process-oriented offices with little discretion and when there are fewer high quality men candidates running (Lublin and Brewer 2003). Taken together, these findings suggest that women are, either by choice or by circumstance, more likely to pursue stereotypical "female" posts and those with less independent authority, which speaks to a process of women shaping candidacies to fit public expectations. This serves at best to perpetuate stereotypes and at worst as a de facto limit on the present and future opportunities women can pursue.

The uneven distribution of women's candidacies indicates that the playing field is not completely level for women, pointing to several fruitful areas of research. We need to look past the number of women holding office at the state and local levels to a closer examination of the offices being held. We also need to examine patterns of candidacy at these levels and to trace the career paths of women from local office on up the pipeline. Alternatively, we need to see whether there is a point in the process where women's advancement is blocked, whether there is a group of offices that do not serve as successful stepping stones to higher office. We also need to know more about the full range of districts and states in which women run, not simply to identify the characteristics of the places from which they win. Do women who lose tend to run in districts in which they are the partisan minority? Do they run in states with less supportive political parties? Does incumbency have the same power for women across the country? As Sanbonmatsu (2005) suggests, women and men are equally likely to win their races. However, if women generally run where they are most likely to win, then the playing field of candidacies is not yet level and will not be until women of every type can contest for a full range of offices everywhere around the country.

Examining when and whether women run for office requires us to acknowledge that these women enter a system that is gendered in its structure and operation. From money networks to political parties to incumbents in office, most aspects of our political system are overwhelmingly male and are dominated by men. This reality provides women candidates with an additional challenge: to navigate a system that sees them as the exception, outside the norm. Women who succeed in this system may do so because of luck, timing, or strategic decisions and behaviors. Determining how women exist in a male-dominated system is still a fruitful area of study.

VOTE CHOICE

For much of our history, public unwillingness to support women candidates at the polls was a significant stumbling block to their success. Traditional ideas about inappropriateness of a public role for women led many voters, male and female, to reject women candidates on principle alone (Dolan 2004). The evidence gathered over the past twenty-five years, however, has demonstrated the increasing electoral viability of women, concluding that similarly situated women and men are equally likely to win elections at both the state and national levels (Burrell 1994; Newman 1994; Seltzer et al. 1997). On the basis of these findings, the question regarding women candidates has shifted from whether people will vote for them to which voters are most likely to do so.

Analysis of data from the National Election Study for candidates for Congress from 1990 to 2000 indicates that there are relatively few consistent gendered patterns of voter support for women candidates (Dolan 2004). The major determinants of vote choice for people faced with a woman candidate are the same as the determinants of the vote in all elections – incumbency and a shared party identification between candidate and voter. This is an important finding because it lets us know that the "typical" election dynamics are not thrown out the window when a woman candidate appears on the scene. Women incumbents earn the same advantage that men incumbents do, and women candidates are embraced by the members of their own party, just as men are. If these factors were not important to voting for a woman, this would signal that candidate sex trumped traditional electoral influences. However, we see no evidence that voters consider candidate sex a primary concern.

Beyond the influence of incumbency and shared party identification, few variables are consistently related to voter support for women candidates since 1990. Voters of a particular political party or ideological persuasion are no more or less likely to support women candidates. Counter to expectations, age, religiosity, and education did not distinguish the voters who chose women candidates from those who did not. Race, however, does serve to influence vote choice, with minority voters being more likely to support women candidates than white voters (Dolan 2004).

The most obvious demographic characteristic related to vote choice for women candidates is the sex of the voter. The notion that women voters should be an automatic base of support for women candidates has been an implicit, and sometimes explicit, assumption of much of the work done on women candidates. Indeed, women have a stronger preference for same-sex representation than do men and a sense of shared gender identity or common concern about issues may motivate women voters to select women candidates (Rosenthal 1995; Sanbonmatsu 2002a; Tolleson-Rinehart 1992). Furthermore, any greater likelihood that women voters will chose women candidates may be based not so much on a shared gender identity but instead on a set of ideological or partisan sympathies, because women in the public and women candidates are more likely to be Democrats than Republicans. Finally, we should acknowledge that women are not a monolithic voting bloc, slavishly being driven by sex and gender considerations. Instead, women may be more likely to choose women candidates than men voters would be, but this dynamic is probably shaped by the same political forces that shape other vote choice decisions – incumbency, political party, race, and the level of office being sought. For example, some studies have demonstrated that certain subgroups of women – African American, liberal, feminist, and well-educated women – are more likely to choose women candidates than are other women (Lewis 1999; Sigelman and Welch 1984; Smith and Fox 2001). Other work has shown that women voters may be more likely to choose women candidates in some circumstances, such as when they are incumbents or when running for a particular office, than others (Cook 1994; Dolan 1998, 2004).

The sometimes conflicting evidence on whether women are more likely to support women candidates than are men raises questions for future research. Sanbonmatsu's work demonstrates that women are more likely to have a "baseline" gender preference for women candidates, whereas other work on vote choice indicates that party identification and incumbency drive voting for women. At the same time, some scholars suggest that some women will cross party lines to support women (Brians 2005; King and Matland 2003). So it would be interesting to know more about what factors pull people away from their baseline preference and what it takes for that to happen. If many women begin predisposed to vote for women candidates, what occurs to cause them to vote counter to that preference? Is political party the key? Is party enough? Is it some combination of party and position on issues? What explains women (or men, for that matter) who cross party lines to vote for a woman? Are Republican or Democratic women equally like to cross? Are minority women pulled more by race or sex in their voting decision in the presence of a woman candidate?

Another area on which we need more information has to do with the impact of voter stereotypes on vote choice. Although we have very clear evidence that people evaluate women and men candidates through gendered lenses, we have less information about how those stereotypes shape people's attitudes and behaviors toward women candidates and whether they influence vote choice. This is particularly important with regard to vote choice. The stereotypes research speaks extensively about the degree to which women candidates can be helped or hurt by the stereotypes people hold. We know little about the degree to which people employ sex stereotypes in their voting decision and where stereotypes might rank among the host of other influences. Understanding whether general sex stereotypes are applied in vote choice regarding a specific candidate could give us a better sense of whether particular electoral or issue climates should be more or less hospitable to women candidates. Also, as with so many other things, we should consider the party of the woman candidate here. It may be the case that sex stereotypes interact with party stereotypes in a way that might make them more or less important to vote choice in different situations.

IMPACT OF WOMEN CANDIDATES ON THE PUBLIC

One final area to consider looks not at how the political system affects women candidates but instead at how the presence of women candidates affects the political system. The increase in the number of women who run for and are elected to office in the United States has been accompanied by an expanding literature that examines the impact these women have on our political system. Much has been written about the impact of women on *substantive* representation, resulting in our understanding that having more women in office tends to lead to different policy outcomes and different procedural pathways (Dodson 1998; Swers 2002; Thomas 1994; but see Reingold 2000).

However, a second aspect of representation, one that is more relevant at the candidacy stage, is that of *symbolic* representation. The presence of women candidates can signal a greater openness in the system and women candidates can also serve as role models or symbolic mentors to women in the public, sending the signal that politics is no longer an exclusive man's world and that female participation is an important and valued act (Dovi, this volume, Reingold 2000; Tolleson-Rinehart 1992). Jane Mansbridge (1999) suggests that the increased representation of marginalized identity groups also affirms that members of these groups are capable of governing and can serve to connect group members more strongly to the polity.

The signals of openness, legitimacy, and identity sent by the presence of women candidates can, in turn, stimulate activity and engagement on the part of those members of the public heartened by an increasingly democratic and representative candidate pool. Indeed, much of the work on the symbolic impact of women candidates finds some, if limited, support for the notion that their presence stimulates greater interest, knowledge, and attentiveness to politics, particularly among women (Atkeson 2003; Hansen 1997; Koch 1997; Sapiro and Conover 1997).

Although previous research suggests a symbolic benefit to mobilization from the presence of women candidates, none of the findings is conclusive. Several focus on one or two elections and on a small number of political variables (with the exception of Atkeson 2003), and none address whether the presence of women candidates mobilizes the public to turn out to vote in higher numbers. Indeed, recent work that more fully explores the impact of women candidates on the public offers little evidence to support a symbolic mobilization hypothesis (Dolan 2006). In a few limited circumstances, people who lived in the presence of women candidates for Congress from 1990 to 2000 experienced increases in some attitudes or activities over those who experienced male-only races. However, there was no consistent pattern to this effect and no strong evidence that the presence of women candidates causes people to sit up, take notice, and engage in politics in a real or different way (Dolan 2006).

Understanding the connection, or lack thereof, of women candidates with the public will allow us a more rigorous examination of our assumptions about the importance of symbolic representation. As Jennifer Lawless (2004) suggests, a woman does not have to be directly represented by Hillary Clinton or Mary Landrieu to experience the symbolic benefits of having more women in elected office. The same may be true for people observing women candidates. Figuring out a way to measure this more general symbolic representation may help us better identify how the presence of women candidates works. We should also examine the characteristics of women candidates and the contexts of the races in which they do have an impact on the public. Women candidates who stimulate public attitudes and behaviors may take certain positions or highlight certain issues, or run in certain areas of the country or particular election years, or even experience certain kinds of opponents. Given that both Dolan (2006) and Lawless (2004) have found evidence that men's attitudes and behaviors can be influenced by women candidates and officeholders, we should work further to examine the impact that women candidates have on men.

CONCLUSION

The field of political science has produced a large and important body of research on the situations facing women candidates in the past forty years. In many ways, we are still at the beginning of a research agenda that seeks to examine more fully the role that sex and gender play in American elections. That these issues play a less formal and decisive role today than they did in the past is clearly evident in the research. Nonetheless, we have many avenues still to pursue. These avenues involve questions raised in the beginning of the chapter, questions that will require us to seek new and better data on a wider range of offices and elections than has been utilized to date, questions that require us to think about the experiences of a more diverse group of women candidates, questions that ask us to untangle the interconnected elements of sex and gender in our social, cultural, and political life. These questions for the future require us to continue to examine the gendered nature of family and professional life, stereotypes, electoral systems, political parties, and the media so that we can more clearly determine whether we are indeed moving toward a time when women candidates are thought of as candidates who happen to be women.

9

Women as Officeholders

Linking Descriptive and Substantive Representation

Beth Reingold

This chapter reviews the wealth of research on the behavior, experiences, and accomplishments of women in elective office in the United States to assess what we have learned and to identify some of the most promising avenues for future research. Motivated in large part by questions and concerns about women's political representation, this research has established a clear, empirical link between women's descriptive and substantive representation.[1] Throughout the policy-making process – and beyond – female officeholders are often more likely than their male colleagues to act for women or women's interests. A closer look at this research also reveals that these links are by no means guaranteed or universal; descriptive representation is neither absolutely necessary nor entirely sufficient for substantive representation to occur. Some female officeholders are more likely than others to act for women; some male politicians are more likely than others to do so; some governing institutions are more likely than others to do so. Although few, if any, researchers would deny the imperfect nature of the relationship between women's descriptive and substantive representation, few (Dodson 2006; Dolan and Ford 1998; Reingold 2000) have made it their central focus.

Future research, I argue, needs to recognize and explore the complex, contingent, and gendered processes by which the linkages between the descriptive and substantive representation of women are strengthened or weakened. More specifically, researchers should pay more attention to numerous factors besides the sex of individual politicians that may promote or inhibit women's substantive representation, including other dimensions of social location and identity, such as race and ethnicity, as well as institutional and political opportunity structures.

The scope of the analysis presented here is necessarily limited in several ways. First, to maintain theoretical and empirical coherence, the discussion focuses on *elected* officials only. Second, I rely heavily on research concerning state legislators and members of Congress, for little research has examined the behavior and impact of women in local elective office. Finally, to maintain the focus on questions about women's substantive representation, I omit much of the more biographical research that examines the "private" and "public" roles of women in public office (see Cammisa and Reingold 2004). For the same reason, I also refrain from discussing the research on women's symbolic representation or the effects female officeholders may or may not have on women's political engagement (e.g., Burns, Schlozman, and Verba 2001; Lawless 2004). (See Dolan, this volume, on the symbolic representation of female candidates.)

REVIEW OF THE LITERATURE: MAKING A DIFFERENCE

Literature on women in office often begins by observing the increasing numbers of women getting elected and asking: what difference does it make? Do the increasing numbers of women in office mean that women's political interests, preferences, and perspectives are better represented? Are public officials who descriptively "stand for" women more likely to "act for" women in a substantive manner (Pitkin 1967)? Empirically, most researchers have addressed these questions by examining whether women and men behave differently in office. The conclusions have been remarkably similar: women in office do make a difference. There are notable exceptions and qualifications, however. Indeed, it is those "ifs, ands, and buts" that pose the most interesting questions for future research.

Policy Preferences

Much of the research on women officeholders began where the more mainstream studies of representation and legislative behavior began: with policy preferences and roll-call voting. Most of these studies reveal that female policy makers are more likely than their male colleagues to represent women's interests in two ways. First, elite policy preferences and roll-call votes tend to match gender gaps in public opinion; thus female officeholders are more likely to take liberal positions on a wide array of issues such as gun control, social welfare, and civil rights, as well as on composite measures of liberalism and conservatism (Barrett 1995; Burrell 1994; Carey, Niemi, and Powell 1998; Clark 1998; Center for American Women and Politics [CAWP] 2001; Diamond 1977; Dodson 2006; Dodson and Carroll 1991; Epstein, Niemi, and Powell 2005; Evans 2005; Johnson and Carroll 1978; Poole and Zeigler 1985; Schumaker and Burns 1988; Welch 1985). Second, even though sex differences in public opinion on many women's rights issues (e.g., abortion and the Equal Rights Amendment) are minimal, women in office are more likely to support such feminist proposals (Barrett 1995; Burrell 1994; CAWP 2001; Day 1994; Diamond 1977; Dodson 2006; Dodson and Carroll 1991; Dolan 1997; Epstein et al. 2005; Hill 1983; Johnson and Carroll 1978;

Leader 1977; Swers 2002; Thomas 1989). Together these studies cover three decades, national, state, and local officials, and most state legislatures. In most instances, the sex-related differences they report withstand controls for party and district-level factors.

Note, however, several important exceptions and caveats. First, some state (Barnello 1999; Reingold 2000), local (Mezey 1978a, 1978b), and congressional studies (Gehlen 1977; Tamerius 1995; Vega and Firestone 1995; Wolbrecht 2002b) report few, if any, sex differences in lawmakers' policy preferences and roll-call votes. Second, the occurrence and magnitude of such gender gaps vary, depending on the issue at hand. For example, Sue Thomas (1989) found sex differences in state legislators' support for women's rights but not on other issues (see also Barrett 1995; CAWP 2001; Dodson 2006; Dodson and Carroll 1991; Johnson and Carroll 1978). Third, there is some evidence that sex differences in congressional voting behavior have decreased over time "primarily because of the reduction in the liberalism of female members" (Welch 1985, 131; see also Clark 1998; Dodson 2006; Swers 2002; Vega and Firestone 1995; but see Wolbrecht 2002b, 196–7). Fourth, numerous studies, particularly of congressional roll-call votes, have found significant gender gaps only or primarily among Republicans (Burrell 1994; Dolan 1997; Evans 2005; Swers 2002; Thomas 1989; Vega and Firestone 1995; Welch 1985; but see Dodson 2006). Finally, with few exceptions (Schumaker and Burns 1988), the sex differences that are revealed are not wide chasms. Rarely is a majority of women pitted against a majority of men.[2] Indeed, most scholars recognize that sex differences in elite policy preferences pale in comparison to party differences. Republican women may be more liberal than GOP men, but rarely are they as liberal as Democrats – male or female.

Policy Leadership

"Voting," Shelah Gilbert Leader pointed out in 1977, "is only one kind of political activity and possibly not the most important. It tells us nothing about who initiates the introduction of feminist legislation and who leads floor fights and mobilizes support" (284). Indeed, women in public office frequently are expected – by voters, activists, and researchers alike – to care more about, know more about, and do more about "women's issues," whether they are defined strictly in feminist terms (e.g., women's rights) or more broadly as issues related to women's traditional roles as caretakers (e.g., social welfare).

A large body of research confirms these popular expectations. Across time, office, and political parties, women, more often than men, take the lead on women's issues, no matter how such issues are defined. In interviews, surveys, press releases, and newsletters, women officeholders are more likely to express concern about such issues and claim them as their own

(Barrett 1995; Boles 2001; Diamond 1977; Dolan and Kropf 2004; Fridkin and Woodall 2005; Garcia Bedolla, Tate, and Wong 2005; Reingold 2000). They are more likely to serve on committees relevant to women's issues (Carroll 2006; Diamond 1977; Reingold 2000; Thomas 1994; Thomas and Welch 1991). They are more likely to introduce or sponsor legislation addressing such issues (Bratton 2002, 2005; Bratton and Haynie 1999; Bratton, Haynie, and Reingold 2006; Carroll 2001; CAWP 2001; Dodson and Carroll 1991; Reingold 2000; Saint-Germain 1989; Swers 2002; Tamerius 1995; Thomas 1994; Thomas and Welch 1991; Wolbrecht 2002b).[3] Christina Wolbrecht (2002b) shows that women in Congress (especially the Democrats) also are more innovative in their approach to women's issues: *they* have been the ones primarily responsible for introducing new women's rights concerns and new policy solutions (see also Kathlene 1995). Congressional research also reveals that women's policy leadership extends far beyond bill introduction. It involves constant vigilance throughout the entire policy-making process – in committee and on the floor, as well as behind the scenes (Dodson 1998, 2006; Hawkesworth et al. 2001; Norton 2002; Swers 2002; Walsh 2002).

Again, there are a few notable cracks in the consensus. Some of the earliest studies found no significant differences in the policy priorities of women and men (Gehlen 1977; Johnson and Carroll 1978; Merritt 1980; Mezey 1978a, 1978b; see also Niven and Zilber 2001). More recent research suggests that sex differences in policy leadership may not extend to all women's issues or to every jurisdiction. Jesse Donahue (1997) and Susan Abrams Beck (2001) have found that at the local level, male and female officials share the same policy priorities; all are faced with the same imperatives, such as minimizing taxes and maintaining infrastructure, leaving little room for women's issues or policy innovation in general. Beth Reingold (2000) reports that gender gaps in policy leadership among Arizona legislators were larger and spanned a wider range of women's issues than did those among California legislators (see also Thomas 1994). Michele Swers (2002) has found variation across both issues and time. Sex differences in policy leadership were more pronounced on feminist issues than on social welfare issues, and women's (especially Republican women's) willingness and ability to advocate for women's issues were more constrained in the Republican-controlled 104th Congress than in the Democratic-controlled 103rd (see also Dodson 2006; Hawkesworth et al. 2001).

Policy Impact and Outcomes

Researchers have paid less attention to the actual impact of women on policy outcomes. Conclusions about whether women's issue bills sponsored by women are more successful than those sponsored by men have been mixed. Some find support (Saint-Germain 1989; Thomas 1994), whereas others fail to uncover significant differences (Bratton 2005; Bratton and Haynie

1999; Reingold and Schneider 2001). More generally, research shows that female legislators, at the state and national level, are at least as successful as (and occasionally more successful than) male legislators in getting their bills passed – regardless of subject matter (Bratton 2005; Bratton and Haynie 1999; Ellickson and Whistler 2000; Jeydel and Taylor 2003; Saint-Germain 1989; Thomas 1994; Thomas and Welch 1991).

Given women's leadership on women's issues and their legislative success rates, one might expect the links between the presence of women and aggregate policy outcomes to be rather strong – especially on women's issues. At the local level, Grace Hall Saltzstein (1986, 144) has found that female mayors, in cities across the nation, made a significant difference "in terms of the equitable provision of municipal jobs to women," but Paul Schumaker and Nancy Burns's (1988) single-city study indicates that policy outcomes were more likely to reflect the preferences of male rather than female policy makers. Most state-level research demonstrates little or no relationship between the proportion of women serving in the legislature and aggregate policy change or innovation (Thomas 1994; Tolbert and Steuernagel 2001; Weldon 2004). Others, however, show that the presence of women does have a significant effect on specific policy adoption, such as child support laws (Crowley 2004), and on the final passage of women's issue bills (Reingold and Schneider 2001). More qualitative, in-depth studies of Congress have detailed the ways in which women's leadership throughout the policymaking process has been critical to the success of numerous initiatives on behalf of women's interests (Dodson 2006; Hawkesworth et al. 2001; Norton 2002).

Clearly, more research on aggregate policy outcomes is needed – not only because of the mixed results produced thus far but also because this type of research has been neglected for far too long. We cannot simply assume that being different and acting differently assures that women will, in fact, make a difference (Dahlerup 2006a, 518). As Saltzstein (1986, 142) argued more than two decades ago, "the answer to the question as to what difference it makes if women are elected to office not only must address what those women *do* in office but also must address what others do in response or reaction to their presence."[4]

Legislative and Leadership Styles

In addition to affecting policy inputs and outputs, women in office often are expected to practice politics differently and, perhaps even alter the policymaking process. In this literature, the "rules of the game" are recognized as inherently gendered. Dominant norms and approaches to policy making and leadership are described in masculine terms: hierarchical, authoritative relationships; zero-sum competition and conflict; and interpersonal dynamics involving coercion and manipulation (see especially Duerst-Lahti

2002; Rosenthal 1998; Thomas 1994). In contrast, women's approaches are expected to emphasize empowering, egalitarian, reciprocal relationships; compromise, consensus building, and cooperation; and honesty, openness, and integrity.

Much research on state legislative leaders confirms these expectations. Lyn Kathlene (1994), for example, finds that female committee chairs in Colorado used their positions to facilitate open discussions among committee members, sponsors, and witnesses, whereas their male counterparts used their positions to control the hearings. Studies of larger, national samples of state legislative leaders reveal similar patterns in which women are more partial to nonhierarchical collaboration and consensus building than men are (Dodson and Carroll 1991; Jewell and Whicker 1994; Rosenthal 1998, 2005). Little research like this has been conducted at the local or national level, but there are some indications that such gendered leadership styles can be found in those contexts as well (Fox and Schuhmann 1999; Swers and Larson 2005; Tolleson-Rinehart 1991).[5]

On the other hand, most studies focusing on rank-and-file politicians reveal few sex differences in leadership approaches or legislative styles. In several studies of state legislators, majorities of both sexes endorse more inclusive and cooperative alternatives for exercising leadership and interacting with colleagues (Blair and Stanley 1991; Dodson and Carroll 1991; Kirkpatrick 1974; Reingold 2000). At the local level, Donahue (1997) finds few differences in the ways school officials participate in policy deliberations, and what few differences do occur show men being more facilitative than women (but see Beck 2001). At the national level, Kim Fridkin and Gina Woodall's (2005) analysis of senators' press releases shows women, more often than men, emphasizing their "male" traits (e.g., strong leader, tough, experienced, consistent), and men more likely to stress their "female" traits (e.g., honest, compassionate, trustworthy, moral) than their "male" traits.

Constituent Responsiveness

Although most research on women in office has focused on policy making, some studies have examined more constituent-oriented matters. Here again, the expectation is that women will practice politics differently and pay more attention to their constituents. Numerous studies have found that female state and local officials are apt to believe they are more responsive to constituents, more approachable, more trusted, and more committed to community relations than their male colleagues are (Beck 2001; Diamond 1977; Flammang 1985; Johnson and Carroll 1978; Merritt 1980; Mezey 1978c). Research comparing the representational priorities and activities of women and men in state and local office confirms these perceptions. For example, in two national surveys of state legislators (Carey et al. 1998; Epstein, Niemi, and Powell 2005), women reported devoting significantly more time than men did to keeping in touch with constituents and helping constituents with their problems – even controlling for a variety of other factors likely to affect how legislators spend their time (e.g., professionalization and size of legislature, seniority; see also Bers 1978; CAWP 2001; Johnson and Carroll 1978; Richardson and Freeman 1995; Thomas 1992).

There are few exceptions, but once again they are notable for the questions they raise. Women and men in Reingold's (2000) study spent equivalent amounts of time on constituent casework and meeting with constituents and were in agreement regarding the importance of such activities. Reingold (2000) and others (Diamond 1977; Githens 1977) also find little support for the notion that women in office are more likely than men to adopt the delegate role and defer to their constituents' wishes (but see CAWP 2001). In fact, the delegate role finds few takers, male or female, in these studies, perhaps because it could easily be associated with passiveness, subservience, weak leadership, and indecisiveness – all gender stereotypes that haunt female politicians in particular. To illustrate, Beck (2001, 56) has found that, whereas the women she interviewed believed their willingness to listen to constituents made them better representatives, their male colleagues criticized them for being "too responsive to feelings and not analytic enough." Thus, in a masculinized world where policy accomplishments are associated with institutional power and political prestige, public officials may very well feel the need to avoid devoting "too much" attention to their constituency (Caldeira, Clark, and Patterson 1993; Hibbing and Thomas 1990; Reingold 2000, 105–6).

Rather than approach the idea of constituency as a single, undifferentiated whole, a few studies have explored the possibility that female officials are more likely than their male colleagues to "see," care about, and respond to their female constituents in particular. Here the research is unanimous: the ties that bind representatives and their constituents are particularly strong among women. For example, almost all the congresswomen interviewed by CAWP said they felt a "special obligation to represent the interests of women" (Carroll 2002, 53; Dodson 1998, 2006; Hawkesworth et al. 2001). Similar inquiries among state legislators confirm that women and men differ significantly in this respect (Barrett 1997; CAWP 2001; Reingold 2000; Thomas 1994). Nonetheless, the women differ among themselves in how they explain and describe that responsibility. "Women differ in the solutions they see to the problems women face, they differ in the kinds of women they represent, and they differ in the extent to which these concerns are salient" (Dodson 1998, 148; see also Reingold 2000). As Susan Carroll (2002, 66–7) explains, this diversity among women has important implications for researchers wondering whether women officeholders make a difference: "All of these differences ... can influence how congresswomen translate their perceived responsibility to represent women's interests into actual policy decisions. As a result, even when women members of Congress act in ways that they perceive as representing women, their actions may not always look the same. They may vote differently, offer different amendments, or favor different legislative solutions. Consequently, the changes in policy making that result from congresswomen's surrogate representation of women's interests will not always be unidirectional, straightforward, or uncomplicated."

DIRECTIONS FOR FUTURE RESEARCH: EXPLAINING VARIATION

What emerges from the literature is clear: the links between women's descriptive and substantive representation are numerous and strong, especially at the individual level. In various ways and across various political jurisdictions – before, during, and after the "Year of the Woman" (1992) – female officials have been more likely than their male counterparts to act for women and women's interests. What emerges from all the caveats and exceptions, however, is equally clear: the link between women's descriptive and substantive representation is not always assured. The existence or strength of that linkage can – and often does – vary across individuals, time, and space. Yet it is this variation – particularly the differences among women and the complicated interactions between individuals and institutions – that has been neglected. Why do some women (and men) make more of a difference than others? What makes some institutions more conducive than others to women's substantive representation – by women or men? Shifting our attention away from the search for sex differences in and of themselves and turning toward a more gendered analysis, we can investigate such questions more extensively.

Some researchers have begun to do just that. For them (and others), the profound changes in the politics of women's representation between the Democratic-controlled 103rd Congress (1993–4) and the Republican-controlled 104th (1995–6) may have served as a wake-up call (Dodson 2006; Hawkesworth et al. 2001; Swers 2002). The election of more conservative women, the new Republican majority, and the more ideologically polarized climate all seemed to conspire to weaken the links between women's descriptive and substantive representation. While women's numbers were increasing (slightly), their willingness and ability to pursue women's issues waned. We could no longer ignore the differences among female public officials and the power of political institutions to shape the policy-making process from beginning to end. As the preceding paragraphs demonstrate, those differences among individual female officeholders, across institutions, and over time were always there. Clear and consistent patterns in those "aberrant" findings are not readily apparent, however, and many of us may be uncertain what to make of them.

On a closer examination, though, the available literature offers a good number of tentative hypotheses and key variables that might help explain varying patterns in the relationship between women's descriptive and substantive representation. Our attention can be directed to three levels of analysis: (1) individual politicians and their social locations, identities, political perspectives, positions, and constituencies; (2) institutional structures within representative policy-making bodies; and (3) sociopolitical forces surrounding those governing bodies, temporally and geographically. These are the sorts of factors that most likely shape the desire and the ability of women (and men) in public office to act for women, as well as their conceptions of what women's substantive representation entails.

Individuals

Party and Ideology. There is no denying that Democratic and Republican women often differ – sometimes profoundly (see especially Evans 2005). Just as there are significant sex differences in legislative behavior within both parties, there are significant party differences among both sexes; in some cases, party and sex interact so that gender gaps are greater in one party than in the other. Thus Democratic women usually appear most committed to women's substantive representation and Republican men the least. Depending on the dimension of representational behavior or the specific issues at hand, Democratic men and Republican women vie for second and third position.

That women's substantive representation depends on both sex and party should come as no surprise, given the persistent gender gaps in partisanship (see Sanbonmatsu and Huddy, this volume) and the fact that most women's issues, as defined in the literature, are at least moderately feminist, liberal, or both. But this suggests that political and gender *ideologies* also play important roles in how public officials define women's issues or interests and how actively they support them (Johnson, Duerst-Lahti, and Norton 2007).

Recent research on women's representation in Congress highlights the significance of political ideology – above and beyond partisanship (see especially Swers 2002). Within both parties, liberals are more likely than conservatives to advocate and support women's issues. Moreover, the election of more conservative Republican women to Congress in recent years has made it clear that most of the efforts and gains on behalf of women and women's interests have depended and will continue to depend on the ability of Democratic and moderate Republican women to forge effective bipartisan coalitions (see especially Hawkesworth et al. 2001).

Few studies have examined in depth the prevalence and impact of feminist identity, or other forms of gender ideology, among public officials. Utilizing national surveys of state legislators, Kathleen Dolan and Lynne Ford (1995, 1998) and Debra Dodson (2001) show that self-identified feminist women are more likely than nonfeminist women to make women's issues their top priority. Dodson (2001) also finds that feminist women are more likely to act for women than even feminist men, both in their policy priorities and their policy preferences (see also Dodson 2006). Although Dolan and Ford's

(1995) multivariate analysis suggests that at least some of these differences between feminist and nonfeminist lawmakers may disappear once we control for political ideology, much more research on the significance of feminist identities and ideologies among public officials is needed.

As early as the 104th Congress, congresswomen interviewed by CAWP recognized the challenges of ideological diversity within their ranks. The Democrats and moderate Republicans "tended to see the major dividing line among women [in Congress] not as party, but rather as ideology. In particular, they saw several of the women in the cohort of conservative freshmen elected in 1994 as ideological outliers" (Carroll 2002, 63–4). In the years since then, the number of conservative Republican women in Congress has increased and "more of these women have taken leading roles in championing antifeminist proposals" (Swers and Larson 2005, 124). What we may be seeing, then, is evidence that gender consciousness among female politicians can come in both liberal/feminist and conservative/antifeminist varieties (125–6). This, in turn, raises some important questions about how researchers define and measure women's political interests and substantive representation. To what extent and how should such antifeminist initiatives be incorporated into our analyses?

Dodson (2005, 2006) suggests that both feminist and antifeminist initiatives could be considered acts of women's representation *if* they reflect a conscious effort to forge responsive connections with women and women's groups (see also Dovi, this volume). However, this means we need to devote more attention to how public officials view and interact with their various constituencies, and how women, women's organizations or movements, and women's interests *of all types* figure into those perceptions and interactions. Taking a cue from Richard Fenno (1978), we must recognize that the constituencies that matter most to electorally minded officials are not those defined strictly in geographic terms. Women may constitute roughly half of all district-level constituents, but they may figure much more prominently in some politicians' winning coalitions than in others. Moreover, elected officials may distinguish certain types of women, women's groups, and women's causes as more or less supportive.[6]

Race and Ethnicity. Although many studies acknowledge at least the potential significance of partisan and ideological differences, few have recognized the potential significance of racial and ethnic diversity. As a result, the experiences of women of color and questions about *their* representation are too often ignored or marginalized, and what we think we know about "women" in public office may be applicable only to the majority of white, non-Hispanic women (see Dovi, this volume). Theories of intersectionality (e.g., Collins 2000; Crenshaw 1998; King 1988), in combination with what little empirical research is available, strongly caution against overgeneralizing from the gendered experiences of the dominant majority to those of marginalized

minority groups. To the contrary, they suggest that research on the representation of women of color may be a particularly fruitful vantage point from
which to consider the fact that sex is only one of many politically significant
dimensions of social location and gender only one of many important social,
political, and institutional forces (see Junn and Brown, this volume).

Most of the empirical research thus far demonstrates that women of color
are uniquely situated to recognize that the demands for both racial/ethnic
and gender representation, although not completely overlapping, are more
likely to be mutually reinforcing and interdependent than mutually exclusive
and independent. The black and white women in Edith Barrett's (1997)
study of Democratic state legislators, for example, were in agreement that
"[w]omen legislators should pay attention foremost to women's issues," and
that "[i]t is necessary to have women in state legislatures to ensure that
women's concerns get addressed" (135–6). Furthermore, the white women
were more likely than the white men to agree with similar statements about
minority legislators (see also Barrett 1995). Carroll (2002, 57) notes that,
although the commitment to representing women was widely shared among
congresswomen, the congresswomen of color "talked in somewhat different
ways" about that responsibility. Some "expressed the inseparability of their
identities as, and their responsibilities to, people of color and women"; others
expressed a particularly strong sense of responsibility to poor and working
class women, or to women outside the United States (see also Garcia Bedolla
et al. 2005).

The latest research on women of color in state legislatures is equally illuminating. Kathleen Bratton, Kerry Haynie, and Beth Reingold's (2006) analysis of bill introductions reveals that African American female lawmakers
are uniquely responsive to both black interests and women's interests. They
sponsor just as many black interest measures as do African American men,
and just as many women's interest measures as do nonblack women; they are
also more likely than any others to sponsor at least one black interest and
one women's interest bill. Luis Fraga and colleagues (2005, 1–2) theorize
that Latina public officials "are uniquely positioned to leverage the intersectionality of their ethnicity and gender" in ways that enable them "to be the
most effective long term advocates on behalf of working class communities
of color." Their initial findings show that, although Latina and Latino state
legislators share the same basic policy priorities, Latinas are more likely to
forge coalitions across ethnic and gender lines and are more likely to attempt
to balance women's interests and Latino interests in situations in which they
come into conflict.

Other researchers, however, caution that women of color in elective
office may face unique and uniquely challenging obstacles as well. Mary
Hawkesworth (2003), Marsha Darling (1998), and Wendy Smooth (2001)
document the ways that institutional racism and sexism interact, in Congress
and in state legislatures, to constrain, marginalize, silence, and discredit

women of color and the interests they attempt to represent. On the other hand, Hawkesworth (2003) notes, the anger and resistance engendered by these experiences may help explain why congresswomen of color adopt the policy priorities they do, especially those that seem doomed to failure but speak forcefully and respectfully on behalf of poor women of color.

Position Power. As the congressional research often demonstrates, positions of institutional power or authority can have significant effects on the policy efforts of the women who occupy them. Noelle Norton (1995, 2002) reveals, for example, how important committee and subcommittee membership can be. Even on highly salient issues such as reproductive health, little significant activity in Congress takes place outside that committee structure. Without access to such positions, congresswomen's ability to participate in, much less influence, reproductive policy making is minimal at best. Others (Dodson 2006; Hawkesworth et al. 2001; Swers 2002) show that the ability of congresswomen to legislate on behalf of women is also constrained by their level of seniority and their status as members of the majority or minority party (which determine their access to positions of power on committees and within party leadership).[7]

Perhaps this comes as no surprise to congressional scholars; those in positions of institutional power are those most likely to influence policy, regardless of sex (e.g., Hall 1996). Yet Swers (2002) offers an additional, important insight: institutional status not only helps determine the success or effectiveness of women's policy efforts but also can affect the decision to pursue those goals in the first place. If one assumes, as Swers does, that legislators (male and female) are strategic actors, then it follows that they will choose to pursue only those policy proposals that are likely to help them reach their goals of reelection, policy change, or institutional influence (Fenno 1973). Access to key committees, key committee positions, majority party status, and party leadership will likely make some policy proposals more strategically viable, and thus worthwhile, than others. In short, we should not assume that policy priorities of public officials are exogenous reflections of pure, sincere preferences. Rather, they are likely to be determined at least in part by strategic assessments of institutional power arrangements and political opportunities.

Institutions

Those who study women in American politics are well aware that political institutions are gendered (Beckwith 2005; Duerst-Lahti 2002; Duerst-Lahti and Kelly 1995; Hawkesworth 2003; Kenney 1996). Historically male-dominated, the norms, procedures, and goals of legislatures, city councils, and school boards all have potentially gendered implications and biases that privilege men and all that is associated with them. Unfortunately, though, too little of the research on women in elective office has focused directly on the inner workings of governing institutions and their gendered characteristics. Although there are myriad institutional arrangements that could affect women's political representation (and vice versa), only the following three have received significant attention.[8]

Critical Mass. Although the fifty state legislatures offer fertile ground for systematic, comparative institutional analyses, relatively few studies of women's representation take advantage of such opportunities. Those that do usually employ some version of "critical mass" theory to explain variation across states in the relationship between women's descriptive and substantive representation. Applying Rosabeth Moss Kanter's (1977) work on the effects of sex ratios in corporate settings, political scientists (most notably Thomas 1994) have theorized that the degree to which women "make a difference" depends on their numbers or proportions within representative institutions. The theory (as adapted) posits that when women constitute a small "token" minority (approximately 15 percent or less), the pressures to conform to male norms are too great, and the collective will and power to resist are too weak. As the numbers and proportions of women in office increase (across states or over time), however, such restrictions will be overcome more easily. In short, female officials will avoid acting for women until they are surrounded by a critical mass of female colleagues, and transformation of state politics by women for women will be unlikely until women constitute at least a substantial minority (20–30 percent) of officeholders.

Although two of the earliest tests of critical mass theory (Saint-Germain 1989; Thomas 1994) produced encouraging results, most other studies have found little confirming evidence (Barrett 1997; Bratton 2002, 2005; Carroll 2001; Considine and Deutchman 1996; Diamond 1977; Ford and Dolan 1995; Thomas and Welch 1991; Tolbert and Steuernagel 2001; Weldon 2004). There is no clear, positive relationship between sex ratios in legislative rosters and (1) the frequency or magnitude of sex differences in legislative behavior or (2) overall levels of policy activity or outcomes promoting women's political interests. Plus, some of the more recent research suggests that, although the growing presence of women "regenders" (Beckwith, this volume) legislative institutions, it does so in different, or at least more complicated, ways than critical mass theory anticipated.

Several studies (Barrett 1997; Kathlene 1994; Rosenthal 1998) suggest that the empowering effects of critical mass may be mitigated by a backlash from male colleagues who feel their dominant status threatened by the influx of women. Kathlene (1994), for example, has found that as the proportion of women participating in committee hearings increased, the men became more verbally aggressive and conversationally dominant. Cindy Simon Rosenthal (1998) also argues that the effects of women's increasing *power* within legislative institutions (namely, their ability to gain leadership positions) may be more significant than the effects of women's increasing numbers.

"[A]s women's share of institutional power increases," Rosenthal (1998, 90) reports, "male committee chairs become less inclined toward such integrative behaviors of leadership as collaboration, inclusiveness, and accommodation, whereas women committee chairs become more likely to embrace these integrative strategies." Women's increasing institutional power thus promoted both the sort of positive, transformative effects among women that critical mass theory predicts and the negative, resistant effects among men that a backlash theory would predict.

Kathleen Bratton (2005) calls explicitly for a reexamination of critical mass theory.[9] She finds no evidence that "token" women are any less likely to introduce women's interest bills or that they are any less successful getting their bills passed or assuming leadership positions – or that women's interest legislation fares better in more gender diverse legislatures. In the few instances in which the sex composition of the legislature mattered, "token" women appeared *more* distinctive in their agenda-setting activity and *more* successful in bill passage (see also Crowley 2004). As Bratton (2005) points out, Kanter (1977) herself recognized that minimization of sex differences (via conformity to masculine norms) may not be women's only response to tokenism. Token women may also respond by overachieving or promoting themselves and their achievements. Furthermore, Bratton argues, in legislative (as opposed to corporate) settings in which female officials "may be regarded as experts on political matters of relevance to women, and may be encouraged to focus on women's issues" the incentives to distinguish oneself as an advocate of women may be greater than the incentives to act like men (103).

Another reason token women may be more rather than less likely to act for women is that they are more likely to feel responsible for doing so. Reingold (2000) and Carroll (2002) note that female officials often explain that their commitment to representing women is a response to the realization that no one else is going to do it. Thus as the number of female colleagues increases, individual women officeholders may perceive less need to assume those responsibilities themselves (Carroll 2001; Reingold 2000). Bratton and colleagues (2006) also have found that African American female state legislators sponsor fewer women's interest bills when surrounded by more female colleagues – because, in all likelihood, the responsibility for women's substantive representation can be shared more easily and evenly than the responsibility for black substantive representation.

Women's Institutional Power. Gaining positions of institutional power can affect not only the individual women occupying them but also the institution as a whole. As mentioned earlier, it could change the way committees are run and how influence in general is wielded. All of these changes, in turn, may have a particularly strong empowering effect on the female members of the institution. In a 2004 online survey, a large majority of female state legislators "acknowledge that their effectiveness and inclusion depends on having women in key positions" (Rosenthal 2005, 211). Most also believed that the men in leadership positions "forget to include women" and "discount women's advice" in their decision making.

Yet women's institutional power (and the gendered nature of policymaking power) may not simply be a function of the number of women or of the number of women occupying leadership positions. It may also be a function of women's capacity to organize collectively. Thomas (1994, 100) was one of the first to draw attention to the power of women's legislative caucuses in particular. Noting that women's issue bills were more likely to pass in state legislatures that had a formal women's caucus, she concluded that such organizations represent "political clout" and establish women's "legitimacy within the wider legislative environment" (see also Carroll 2001; CAWP 2001; but see Weldon 2004). Studies of congressional policy making by and for women also demonstrate that success was often dependent on the willingness and ability of congresswomen to coalesce, which in turn depended (in part) on the organizational resources and institutional clout of the (now defunct) Congressional Caucus for Women's Issues (CCWI) (Dodson 1998; Hawkesworth et al. 2001). The links between women's descriptive and substantive representation appeared strongest when the CCWI was able to reach a bipartisan consensus on a specific agenda of women's issues and to promote it aggressively as such.

Party Control and Dominant Factions. The demise of the CCWI may be attributed, as Irwin Gertzog (2004) suggests, to growing divisions among congresswomen and their increasing numbers, ambition, and access to positions of power. In other words, it may have lost its usefulness as a mechanism by which women could gain institutional power and link women's descriptive and substantive representation. Perhaps the biggest blow to the CCWI, however, came when the Republicans took control of the House of Representatives in 1995 and stripped it and all other legislative service organizations (LSOs) of their institutional resources. This move to abolish the LSOs may have appeared neutral on its face, but it was clearly perceived as gendered and raced by many of the congresswomen involved (Hawkesworth 2003). It also illustrates one of several ways that researchers have documented the effects of that transition of party control on women's substantive representation in Congress.

The all-important committee leadership positions switched, taking power "most directly relevant to the substantive representation of women" away from sympathetic Democratic men and concentrating it "in the hands of conservative men" (Dodson 2005, 138). Dodson (2006, 37) also notes how the Republican leadership shifted power away from standing committees to even more male-dominated "ad hoc task forces comprised of loyal [conservative] Republicans." Losing majority-party status thus severely restricted the policy-making efforts of Democratic women, especially on women's issues. Yet gaining majority party status did not exactly free Republican women to take over leadership on women's issues (Dodson 2006; Evans 2005; Swers 2002). Of course, conservative Republican women were never eager to take the lead on women's issues, and moderate Republican women had long risked ruffling the feathers of the party leadership by initiating and supporting women's issues, especially the more feminist ones (Evans 2005). Gaining majority status made pushing women's issues – and thus defecting from the increasingly rigid, conservative party line – even riskier. Much more was at stake for these moderate Republican women (especially the more senior ones), including their own leadership status within the party and their new-found ability to pursue other district and policy priorities (Dodson 2006; Swers 2002).[10]

In sum, the potential effect of party control on women's substantive representation is not only a matter of whether Democrats are in the majority or how many women happen to reap the benefits of majority party status. It is also a matter of which faction within the majority party holds sway and how tightly it controls the caucus and the institution as a whole.

Political Context

Even though "various measures of political culture" are the "best predictors" of how many women get elected to state legislatures (Norrander and Wilcox 1998, 116), the research on women in state and local office has had little to say about whether or how the "outside" political world might affect choices, processes, and outcomes "inside" governing institutions. With few exceptions (Ford and Dolan 1995; Reingold 2000; Rosenthal 1998), political culture – defined only in terms of Daniel Elazar's (1984) three-part typology – is included only as a control variable, if at all.

Ford and Dolan's (1995) study of regional differences among female state legislators provides one of the most interesting exceptions. Southern women, they find, are much less likely to identify themselves as feminists but, at the same time, are more likely to list women, children, and family issues as legislative priorities. Southern women's leadership on women's issues may seem contrary to common assumptions about "traditionalistic" southern political culture (Elazar 1984), but, as Ford and Dolan point out, such expectations are usually based on the assumption that women's issues are feminist and transformational. If leadership on such issues is instead seen as congruent with women's traditional roles "as guardians of domesticity and the sanctity of the family," then the higher levels of such activity among southern women may make more sense (345). This further suggests that the larger political context surrounding public officials can shape the very meaning of women's interests, how "women's issues" are framed, and which women's issues are more viable than others.

Not surprisingly, the comparisons of women's policy making in the 103rd and 104th Congresses have a lot to say about the impact of the larger political context (Dodson 2005, 2006; Hawkesworth et al. 2001; Swers 2002; Swers and Larson 2005). They leave little doubt that an increasingly partisan, polarized, and conservative political environment can take a toll on advocates of women's substantive representation. It is that environment that produced, shaped, and reinforced the conservative Republican majority in Congress and its effects on the women's issue agenda, the CCWI, and moderate Republican women in particular. However, this research points to another important dimension of contemporary American politics: the gender gap among voters and the issues, organizations, and movements thought to fuel it.

The gender gap and the ensuing competition for women's votes give both parties a stake in women's substantive representation, and they empower women in office who seek to provide that representation. According to Swers (2002, 24), party leaders often turn to their female colleagues "to act as spokespersons on women's, children's, and family issues" and to attract women voters (see also Dodson 2006). "Thus, substantive representation of women is facilitated not only by increasing women's presence as members of Congress, but also by a strong and vibrant women's movement that can mainstream what was once nontraditional, raise the consciousness of women voters and women members, and fuel gender gap pressures that legitimize women members' contributions to gender difference in the eyes of male colleagues" (Dodson 2005, 134).

The power of the gender gap can be elusive, though. First, it only works "for those congresswomen who agree with their party's position on specific issues"; those who stray too far from the party line will not be able to leverage gender gap politics to their advantage (Swers 2002, 29). Second, as the post–September 11 world so clearly demonstrates, gender-gap politics come and go. As Swers (2002, 132) predicted, "the power derived from electoral sources such as the gender gap is highly contingent on the centrality of the group and its interests to the party's voting coalition. As concerns about defense and ways to combat terrorism dominate the Congressional agenda, the ability of women to capitalize on issues related to the gender gap is diminished" (see also Dodson 2005, 137).

Consideration of gender-gap politics also sheds much needed light on the role of women's organizations, interest groups, and movements in effecting women's substantive representation within and by governing institutions. As Banaszak (this volume) notes, "first wave" women's movements were instrumental in the development of modern interest group approaches to legislative influence (e.g., lobbying, petition drives), yet hardly any research on women officeholders focuses on their connections to and interactions with such groups and movements. S. Laurel Weldon (2004) comes close when she observes that state government efforts to combat violence against women are much more responsive to women's organizing outside the state ("feminist civil society") than to either the presence or the organization of women inside the state legislatures – but she neglects the possibility that women inside the state were conduits for women's organizations outside the state (see Dodson 2006).

CONCLUDING RECOMMENDATIONS

The willingness and ability of women (and men) in public office to enhance the substantive representation of women, as well as their conceptions of what that should entail, vary quite a bit. This chapter offers numerous suggestions for understanding and, perhaps, explaining that variation. At the individual level, we could examine more closely and thoroughly the differences in party affiliation, ideology (political and gender), race, ethnicity, and position power among female officeholders. We would also do well to think harder about the nature of constituencies and winning electoral coalitions and women's visibility within them. At the contextual level, we could benefit from more historical and comparative approaches that might account for the effects of changes in interest group and social movement formation, public opinion, voting behavior, and issue cycles.

It is at the level of institutions, however, that some of our most challenging and creative efforts could be directed. We could capitalize on the most recent critiques of critical mass theory and consider the numerous ways in which the gender – and racial and ethnic – diversity of a political institution might (or might not) affect individual and collective behavior on behalf of women and women's interests. Beyond questions of numbers and proportions, we could examine more closely the collective resources of female officeholders – how those resources are amassed and with what effect. We should always keep in mind the powerful ways political parties and dominant coalitions structure – and gender – most aspects of policy making and representational behavior. Finally, we should be open to considering the gender dynamics of other institutional forces and characteristics, including electoral incentives, professionalization, procedural rules and regulations, committee structure, fiscal and budgetary imperatives, interinstitutional relations (between legislative, executive, and judicial branches), and intergovernmental relations (between national, state, and local governments).

Tackling this research agenda will enable and require us to build on many of the strengths of the existing research, most notably its epistemological and methodological pluralism. Maintaining an open dialogue with other subfields in the discipline – including legislative studies, state politics and policy making, urban politics, and race and ethnic politics – is key. Each of these subfields can offer additional theoretical, conceptual, empirical, and analytic tools. Each also could benefit from a better understanding of sex, gender, and processes of group representation. The research on women in public office also has successfully employed a multitude of methodological approaches (from in-depth, qualitative case studies to large N, multivariate statistical analyses) and measurement tools (in-depth interviews, surveys, legislative records, etc.). Maintaining that diversity of approaches and that large toolkit is also key. Paying more attention to variation across individuals, institutions, and time, however, will require us to undertake more systematic comparative analyses and more historical or longitudinal approaches as well. Those types of analyses and approaches, in turn, would benefit from greater collaboration and coordination among scholars, especially when it comes to case selection and data collection.

The central, underlying lesson for future research lies at the theoretical and conceptual level, in the way we think about the links between women's descriptive and substantive representation. Like the relationship between sex and gender (Beckwith 2005, 131), the strength and the nature of the relationship between women's descriptive and substantive representation must be recognized as potentially uncertain and fluid (Reingold 2000, 49). Gendered representation is not simply a matter of sex differences; like gender itself, it can and does vary across individuals of all sorts, across institutional and cultural contexts, and over time. Capturing, understanding, and explaining that variation is what lies at the forefront of current and future research on women as officeholders in the United States.

Notes

1. See Dovi (this volume) for a full discussion of the various concepts of political representation, including definitions of "descriptive" and "substantive" representation.

2. Of course, when it comes to roll-call votes, even a small gender gap could mean the difference between passage and failure. Almost no research examines whether women's votes make such a difference.

3. Some studies also report that male legislators are more active on "men's issues" (e.g., fiscal affairs, commerce) than are female legislators (Fridkin and Woodall 2005; Reingold 2000; Thomas and Welch 1991).

4. Dahlerup (2006a) and Dodson (2006) advocate abandoning altogether the question of whether women "make a difference" precisely because it is too often and too simplistically conflated with the existence of sex differences in legislative behavior.

5. Although Fox and Schuhmann (1999) studied unelected city managers, they ask similar questions about gendered leadership styles.

6. See also recent discussions of surrogate representation (Carroll 2002; Dodson 2006; Dovi, this volume; Mansbridge 2003).

7. Saltzstein (1986) also shows that the impact of female mayors on gender parity in municipal employment is greater when they have greater institutional authority – that is, in the absence of city managers.

8. The only other institutional variable discussed at any length, institutional professionalization, is specific to state legislative research (see Cammisa and Reingold 2004).
9. See also the "Critical Perspectives" symposium on critical mass in *Politics & Gender* 2(2006): 491–530.
10. An added concern, according to Evans (2005), was their electoral vulnerability.

Theorizing Women's Representation in the United States

Suzanne Dovi

From the perspective of women's experiences, it is easy to see that democratic representative institutions can be tools of oppression.[1] After all, formal democratic institutions have been either a form of governance that has *only* ruled over women (e.g., women were formally prohibited from holding elected offices) or a form of governance in which women have ruled and been ruled *unequally* (e.g., the number of female representatives have been significantly lower than the number of male representatives).[2] Moreover, there is good reason to believe that informal representative institutions, such as interest groups, do not work as well for multiply disadvantaged groups (Strolovitch 2007). These facts suggest that democratic representative institutions need to be viewed with suspicion. We need to know why democratic representative institutions do not work for women as well as they work for powerful men, and we need to know what conditions contribute to those institutions working better for women. We also should not assume that representative institutions in democracies necessarily benefit all women. In fact, we need to recognize how representative institutions can divide women, pitting some women's interests and preferences against other women's interests and preferences. Democratic representative institutions can function to preserve the status quo, distributing benefits unjustly and inequitably among different groups of women.

Knowing if and how well representative institutions are working for women in democracies depends, in part, on one's understanding of what counts as the adequate representation of women in a democracy. Does the

I thank Christina Wolbrecht, Karen Beckwith, and Lisa Baldez for their helpful comments. In addition, I thank Sigal Ben-Porath, Amanda Driscoll, Kara Ellerby, Kris Kanthak, Jane Mansbridge, Barbara Norrander, Trina Running, and the participants in the "Political Women and American Democracy" conference as well as in my graduate seminar for their comments and conversations. Most of all, I thank Houston Smit, whose conversations, support, and help made this chapter possible.

adequate representation of women require female representatives? If so, how many? Do the opinions, interests, and perspectives of these female representatives matter? Does the adequate representation of women depend on simply the passing and implementation of policies that most women consider to be "women-friendly"? Does the adequate representation of women require outside pressure on both male *and* female representatives? Does such outside pressure need to come from women?

Any conscientious attempt to answer these questions requires, as Iris Marion Young (1994) wisely recommends, attending to "questions about how and whether women in a particular time and place suffer discrimination and limitation on their action and desires" (715). Following Young's advice, in this chapter I focus on the representation (or lack thereof) of U.S. women. More specifically, I survey recent theoretical and empirical research on representation in general and the representation of U.S. women in particular to identify those conceptual tools that can best help us understand whether and when U.S. women are being adequately represented.[3] My intent is not to compare the representation of U.S. women with the representation of other women (e.g., the parité movement in France) but rather to focus on the representation of U.S. women specifically.[4] I do so partially because the U.S. falls behind many other democracies in its attempt to increase the number of women in public office.[5]

My focus on the political representation of U.S. women is motivated by two main considerations. First, it will help us rethink a common bias among U.S. political scientists that increasing descriptive representation will promote further democraticization and improve the substantive representation of U.S. women.[6] Such scholars treat the representation of women as a numbers game – the more women, the better the democracy. Such thinking has been used to justify institutional reforms, such as party list quotas and gender quotas that are specifically aimed at increasing the number of female representatives. Although the inclusion of *some* women does have some advantages, as I discuss later, the assumption that increasing the number of women improves the level of democraticization fails to treat seriously how democratic representative institutions can distribute benefits unjustly among different groups of women. It naively assumes that the benefits and privileges of some women will translate into giving all women a voice in the United States. It also ignores how the opinions, interests, and perspectives of those female representatives influence the degree to which democratic institutions approximate their ideals.

Second, I understand political representation to be a major, albeit limited, way that power is distributed in the United States. In stating this, I want to avoid being understood as simply reducing democracy to political representation.[7] Examining the representation of U.S. women, be it in formal or informal political institutions, is an important starting place for reevaluating both the oppressive and the liberating potential of democratic institutions for U.S. women.[8] By surveying recent theoretical and empirical work, we can be in a better position to identify the costs (and possibly even some benefits)[9] of having relatively few U.S. women among the political elites. As this chapter shows, improvements to the substantive representation of women and to democratic institutions can depend on *which* women hold offices, as well as on how representative institutions are gendered. It is not enough to assume that competitive elections will safeguard women's needs.

I begin with a broad question: What do we mean by the representation of women? For its answer, I turn to the theoretical literature on political representation as well as to recent feminist contributions to that literature. After exposing two persistent problems facing those who wish to assess the representation of U.S. women, what I call "the standards problem" and "the inclusion problem," I recommend several ways that those who wish to study the representation of U.S. women might proceed. Finally, I conclude by summarizing the insights in the theoretical literature on representation that are vital to studying and assessing the representation of U.S. women.

THE POLITICAL REPRESENTATION OF U.S. WOMEN

Most theoretical discussions of political representation begin with Hanna Pitkin (1967). Pitkin's classic work sets the terms of how we think about political representation. In particular, she identifies four alternative views of representation: (1) the formalistic view, which focuses on the processes of authorization and accountability; (2) descriptive representation, which focuses on the extent to which representatives "resemble" or share certain experiences with the represented; (3) symbolic representation, which examines the emotional response of the represented to the representative; and (4) substantive representation, which focuses on the activity of advancing the interests of those represented.

Each view of representation provides an alternative approach for assessing the quality and success of the representation of U.S. women. U.S. women could vote their representatives in and out of office (formalistic view). U.S. women could resemble or share certain experiences with their representatives (descriptive representation). U.S. women can feel represented (symbolic representation). Finally, U.S. representatives can act on women's behalf, advancing "women's interests" (substantive representation).

Pitkin's discussion of political representation also shows why evaluating the representation of U.S. women is such a difficult task. The concept of representation is itself paradoxical: each view of representation contains different and sometimes contradictory standards for how representatives should behave. For instance, the descriptive view of representation assesses representatives by their similarities to their constituents, for example, their shared racial or ethnic characteristics. In contrast, substantive representation evaluates representatives by whether they are good delegates (those who follow the expressed preferences of their constituents) or good trustees (those who follow their own understanding of their constituents' best interests). Pitkin suggests reconciling these contradictory standards by evaluating representatives according to the "best interests" of the represented. However, establishing commonly agreed-on criteria would be necessary for determining the "best interests" of the represented, and unfortunately, Pitkin never specifies how we are to identify such criteria.

Those who study the representation of U.S. women face similar difficulties.[10] Not only can the standards for evaluating the representation of U.S. women contradict each other, but there are also no commonly agreed-on criteria for identifying "women's interests" (Diamond and Hartstock 1981; Jónasdóttir 1989; Sapiro 1981). In fact, by attending to the differences among U.S. women, it becomes clear that benefits from democratic institutions can be distributed unfairly among different groups of women (Collins 2000; Crenshaw 1991, 1989; Hancock 2007; McCall 2005). As a result, there can be an infinite regress of different women's interests, thereby dissolving the category of women into mere individuals (Young 1994, 721). Although useful for identifying various ways that women can be represented, Pitkin's analysis is less helpful for determining which women are *adequately* represented in the United States or whether U.S. women can be adequately represented.[11]

Recent empirical and theoretical research holds at least three important insights into how political scientists should approach the question of whether U.S. women are being adequately represented. The first insight is that the adequate representation of U.S. women will not occur exclusively in legislative bodies. In particular, Laurel Weldon (2002b) argues persuasively that political scientists should not simply "count bodies" in legislatures – that is, count the number of women in legislatures – to determine how well women are being represented. The representation of U.S. women depends on nongovernmental actors, such as women's movements and interest groups. In fact, one of the many important contributions of this volume is its focus beyond the mere presence of women in the U.S. Congress. Weldon's work suggests that the activities within civil society are crucial to the adequate representation of U.S. women. Building on her insights, it is important to recognize how other features of a political society, such as the right to association and the availability of political resources, can influence the quality of the representation of U.S. women.

A second important insight into our understanding of whether women are adequately represented comes from Jane Mansbridge (2003). Mansbridge identifies four forms of democratic representation in the United States (promissory, anticipatory, gyroscopic, and surrogacy).[12] Mansbridge claims that the normative criteria for each form of democratic representation vary. For example, promissory representation would require representatives to keep their campaign promises to women, whereas gyroscopic representation would require representatives to provide opportunities for women to assess the candidate's character for them to represent U.S. women adequately. The proper criteria for determining whether U.S. women are adequately represented partially depend on which form of democratic representation is being employed. Those concerned with the adequate representation of U.S. women will need to specify which form or forms of representation they are examining and determine whether the representative is acting consistently with the normative criteria specific to that form. For our purposes here, Mansbridge's classification system is important because it opens the possibility that U.S. women can be adequately represented *in more than one way*. It also reveals the need to identify indicators that would signal *which* women are *not* being adequately represented according to each of these forms.

One final insight is implicit within the recent theoretical literature on representation: improving the representation of U.S. women (or at least increasing the number of female elected officials) does not automatically mean that the U.S. political system will better approximate democratic ideals. After all, political representation is not necessarily democratic (Rehfeld 2006);[13] thus, improving the representation of some women does not necessarily mean that the society as a whole is becoming more democratic. This is true not only because women do not necessarily value democratic institutions (Dovi 2007) but also because improving the representation of some women can come at a cost to other women (Cohen 1999; Dovi 2002; Young 2000). Moreover, improving the representation of women can also come at a cost to other groups – racial minorities, sexual minorities, or even the dominant white male majority. Increases in the number of female public officials by themselves should not be taken as evidence of further democratization.

In addition, as Adolph Reed Jr. (1986) argues, mass mobilization around identity might constitute a new mode of domination, an "artificial negativity" that creates an illusory opposition so that the social management system can control that opposition. Reed's work implies that the inclusion of U.S. women in representative institutions could function to preserve the status quo and thereby the inequalities within the U.S. political system. Reed's work also suggests that an increase of female representatives will only be likely to improve democracies if those representatives (and the people who support them) value certain things – such as democratic representative institutions that proactively address gender inequalities and reconcile political conflicts fairly.

FEMINIST CONTRIBUTIONS TO UNDERSTANDING THE REPRESENTATION OF WOMEN

Feminist theorists have made many important and shamefully overlooked contributions to democratic theory. To view democratic institutions from feminist perspectives is to enter a much richer and more complicated vision of politics than the one typically held by political scientists (Childs 2006). Anne Phillips (1991) captured this insight, writing, "Feminism multiplies the places within which democracy appears relevant, and then it alters the dimensions as well. 'Details matter'" (159). Not only have feminist theorists challenged conventional ways of knowing and researching political life (Zerilli 1998), but they have also expanded the proper scope of democratic theory: broadening the unit of analysis from the individual to the family unit (Okin 1989), rejecting simplistic divisions between the public/private arena (Elshtain 1981; Landes 1988), criticizing the gendered assumptions of political research (Phillips 1991; Sapiro 1979, 1987), and providing a more fluid and complex understanding of our political identities.

Recognizing all of the feminist contributions to democratic theory is clearly beyond the proper scope of this chapter. For this reason, I concentrate on only four feminist contributions that improve our understanding of the adequate representation of U.S. women: (1) feminist theorists have expanded our understanding of *what* needs to be represented; (2) feminist theorists have identified formal as well as informal barriers to the representation of U.S. women; (3) feminist theorists have recognized how the gendered nature of political institutions affects the representation of women; and (4) feminist theorists have identified specific representative functions that are more likely to be performed by female than by male representatives.

First, feminist theory has expanded our understanding of *what* needs to be represented. Traditionally, political theorists writing on representation have focused on interests (e.g., Barry 1965/1990). Of course, the concept of interest can be based on subjective criteria, for example, on what a person actually wants, or on objective criteria, for example, on a standard of what is a justifiable interest. Problems arise when objective criteria and subjective criteria conflict. Such problems have led political scientists to set aside the issue of interests and to focus merely on the expressed preferences of constituents (Achen 1975).

Feminist theorists have refined our understanding of what needs to be represented in two important ways. The first refinement occurs in their recognition of the problem of essentialism.[14] Feminists noted that conceptions of "women's interests" often assume some essential understanding of women; that is, they assume all women possess a common identity or shared set of interests. Feminists argue that we should not assume that all women view political issues from the same perspective. We should not evaluate representatives by whether they enact a laundry list of feminist or even "women-friendly" public policies. In fact, the easier it is to identify a list of policies that all women should or do support, the less important it is to have female representatives. After all, male representative could also advance such a laundry list according to Phillips (1998). In this way, Phillips would reject attempts to evaluate the adequate representation of U.S. women by appealing to a particular list of policies.

In response to the problem of essentialism, feminists have introduced two important distinctions: (1) the sex/sexuality/gender distinction and (2) the woman/feminist distinction. The sex/sexuality/gender distinction is important because it differentiates sex (biology, physiology) from sexuality (sexual preferences, sexual orientation, sexual practices) from gender (social roles and status). In particular, the concept of gender focuses on "all those cultural expectations associated with masculinity and femininity that go beyond biological sex differences" (Lipman-Blumen 1984, 3). These distinctions allow us to recognize how gender is socially constructed within any given society: what women are depends on the norms and practices of their society.[15] The woman/feminist distinction emerges because not all women are committed to gender equality, let alone to the elimination of gender hierarchies.[16]

Both the gender/sex/sexuality distinction and the woman/feminist distinction reveal that conceptions of "women's interests" are deeply ideological. Evaluations of the representation of U.S. women in terms of "women's interests" will reflect a particular political bias of the researcher. How we identify interests reflects our commitment (or lack thereof) to feminism.

Iris Marion Young (2000) is responsible for the second feminist refinement about what needs to be represented. For Young, women are represented when their *interests*, *opinions*, and *perspectives* are being advanced. For Young, interests determine the life prospects of individuals, for example, how material resources affect a person's opportunities. Opinions are the values, principles, and priorities of individuals. Perspectives are understood as particular kinds of social meanings, apparent in the types of questions being asked during public deliberations. Women's perspectives are present when participants in public deliberations inquire about the specific impact public policies have on different women. As can be seen, identifying how issues are being framed and whose values are being appealed to are vital for assessing the adequate representation of U.S. women. The adequate representation of U.S. women requires more than satisfying U.S. women's policy preferences.

The second contribution of feminists to our understanding of whether U.S. women are adequately represented is their analysis of the formal and informal barriers to the representation of women.[17] Feminists have denounced such formal barriers as simply unacceptable to the proper functioning of democratic institutions, be those barriers formal prohibitions against women voting or against women running for office.[18]

Feminists have also identified informal barriers to "real representation." For example, Iris Marion Young's (1990) discussion of the five faces of oppression is particularly instructive for understanding the barriers that can prevent citizens from expressing their interests, opinions, and perspectives. According to Young's work, representation would not be adequate when U.S. women face violence, powerlessness, exploitation, cultural imperialism, marginalization, or a combination of these. Admittedly, Young's faces of oppression could be updated. For example, her account of exploitation needs to take better account of the effects of globalization. Nevertheless, Young's analysis of the faces of oppression identifies several existing mechanisms within the U.S. political system that prevent the adequate representation of U.S. women.

For many feminists, formal and informal barriers to women's representation can be detected when rates of participation of women or numbers of women in public office do not reflect the number of women in the population as a whole. As Catharine MacKinnon (1987) wrote, "Feminists have this nasty habit of counting bodies and refusing not to notice their gender" (35). Differences, specifically relative lower numbers of women, are seen as evidence of discrimination.[19]

Third, feminists have provided an analytical framework for assessing how the adequate representation of U.S. women depends on how existing governmental institutions are gendered. For a particularly instructive discussion of gender within the U.S. political system, see Gretchen Ritter's chapter in this volume. It is not enough to examine male-female differences, such as the numbers of women voting or elected to office or leadership-style differences. In particular, it is important to recognize how sex differences become politically relevant to gender experiences. For example, Karin Tamerius (1995) identifies four gendered aspects of representatives' experiences that result from sex differences: (1) the content of sexual divisions of society, (2) their subjective perspectives, (3) mutuality (shared experiences of same-sex groups), and (4) associations including sexually exclusive groups. Tamerius argues that the gendered experiences of legislators will affect their attitudes (support and commitment), as well as their resources (awareness and expertise). Such insights about the complex relationship between sex and gender suggest that political scientists should not treat sex and gender interchangeably. We should not extrapolate gender from the variable of sex (Duerst-Lahti and Kelly 1995a). Joan Acker (1992) provides a particularly fruitful way of analyzing gender in institutional processes, practices, ideologies, and the distribution of power. For instance, Acker helps us see how the meaning of being female – whether positive, negative, or even neutral – can influence the distribution of gender power in representative institutions.[20] Gender needs to be understood as a fluid concept, the substance of which depends on the particular context. (See Beth Reingold's discussion in this volume of how gender might differ when two women run against each other versus when a female candidate runs against a male one.) Feminist theorists have improved our understanding of the adequate representation of U.S. women by revealing how gender norms can constrain and prescribe certain behavior in political institutions (Duerst-Lahti and Kelly 1995b; Rosenthal 2002).

Finally, feminist theorists have improved our understanding of the adequate representation of U.S. women by specifying certain functions that female representatives are more likely to perform than male representatives. These functions emerge in feminist explanations of why women are needed to represent women (e.g., Diamond and Hartsock 1981; Gould 1996; Mansbridge 1999; Phillips 1991, 1995, 1998; Sapiro 1981; Williams 1998;

Young 1990, 2000). To contend that female representatives are necessary for democratic institutions, as these feminists do, contradicts the faith that democratic theorists place in institutional design. For instance, Joseph Schumpeter (1976) argued that the actual choice of representatives is less important than having an institutional design that promotes competition and thereby provides institutional incentives to be accountable and responsive to the electorate. Feminists' arguments for the descriptive representation of women reveal why even the best institutional design for promoting competition is not enough: it matters whether the people who occupy institutional position are women.

In particular, there are at least six distinct arguments for why female representatives are necessary for the adequate representation of U.S. women: *the role-model argument, the justice argument, the trust argument, the legitimacy argument, the transformative argument,* and *the overlooked interests argument.*[21] Each of these arguments points to a different function that female representatives can have in the United States.

The role-model argument contends that the presence of female representatives in the U.S. political system improves female citizens' self-esteem and sense of political efficacy. Seeing Hillary Clinton or Nancy Pelosi in leadership positions increases female citizens' sense of the possible, expanding their career choices to include the highest positions of political power and inspiring other female citizens to imitate their career paths.[22] The role-model argument also captures how female representatives can "mentor" other females. For instance, senior female representatives can mentor their junior female colleagues by teaching them how to raise money (Driscoll and Kanthak n.d.).

The justice argument contends that fairness demands that men and women be present in roughly equal numbers among political elites. As Anne Phillips (1998) asserts, "it is patently and grotesquely unfair for men to monopolize representation" (229). Descriptive representation of women compensates for existing inequalities and combats the formal and informal barriers to participation by supplementing women's access to the political arena. The justice argument links the need for female representatives to U.S. citizens' sense of fairness.[23]

The trust argument focuses on the past betrayals of female citizens by male representatives in the United States. According to the trust argument, increasing the number of female representatives is necessary for female citizens to put their confidence in their representatives.[24] In this regard, U.S. women will only be adequately represented when they have representatives whom they trust. Such trust is likely to have an additional benefit – namely, increasing the participation of female citizens. Having more female representatives is likely to increase the number of women who vote, lobby, and get involved in politics.[25]

The legitimacy argument contends that the presence of female representatives increases the legitimacy of the U.S. democratic institutions (Phillips

1995, 1998).[26] Put simply, the legitimacy of the U.S. government depends on who is present, and thus an all-female Congress could not legitimately represent U.S. men, and an all-male Congress could not legitimately represent U.S. women. In terms of adequate representation, knowing how many of which women is necessary to increase the legitimacy of the U.S. government is critical. Is having a female president sufficient for guaranteeing the adequate representation of U.S. women, or does the adequate representation of U.S. women rely on a critical mass of women being distributed throughout formal and informal representative institutions?

The transformative argument maintains that the presence of female representatives allows representative institutions to approximate better their democratic ideals. Women make representative institutions more democratic. According to the transformative argument, the presence of U.S. female representatives not only changes the norms and political practices of those institutions (Phillips 1998) but also is only possible when the political system has substantially changed (Diamond and Hartsock 1981).[27] This argument implicitly assumes that female representatives will behave in a more democratic fashion (e.g., attending to political inequalities and facilitating democratic deliberations) than existing male representatives. The transformative argument suggests that the adequate representation of U.S. women will depend on systemic changes that make the U.S. political system more democratic.

Finally, the overlooked interests argument holds that democratic deliberations and political agendas can be improved by having more female representatives in public office. (For a discussion of the links between descriptive representation and substantive representation, see Beth Reingold, this volume.) Put bluntly, male representatives are not always aware of how public policies affect female citizens. For this reason, the presence of female representatives can contribute to "the feminization of the political agenda" (the articulation of women's concerns and perspectives in public debates), as well as "the feminization of legislation" (public policies that take into account their effect on women; Childs 2006, 9).[28]

Recently, an important qualification has been introduced about the need for descriptive representation. In particular, Jane Mansbridge (1999) contends that the need for descriptive representation is contingent. The presence of female representatives in the United States would only be necessary under certain conditions. More specifically, Mansbridge identifies four contexts in which descriptive representatives perform certain functions. It follows that U.S. female citizens should prefer female representative when they need

1. to foster adequate communication in contexts of mistrust;
2. to promote innovative thinking in contexts of uncrystallized, not fully articulated interests;[29]

3. to create a social meaning of "ability to rule" for members of a group in historical contexts where that ability has been seriously questioned; and

4. to increase the polity's de facto legitimacy in contexts of past discrimination (Mansbridge 1999, 628).

Note that descriptive representation will only improve the substantive representation of women in the first and second context. The third and fourth contexts promote goods other than substantive representation. Mansbridge reiterates that assessments about whether U.S. women are adequately represented should not focus exclusively on substantive representation. Increasing the number of female representatives in the United States can enhance the capacities of some women to rule themselves and can even increase the legitimacy of U.S. democratic institutions. The need for more women among U.S. political elites depends on the political context. (For a discussion of how political scientists can construct a theory of politicized context around gender, see Nancy Burns's chapter in this volume.) Mansbridge's work suggests that under some conditions, U.S. women could be adequately represented in the absence of female representatives.

THE STANDARDS PROBLEM AND THE INCLUSION PROBLEM

Despite these important insights about assessing the representation of U.S. women, two persistent problems remain: *the standards problem* and *the inclusion problem*. Although these problems are interrelated, by separating them out, it is possible to see how each of these problems can plague assessment of the representation of U.S. women.

The standards problem addresses the difficulty of identifying a proper benchmark for assessing women's political performance in democracies. Should we evaluate men's behavior differently from women's? What standard, if any, should be applied to all female representatives' behavior, or should standards for evaluating female representatives be contingent (and if so, contingent on what)? The standards problem arises because the proper comparison class of female representatives is unclear: should female representative's performance be measured against democratic ideals, male representatives' behavior, other female representatives' behavior, powerful male representative's behavior, or some different standard altogether? There are limitations to adopting all of these standards.

For instance, crafting standards that treat male representatives' behavior as the norm – what Catharine MacKinnon (1988) called the "difference approach" – can ignore the particular barriers experienced by female representatives. Moreover, the difference approach can hide problems that occur when gender roles of male citizens and female citizens converge (Swers 2002).

However, holding female representatives to a set of standards derived from female experiences has its own difficulties. In particular, such standards often focus our attention on outliers (those female representatives who fail to meet those standards adequately) at the expense of paying attention to how such female experiences are tied to gender hierarchies and how adopting such standards can perpetuate gender hierarchies. After all, standards for evaluating female representatives that incorporate – let alone affirm – gender differences can inadvertently incorporate structural injustices. As Kathy Dolan observes in this volume, female candidates are often more qualified than male candidates to achieve the same electoral success. To ignore the different qualifications necessary for female representatives to succeed is to overlook the gender bias within the existing political system. To acknowledge that bias of the existing political system and thereby the need for a two-tier system of standards for male and female candidates seems to hold women to higher standards. To the extent that standards for evaluating female representatives reflect the status quo, and to the extent that the status quo rests on the systemic injustices, standards for evaluating female representatives can be part of the problem, products of systemic injustices.

The second persistent problem that haunts evaluations of the representation of U.S. women is the inclusion problem. The inclusion problem recognizes the costs that come with becoming political insiders. The inclusion problem can take at least two forms. The first emphasizes the costs of including some women rather than other groups of women. The second emphasizes the dangers that accompany the political inclusion of women. Both forms recognize that political inclusion may not always be desirable. Political scientists should not assume that increasing the number of women among the political elites will necessarily improve the substantive representation of women or will necessarily make a polity more democratic.

The first form of the inclusion problem results because of the significant differences among women. Women differ when they have children or do not, are married or not, have been raped or not, are straight or gay, obese or thin, Muslim or Christian, menopausal or prepubescent. These differences matter to the degree that attempts to increase descriptive representation of one group cannot be enacted without marginalizing further other vulnerable subgroups of women. For instance, Young (2000) discusses how the increased representation of Latinos can come at the expense of the representation of gay and lesbian Latinos. Young emphasizes that this is a problem for all representatives, not simply for descriptive representatives. It occurs because one person cannot adequately capture the differences among the many. Cathy Cohen (1999) refers to how including some representatives from marginalized groups leads to marginalization of other members as "secondary marginalization" (70). Members of marginalized groups construct and police group identity so as to regulate behavior, attitudes, and the public image of those groups. To the degree that "women" is a heterogeneous category, democratic institutions can advantage some women as they disadvantage others. Those who study the representation of women must attend to the ways in which female representatives can perpetuate unjust inequalities.

The second form of the inclusion problem focuses on the costs that come with political incorporation. John Dryzek (1996) argued that marginalized groups should be strategic about when and how they want to be included in the state. For Dryzek, marginalized groups should only aim at inclusion in the state when "a group's defining concern can be assimilated in an established or emerging state imperative and . . . civil society is not unduly depleted by the group's entryway into the state" (475). Otherwise, political inclusion can lead to the group being "co-opted or bought off cheaply" (480). Before concluding that increased numbers of female representatives are good for democracy, political scientists need to examine the state imperatives, as well as how much outside pressure is placed on female representatives.

Political scientists also need to differentiate between female representatives as inside players, who can potentially transform the political system, and female representatives who are merely tokens. The election of female legislators "does not guarantee their influence over policies that differentially affect the genders" (Norton 1995, 115). Noelle Norton's work shows how the structure of legislative committee systems and the power of male committee and subcommittee leaders can create institutional roadblocks to female representatives gaining the institutional power position necessary to "exert gender power over policies of importance to women" (115). However, other obstacles to gender power can be more coercive.[30] Eliminating the institutional forms that distribute and maintain hierarchical gender power is crucial for the adequate representation of U.S. women.

FUTURE DIRECTIONS FOR STUDY

I make three concrete recommendations for how we should assess the adequate representation of U.S. women in light of the standards problem and the inclusion problem. First, those who study the relationship between women and democracy should not focus simply on the disadvantages that all women share. Rather, four additional considerations need to be examined:

1. How do representative institutions confer benefits on some men at the expense of conferring the same or different benefits on other women?
2. How do representative institutions confer benefits on some women at the expense of conferring the same or different benefits on other women?
3. How do representative institutions affect *most* women?
4. How do representative institutions impact *the most vulnerable* women?

Because representative institutions create political winners and losers, political scientists need to attend to patterns of privileging, ones that transform and improve the lives of some U.S. women as they disadvantage and marginalize other women.

Second, it is necessary to consider the ability of U.S. women to hold their representatives accountable. As Judith Squires (2005) and Sarah Childs and Mona Lena Krook (2006) suggest, it is important not only to assess *who* represents and *what* gets represented but also to examine *how* the substantive representation of women occurs. It matters whether the substantive representation occurs because women have political influence and can sanction their representatives. It is necessary to look beyond formal mechanisms of authorization and accountability to alternative forms of accountability.

Here Ruth Grant and Robert Keohane's (2005) discussion of accountability in the international arena is particularly instructive. They suggest that in the international arena, we should not assume that the ballot box is necessary for preventing the abuse of power. Sometimes indirect forms of accountability, such as relying on experts to monitor each other (peer accountability) or on public opinion (public reputational accountability), can be effective. Grant and Keohane's insights about alternative forms of accountability suggest that political scientists need to track not only what women's representatives are doing, but also to whom they are responsive and who holds them accountable. Do women's opinions of their representatives count as much as men's opinions? For example, do women lack the peer and reputational forms of accountability needed to sanction their representatives? Does the adequate representation of women require women to possess a certain combination of accountability forms? Which forms of democratic representation enhance the ability of which female citizens to sanction their representatives, and which forms of democratic representation promote representatives' responsiveness to female citizens? Are certain groups of women helped or harmed by having women exercise accountability, be it directly or indirectly? As can be seen, we need more research assessing how well different groups of women can influence and sanction their representatives (if they are able to at all).[31] Because there are different standards for assessing the representation of U.S. women, it is important to examine whether institutional reforms aimed at increasing the number of women in the public arena possess adequate mechanisms of accountability. Here I posit that one factor that matters most for the adequate representation of U.S. women is having sufficient power to sanction their representatives.

Third, it is necessary to create a theoretical framework for determining when and how differences among women matter in representative practices. Should those who study the representation of women simply assume that white female representatives cannot represent black women? Or should they assume that white female representatives can *under certain conditions* represent black women just as black female representatives can *under certain conditions* represent white women? For this second area of research to advance, it is important to understand the conditions that divide and unite different groups of women. Understanding the differences between descriptive representation of women and descriptive representation of race is one important step (Htun 2004). The creation of "intercategorical complexity," as Jane Junn and Nadia Brown's chapter in this volume suggests, is another important step. What is clear from recent theoretical and empirical research is that if we are to take the heterogeneity of gender seriously (and the dangers of secondary marginalization), then assessments of the representation of women cannot treat all women the same.

Consequently, we need to move beyond identifying those groups that need descriptive representation by simply pointing to a group's historical exclusion. For example, Melissa Williams (1998) identifies those groups that need descriptive representation by whether the group has experienced discrimination *over multiple generations*. Such an understanding of which groups require more descriptive representation, though, does not adequately consider how democratic citizens must sometimes choose between different disadvantaged groups (black women or white women) to receive more descriptive representation. Democratic citizens need to forgo simplistic oppressor-oppressed distinctions that fail to acknowledge how women participate in and can benefit from gender hierarchies. Improving the representation of some U.S. women can be inextricably tied to the exclusion of other women.

This means that new modes of domination and existing forms of exclusion are relevant for assessing who needs more descriptive representation. Groups that have been marginalized over multiple generations are not the only ones who lack adequate representation. In fact, if the need for descriptive representation is contingent, feminist theorists need to confront the fact that present forms of exclusion might sometimes outweigh historical ones. Determining which vulnerable subgroups of women should be prioritized is certainly not easy. However, such questions are integral for determining whether certain groups of U.S. women are being adequately represented.

In particular, we need to reconsider the importance of ideological and religious differences among women. (For a discussion of conservative women's movements, see Lee Ann Banaszak's article in this volume.) Here we need more scholarship on how conservative women can advance the interests of some women despite the opposition from some feminist women. We need a better understanding of the relationship between a politics of presence (what Phillips calls descriptive representation) and the politics of ideas.[32] One place to begin is with political ideologies that contribute to the exclusion of certain groups. We need to differentiate representatives who promote gender hierarchies, for example, in justifying policies by presuming certain gender hierarchies or in inciting violence toward women from those that seek to undermine gender hierarchies. A lot more needs to be said about how empirical research and theoretical accounts should account for differences among women. What I can say here is that feminists should not presume that privileged representatives – whether those representatives are white males or white females – promote hierarchies or that all representatives from disadvantaged groups seek to undermine hierarchies.

What may be most necessary for a proper assessment of the representation of U.S. women is an analysis of how the institutional conditions constrain different women's choices of their representatives (Hayward 2000). Understanding how norms and informal practices can prevent U.S. representative institutions from living up to democratic ideals is crucial for creating realistic expectations of any female or male representative. Such an understanding can benefit from recognizing the inclusion problem – specifically, how the pursuit of one political strategy (e.g., incorporation) may serve some women while harming others. If this is true, perhaps one of the most enduring lessons from feminist theorists is that we need to continue to be suspicious of how U.S. representative institutions distribute privileges. Feminist contributions to our understanding of representative institutions provide an important check on the rhetoric of democracy, exposing the ways our democratic rhetoric is overinflated and highlighting the need to proceed cautiously.

CONCLUSION

So what does it mean for U.S. women to be adequately represented? My survey of the literature has provided only a tentative answer to that question. First, we cannot determine whether U.S. women are adequately represented simply by examining the substantive representation of women. This is true because attempts to define "women's interests" are likely to be deeply ideological and controversial, but also because the opinions and perspectives of women are vital to their adequate representation. Political scientists need to attend to how U.S. policies are framed, which values are expressed and which questions are asked within representative institutions, and how these can potentially work against certain women. It is not enough for just some women's interests, opinions, and perspectives to be present: the adequate representation of women requires the presence of women's *multiple* interests, opinions, and perspectives.

Second, those who wish to determine whether U.S. women are being adequately represented must pay attention to context. The institutional legacy of representative institutions is relevant. For instance, the historical prohibitions against women voting influence the extent to which female representatives are needed. So do the institutional norms and practices that continue to constrain women's choices about their representatives and their capacities to sanction their representatives. The political inclusion of more women alone is not necessarily a sign of democratic progress. Furthermore, to pay attention to the relevant political context means examining political behavior outside formal governmental institutions. Finally, the importance of context to evaluations of the representation of women suggests that the adequate representation of U.S. women is likely to take different forms.

This leads to my third and final point: evaluations about the adequate representation of U.S. women depend on what is properly considered possible.

Without better empirical evidence on how many, and which, female representatives are necessary to make U.S. women's multiple interests, opinions, and
perspectives present and to give them adequate voice in democratic representative institutions, political scientists risk holding female representatives to
too high – or possibly even too low – a standard. To reduce such risks, political scientists must keep in mind how democratic representative institutions
can be both potential tools of oppression *and* tools of liberation.

Notes

1. By democratic representative institutions, I mean those formal as well as informal
   political institutions used to advance public policies within democratic states.
   For a full discussion of my understanding of democratic representation, see Dovi
   (2007).
2. For a discussion of how men disproportionately represent women in all democratic states, see Inglehart and Norris (2003) and Nelson and Chowdhury (1994).
3. Of course, not all feminists support such a project. Those who reject liberal
   democracy or who embrace some radical forms of feminism could argue that
   women can never be adequately represented within the current U.S. system. I do
   not wish to argue here for whether the United States is sufficiently democratic to
   represent U.S. women. Instead I presuppose the legitimacy of liberal democracy
   and intend to articulate the theoretical assumptions necessary for assessments
   of whether the current U.S. system adequately represents women.
4. For a comparative perspective, see Lisa Baldez (this volume).
5. According to Pippa Norris (2000), women generally do better in Nordic countries, averaging 38.3 percent, whereas other countries such as Kuwait or the
   United Arab Emirates have few or no female representatives. In the U.S. Congress
   at the time of this writing, a record total of sixteen women serve in the Senate and
   seventy-one women sit in the House. In the United States, seventy-six women
   hold statewide elective executive posts, and the proportion of women in state
   legislatures is at 23.5 percent (Center for American Women and Politics 2007a).
6. Christine di Stefano (1997) contends that democraticization does not necessarily
   improve the conditions of women.
7. For more robust visions of democracy, see Carole Pateman (1970) and Chantal
   Mouffe (1992).
8. Not everyone considers getting more women into elected offices to be politically
   significant. For some, the integration of women into the political system is only
   significant to the degree to which such integration changes the structure of the
   political system. See Cohen, Jones, and Tronto (1997).
9. For instance, Virginia Woolf (1966) recognizes the value of women having "a
   society of outsiders" for transforming political relations.
10. Some feminists contend that women have distinctive interests from men. For
    instance, according to Kathy Ferguson (1984), such distinctive interests emerge
    from women's disproportionate association with mothering and reproduction,
    the political economy of the gendered division of labor, and the arrangement
    of the female body. Others argue that women's distinctive interest is in ending
    gender oppression.

11. Pitkin's account does not capture the changing political realities about how democratic citizens are currently represented. For helpful discussions of the various ways that contemporary democratic citizens are represented, see Rehfeld (2006) and Warren and Castiglione (2004).

12. This classificatory scheme of how women are being represented in the United States raises new and interesting research questions: Are female citizens more likely than male citizens to rely on surrogate representation – that is, on representatives whom they did not directly authorize? Do U.S. women require all four forms of democratic representation to be adequately represented?

13. In contrast, David Plotke (1997) argues that representation is democracy.

14. For discussions of the problem of essentialism, see Fuss (1989) and Williams (1998).

15. A tremendous amount of feminist attention ranging from Simone de Beauvoir (1952) to Judith Butler (1990) has been paid to how we define women. For interesting contemporary discussions, see Young (1994), Moi (2002b), and Zerilli (1998, 2005). Patricia Mann contends that feminists should "stop worrying about issues of identity and focus on issues of agency, or significant action" (1997, 225). According to Mann, it is more important to understand why people are uncertain about how to act and what is considered meaningful action than it is to define the category of women.

16. Debra Dodson (2006) offers the terms "feminale" and "feminalism" as a conceptualization that avoids putting women in the feminist-antifeminist box. This terminology is particularly helpful for analyzing conservative women and women who deny being feminists but support gender equality because it recognizes the possibility that women do not identify themselves as feminist even though they advance public policies that support gender equality.

17. Feminists have also identified various barriers that prevent women from participating in numbers equal to those of men, such as political recruitment (Norris 1995) and socialization (Jennings 1983).

18. Famously, Joseph Schumpeter (1976) argues that democracies should be able to determine the scope of who participates. Because democracies are allowed to decide who counts as the people, a democracy can legitimately decide to rule out women as full citizens.

19. Of course, feminist analyses of discrimination should not be and are not limited to observable and measurable sex differences in the behavior of female representatives or of female citizens (Lovenduski and Norris 2003). After all, the absence of sex differences does not mean that the political arena is free from structural forms of discrimination (Randall 2002; Squires 1999). For example, women's presence in legislatures may cause men to be more concerned about women's issues, thereby masking actual sex differences (Reingold 2000).

20. Because the meaning and importance of gender varies, feminist scholars need to continue to create methodologies that can accommodate the dynamic nature of gender inequalities, as Lee Ann Banaszak calls for in this volume.

21. Anne Phillips (1998) identifies four main arguments for representation: overlooked interests, justice, revitalized democracy, and role-model argument. My six arguments expand on Phillips's four arguments in light of recent empirical and theoretical findings. Note that the trust argument and the legitimacy argument both suggest that descriptive representation holds certain benefits to the

U.S. political system as a whole, suggesting that the adequate representation of U.S. women depends on the quality of the entire political system.

22. For an alternative explanation of the role-model effect, see Campbell and Wolbrecht (2006).

23. For this reason, we need to explore whether women feel unfairly represented by male representatives, as well as whether men feel unfairly represented by female representatives.

24. For an alternative explanation of the impact of descriptive representatives on trust, see Claudine Gay (2002).

25. Empirical evidence seems to support that the number of women in elective office or the number of credible female candidates increases the political interest and participatory attitudes on women in the electorate. See Atkeson (2003); Burns, Schlozman, and Verba (2001); Schwindt-Bayer and Mishler (2005); and Verba, Burns and Schlozman (1997).

26. The extent to which increasing trust in representatives also increases the legitimacy of democratic institutions is the extent to which the trust argument will resemble the legitimacy argument.

27. It is unclear whether women have a transforming effect on representative institutions or whether representative institutions need to be transformed to include women.

28. The presence of female representatives improves the quality of deliberations because female representatives are presumed to have more insight and concern about female issues than do male representatives. According to such logic, the reason that some U.S. states make female prisoners give birth in shackles is because male representatives do not adequately appreciate the inconvenience or hardship that such shackles place on women giving birth.

29. As Jane Mansbridge (1999) points out, the need for descriptive representation depends on the degree to which interests are crystallized. The more we know what disadvantaged groups want, the less descriptive representation is necessary. This argument often relies on the example of Senator Carol Braun's refusal to renew the Daughter of the American Revolution's patent of the confederate flag. However, this example is somewhat misleading because the issue of the confederate flag was crystallized *within* the African American community. The problem was that white Senators did not have sufficient understanding and appreciation of this crystallized interest.

30. For instance, Malalai Joya, a female member of the Afghan Parliament, describes how her "microphone has been cut off a number of times when I criticize the situation and want to express my point of view. Once they even physically attacked me inside the Parliament and one of them called (quote) 'Take and rape this prostitute'" (Mulvad 2007).

31. Such evaluations are likely to be complicated by the fact that even when representatives advance what are considered to be women's interests, it is difficult to determine whether those representatives are responding to their female constituents or to other pressures, for example, party demands or instrumental interests. See Mansbridge (2003).

32. For Phillips (1995, 1998), democratic politics occurs when both a politics of presence and a politics of ideas are represented in a democratic polity, but she does not specify how they relate to each other.

11

Political Women in Comparative Democracies

A Primer for Americanists

Lisa Baldez

The United States is often heralded as an exemplary model of democracy, and this vision prompts many to assume that women in the United States enjoy greater equality than women anywhere else. As Gretchen Ritter (this volume) notes, "As the world's first modern democracy, one might expect that the United States has led the way in granting equal rights to women." Women in the United States have come a long way, but we still have far to go before men and women gain political equality, as many of the chapters in this volume make clear. How does the United States compare with other countries in this regard? Any remaining expectation that the United States leads the world in terms of women's rights evaporates when you look at the United States in terms of the indicators now used to compare the status of women worldwide. Consider the percentage of women in elective office. The number of women elected to the U.S. House of Representatives has registered steady gains over time and, as of this writing, stands at 17.1 percent. In terms of the worldwide ranking of women in the lower houses of parliament, however, the United States stands in sixty-eighth place, between Zimbabwe and Turkmenistan. Because of ties among nations, the United States is actually eighty-first in the ranking; eighty nations have better records of electing women to national legislatures (Inter-Parliamentary Union 2007). The United States is one of only a handful of countries that have not ratified the Convention to End All Forms of Discrimination Against Women (CEDAW), the United Nations' (UN's) women's rights treaty. More than 96 percent of UN member countries, 185 in all, have ratified CEDAW. Failing to ratify this document puts the United States in the company of Sudan, Somalia, Qatar, Iran, Nauru, Palau, and Tonga (Amnesty International 2007). Moreover, the U.S. Constitution does not guarantee equal rights between men and women, whereas the constitutions of South Africa, Chile, Afghanistan, and scores of other countries contain explicit statements that affirm sex equality. When it comes to protecting the rights of women, American democracy is far from exemplary.

What might Americanists learn from engaging with the comparative literature? By looking at the United States from the perspective of research on comparative gender and politics, we can expand the range of topics to study, questions to ask, and data to mine. We increase the validity of the inferences we can draw about the United States by including it in cross-national studies. Whereas Americanists by definition do not look beyond the fifty states, comparativists routinely include the United States as another case in multinational studies, both qualitative (Banaszak 1996b; Bashevkin 1998; Elman 1996; Gelb 1989, 2004; Katzenstein and Mueller 1987) and quantitative (Inglehart and Norris 2003; Matland 1998; Reynolds 1999; Welch and Studlar 1990; Weldon 2002a).[1] Many factors that are static within the United States vary in the comparative context. Although primary elections are a fixture of U.S. politics, for example, they are extremely rare in the rest of the world (but becoming more prevalent, as I discuss later). We take the "first-past-the-post" electoral system as a given in the United States, but most countries have proportional representation (PR) systems. Comparative research shows that the single-member districts we have in the United States are much less conducive to the election of women than the multiple-member districts in wide use around the globe. The United States has not had a female president, but more than fifty other countries have had female presidents or prime ministers. For Americanists, looking beyond U.S. borders can expand the sense of what kinds of political arrangements are possible and inspire creative new research.

In this chapter, I evaluate some of the main findings about women in the United States in the context of the comparative literature about sex/gender and politics. I assess some of the comparative scholarship on political women and democracy in terms of the areas of empirical research covered in the other chapters in this volume: public opinion and voting behavior; women's movements; elective office, including campaigns, legislative behavior, and political parties; and public policy.[2] In doing so, I hope to encourage cross-subfield pollination and to highlight fruitful areas for future research, for comparativists and Americanists alike.

PUBLIC OPINION AND VOTING BEHAVIOR

In comparative politics, the earliest work on women focused on public opinion and voting behavior, starting with Maurice Duverger's oft-cited *The Political Role of Women* (1955), a study that compared the status of men and women in four countries: France, Norway, West Germany, and Yugoslavia.[3] The Duverger study revealed a gap between formal laws that established gender equality and cultural mores that connected women to the home (see Burns's discussion of Duverger, this volume). Up until the 1970s, most other early comparative studies did not focus primarily on sex, but a few did include sex as a variable; these tended to confirm the conventional and as yet unproblematic wisdom that women tended to vote more conservatively than men (Almond and Verba 1963; Lipset and Rokkan 1967; Tingsten and Hammarling 1937). In the 1980s and 1990s, literature focused on a realignment of the gender gap by which women now tend to be more liberal than men (Jelen, Thomas, and Wilcox 1994). Ronald Inglehart and Pippa Norris (2000) identify this shift from a "traditional" gender gap to a "modern" one as a worldwide trend, prompted by cultural change.

Gender gaps have been the focus of significant scholarly and media attention in the past several years. As in the United States, gender gaps in voting behavior abroad remain far smaller than class or race gaps, but they can prove influential in elections decided on the margins. The U.S. literature tends to explain the gender gap in terms of contextual political factors, particularly party strategy. Comparative scholars have identified a somewhat wider range of factors that explain the difference between men's and women's voting behavior, including socialization and socioeconomic status, as well as political factors (Studlar, McAllister, and Hayes 1998). Inglehart and Norris (2000) maintain that the contemporary gender gap reflects changes in women's attitudes that have resulted from structural change and the economic transformations of postindustrial societies. As women enter the labor force, the rigid gender-role differentiation associated with traditional societies begins to erode and women's views shift leftward. Torben Iversen and Frances Rosenbluth (2006) make a similar argument, maintaining that attitudinal differences between men and women reflect the kinds of economic opportunities afforded to women, but they highlight the role that political factors play in making those opportunities available, particularly a country's welfare policies and its position in the international division of labor.

Although we know more and more about the causes of gender gaps worldwide, we understand less well the degree to which they fuel electoral connections between voters and elected officials. The gender gap, although not the same as a women's (or a men's) voting bloc, can force political parties to be more responsive to the collective concerns of women (or men). As Inglehart and Norris (2000, 459) note: "The gender gap in the United States has served to expand media attention and public debate about gendered issues, to heighten party competition in an attempt to gain 'the women's vote,' and to increase the attractions of nominating women for public office." As Beth Reingold (this volume) notes, "the power of the gender gap can be elusive." The extent to which gender gaps translate into substantive change depends on context, as well as mobilization by activists and public officials (Mueller 1988b).

Iversen and Rosenbluth (2006, 18) break new ground by identifying the mechanisms that connect gender gaps to concrete policy outcomes. They maintain that "women everywhere want the government to take a more active role in public employment creation" on the grounds that public sector jobs "counter the disadvantages of women" in some countries. If this is true, then we should expect the gender gap to widen as governments shift public expenditures away from welfare spending, which is a widespread trend in developed and developing countries alike. This study also illustrates how the gender gap is relevant to the issue of democratization within the family. The authors assert that "female labor-force participation and higher female income do in fact shift the burden of household work a bit further onto men's shoulders" (2006, 18). The sexual division of labor within the household changes as women join the paid labor force, although all evidence indicates that it does not approach equality. Women's shift leftward reflects the kinds of economic opportunities afforded to women by virtue of a country's welfare policies and its position in the international division of labor. Comparative research on the gender gap thus suggests several questions and hypotheses about the political significance of the gender gap that might fruitfully be examined in the context of the U.S. case. Does the political salience of economic issues and the welfare state correlate with the width of the gender gap? Does the salience of a gender gap itself correlate with the width of the gap? Future research might take up the issue of what we might expect to follow from smaller or larger gaps between men and women's views.

Comparative survey research has also identified gaps between support for women's rights and support for democracy overall. In stable democracies, "a majority of the public disagrees with the statement that 'men make better political leaders than women,'" but this is not the case in many developing societies (Inglehart and Norris 2003, 71). What policy consequences might flow from this gap? What does it bode for efforts to promote democracy abroad, especially those made by the United States in the Islamic world? Research that connects individual behavior to aggregate institutions in this way, along the lines described by Nancy Burns in her contribution to this volume, will better equip us to answer these important questions.

WOMEN'S MOVEMENTS

The past couple of decades have witnessed a dramatic expansion of women's organizations in every region of the world, as well as the formation of transnational women's movements.[4] Comparative gender research has documented the emergence, evolution, and impact of new women's movements and has demonstrated a high degree of women's mobilization in a wide array of political environments, challenging what we might call the "homogendered bias" of mainstream comparative research. The impressive growth of new women's movements can be attributed to three factors: political opportunities afforded by periods of regime change, resources available through international organizations, and networking facilitated by international conferences and new technologies. These three factors are far more significant for women's movements outside the United States than for those within it, for reasons I discuss later.

Throughout the developing world, transitions from authoritarian to democratic regimes provided an opportunity for the mobilization of women along gender lines (Basu 1995; Bystydzienski and Sekhon 1999). In Latin America, women seized on the profound transitions afforded by the establishment or restoration of democratic rule to demand that women assume positions of political authority and that women's concerns be placed high on the agendas of new democratic governments (Alvarez 1990; Baldez 2002; Bayard de Volo 2001; Friedman 2000; Jaquette 1994; Jelín 1991; Kampwirth 2002, 2004; Kampwirth and Gonzalez 2001; Kaplan 1997; Luciak 2001; Stephen 1997; Waylen 1993). Women in these movements claimed that political systems that do not incorporate women and do not espouse human rights and sex equality are not legitimate democracies. The slogan "without women, there is no democracy"[5] epitomizes the effort to link women's inclusion to democratic viability. According to this literature, women's historical exclusion from politics and consequent lack of association with prior authoritarian governments boosted the legitimacy of women's claims for greater participation. Efforts to promote policy change in posttransition periods have born mixed results (Franceschet 2003; Friedman 1998; Jaquette and Wolchik 1998; Ríos Tobar 2003).

A different dynamic emerged (or failed to emerge) amid democratic transition in the Soviet Union and in Eastern and Central Europe. Under communist regimes, governments essentially monopolized claims to represent women and women's issues, rendering sex equality unavailable as a basis for antiregime mobilization (Einhorn 1993; Funk and Mueller 1993; Matland and Montgomery 2003; Sperling 1999; Tatur 1992; Young 1999). Communist leaders claimed to have achieved "women's emancipation," defined (solely) as full female employment, but their claims rang ridiculously hollow over the years. Women rejected this ostensible emancipation because they experienced it as the "double burden": a full day of work in the formal labor force added to full responsibility for maintaining the family and the household. Many women opposed communism to be sure, but they found it difficult to mobilize against communism along gendered lines. The high degree to which communist regimes "owned" claims to represent women made it politically unfeasible for women to frame their opposition in gendered terms. Democratic regime change thus did not promote the formation of women's movements in the former Soviet Union and in Eastern and Central Europe to the same degree it did in Latin America (Baldez 2003; Waylen 1994). Since then, however, efforts to mobilize around gender concerns have emerged and have met with varying levels of success throughout the former Soviet Bloc (Einhorn and Sever 2003; Sloat 2005). In communist countries that have not undergone reform, women's movements exist, but they tend to be more closely linked to state institutions, particularly official state-run women's organizations (Fernandes 2005; Howell 2003; Judd 2002).

In Africa, the decline of single-party authoritarian states paved the way for the emergence of new political cleavages and competing political parties. Women took advantage of this political realignment to organize at record levels in every arena of society (Britton 1998; Hassim 2006; Kaplan 1997; Tétreault 1994; Tripp 2003). Women throughout Africa, the Middle East and other conflict-ridden societies participated in revolutionary movements, nationalist movements, and collective efforts to rebuild in the wake of violent conflict (P. Campbell 2003; Chatty and Rabo 1997; Moghadam 1993; Tétreault 1994; West 1997).

Transitions from one regime type to another are not relevant in studies of women's movements in Western, industrialized countries. Although it makes sense to think about the United States as always involved in a process of deeper democratization, as Ritter (this volume) provocatively suggests, the United States has not undergone a change in regime for some time; thus the political opportunities that have fostered women's mobilization in the developing world differ fundamentally from those in the United States. Nonetheless, as Lee Ann Banaszak (this volume) demonstrates, studies of the United States and other developed countries consistently emphasize the importance of the state and consistently argue that political opportunities shape the emergence, evolution, and outcomes of women's movements, from the conservative governments of Canada, the United States, and the United Kingdom in the 1980s (Bashevkin 1998) to the "reconfigured state" of the new millennium (Banaszak, Beckwith, and Rucht 2003; see also Beckwith 2000; Gelb 1989; Katzenstein and Mueller 1987; Threlfall 1996).

The emergence and growth of global women's movements has been fostered by resources provided by international organizations (Hawkesworth 2006; Keck and Sikkink 1998; Moghadam 2005; Naples and Desai 2002). Activities organized by the UN precipitated the formation of transnational women's movements, as well as domestic ones, beginning in 1975 with the convocation of the International Year of the Woman and the First World Conference on Women in Mexico City. Gathering data on the status of women, a prerequisite for participating in the UN conferences, revealed far greater gender inequities than many people anticipated; these discrepancies turned many skeptics into feminist activists. Over the past thirty years, participants at the UN World Conferences on Women – in Nairobi (1985), Copenhagen (1992), and Beijing (1995) – formed increasingly dense networks at the regional and transnational levels (Friedman, Hochstetler, and Clark 2005). UN support gave women's issues an imprimatur they lacked, legitimizing the demands of women's rights activists at home and prompting previously recalcitrant national governments to take action, exemplifying the "boomerang effect" (Keck and Sikkink 1998). The use of the Internet by women's advocacy groups has helped maintain international networks and expand democracy to the extent that it provides a space for political participation among "outcast" groups, the agendas of which are not widely supported at home (Friedman 2005).

Although Burns (this volume) maintains that preexisting networks foster women's mobilization, transnational networks can also inhibit the formation or consolidation of women's movements. Movement organizations dependent on funding from international agencies necessarily orient their work at least somewhat toward the agendas of donor agencies. A shift in focus toward the international arena can cripple activists' ability to build grassroots support, the currency in which domestic policy makers frequently trade (Fernandes 2005). Women's groups that receive funding to provide service delivery and to implement policy (either from international sources or their own governments) face strong incentives to maintain the political status quo, a phenomenon that has come to be known as the "NGO-ization" of the women's movement (Alvarez 1998; Lang 1997). One avenue for future research would focus on developing a better understanding of the relationship between transnational and domestic movements and specifying the conditions under which a boomerang effect will take place. As Banaszak and also Ritter (this volume) point out, ample research documents the transnational networks that shaped the American women's movement prior to World War II, but the relative lack of involvement by American feminists in transnational movements is either a puzzle that merits greater attention or a literature that warrants greater development. Women's organizations in the United States have participated actively in transnational women's movements, but they tend to depend far less heavily on the international arena than do their peers elsewhere in the world. Most U.S. organizations can draw their budgets from individual membership dues and do not need to rely on external funding.

ELECTIVE OFFICE

The comparative literature on sex and legislative office mirrors the U.S. literature in terms of its focus on two primary questions: what factors promote women's electoral chances and under what conditions does the descriptive representation of women lead to the substantive representation of women's concerns? The comparative literature on cross-national variation in the percentage of women elected to national-level office, for example, is analogous to studies that compare the election of women across the fifty states (see the chapters by Dolan and Reingold, this volume). Existing comparative research points to institutional factors (Reynolds 1999), socioeconomic differences (Matland 1998), and culture as key explanatory variables (Inglehart and Norris 2003; Matland 1998; Paxton 1997; Paxton and Kunovich 2003). As Miki Caul Kittilson (2006) points out, these studies generally rely on "snapshot" data – that is, the percentage of women in office in an array of countries at a given point of time; she explains change over time as a function of decisions made by political parties (see also Kunovich and Paxton 2005).

Comparative research frequently tests hypotheses derived from observation of the U.S. legislatures. This form of borrowing often entails more than merely testing old arguments against new data. Leslie Schwindt-Bayer and William Mishler (2005), for example, have found that women legislators around the world prioritize women's issues to a greater extent than men do; their study confirms findings from the United States (see Reingold, this volume) and elsewhere (Bratton and Ray 2002; Childs 2002; M. Jones 1997; Taylor-Robinson and Heath 2003). Because of its broad comparative focus, Schwindt-Bayer's work allows us to test the validity of United States–centric claims; she argues that gender differences in legislative behavior transcend national and political context (see also Cornwall and Goetz 2005; O'Regan 2000). Moreover, Schwindt-Bayer's analysis adds a theoretical innovation to this literature by comparing legislators' *attitudes* with legislators' *behavior*; men and women legislators prioritize issues differently, but women tend not to act on their preferences, which Schwindt-Bayer interprets as evidence for the marginalization of women within legislatures.

The comparative literature on gender and elective office diverges from the U.S. literature due to its focus on institutions that are not relevant in the U.S. case, two in particular: electoral laws and gender quotas. One of the strongest findings about elective office in the comparative literature (i.e., not just on gender) is that electoral rules play a critical role in determining who gets elected and how they serve their constituents. Proportional representation systems are considered to be more conductive to the election of women (and other underrepresented groups; Beckwith 1992; Bystydzienski 1995; Matland and Studlar 1996; Matland and Taylor 1997; Rule and Zimmerman 1994). District magnitude – the number of legislators within a particular district – significantly affects women's chances for election and shapes the degree to which women's demands will be met, with women's chances for candidate nomination being better in multimember districts than in single-member ones (Matland 1993; Matland and Brown 1992). Thus female candidates in the United States compete in a comparatively unfavorable environment.

Gender quotas – affirmative action measures applied to candidates for legislative office – are becoming increasingly prevalent worldwide. More than 40 countries and 168 political parties have adopted gender quotas, most of them since 1991 (International IDEA 2007). Gender quota *laws* require political parties to ensure that women fill a certain percentage of candidate slots; the percentage ranges from 5 percent in Nepal to 50 percent in France.[6] Gender quota laws apply to all parties within a given system, which distinguishes them from *voluntary quotas* adopted by individual parties (Caul 2001), and they apply to candidates, which distinguishes them from *reserved seats* set aside for legislators (Htun 2004). On average, gender quota laws generate a 10 percent increase in the number of women elected to office (Htun and Jones 2002). The Quota Project, a comprehensive database on quotas around the world, has greatly facilitated comparative research on this topic (International IDEA 2007).

Case studies have identified a range of variables that lead to the adoption of gender quota laws, including international diffusion (Dahlerup 2003, 2006b; Towns 2003), presidential support (Htun and Jones 2002), and the advent of electoral competition within a party system (Baldez 2004). Institutional variables account for much of the variation in quota law effectiveness. Quota laws tend to be more effective in multimember district electoral systems with high district magnitude, and where quota laws stipulate a placement mandate and a high quota (Jones 1996, 1998, 2004; Jones and Navia 1999). Quota laws can increase the number of women in both open-list and closed-list PR systems (Schmidt and Saunders 2004). In other words, quotas are more likely to be effective where voters choose from among lists of candidates created by political party leaders, where such lists are long, and where women cannot be clustered at the bottom and where the percentage of women that appears on them is relatively high. Scholars are beginning to examine how holding primary elections, which are becoming much more widespread, interact with quotas (Baldez 2007; Hinojosa 2005; Piscopo 2005). Americanists have also begun to examine the gendered impact of primary elections in the United States as well (Pearson and Lawless, forthcoming).

Although few people in the United States have heard of them, gender quotas constitute an important part of the history of American political parties. Both the Democratic and Republican parties adopted regulations requiring that equal numbers of men and women serve on party committees in the context of the passage of the suffrage amendment. The Democratic Party adopted a "fifty-fifty rule" at its 1920 convention, and the GOP followed suit in 1924. Although the Republicans removed this requirement in 1952, the Democratic statute still applies to delegates to the party's National Convention (Freeman 2000, 111–12; see also Andersen 1996).[7]

In addition to formal rules, political parties also significantly shape the representation of women in politics (Bruhn 2003; Lovenduski and Norris 1993, 1996). Kira Sanbonmatsu (this volume) invites us to think about party agendas and women's representation as two sides of the same coin. Caul Kittilson (2006) confirms earlier findings that parties representing "leftist ideological values" offer the most hospitable environment for women politicians and furthermore shows that "the more factionalized parties have more women on the top decision-making committees." Elisabeth Friedman (1998) shows how Venezuelan political parties sought to shut women's movements down after the transition to democracy to establish monopoly control over the female electorate.

In terms of women and political office, this volume gives short shrift to two important areas within the Americanist literature on women and gender:

the executive and judicial branches, both of which constitute viable potential growth areas for comparative gender scholars. Those concerned with the
prospects for a woman to become president in the United States might fruitfully examine the conditions that have allowed women to win highest office
in other countries; actually, the same holds true for comparativists because
there is not much comparative literature on this topic either. There is a scant
comparative literature on women in executive cabinets, but Maria Escobar-
Lemmon and Michelle Taylor-Robinson's (2005) study of portfolios in Latin
America illustrates the potential for more excellent work in this area. Comparative scholars could take leads from the voluminous research on gender
and judicial politics in the United States to examine the role of women judges,
following the work that Sally Kenney has done on the European Court of
Justice, for example (Kenney 2002, 2004).

PUBLIC POLICY

CEDAW has played a crucial role in putting women's issues on the public policy agendas of many governments. Despite its nonbinding status as
a UN convention, perhaps no other document has done so much to legitimize the issue of women's rights and to push governments to take action
to correct gender inequalities (Zwingel 2005). The policy statements drafted
at the various UN World Conferences on Women, particularly the Beijing
Platform for Action, have provided benchmarks for policy implementation
adopted by many countries and incorporated, at times verbatim, into the
text of domestic legislation. Unifem, the UN agency created to oversee adherence to CEDAW, collects periodic reports on the status of women from all
states-parties to CEDAW. This rich and underutilized data could be mined
for future research. President Jimmy Carter signed CEDAW in 1980, but
U.S. ratification awaits a two-thirds vote of the Senate. Awareness of the
UN's support for women's issues surged when Hillary Clinton addressed the
Fourth World Women's Conference in Beijing in 1995 – but efforts to mobilize support for CEDAW remain extremely weak in the United States. Why?

A great deal of research on public policy in comparative falls under the
category "comparative state feminism." This area of research analyzes state
commitment to policies that promote women's rights in terms of the level
of cooperation between women's movements, political actors, and government agencies. One component of this literature focuses on the formation
of bureaucratic agencies dedicated to the promotion of women's issues,
known as women's policy agencies (Franceschet 2003; Okeke-Ihejirika and
Franceschet 2002; Stetson and Mazur 1995). Another area examines interaction between women's movements and state actors with regard to specific
policy issues.

Comparative gender scholars have emulated the example set by activists:
building networks, collaborating on research, sharing ideas, scholars from

developed countries supporting scholars from developing countries, all seeking to promote legitimacy of research on gender and women. Research on feminist comparative policy is plagued by a lack of standard methodologies and metrics. As Amy Mazur writes, "much of the literature is more concerned with describing the unfolding of specific policies within national contexts than addressing any larger theoretical puzzles about feminist government action" (Mazur 2002, 34). The lack of cross-national data and absence of shared analytical frameworks has spurred scholars to form large scholarly teams who commit to gather data according to a common rubric (Nelson and Chowdhury 1994; Research Network on Gender Politics [RNGS] and the State Project 2007). Many of these projects have demonstrated a strong commitment to fostering scholarly collaboration among women across various countries and between women from developed and developing countries. One such network, the RNGS project, has produced six cross-national studies in this vein, on job-training programs (Mazur 2001), prostitution (Outshoorn 2004), abortion (Stetson 2001), political representation (Lovenduski 2005), and globalization (Haussman and Sauer 2006). An additional volume explicates the theory behind the series and provides a useful meta-analysis of research in comparative state feminism (Mazur 2002). Each of the RNGS volumes systematically classifies various aspects of the policy-making process in a range of Western industrialized countries, according to movement impact, the activities and characteristics of the women's policy agency, characteristics of the women's movement, and the overall policy environment. Laurel Weldon's study of domestic violence policy worldwide incorporates comparative state feminist variables such as women's policy machinery and women's movement strength into a quantitative policy analysis model (Weldon 2002a); for a qualitative study that compares domestic violence policy in Sweden and the United States, see Elman (1996).

Other aspects of state feminism examine efforts to promote equality between men and women into non-sex-specific areas of policy. The term "gender mainstreaming" refers to the effort to incorporate sex equality into all areas of governance. It represents a commitment to expand concern for women's rights beyond issues traditionally considered to be specific to women (*International Feminist Journal of Politics* 2005; True 2003; Van de Vleuten 2005). The European Union Treaty, for example, requires member states to commit to the "aim to eliminate inequalities, and to promote equality, between men and women" in all government activities (European Union 1997). "Gender budgeting" represents a specific aspect of mainstreaming; research in this area compares the allocation of government resources between men and women (Elson 2004; Sharp and Broomhill 2002). In this area, as in others, the United States remains anomalous in its inattention to this issue. "More than 60 countries have answered this call by implementing gender-responsive budgets at the national and subnational levels. However, gender-responsive budgeting is virtually unheard of among public finance scholars and U.S. public administration scholars and practitioners" (Rubin and Bartle 2005, 259). Institutional analysis examines how the formal and informal rules in place in different political systems affect the adoption and implementation of gender-related public policy (Baldez 2001). A central premise of this approach is that the adoption of policy on women's issues does not necessarily flow exclusively from the efforts of women's movements but can depend on coalitions of support that includes issue experts, lawyers, and interested legislators. Advances in gender equality do not necessarily even occur under democratic governments. Authoritarian regimes in Argentina, Brazil, and Chile adopted significant changes in family policy that benefited women (Htun 2003).

CONCLUSION

When we examine American democracy in comparative perspective, we learn that the status of women in the United States is often anomalous and sometimes similar to that of women elsewhere but is rarely exemplary. The gender gap, for example, is not unique to the United States and perhaps cannot be best explained with reference to factors specific to this country. Around the world, women espouse more progressive views than men across a range of issues. Women may become more progressive, increasing their support for welfare state policies as they join the formal labor force. If this hypothesis is true, we should expect to see the gender gap widen in the wake of the contraction of state-provided social services and expansion of women as a percentage of the world's workers, two of the central consequences of globalization, and the adoption of neoliberal economic policies. Looking at the gender gap from a comparative perspective suggests that women in the United States have a great deal in common with women elsewhere.

A comparative perspective draws our attention to the possibility that the reason the United States has comparatively few women in its national legislature is not (entirely) a failure of women to put themselves forward, but (also) a set of institutional rules (primary elections, first-past-the-post elections, gender quotas) that work against women's election. A candidate-centered approach dominates much of the candidate emergence literature and policy practices right now). If the focus shifted to the way in which formal rules constrain outcomes, maybe more American women would put themselves out there as candidates. Perhaps those seeking to increase the percentage of female politicians in the United States would be well served to consider electoral reform and some kind of gender quota rule as viable strategies.

Comparative research helps us understand and explain the various ways in which gender constructs politics, and vice versa. As Nancy Burns (this volume) maintains, "politics [builds] assumptions about women's place into policy," but the gendered nature of politics is often invisible – to ordinary people, to political elites, and to many political scientists. Furthermore, seeing gender in the state requires comparison across space and time. The emergence of women's movements in other regions of the world provides one example. Some types of regime change – from authoritarian to democratic – prompted women to mobilize on the basis of their gender identity, whereas others – from communist to capitalist – did not. Such examples highlight the gendered nature of the state. In a context in which regime change has not occurred (such as the United States), gender might appear to have a more static relationship with the state and might be more difficult to perceive.

Viewing the United States from the perspective of comparative research highlights the ways in which political women in American democracy are unique, which in turn suggests new research questions about how to explain various anomalies. What explains American immunity from global patterns of policy diffusion? Why has the United States not adopted gender quotas? Why hasn't the United States ratified CEDAW? Why have efforts to promote the ratification of CEDAW remained weak? How might electoral rules in the United States be made more "woman-friendly?" Further cross-pollination between American and comparative politics will yield additional fertile ground for new research. Myriad changes in women's lives have been attributed to globalization, yet the United States remains curiously unaffected by some of the profound changes in policies toward women that have occurred elsewhere in the world. It can be humbling, if not humiliating, to comprehend the ways in which the United States falls short on various measures of gender equality and women's rights, but better awareness of our limitations may be a necessary prerequisite to more profound change at home and to the elimination of stereotypes about the status of women abroad.

Notes

1. Some comparativists also do research that focuses exclusively on the United States (Baldez, Epstein, and Martin 2006; Matland and Brown 1992; Schwindt-Bayer and Corbetta 2004).
2. The magnitude of research in this field is too great to cover it adequately in a single chapter. Space constraints necessitated leaving out a lot of important work, and I apologize to the authors whose work I could not include. I encourage others to take up the important task of writing an appropriately comprehensive "state-of-the-field" essay on gender and comparative politics. For other perspectives on doing comparative research on gender, see the essays by Chappell, Weldon, and Tripp in "Critical Perspective on Gender and Politics: Moving to a Comparative Politics of Gender" in *Politics & Gender* 2(June 2006):221–63.
3. For details about the UN Educational, Scientific and Cultural Organization study, see Freeman (2006).

4. For a cogent review of the literature on women's movements in the United States and abroad, see Beckwith (2000).
5. This slogan makes more sense in Spanish because it rhymes: "Si la mujer no está, la democracia no va."
6. The French law requires parity between men and women and is technically not a quota; see Scott (2005).
7. For a discussion of why the United States has so far remained immune to the quota wave, see "Critical Perspectives on Gender and Politics: Gender Quotas" in *Politics & Gender* 1(December 2005):621–52 and 2(March 2006):101–28.

12

Conclusion: Between Participation and Representation

Political Women and Democracy in the United States

Karen Beckwith

> We need to know why democratic representative institutions do not work for women as well as they work for powerful men, and we need to know what conditions contribute to those institutions working better for women.
>
> (Dovi, this volume, 148)

How democratic has U.S. democracy been for women? How political have U.S. women become since "the revolution" (Wolbrecht, this volume)? Certainly since the publication of Jeane J. Kirkpatrick's *Political Woman* in 1974, there has been a revolution in women's political and legal status, mass participation, feminist movement activism, and voting behavior. *Political Woman*, politically active women, and a highly political women's movement emerged alongside important legislative achievements (e.g., the proposal of the Equal Rights Amendment in 1972 and passage of Title IX in 1974), landmark Supreme Court decisions (most notably *Roe v. Wade* in 1973), and significant implementation of antidiscrimination laws by the Equal Employment Opportunity Commission.

What have been the subsequent impacts and political trajectory of this revolution of political women? What do we know about political women and democracy in the United States? The chapters in this volume, in answering these questions, share two major commonalities at their outset: their attention to distinctions of "sex" and "gender," and their appreciation of the impact of gendered institutions on political women and of political women's influence in gendering political parties, policy processes, and state structures. Their consistent focus on women and on gender in regard to U.S. democracy signals a further revolution: the movement of gender into the core of political science research and democratic political theory.

First, each chapter recognizes and offers a sophisticated analytical distinction between "sex" and "gender." Lee Ann Banaszak (this volume) positions women's movements in a larger consideration of social movements generally, arguing convincingly that political movements of *women* – women's movements – have also led to the importance of *gender* in understanding all movements "by highlighting the gendered aspects of ... social movement concepts" (see also Burns, this volume). In a manner rare for studies of women's electoral candidacies, Kathleen Dolan focuses explicitly on questions of sex *and* gender, asking, "How do we account for the interconnectedness of sex and gender effects" in women's candidacies (Dolan, this volume)? Second, each author investigates this distinction in terms of individuals and of gender as a feature of state institutions (Ritter, this volume), recognizing that gender may accrue in individuals and their behaviors but also that institutions can be structured by sexed and gendered actors and by processes that work their way through the gendered nature of institutional political histories, their routine practices, and their prevailing strategies.

These chapters differ, however, in their emphasis on different components of democracy. Several chapters focus on political women and on *democracy as participation*, reviewing the literature on women's mass political participation (Burns; Junn and Brown), which is often expressed through political movements and political parties (Banaszak; Burns; Sanbonmatsu). Other chapters emphasize *democracy as representation* (Dovi), which is generally expressed through electoral and political institutions, and focus on the literature on women's candidacies (Dolan), women in political parties (Sanbonmatsu), and women holding public office (Reingold). With these two emphases of democracy, how can we assess political women in the context of democracy in the United States?

This distinction between participatory and representative visions of democracy reflects the reality for political women in the United States.[1] If our theoretical starting point is that democracy depends on political *participation* (Mansbridge 1980; Pateman 1970; Phillips 1991; Young 2000), then U.S. democracy has come to include political women,[2] who vote in large numbers (relative to men; see Center for American Women and Politics [CAWP] 2007f), have increased their voting turnout (CAWP 2007f; see also Dolan, this volume), evidence a distinctive trajectory of vote choice and policy preference (Burns, this volume; Dolan, this volume; Reingold, this volume), and initiated – and now sustain – involvement in the second (and perhaps third) wave of the U.S. feminist movement (Banaszak, this volume; Ritter, this volume).[3]

If, however, our theoretical starting point is that democracy relies on political *representation* (Dovi, this volume; Mansbridge 2003; Phillips 1991), U.S. democracy has been less helpful to political women, impeding women's access to, and excluding women from, elective office. As chapters in this volume (Dolan; Sanbonmatsu) demonstrate, women's candidacies have increased across the past three decades[4] and differ little from men's candidacies (Dolan, this volume); women raise as much money as do their male counterparts running for office (Burrell 2005; Dolan, this volume; Sanbonmatsu, this volume); women enjoy an incumbency rate equivalent to that of men (Dolan, this volume; see also Palmer and Simon 2005); and female candidates attract as much voter support as do their male counterparts – and sometimes more support, depending on the ethnicity, race, educational and/or marital status of the voter, and campaign-specific issues (see Dolan, this volume; Thomas 2005, 9).

Nonetheless, women's political representation remains strikingly low.[5] For all the effort and expense and mobilization by women seeking representation in elective office, the sad result has been the record "high" of seventy-one women (16.3 percent) in the U.S. House of Representatives, and sixteen women (16 percent) in the U.S. Senate (CAWP 2007a), placing the United States only eighty-first among representative democracies worldwide (Inter-Parliamentary Union 2006).[6] In U.S. state legislatures, the percentage of elected women reached a high of 22.7 percent in 2002 and 2005 (CAWP 2007d); as Kira Sanbonmatsu notes (2006, 191), this percentage has reached a plateau. Percentages of female state legislators have hovered between 20.8 and 22.7 percent since 1996 (CAWP 2007d), a 1.9 percent gain in the past decade.[7] To date, the effort to increase women's political representation has been disproportionate to the result (Beckwith 2003, 194–7; see also Chappell 2002, 51).

In short, U.S. democracy has been better for U.S. women in terms of their mass participation than it has been for their political representation. As Christina Wolbrecht (this volume) observes, there has been a revolution for political women in the past three decades. It has been, however, more a revolution of participation than of representation.

POLITICAL PARTICIPATION, POLITICAL VOICE, AND WOMEN'S MOVEMENTS

What are the U.S. democratic institutional arrangements that might encourage women's mass political participation? In considering *American* democracy, are there any distinctive features of the political system that support political women at the mass level? Structural arrangements of the U.S. political system, although they may not "invite women's rebellion" (Costain 1992), certainly offer points of entry, facilitating and encouraging women's political participation, by presenting an open set of political opportunity structures that can facilitate mass participation (Kitschelt 1986, 58). These include the presence of a large number of organized groups and political parties "that effectively articulate different demands in electoral politics"; the larger the number of contending groups, the more open the political system – and the greater difficulty in limiting "electoral interest articulation" to only a few interests (Kitschelt 1986, 63). Second, because Congress is independent of the executive branch, elected from and accountable to a structurally separate electoral base, the national legislature is relatively open to hearing demands from organized groups, including, presumably, women's groups and women's movements (but see Ritter, this volume). Similarly, flexible, multiple linkages between groups in civil society and executive branch agencies in the United States facilitate openness and access, again including for women. Fourth, "viable procedures [for building] effective policy coalitions" are a final component of state "openness" to mass efforts at political influence (Kitschelt 1986, 63).

In *Power in Movement*, Sidney Tarrow (1998) identifies additional "stable aspects" of political opportunity. In regard to the United States, the most important, in the context of political women, are federalism and the decentralized nature of the U.S. state. Federal states encourage participation by providing multiple venues for making demands and attempting influence (see Beckwith 2003, 197–202; Elman 2003, 102). Decentralized states, such as the United States, "provide a multitude of targets" for mass participation and influence; they "invite...participation" (Tarrow 1998, 81). Furthermore, Tarrow, citing Hanspeter Kriesi and colleagues (1995), suggests that the U.S. state generally has a "prevailing state strategy" of inclusion, where the state's stance toward activists and participants further invites their involvement and "facilitates their entry into the polity" (1998, 82). Tarrow cautions, however, that a state's prevailing strategy will vary according to who the actors are and what issues are raised, concluding that "the American state presents an open door to groups that advance modest goals but sets up a barricade against those which challenge capital or national security" (1995, 83).[8] It is worth noting that a prevailing strategy of including women as political actors at the mass level is a relatively new phenomenon; in this regard, the "open" U.S. system had to be "broken open" by activist women across the past two centuries (see also Junn and Brown, this volume; Ritter, this volume).[9] It is also worth noting the prevailing strategy of excluding women of color, particularly African American women, from mass participation (see, e.g., Smooth 2006; Junn and Brown, this volume; Ritter, this volume).

Arrangements of political institutions and their prevailing strategies are not the only measures of a favorable political opportunity structure for women's mass participation in the United States. Tarrow further identifies "consistent...dimensions of the political environment that provide incentives for collective action by affecting people's expectations for success or failure" (Tarrow 1998, 76–7). These include the "expansion of access [to participation]"; electoral instability "based on new coalitions"; evident splits among political elites; and the emergence of influential allies, the most important of which are political parties, particularly leftist and New Left parties (1998, 77–80). This combination of institutional structures (such as federalism and separation of powers), the availability of alliances and coalition possibilities, generally increasing access to politics, and a prevailing state strategy of inclusion (and, perhaps, assimilation and cooptation; see Kriesi et al. 1995, 33–7) has constructed relatively conducive political opportunities for women's mass political participation. In short, in terms of *participation*, political women now face a relatively open and accessible state.

This may be especially the case for women's movements. Women's movements have generally been reformist in their policy demands on the state, many of which were framed as "rights" issues (see Banaszak 1996b; Beckwith 2001, 384–5; Katzenstein 1998; Luker 1984, chap. 5). The U.S. feminist movement has been successful in crafting coalitions with labor unions, environmental groups, health-care professionals, and others in advancing its issues in state arenas. As the "left" party in the United States, the Democratic Party has been more supportive and inclusive of women and the feminist movement than has the Republican Party (Freeman 2000; Sanbonmatsu, this volume; Wolbrecht 2000). Moreover, U.S. women's movements are generally inclusive (Beckwith 2005) and tend to employ the classic Schattschneiderian strategy of socialization of the scope of the conflict (Schattschneider 1975). As Anne Phillips observes, "The contemporary women's movement has been almost an experiment in participatory democracy, with a politics of grass-roots activism, a radical critique of authority and a commitment to collective decisions" (1991, 41). By including new participants and by expanding the range of activists, women's movements not only have benefited from "expansion of access" (Tarrow 1998, 77–80) but also have contributed to it. In this regard, the feminist movement has influenced and actively gendered the U.S. political opportunity structure. By doing so, the U.S. women's movement has been directly involved in building the very democracy from which it seeks full inclusion.

Women's political participation and its potential for further impact specifically on democracy also have theoretical underpinnings (see Mansbridge 1980; Pateman 1970; Phillips 1991; Young 2000). Carole Pateman asserts that participatory democracy involves

an ambitious purpose, "the education of an entire people to the point where their intellectual, emotional, and moral capacities have reached their full potential and they are joined, freely and actively in a genuine community," and that the strategy for reaching this end is through the use of "political activity and government for the purpose of public education." ... [T]he "unfinished business" of democratic theory is "the elaboration of plans of action and specific prescriptions which offer hope of progress towards a genuinely democratic polity." (Pateman 1970, 21)

One "ambitious purpose," a focus of this volume, is the full inclusion of women in governance. The irony is that an increasingly gendered political participation in the United States comes up against a democratic system of representation that continues, structurally, to disadvantage and to exclude women. Where is the revolution for women's political representation?

POLITICAL REPRESENTATION, POLITICAL WOMEN,
AND U.S. DEMOCRACY

Democracy in one sphere may have little or no consequences for democracy in the other. (Phillips 1991, 39)

More than a decade ago, Najma Chowdhury and Barbara Nelson observed that "*in no country do women have political status, access or influence equal to men's*. The sweep of women's political subordination encompasses the great variety of cultures, economic arrangements, and regimes in which they live" (Chowdhury and Nelson 1994, 3; emphasis in original). Democracy in the United States is no exception. Indeed, in structural terms, U.S. democracy is much less welcoming to women who seek elective office than it is to women's mass political participation[10] and less welcoming to women's political representation generally than are many other democratic nations. Why is this the case?

The evidence summarized in the chapters in this volume leads me to conclude that, in contrast to democracy as participation, in representational democracy in the United States, women are confronted with sets of interlocking institutions and practices that are only modestly democratic, that exclude them, and that are difficult to regender in ways that will encourage women's electoral success and garner representation for women's interests. Kathleen Dolan (this volume) observes a paradox of women's political representation: female candidates are as successful as their male counterparts, yet the number of women running for office and winning elections has not increased, signaling "that sex and gender still matter in very real ways."

Suzanne Dovi identifies additional disadvantages regarding women's access to political office in cases in which political women must match the prevailing (male) standard for successful candidacies, meaning that "standards for evaluating female representatives can be part of the problem, products of systemic injustices" (this volume). Furthermore, where women win, there is an add-on effect of increasing women's political interest and participation at the mass level – providing a positive feedback link between women's political representation and their political participation. Where structural constraints disadvantage or impede women's candidacies and election, a negative feedback process develops: opportunities are not merely closed for representation but the capacity for mass democratic participation among women to advance women's political representation is blocked. Kira Sanbonmatsu's review of "representation by gender and parties" reveals a trade-off for women between political party activism and interest group involvement, where a democracy of group-based participation is the price of little access to political party power and influence and, ultimately, political office – in a political system in which "[m]odern democracy is... unthinkable save [in terms of] political parties" (Schattschneider 1942, quoted in Sanbonmatsu, this volume).

What is the political opportunity structure for women's elective access in the United States? The chapters in this volume, and comparative evidence regarding women's electoral success in other nations (see Baldez, this volume), suggest a set of party and electoral structures relatively closed to women. Three major factors structure women's representational disadvantage in the context of U.S. democracy: (1) the party system, (2) the electoral system, and (3) incumbency history. These factors are interrelated and mutually reinforcing, functioning to gender representational opportunities to political women's disadvantage.

A Gendered Party System?

Kira Sanbonmatsu (this volume) discusses multiple tensions between political women and political parties, as women have tried to advance candidacies, coalitions, and issues in U.S. democracy. She concludes that "there is no direct correspondence between women's descriptive representation and party representation in the United States" and reminds us that committees in Congress are not organized around women's interests or issues but rather around "issues that benefit the majority party." A step back from the specific, gendered nature of U.S. parties further indicates, in comparative perspective, the distinctive nature of U.S. parties at the national level as relatively weak, disciplined primarily in regard to leadership contests in Congress, and laissez-faire in regard to candidate selection and reselection (see Norris 1993). A persisting lacuna in women and politics scholarship concerns a gendered analysis of political party structures in the United States and of political party theory concerning U.S. parties specifically (see, however, Burrell 2006; Sanbonmatsu 2006). Access to party leadership and to party nomination and support is structurally gendered in the United States by, for example, the absence of clear, uniform routes to party nomination for national office; no centralized national party selection procedures for nominations for national legislative office (see Kittilson 2006); no concomitant deselection mechanisms and procedures; no standards for access to national party campaign finance funding; and little coordinated control over candidate financing, including party prohibitions on incumbents' financing of other congressional candidates.[11] Clear routes to candidacy would provide all potential contestants with a map to nomination. In contrast, informal, insider, independent, and often invisible routes to nomination advantage those who are already inside party circles and who understand the hidden pathways to successful nomination.[12] The concept of the "tyranny of structurelessness," employed as a critique of the political power embedded in second wave feminist consciousness-raising groups in the United States (Freeman 1972), is surprisingly applicable to contemporary U.S. political parties regarding the gendered implications of informal and decentralized party structures.[13]

The party context in which women stand for office is further tempered by the U.S. party system, dominated by two major parties. Although not terribly strong or disciplined in comparative context, the Democratic and Republican parties have captured all electoral competition on the national level (and have institutionalized party competition and electoral access in ways that make new party incursion extremely difficult; see Sanbonmatsu, this volume; see also Ritter, this volume).[14] Neither party offers a formal, visible, institutionalized route to nominations, which depend instead on elite networks, individual wealth, and independent candidacy (Burrell 2006, 166; Norris 1996, 205–6, esp. 203, figure 7.2; Sanbonmatsu 2006, 200–4; Smooth 2006b, 138). Access is closed to newcomers, even to talented and otherwise qualified likely candidates. In the absence of other potential party venues for political representation (i.e., third parties), political women face a relatively closed political opportunity structure in U.S. political parties and the party system.[15]

A Gendered Electoral System?

Writing more than a decade ago in *Women, Elections and Representation*, R. Darcy, Susan Welch, and Janet Clark remarked (1994, 169): "It is curious that women, perhaps *the* most underrepresented group in American politics, have subjected electoral systems to very little challenge. Other groups do not hesitate to cry foul when they perceive a disadvantage for themselves in the methods adopted for conducting elections. Yet, there are electoral circumstances under which women candidates are more likely than others to run and be elected." Half a century ago, the single-member plurality electoral system was identified as inconducive to women's election to parliaments (Duverger 1955). Extensive research across the past two decades details the strongly gendered impact of electoral systems on women's political representation (Baldez, this volume; Darcy, Welch, and Clark 1994, 138–71; Dolan, this volume; see also Dahl 2002, 60; Kittilson 2006; Norris and Inglehart 2005, 248–50; Rule and Zimmerman 1992, 1994; Welch and Studlar 1990).[16] This research concludes that the single-member first-past-the-post electoral system is the least propitious for new entrants among all electoral systems and is particularly disadvantageous for women. In the United States, the electoral system for the U.S. Congress – House and Senate – is, in relative terms, a barrier to women's nomination and to their election, a barrier that functions regardless of women's race (Schroedel and Godwin 2005, 275–6; Thomas 2005, 9–10). This particular electoral arrangement is unusual in comparative perspective: few nations rely on single-member plurality arrangements for electing members to national legislatures (Blais and Massicotte 1996, 52–5; Lijphart 1984).[17]

Gendered Incumbency?

Incumbency status and patterns are related to both the electoral system and to parties in the United States. Miki Caul Kittilson (2006, 27) reminds us that because "[e]lectoral rules pace the rate of turnover among elected officials ... single-member districts can act as a drag on women's progress." In the U.S. Congress, incumbency – particularly male incumbency – is strong and nearly exclusive of new entrants (see Dolan, this volume). The strong and persistent incumbency effect on candidate election is unrelated to candidate sex; female incumbents fare as well as incumbent men in reelection. Instead, the incumbency effect works through the presence of men, in large numbers, already in national office. Political parties are also implicated in the gendered incumbency effect; parties structure the ability of all incumbents (male or female) to gain renomination through nominating processes that free incumbents from any organized party deselection powers and by primary electoral processes that favor a limited, unrepresentative party electorate that advantages candidates, like incumbents, with high name recognition.[18]

Shifting Gendered Structures?

Given electoral and party structures that impede women's political representation, what opportunities exist for activist women to regender these structures? Tarrow suggests that political opportunity structures, including state structures, are malleable and that political actors can shift structural opportunities to their own advantage. Lee Ann Banaszak, Dieter Rucht, and I have argued that women's movements (and, more specifically, feminist movements) are as much agents in facilitating state reconfiguration as they have been affected by it (Banaszak, Beckwith, and Rucht 2003). Can political women bridge the gap between their extensive political participation at the mass level and their underrepresentation in Congress?

A major means of increasing women's political representation in other countries has been the introduction of gender quotas (see Darcy et al. 1994, 169; Kittilson 2005, 644). Lisa Baldez shows that comparative research has found gender quotas to be a successful means of increasing the numbers of women elected to national legislatures, *"thus enhancing democracy"* (2006, emphasis added).

Baldez adds, however, that gender quotas are generally employed in party systems where, unlike the case for the United States, party leaders control nominations (Baldez, this volume). Mark Jones argues that gender quotas are most likely to be effective under additional restrictive conditions, including "placement mandates (in concert with closed [party] lists), ... [and] the employment of quotas within the context of moderate-to-large multimember electoral districts" (2005, 647). These key conditions for implementing gender quotas do not obtain in the United States, given the single-member plurality electoral system by which members of Congress are elected and the party system that nominates congressional candidates. The congressional electoral system is constitutionally constructed and unlikely to change. As Jones writes in regard to parties nominating a mandated number of women for congressional seats, this alternative is "sufficiently at odds with political and constitutional reality in the United States that it is unrealistic even to consider them as potential remedies" (Jones 2005, 649).

Women's Movements as Key Actors

In the United States, political women are caught at the intersection of an open participation system and a closed representational system. Gender quotas are an unlikely mechanism for opening representational opportunities for women, despite their success in other nations. What are the opportunities for activist women to regender these structures? Are there other means of increasing representational democracy by and for women? Baldez, Banaszak, Ritter, Sanbonmatsu (all from this volume), and others identify the U.S. women's movement as the key to gendering U.S. politics toward women's political representation and to working political parties and electoral gender gaps to women's political advantage. When targeted at specific policy objectives, related to the electoral and policy success of legislators, the U.S. women's movement has been crucial to major policy changes and to increases in women's election to Congress and to state legislatures over the past two decades (see Sanbonmatsu, this volume). Baldez (2006) hypothesizes that "[t]he degree to which women's movements enhance the substantive representation of women depends on how autonomous women's organizations are from state institutions" (see also Banaszak, this volume). My own work suggests that the U.S. feminist movement "[turned] toward the state and state-affiliated groups, such as political parties and [began] employing a strategy of state involvement and electoral orientation" (Beckwith 2003, 200–1). In short, an activist women's movement may be the key not only to increasing women's descriptive representation in Congress and state legislatures but also to linking women's mass-level participation to women's electoral participation in ways that may advance women's substantive representation.[19]

Furthermore, women's movement activists are also positioned to build democracy. As Baldez shows in this volume, women's movements, in their practice, are inclusive, participatory, and democratic (see also Beckwith 2005; but see Htun 2003). Women's movement activists in the United States have furthered democracy by insisting on women's full political inclusion in U.S. politics; by constructing a political context within which women are recognized as legitimate actors; by creating a political discourse, within and outside institutions and organizations, that includes women and women's concerns (see Katzenstein 1998); by creating attitudinal change and transforming the U.S. political agenda (Banaszak, this volume); by engaging in grassroots community building (Banaszak, this volume); and by creating multiple organizations and groups for mobilizing women. The key to increasing women's political representation, and to regendering the structures that inhibit it, may also be the means of strengthening U.S. democracy generally: through the participatory, highly democratic mass base of women's activism in women's movements.

CONCLUSION: PROSPECTS FOR FUTURE RESEARCH?

Given the extensive array of research on women, gender, and politics, across individuals and institutions, recounted and critiqued in this volume, what remains to be done? What research questions might illuminate the intersection of women's mass participation and electoral representation? The individual chapters in this volume propose an extensive list of potential research questions, hypotheses for testing, areas of continuing research that are still incomplete, and prospects for the development of new questions and concepts. In this conclusion, I summarize these proposals under a rubric of six general research frames and foci for further research on political women and American democracy: (1) political women, (2) patterns of change, (3) political space and context, (4) processes of gender, (5) political theory, and (6) a comparative politics of gender. I discuss each of these, briefly, and identify questions that emerge not only from the chapters in this volume but also from the discussions at the conference that preceded it and from the wider and continuously developing scholarship on political women and democracy in the United States.

The Full Range of Political Women

Scholars have yet to analyze the political behavior, participation, quiescence, and mobilization of women in the United States across the range of women's diversity on several key politically relevant demographic variables. It is a welcome commonplace to insist on more attention to the intersections of gender and race in U.S. political research, but such insistence has yet to be matched with the scholarly consideration it deserves (see Burns, this volume; Junn and Brown, this volume). We still know less than is necessary about how gender is racialized in individuals. We do not understand fully the constraints and advantages that adhere to women in regard to their racial identity, how women and feminists mobilize in movements by and across race, and how political women benefit from race-based differences in political participation, voter turnout, and vote choice (and the bases for such differences; see Dolan, this volume; see also Reingold, this volume). Ritter (this volume) offers a template for further analysis of race and gender as these concepts are worked through political individuals and practices in the continuing development of the U.S. political system.

In addition, there is ample scope for political theorizing on gender and race. Dovi (this volume) calls for feminist scholars to theorize not just about issues of inclusion and exclusion but to "consider how democratic citizens must sometimes choose between different disadvantaged groups (black women or white women) to receive more descriptive representation." Dovi, Ritter, and Junn and Brown (all this volume) encourage further theorizing about structural inequalities based on gender, race, and racialized differences.

Similar questions, again intersecting with race and gender, arise in regard to women and class. Class is perhaps the most undertheorized component of women, gender, and politics research. Among the topics that warrant exploration are questions of how women experience politicized class differences, how class status and class identity are politically constructed, and how class and race identities (including identities framed by others) interact to produce distinctive (or invisible) political differences among women.

Finally, scholars are increasingly realizing that a focus on women's political agency, autonomy, and activism, taking into account ideological differences among women, must include research on conservative and right-wing women and their mobilization into conservative and antifeminist women's movements and organizations (see Banaszak, this volume; Beckwith 2005; Blee 2002; Klatch 1987; Schreiber 2002a, 2000b). Much of what we know about women's movements concerns more explicitly *feminist* movements; most women who have run for and have been elected to state legislatures and Congress are Democrats; in the aggregate, women are more supportive of a variety of social welfare issues than are men (see Huddy et al., this volume). What might we learn about political women if we focused more attention on conservative women and right-wing women?

Patterns of Change

More research is necessary to develop and to test models of the pattern of change and continuity for political women over time. Several potential models might explain patterns of change: critical mass, political learning, political generations, political opportunity, and punctuated equilibrium. All of these models are implicit in the literature reviewed in the chapters in this volume; all suggest a range of questions, both empirical and theoretical, for future research.[20] For example, in regard to women's electoral success over time, is the slow increase of women in office in the United States a response to individual mobilizing, fund-raising, and strategizing, or is this pattern better explained as *punctuated equilibrium*, with substantial, time-specific jumps in women's representation followed by a period of stasis? Are patterns of change based on some *critical mass* of women's political attitudes, voting preferences, and electoral achievement, the preponderance of which then have an impact on other attitudes? Are there particular structural openings for women's election to office (a *political opportunity* model), or are there instead particular issues that facilitate their election? Are women, in the aggregate, learning over time how to be good candidates, as individuals, suggesting a pattern of *political learning* and success? In regard to women's political attitudes and preferences, are these similarly located in the individual and conditioned by individual experience of, for example, class, education and race (Burns, this volume; but see Junn 2007), evidencing a slow pattern of progress over time? Are there instead *generational effects* for political attitudes and preferences of U.S. women, with intense changes that are confirmed as quasi-permanent, major attitudinal transformation? If so, how do these changes affect the ebb and flow of women's movements?

Specifying these models – critical mass, political learning, political genera-tions, political opportunity, and punctuated equilibrium – and testing and evaluating them against each other would be a major contribution to the study of U.S. political women and democracy, and would constitute frontier modeling work in the subfield of women, gender, and politics.

Political Space and Context

What can political scientists add to a geography of political women? Are there specific spaces and contexts that favor women's interests and advance their election to office? Several chapters identify an increasing importance of state governments, and of specific states and regions,[21] in shaping women's political behavior and chances for governing (see Ritter; Reingold; Dolan).[22] Christina Wolbrecht (this volume) raises additional questions about gender and political space, noting a distinctiveness of gender compared to "other politically relevant divisions," especially in comparison to African American activists and the civil rights movement. Mary Fainsod Katzenstein (1998) has analyzed women's political activism in the distinctive male-dominant insti-tutional spaces of the U.S. military and Catholic Church. My own work (1996) on women in male-dominant organizations details the ways in which working-class women construct their own spaces for advancing community goals.

Lee Ann Banaszak (this volume) offers an additional perspective on polit-ical space, focusing on women as political insiders – literally, inside the state. A range of research remains to be done regarding this conception of politi-cal space. What does it mean for women to be located as political insiders in the state? What is the relationship between women's movement activists inside executive branch agencies and women present in small numbers, and increasingly partisan, in Congress? Are women in these state locations inside in the same way as are men? What is the relationship between women as political insiders and activist women on the outside?

Political women also target different governmental arenas for candi-dacy and policy influence. This suggests that some state spaces are more women-friendly than others, especially as states reconfigure their authority and policy responsibility (see Banaszak, Beckwith, and Rucht 2003, 1–29; Beckwith 2003, 191). Political women are not equally distributed across national institutions, nor are they equally distributed across the federal boundaries between national and state governments; this inequality of insti-tutional spatial distribution varies among women by race as well. Within state governments, especially state legislatures, as Dolan (this volume) observes, female candidates and elected women are not equally distributed across the country. Some states in this nation, and specific types of electoral districts (even within the same electoral system), are more receptive to female candidacies and produce higher percentages and numbers of elected women.

Women of color are spatially distinctive among state legislators. Constituting 19.8 percent of all female state legislators in 2007, they are overwhelmingly located in the Democratic Party (93.3 percent) and are geographically concentrated in a subset of states (CAWP 2007d, 2007e).[23] Clearly there is more work to be done, and questions raised, about the nature of specific political spaces that create "women-friendly" contexts (Palmer and Simon 2006). Furthermore, such work will need to take into account the potential malleability of political spaces, the ways in which political spaces function dynamically rather than statically, and how activist women can regender political spaces to their advantage.

Processes of Gender

The most important and least developed arena of research on political women concerns gender as a process. How do women actively gender democracy? How do they create gendered opportunities for their further participation as citizens and as officeholders? How do they gender state institutions? How do other actors, including organized groups, political parties, male legislators, and judicial elites, gender U.S. democracy – and with what results? Recent research is beginning to trace provocative links between increases in women's education and election of women to office; between numbers of women in a legislature and women's political interest and efficacy; between women's political representation and introduction and support of women-friendly public policies. There are also gendered processes that are structured and enacted to disadvantage political women; new research is necessary to identify what might be termed negative processes of gender. Reingold (this volume) suggests a similar range of potential research, writing, "We should always keep in mind the powerful ways political parties and dominant coalitions structure – and gender – most aspects of policy making and representational behavior," listing "electoral incentives, professionalization, procedural rules and regulations, committee structure, fiscal and budgetary imperatives, interinstitutional relations (between legislative, executive, and judicial branches), and intergovernmental relations (between national, state, and local governments)" as gendered processes and practices that are potentially susceptible to regendering to advantage political women.

Feminist Democratic Theory, State Theorizing, and Gender

The importance of political theory in undergirding and inspiring empirical research can hardly be overstated. As empirical political scholars advance the boundaries of our knowledge about women, gender, and politics, feminist and democratic political theorists have considerable scope for theorizing specifically about political women and democracy and about gender and democracy. Suzanne Dovi (2006, 23–4) observes the continuing "need

[for] a theoretical apparatus for determining how gender is a relevant category of analysis," for identifying the "fluid aspects of gender," and for "[determining] when gender is *not* relevant to understanding political behavior." Furthermore, democratic theorizing can integrate aspects of gender into historical institutional theoretical analyses in ways that have yet to be undertaken (see Chappell 2006; Hawkesworth 2003; Kittilson 2006; Ritter, 2006, this volume). Finally, as the empirical evidence in this volume evidences, theorists have yet to undertake a gendered democratic theory that accounts for the gendered discrepancies between women's participation and women's representation.

Comparative Politics of Gender

As Ritter writes (this volume), "From a comparative perspective today, the United States is far behind other Western democracies in extending social rights that particularly benefit women or in the proportion of women who hold office in the national government." Any analysis of political women in the context of U.S. democracy must eventually take into account how democracy is built, rebuilt, transformed, and defeated by activist women in other national contexts – as well as in the larger international context (Baldez, this volume; Beckwith 2005; Chappell 2006). Furthermore, comparative political research on political women and democracy will "increase the validity of the inferences we can draw about the United States" (Baldez, this volume). Our ability to identify differences and similarities for political women across national boundaries – and within transnational activism – will be a measure of how distinctive political women are in the context of a specifically U.S. democracy.

To reiterate the question that Christina Wolbrecht raises as the outset of this volume, what did we see at the revolution? We have seen a major transformation in political science scholarship and the revolutionary construction of a new political concept of both category and process: gender. We have seen (and participated in) the creation of a body of literature that demonstrates how far political women have come in U.S. democracy, how they have contributed to U.S. democratic development, and how far political women have yet to go to achieve their (our) democratic ends.

Finally, what are the prospects for future research on political women and American democracy? As this volume both demonstrates and initiates, the prospects are, quite simply, revolutionary.

Notes

1. This distinction also maps to a mass versus elite participation dichotomy. In discussing women's political representation, I focus on women's descriptive rather than substantive policy representation, the latter being beyond the scope of this chapter.

2. The inclusion of U.S. women in mass participation, especially but not only in regard to voting, has come as the result of "centuries of struggle" (Flexner 1975) and concerted campaigns by activist women.

3. In *Voice and Equality*, Verba, Schlozman, and Brady (1995, 254) found "a consistent gender difference with women less active than men," with the exception of protest activity (254). Other activities, such as voting, campaign work, and "serving on a local board," showed no gender-related statistically significant differences (254). Differences between men and women were found in terms of campaign contributions, elite contacting, political organizational membership, and informal community work. The average differences between women and men in reported acts of political participation was 0.3 (2.3 for men and 2.0 for women) – "about one-seventh the size of the participatory difference between a high school and a college graduate." They further conclude that there is no difference between participant women and men in the amount of time they devote to voluntary group activism (259). In general, participation differences between women and men persist within racial groups.

4. Note, however, a pattern of stability in women's statehouse candidacies from 1994 to 2004, and a substantial decline in 2006. See CAWP 2007a.

5. Note that in this concluding chapter, I focus primarily on representation as women's presence and am silent on other means of representation, for example, surrogate representation of women by men (see Mansbridge 2003) or women's political representation through judicial or executive action.

6. In comparative perspective, the United States shares sixty-seventh place in a ranking of nations by percentage of women holding national legislative office in the lower house; given ties in the Inter-Parliamentary Union data set, the United States actually ranks eighty-first among nations ("Women in National Parliaments").

7. The percentage of elected female state legislators did not reach 20 percent until 1993, when 1,524 women were elected to state legislatures (20.5 percent; CAWP 2007d).

8. The United States state can be seen as having little autonomy regarding "dominant-class issues" and as closed, in issue terms, to challenges to capitalism. See Evans et al. 1985, 350–1.

9. My thanks to Kathleen Dolan for this observation.

10. For a discussion of the impact of the presence of female officeholders on women's mass political participation, see Burns, Schlozman, and Verba 2001, 334–56; but see Lawless 2004.

11. John Aldrich observes an interesting contradiction in regard to political party organizational strength in the United States. He argues that political party formal organizations are "stronger, better financed, and more professional at all levels now," yet also remarks that party organizational "importance to candidates may be less than in the past" (1995, 15). These very circumstances undergird candidate free rein in regard to self-nomination and self-financing, conditions that advantage the most experienced, wealthiest, or best financed in initial rounds of competition, including those candidates who can deter underfinanced potential opponents.

12. Jean Reith Schroedel and Marcia L. Godwin suggest that differences between the two major parties and across geographic regions in the United States may be

the result of resistances by party leaders and gatekeepers to women's candidacies (2005, 265–75; see also Duerst-Lahti 2005, 232–4).

13. Kittilson includes party system and internal party organization as part of the "institutional opportunity structure" faced by political women in her study of women and fifty political parties in ten West European nations (2006, 26).

14. Sanbonmatsu (this volume) identifies a structural dilemma for political women: although third parties have generally been sympathetic to women's issues and women's representation, because of their exclusion from the party system, they can offer only symbolic support for women's election. She writes, "Third parties were the key supporters of women's suffrage, suggesting the inherent limitations of working with the two major parties. Yet forming a third party – which the National Organization for Women (NOW) contemplated in the early 1990s – seems impractical."

15. Nonetheless, the news is not completely depressing. Writing in 1984, Kristi Andersen and Stuart Thorson developed a predictive simulation model, based on women's representation in the U.S. House of Representatives in 1948 and in 1980, in an attempt to assess women's likely electoral progress. Under the most generous assumptions of weak incumbency effect and number of female nominees, the authors concluded that the slope for their model of women's political representation in the United States was so shallow that it would take forty years – until the year 2020 – for as many as fifty-three women to hold seats in the U.S. House. The actual evidence shows that, by 1996, fifty-four women were elected to the 105th Congress and, in 2004, sixty-seven women were elected, a greater number than Andersen and Thorson's models predicted, even by the year 2030 (see figure 4, 152).

16. Robert Dahl also identifies the ways in which the U.S. Constitution differs from other political systems, with democratic implications, including an electoral system of single-member plurality districts (2002, 60). In comparison among twenty-two nations that have been consistently democratic since 1950, Dahl finds, the United States fares badly in terms of women's political representation, specifically women's cabinet representation 1993–5 (eighth out of twenty-two) and women's national legislative representation 1971–95 (eighteenth out of twenty-two; see Dahl, table 5, 168–9).

17. Among twenty-two democracies studied by Arend Lijphart (1945–80), only four employed a single-member plurality electoral system, one of which (New Zealand) changed to a proportional system in 1996 (Lijphart 1984, 152, figure 9.1). Among fifty-three democracies studied by LeDuc, Niemi, and Norris (1996, 53), four used a plurality system for presidential elections, and thirteen employed a plurality system for legislative elections.

18. See, however, Palmer and Simon (2005) on the gendered effects of incumbency on women's renomination prospects.

19. My thanks to Kira Sanbonmatsu for suggesting this possibility.

20. See Caraway's discussion of women's enfranchisement in the sequencing of comparative democratization (2004). See also Hughes and Paxton 2007; Tripp and Kang, forthcoming.

21. See the discussion of the Southern and the Far West states in Dolan, this volume.

22. Note an earlier related literature on the political geography of women's representation in political science (e.g., Diamond 1977; Nechemias 1985; Rule 1981).

See the more recent work on women, feminism and political geography among political geographers and political development scholars (e.g., J. P. Jones 1997; Momsen and Kinnard 1993; Paxton and Hughes 2007; Staeheli, Kofman, and Peake 2004).

23. For example, Latina state legislators serve in twenty-two states but are concentrated in Arizona (seven), California (ten), Illinois (six), New Mexico (thirteen), and Texas (eight; CAWP 2007c).

References

Abramowitz, Mimi. 1996. *Regulating the Lives of Women: Social Welfare from Colonial Times to the Present*. Boston: South End Press.

Achen, Christopher. 1975. "Mass Political Attitudes and the Survey Response." *American Political Science Review* 69:1218–31.

Acker, Joan. 1992. "Gendered Institution: From Sex Roles to Gendered Institutions." *Contemporary Sociology* 21(September):565–9.

Adams, Greg D. 1997. "Abortion: Evidence of Issue Evolution." *American Journal of Political Science* 41:718–37.

Adams, Julia, and Ann Shola Orloff. 2005. "Defending Modernity? High Politics, Feminist Anti-Modernism and the Place of Gender." *Politics & Gender* 1: 158–72.

Aday, Sean, and James Devitt. 2001. "Style over Substance: Newspaper Coverage of Elizabeth Dole's Presidential Bid." *Harvard International Journal of Press/Politics* 6:52–73.

Aldrich, John H. 1995. *Why Parties? The Origin and Transformation of Party Politics in America*. Chicago: University of Chicago Press.

Alexander, Deborah, and Kristi Andersen. 1993. "Gender as a Factor in the Attribution of Leadership Traits." *Political Research Quarterly* 46:527–45.

Almond, Gabriel A., and Sidney Verba. 1963. *The Civic Culture*. Princeton, NJ: Princeton University Press.

Alvarez, Sonia E. 1990. *Engendering Democracy in Brazil: Women's Movements in Transition Politics*. Princeton, NJ: Princeton University Press.

Alvarez, Sonia E. 1998. "Latin American Feminisms 'Go Global'." In *Cultures of Politics, Politics of Cultures: Re-visioning Latin American Social Movements*, ed. Sonia E. Alvarez, Evelina Dagnino, and Arturo Escobar. Boulder, CO: Westview Press, pp. 293–324.

Amnesty International. 2007. *Ratify the Treaty for the Rights of Women, CEDAW*. Accessed June 15, 2007. http://www.amnestyusa.org/Ratify_the_Treaty_for_the_Rights_of_Women_CEDAW/About_this_campaign/page.do?id=1021185&n1=3&n2=39&n3=719.

Andersen, Kristi. 1975. "Working Women and Political Participation, 1952–1972." *American Journal of Political Science* 19:439–53.

Andersen, Kristi. 1990. "Women and Citizenship in the 1920s." In *Women, Politics, and Change*, ed. Louise A. Tilly and Patricia Gurin. New York: Russell Sage Foundation, pp. 177–98.

Andersen, Kristi. 1996. *After Suffrage: Women in Partisan and Electoral Politics before the New Deal*. Chicago: University of Chicago Press.

Andersen, Kristi, and Elizabeth A. Cook. 1985. "Women, Work, and Political Attitudes." *American Journal of Political Science* 29:606–25.

Andersen, Kristi, and Stuart J. Thorson. 1984. "Congressional Turnover and the Election of Women." *Western Political Quarterly* 37(1):143–56.

Anzaldúa, Gloria. 1987. *Borderlands/La frontera: The New Mestiza*. San Francisco: Aunt Lute Books.

Ardrey, Saundra. 1994. "The Political Behavior of Black Women: Contextual, Structural, and Psychological Factors." In *Black Politics and Black Political Behavior: A Linkage Analysis*, ed. Hanes Walton. Westport, CT: Praeger, pp. 219–34.

Ards, Angela. 1991. *Stories of Art and Power: Toni Morrison's "Tar Baby."* Unpublished honors essay, Department of English, University of North Carolina, Rayleigh-Durham.

Aretxaga, Begoña. 1997. *Shattering Silence: Women, Nationalism, and Political Subjectivity in Northern Ireland*. Princeton, NJ: Princeton University Press.

Atkeson, Lonna Rae. 2003. "Not All Cues Are Created Equal: The Conditional Impact of Female Candidates on Political Engagement." *Journal of Politics* 65:1040–61.

Baer, Denise. 1993. "Political Parties: The Missing Variable in Women and Politics Research." *Political Research Quarterly* 46:547–76.

Baer, Denise L. 2003. "Women, Women's Organizations, and Political Parties." In *Women and American Politics: New Questions, New Directions*, ed. Susan J. Carroll. Oxford, UK: Oxford University Press, pp. 111–45.

Baer, Denise L. 2006a. "Party-Based Leadership and Gender: Beyond the Chinese Box Puzzle of Women's Recruitment to Political Office." Paper presented at the Women and Leadership Conference at the Women and Politics Institute, American University, Washington, DC.

Baer, Denise L. 2006b. "What Kind of Women's Movement? Community, Representation, and Resurgence." In *Women in Politics: Outsiders or Insiders?* ed. Lois Duke Whitaker. 4th ed. Upper Saddle River, NJ: Pearson Prentice Hall, pp. 96–114.

Baer, Denise L., and David A. Bositis. 1988. *Elite Cadres and Party Coalitions: Representing the Public in Party Politics*. New York: Greenwood Press.

Baer, Denise L., and Julie A. Dolan. 1994. "Intimate Connections: Political Interests and Group Activity in State and Local Parties." *American Review of Politics* 15:257–89.

Baer, Denise L., and John S. Jackson. 1985. "Are Women Really More 'Amateur' in Politics than Men?" *Women & Politics* 5:79–92.

Baker, Paula. 1984. "The Domestication of Politics: Women and American Political Society, 1780–1920." *American Historical Review* 89:620–47.

Baldez, Lisa. 2001. "Coalition Politics and the Limits of State Feminism." *Women & Politics* 22:1–28.

Baldez, Lisa. 2002. *Why Women Protest: Women's Movements in Chile*. New York: Cambridge University Press.

Baldez, Lisa. 2003. "Women's Movements and Democratic Transition in Chile, Brazil, East Germany and Poland." *Comparative Politics* 35:253–72.

Baldez, Lisa. 2004. "Elected Bodies: The Gender Quota Law for Legislative Candidates in Mexico." *Legislative Studies Quarterly* 29:231–58.

Baldez, Lisa. 2007. "Primaries vs. Quotas: Gender and Candidate Nomination in Mexico." *Latin American Politics and Society* 49(3):69–96.

Baldez, Lisa, Lee Epstein, and Andrew D. Martin. 2006. "Does the U.S. Constitution Need an Equal Rights Amendment?" *Journal of Legal Studies* 35:243–83.

Baldez, Lisa, and Celeste Montoya Kirk. 2005. "Gendered Opportunities: The Formation of Women's Movements in the United States and Chile." In *The US Women's Movement in a Global Perspective*, ed. Lee Ann Banaszak. Lanham, MD: Rowman and Littlefield, pp. 133–50.

Banaszak, Lee Ann. 1996a. "When Waves Collide: Cycles of Protest and the Swiss and American Women's Movements." *Political Research Quarterly* 49:837–60.

Banaszak, Lee Ann. 1996b. *Why Movements Succeed or Fail: Opportunity, Culture, and the Struggle for Woman Suffrage*. Princeton, NJ: Princeton University Press.

Banaszak, Lee Ann. 1998. "Use of the Initiative by Woman Suffrage Movements." In *Social Movements and American Political Institutions*, ed. Anne Costain and Andrew McFarland. Boulder, CO: Rowman and Littlefield, pp. 99–114.

Banaszak, Lee Ann. 2004. "Mobilizing in and out of the State: Feminist Bureaucrats and the Creation of Women's Movement Organizations." Presented at the American Political Science Association Annual Meeting, Chicago.

Banaszak, Lee Ann. 2005. "Inside and outside the State: How Feminist Activists inside the Federal Bureaucracy Changed Policy." Paper presented at the American Political Science Association Annual Meeting, Washington, DC.

Banaszak, Lee Ann. 2007. *In and Out of the State: The Women's Movement and the Washington Feminist Underground*. Unpublished manuscript, Pennsylvania State University, University Park.

Banaszak, Lee Ann, Karen Beckwith, and Dieter Rucht, eds. 2003. *Women's Movements Facing the Reconfigured State*. New York: Cambridge University Press.

Banaszak, Lee Ann, and Eric Plutzer. 1993. "Contextual Determinants of Feminist Attitudes: National and Subnational Influences in Western Europe." *American Political Science Review* 87:147–57.

Barakso, Maryann. 2004. *Governing NOW: Grassroots Activism in the National Organization for Women*. Ithaca, NY: Cornell University Press.

Barakso, Maryann. 2005. "Diminished Democracy? Comparing Opportunities for Participation in Women's Voluntary Associations." Paper presented at the American Political Science Association Annual Meeting, Washington, DC.

Barnello, Michelle A. 1999. "Gender and Roll Call Voting in the New York State Assembly." *Women & Politics* 20:77–94.

Barnett, Bernice McNair. 1995. "Black Women's Collectivist Movement Organizations: Their Struggles during the 'Doldrums.'" In *Feminist Organizations: Harvest of the New Women's Movement*, ed. Myra Marx Ferree and Patricia Yancy Martin. Philadelphia: Temple University Press, pp. 199–219.

Barrett, Edith J. 1995. "The Policy Priorities of African American Women in State Legislatures." *Legislative Studies Quarterly* 20:223–47.

Barrett, Edith J. 1997. "Gender and Race in the State House: The Legislative Experience." *Social Science Journal* 34:131–44.

Barry, Brian. (1965) 1990. *Political Argument,* 2nd ed. Herefordshire, UK: Harvester Wheatsheaf.

Bashevkin, Sylvia. 1998. *Women on the Defensive: Living through Conservative Times.* Chicago: University of Chicago Press.

Basu, Amrita. 1995. *The Challenge of Local Feminisms.* Boulder, CO: Westview Press.

Batson, C. Daniel, Patricia Schoenrade, and W. Larry Ventis. 1993. *Religion and the Individual: A Social Psychological Perspective.* New York: Oxford University Press.

Baumgartner, Frank, and Bryan Jones. 1993. *Agendas and Instability in American Politics.* Chicago: University of Chicago Press.

Baxter, Sandra, and Marjorie Lansing. 1983. *Women and Politics: The Visible Majority,* rev. ed. Ann Arbor: University of Michigan Press.

Bayard de Volo, Lorraine. 2001. *Mothers of Heroes and Martyrs: Gender Identity Politics in Nicaragua, 1979–1999.* Baltimore: Johns Hopkins University Press.

Beck, Susan Abrams. 2001. "Acting as Women: The Effects and Limitations of Gender in Local Governance." In *The Impact of Women in Public Office,* ed. Susan J. Carroll. Bloomington: Indiana University Press, pp. 49–67.

Beckwith, Karen. 1986. *American Women and Political Participation: The Impacts of Work, Generation, and Feminism.* New York: Greenwood Press.

Beckwith, Karen. 1992. "Comparative Research and Electoral Systems: Lessons from France and Italy." *Women & Politics* 21:1–33.

Beckwith, Karen. 1996. "Lancashire Women against Pit Closures: Women's Standing in a Men's Movement." *Signs* 21:1034–68.

Beckwith, Karen. 1998. "Collective Identities of Class and Gender: Working-Class Women in the Pittston Coal Strike." *Political Psychology* 19:147–67.

Beckwith, Karen. 2000. "Beyond Compare? Women's Movements in Comparative Perspective." *European Journal of Political Research* 37:431–86.

Beckwith, Karen. 2001. "Gender Frames and Collective Action: Configurations of Masculinity in the Pittston Coal Strike." *Politics & Society* 29:297–330.

Beckwith, Karen. 2002. "Women, Gender, and Nonviolence in Political Movements." *PS: Political Science and Politics* 35(March):71–82.

Beckwith, Karen. 2003. "The Gendering Ways of States: Women's Representation and State Transformations in France, Great Britain and the United States." In *Women's Movements Facing the Reconfigured State,* ed. Karen Beckwith, Lee Ann Banaszak, and Dieter Rucht. Cambridge: Cambridge University Press, pp. 169–202.

Beckwith, Karen. 2005. "A Common Language of Gender?" *Politics & Gender* 1(1):128–37.

Beckwith, Karen. 2007a. "Mapping Strategic Engagements of Women's Movements." *International Feminist Journal of Politics* 9(3):312–39.

Beckwith, Karen. 2007b. "Gender and Politics." Unpublished manuscript, Case Western Reserve University, Cleveland, OH.

Bederman, Gail. 1995. *Manliness and Civilization: A Cultural History of Gender and Race in the United States, 1880–1917.* Chicago: University of Chicago Press.

Bedolla, Lisa Garcia. 2007. "Intersections of Inequality: Understanding Marginalization and Privilege in the Post-Civil Rights Era." *Politics & Gender* 3(2):4–20.

Beltrán, Cristina. 2004. "Patrolling Borders: Hybrids, Hierarchies and the Challenge of Mestizaje." *Political Research Quarterly* 57(December):595–607.

Bem, S. L. 1981. "Gender Schema Theory – A Cognitive Account of Sex Typing." *Psychological Review* 88:354–64.

Bendyna, Mary E., Tamata Finucane, Lynn Kirby, John P. O'Donnell, and Clyde Wilcox. 1996. "Gender Differences in Public Attitudes toward the Gulf War: A Test of Competing Hypotheses." *Social Science Journal* 33:1–22.

Bennett, Linda, and Stephen Earl Bennett. 1989. "Enduring Gender Differences in Political Interest." *American Politics Quarterly* 17:105–22.

Berch, Neil. 2004. "Women Incumbents, Elite Bias, and Voter Response in the 1996 and 1998 U.S. House Elections." *Women & Politics* 26:21–33.

Berelson, Bernard, Paul. F. Lazarsfeld, and William McPhee. 1954. *Voting: A Study of Opinion Formation in a Presidential Campaign*. Chicago: University of Chicago Press.

Bernardino, Minerva. 1947. "Women of Latin America Advancing toward Equality." *Equal Rights* (May–June):4.

Bernstein, Mary. 1997. "Celebration and Suppression: The Strategic Uses of Identity by the Lesbian and Gay Movement." *American Journal of Sociology* 103:531–65.

Bernstein, Mary. 2002. "The Contradictions of Gay Ethnicity: Forging Identity in Vermont." In *Social Movements: Identity, Culture and the State*, ed. David. S. Meyer, Nancy Whittier, and Belinda Robnett. New York: Oxford University Press, pp. 85–104.

Berry, Mary Frances. 1988. *Why ERA Failed: Politics, Women's Rights, and the Amending Process of the Constitution*. Bloomington: Indiana University Press.

Bers, Trudy Haffron. 1978. "Local Political Elites: Men and Women on Boards of Education." *Western Political Quarterly* 31:381–91.

Best, Deborah L., and John E. Williams. 1982. *Measuring Sex Stereotypes: A Thirty-Nation Study*. Beverly Hills, CA: Sage.

Bettencourt, B. Ann, and Norman Miller. 1996. "Gender Differences in Aggression as a Function of Provocation: A Meta-Analysis." *Psychological Bulletin* 119(3):422–47.

Beutel, Ann M., and Margaret Mooney Marini. 1995. "Gender and Values." *American Sociological Review* 60:436–48.

Bianchi, Suzanne M., Melissa A. Milkie, Liana C. Sayer, and John P. Robinson. 2000. "Is Anyone Doing the Housework? Trends in the Gender Division of Household Labor." *Social Forces* 79:191–228.

Biersack, Robert, and Paul Herrnson. 1994. "Political Parties and the Year of the Woman." In *The Year of the Woman: Myths and Realities*, ed. Elizabeth Adell Cook, Sue Thomas, and Clyde Wilcox. Boulder, CO: Westview Press, pp. 161–80.

Blair, Diane D., and Jeanie R. Stanley. 1991. "Personal Relationships and Legislative Power: Male and Female Perceptions." *Legislative Studies Quarterly* 16:495–507.

Blais, Andre, and Louis Massicotte. 1996. *Electoral Systems*. Thousand Oaks, CA: Sage.

Blee, Kathleen M. 2002. *Inside Organized Racism: Women in the Hate Movement*. Berkeley: University of California Press.

Boles, Janet. 1979. *The Politics of the Equal Rights Amendment: Conflict and the Decision Process.* New York: Longman.

Boles, Janet K. 1994. "Local Feminist Policy Networks in the Contemporary American Interest Group System." *Policy Sciences* 27:161–78.

Boles, Janet K. 2001. "Local Elected Women and Policy-Making: Movement Delegates or Feminist Trustees?" In *The Impact of Women in Public Office,* ed. Susan J. Carroll. Bloomington: Indiana University Press, pp. 66–88.

Bonk, Kathy. 1988. "The Selling of 'The Gender Gap.'" In *The Politics of the Gender Gap: The Social Construction of Political Influence,* ed. Carol M. Mueller. Newbury Park, CA: Sage, pp. 82–101.

Boris, Eileen. 2003. "Mothers and Other Workers: (Re)Conceiving Labor, Maternalism, and the State." *Journal of Women's History* 15:90–117.

Boris, Eileen. 2005. "On the Importance of Naming: Gender, Race, and the Writing of Policy History." *Journal of Policy History* 17:72–92.

Bourque, Susan, and Jean Grossholtz. 1974. "Politics as Unnatural Practice: Political Science Looks at Female Participation." *Politics and Society* 4(Winter): 225–66.

Box-Steffensmeier, Janet M., Suzanna De Boef, and Tse-Min Lin. 2004. "The Dynamics of the Partisan Gender Gap." *American Political Science Review* 98:515–28.

Bratton, Kathleen A. 2002. "The Effect of Legislative Diversity on Agenda Setting: Evidence from Six State Legislatures." *American Politics Research* 30:115–42.

Bratton, Kathleen. 2004. "The Role of Gender in Nominating Contests for the U.S. House of Representatives." Paper presented at the Southern Political Science Association Annual Meeting, New Orleans, LA.

Bratton, Kathleen A. 2005. "Critical Mass Theory Revisited: The Behavior and Success of Token Women in State Legislatures." *Politics & Gender* 1:97–125.

Bratton, Kathleen A., and Kerry L. Haynie. 1999. "Agenda Setting and Legislative Success in State Legislatures: The Effects of Gender and Race." *Journal of Politics* 61:658–79.

Bratton, Kathleen A., Kerry L. Haynie, and Beth Reingold. 2006. "Agenda Setting and African American Women in State Legislatures." *Journal of Women, Politics, and Policy* 28(3/4):71–96.

Bratton, Kathleen, and Leonard P. Ray. 2002. "Descriptive Representation, Policy Outcomes, and Municipal Day-Care Coverage in Norway." *American Journal of Political Science* 46:428–37.

Breckinridge, Sophonisba. 1933. *Women in the Twentieth Century: A Study of Their Political, Social, and Economic Activities.* New York: McGraw-Hill.

Brians, Craig Leonard. 2005. "Voting for Women? Gender and Party Bias in Voting for Female Candidates." *American Politics Research* 33:357–75.

Britton, Hannah E. 1998. "The Struggle Continues: Women's Role in the Democratization of South Africa." Paper presented at the Midwest Political Science Association Annual Meeting, Chicago.

Brock-Utne, Birgit. 1989. *Feminist Perspectives on Peace and Peace Education.* Oxford: Pergamon.

Brown, Michael K., Martin Carnoy, Elliott Currie, Troy Duster, David B. Oppenheimer, Marjorie M. Shultz, and David Wellman. 2003. *Whitewashing Race: The Myth of a Color-Blind Society.* Berkeley: University of California Press.

Brown, Michael K. 1988. *Manhood and Politics.* New York: Rowman and Littlefield.

Brown, Wendy. 1995. *States of Injury: Power and Freedom in Late Modernity.* Princeton, NJ: Princeton University Press.

Brubaker, Rogers, and Frederick Cooper. 2000. "Beyond 'Identity.'" *Theory and Society* 29:1–47.

Bruhn, Kathleen. 2003. "Whores and Lesbians: Political Activism, Party Strategies, and Gender Quotas in Mexico." *Electoral Studies* 22:101–19.

Buechler, Steven. 1986. *The Transformation of the Woman Suffrage Movement.* New Brunswick, NJ: Rutgers University Press.

Burns, Nancy. 2005. "Finding Gender." *Politics & Gender* 1(1):137–41.

Burns, Nancy, and Donald Kinder. 2002. "Conviction and Its Consequences." Unpublished manuscript, University of Michigan, Ann Arbor.

Burns, Nancy, Kay Lehman Schlozman, and Sidney Verba. 1997. "The Public Consequences of Private Inequality: Family Life and Citizen Participation." *American Political Science Review* 91:373–89.

Burns, Nancy, Kay Lehman Schlozman, and Sidney Verba. 2001. *The Private Roots of Public Action: Gender, Equality, and Political Participation.* Cambridge, MA: Harvard University Press.

Burrell, Barbara C. 1993. "Party Decline, Party Transformation and Gender Politics: the USA." In *Gender and Party Politics*, ed. Joni Lovenduski and Pippa Norris. London: Sage, pp. 291–308.

Burrell, Barbara C. 1994. *A Woman's Place Is in the House: Campaigning for Congress in the Feminist Era.* Ann Arbor: University of Michigan Press.

Burrell, Barbara. 2005. "Campaign Financing: Women's Experience in the Modern Era." In *Women and Elective Office: Past, Present, and Future*, ed. Sue Thomas and Clyde Wilcox. 2nd ed. New York: Oxford University Press, pp. 26–37.

Burrell, Barbara. 2006. "Political Parties and Women's Organizations: Bringing Women in the Electoral Arena." In *Gender and Elections: Shaping the Future of American Politics*, ed. Susan Carroll and Richard Fox. New York: Cambridge University Press, pp. 143–68.

Burrell, Barbara, and Brian Frederick. 2006. "Windows of Opportunity: Recruitment Pools, Gender Politics, and Congressional Open Seats." Paper presented at the Southern Political Science Association Annual Meeting, New Orleans, LA.

Butler, Judith. 1990. *Gender Trouble: Feminism and the Subversion of Identity.* New York: Routledge.

Byrd, Ayana D., and Lori L. Tharps. 2001. *Hair Story: Untangling the Roots of Black Hair in America.* New York: St. Martin's Press.

Bystrom, Dianne. 2006. "Advertising, Web Sites, and Media Coverage: Gender and Communication along the Campaign Trail." In *Gender and Elections: Shaping the Future of American Politics*, ed. Susan Carroll and Richard Fox. New York: Cambridge University Press, pp. 169–88.

Bystrom, Dianne, Mary Christine Banwart, Lynda Lee Kaid, and Terry Robertson. 2004. *Gender and Candidate Communication.* New York: Routledge.

Bystrom, Dianne, Terry Robertson, and Mary Christine Banwart. 2001. "Framing the Fight: An Analysis of Media Coverage of Female and Male Candidates in Primary Races for Governor and U.S. Senate in 2000." *American Behavioral Scientist* 44:1999–2013.

Bystydzienski, Jill M. 1995. *Women in Electoral Politics: Lessons from Norway.* Westport, CT: Praeger.

Bystydzienski, Jill M., and Joti Sekhon, eds. 1999. *Democratization and Women's Grassroots Movements.* Bloomington: Indiana University Press.

Caldeira, Gregory A., John A. Clark, and Samuel C. Patterson. 1993. "Political Respect in the Legislature." *Legislative Studies Quarterly* 18:3–28.

Cammisa, Anne Marie, and Beth Reingold. 2004. "Women in State Legislatures and State Legislative Research: Beyond Sameness and Difference." *State Politics & Policy Quarterly* 4:181–210.

Campbell, Andrea. 2003. *How Policies Make Citizens: Senior Political Activism and the American Welfare State*. Princeton, NJ: Princeton University Press.

Campbell, Angus, Philip E. Converse, Warren E. Miller, and Donald E. Stokes. 1960. *The American Voter*. Chicago: University of Chicago Press.

Campbell, David, and Christina Wolbrecht. 2006. "See Jane Run: Women Politicians as Role Models for Adolescents." *Journal of Politics* 68:233–47.

Campbell, Patricia. 2003. "Gender and Post-Conflict Civil Society: Eritrea." *International Feminist Journal of Politics* 7:377–99.

Caraway, Teri L. 2004. "Inclusion and Democratization: Class, Gender, Race, and the Extension of Suffrage." *Comparative Politics* 36(4):443–60.

Carey, John M., Richard G. Niemi, and Lynda W. Powell. 1998. "Are Women State Legislators Different?" In *Women and Elective Office: Past, Present, and Future*, ed. Sue Thomas and Clyde Wilcox. New York: Oxford University Press, pp. 87–102.

Carroll, Susan J. 1985. *Women as Candidates in American Politics*. Bloomington: Indiana University Press.

Carroll, Susan J. 1988. "Women's Autonomy and the Gender Gap: 1980 and 1982." In *The Politics of the Gender Gap: The Social Construction of Political Influence*, ed. Carol M. Mueller. Newbury Park, CA: Sage, pp. 236–57.

Carroll, Susan J. 1994. *Women as Candidates in American Politics*, 2nd ed. Bloomington: Indiana University Press.

Carroll, Susan J. 1999. "The Disempowerment of the Gender Gap: Soccer Moms and the 1996 Elections." *P.S.: Political Science and Politics* 32:7–11.

Carroll, Susan J. 2001. "Representing Women: Women State Legislators as Agents of Policy-Related Change." In *The Impact of Women in Public Office*, ed. Susan J. Carroll. Bloomington: Indiana University Press, pp. 3–21.

Carroll, Susan J. 2002. "Representing Women: Congresswomen's Perceptions of Their Representational Roles." In *Women Transforming Congress*, ed. Cindy Simon Rosenthal. Norman: University of Oklahoma Press, pp. 50–68.

Carroll, Susan J. 2006. "The Committee Assignments of State Legislators: An Underexplored Link in Understanding Gender Differences." Paper presented at the Women in Politics: Seeking Office and Making Policy Conference sponsored by the Center for Politics (University of Virginia) and the Institute of Governmental Studies (University of California, Berkeley), Berkeley, CA.

Caul, Miki. 2001. "Political Parties and the Adoption of Candidate Gender Quotas: A Cross-National Analysis." *Journal of Politics* 63:1214–29.

Caul, Miki, and Katherine Tate. 2002. "Thinner Ranks: Women as Candidates and California's Blanket Primary." In *Voting at the Political Fault Line: California's Experiment with the Blanket Primary*, ed. Bruce E. Cain and Elisabeth R. Gerber. Berkeley: University of California Press, pp. 234–47.

Cavin, Susan. 1990. "The Invisible Army of Women: Lesbian Social Protests, 1969–1988." In *Women and Social Protest*, ed. Guida West and Rhoda Blumberg. Oxford: Oxford University Press, pp. 321–31.

Center for American Women and Politics (CAWP). 2001. "Women State Legislators: Past, Present and Future." New Brunswick, NJ: Eagleton Institute of Politics, Rutgers University.

Center for American Women and Politics (CAWP). 2005. "Women in Congress: Leadership Roles and Committee Chairs." Fact sheet by the Center for American Women and Politics, Eagleton Institute of Politics, Rutgers University.

Center for American Women and Politics (CAWP). 2006. "Summary of Women Candidates for Selected Offices 1970–2006." Accessed June 8, 2007. http://www.rci.rutgers.edu/~cawp/Facts/CanHistory/can_histsum.pdf.

Center for American Women and Politics (CAWP). 2007a. "Women in Elective Office 2007." Accessed June 8, 2007. http://www.cawp.rutgers.edu/Facts/Officeholders/elective.pdf.

Center for American Women and Politics (CAWP). 2007b. "Women Appointed to Presidential Cabinets." Accessed June 8, 2007. http://www.cawp.rutgers.edu/Facts/Officeholders/fedcab.pdf.

Center for American Women and Politics (CAWP). 2007c. "Elección Latina: State Legislature." Accessed June 28, 2007. www.cawp.rutgers.edu/Eleccion/elecleg.htm.

Center for American Women and Politics (CAWP). 2007d. "Women in State Legislatures 2007." Fact sheet by the Center for American Women and Politics, Eagleton Institute of Politics, Rutgers University.

Center for American Women and Politics (CAWP). 2007e. "Women of Color in Elective Office 2007." Fact sheet by the Center for American Women and Politics, Eagleton Institute of Politics, Rutgers University.

Center for American Women and Politics (CAWP). 2007f. "Sex Differences in Voter Turnout." Fact sheet by the Center for American Women and Politics, Eagleton Institute of Politics, Rutgers University.

Chaney, Carole Kennedy, R. Michael Alvarez, and Jonathan Nagler. 1998. "Explaining the Gender Gap in U.S. Presidential Elections, 1980–1992." *Political Research Quarterly* 51:311–39.

Chappell, Louise. 2002. *Gendering Government*. Vancouver: University of British Columbia Press.

Chappell, Louise. 2006. "Comparing Political Institutions: Revealing the Gendered 'Logic of Appropriateness.'" *Politics & Gender* 2(2):223–35.

Chatty, Dawn, and Annika Rabo, eds. 1997. *Organizing Women: Formal and Informal Women's Groups in the Middle East*. Oxford: Berg.

Childs, Sarah. 2002. "Hitting the Target: Are Labour Women MPs 'Acting for' Women?" *Parliamentary Affairs* 55:143–53.

Childs, Sarah. 2006. "The Complicated Relationship between Women's Descriptive and Substantive Representation." *European Journal of Women's Studies* 13: 7–21.

Childs, Sarah, and Mona Lena Krook. 2006. "Gender and Politics: The State of the Art." *Politics* 26(1):18–28.

Chowdhury, Najma, and Barbara J. Nelson. 1994. "Redefining Poltiics: Patterns of Women's Poltiical Engagement from a Global Perspective." In *Women and Politics Worldwide*, ed. Barbara J. Nelson and Najma Chowdhury. New Haven, CT: Yale University Press, pp. 3–24.

Christensen, James A., and Riley E. Dunlap. 1984. "Freedom and Equality in American Political Ideology: Race and Gender Differences." *Social Science Quarterly* 65:861–7.

Christy, Carol. 1987. *Sex Differences in Political Participation.* New York: Praeger.

Clark, Cal, and Janet Clark. 1986. "Models of Gender and Political Participation in the United States." *Women & Politics* 6:5–25.

Clark, Cal, and Janet Clark. 1996. "Whither the Gender Gap? Converging and Conflicting Attitudes among Women." In *Women in Politics: Insiders or Outsiders? A Collection of Readings,* ed. L. L. Duke. Englewood Cliffs, NJ: Prentice-Hall, pp. 78–99.

Clark, Janet. 1998. "Women at the National Level: An Update on Roll Call Voting Behavior." In *Women and Elective Office: Past, Present, and Future,* ed. Sue Thomas and Clyde Wilcox. New York: Oxford University Press, pp. 118–29.

Clark, Janet, and Cal Clark. 1993. "The Gender Gap 1988: Compassion, Pacifism, and Indirect Feminism." In *Women in Politics: Insiders or Outsiders? A Collection of Readings,* ed. L. L. Duke. Englewood Cliffs, NJ: Prentice-Hall, pp. 32–45.

Clark, Janet, Charles D. Hadley, and R. Darcy. 1989. "Political Ambition among Men and Women State Party Leaders: Testing the Countersocialization Perspective." *American Politics Quarterly* 17:194–207.

Clarke, Cheryl. 1983. *Narratives: Poems in the Tradition of Black Women.* New York: Kitchen Table Press.

Clawson, Rosalee A., and John A. Clark. 2003. "The Attitudinal Structure of African American Women Party Activists: The Impact of Race, Gender, and Religion." *Political Research Quarterly* 56:211–21.

Clemens, Elisabeth. 1993. "Organizational Repertoires and Institutional Change: Women's Groups and the Transformation of U.S. Politics, 1890–1920." *American Journal of Sociology* 98:755–98.

Clemens, Elisabeth S. 1997. *The People's Lobby: Organizational Innovation and the Rise of Interest Group Politics in the United States, 1890–1925.* Chicago: University of Chicago Press.

Cohen, Cathy J. 1999. *The Boundaries of Blackness: AIDS and the Breakdown of Black Politics.* Chicago: University of Chicago Press.

Cohen, Cathy, Kathleen Jones, and Joan Tronto, eds. 1997. *Women Transforming Politics.* New York: New York University Press.

Coleman, John J. 1996. "Resurgent or Just Busy? Party Organizations in Contemporary America." In *The State of the Parties: The Changing Role of Contemporary American Parties,* ed. John C. Green and Daniel M. Shea. Lanham, MD: Rowman and Littlefield, pp. 367–84.

Collins, Patricia Hill. 1989. "The Social Construction of Black Feminist Thought." *Signs* 14(August):745–73.

Collins, Patricia Hill. 1990. *Black Feminist Thought: Knowledge, Consciousness, and the Politics of Empowerment.* New York: Routledge.

Collins, Patricia Hill. 2000. *Black Feminist Thought: Knowledge, Consciousness, and the Politics of Empowerment,* 2nd ed. New York: Routledge.

Combahee River Collective. 1977. "A Black Feminist Statement." In *Words of Fire,* ed. Beverly Guy-Sheftall, 1995. New York: New Press, pp. 232–40.

Committee on Political Parties of the American Political Science Association. 1950. *Toward a More Responsible Two-Party System. A Report of the Committee* on *Political Parties of the American Political Science Association.* New York: Rinehart.

Committee on the Status of Women in the Profession. 2001. "The Status of Women in Political Science: Female Participation in the Professoriate and the Study of Women and Politics in the Discipline." *PS: Political Science and Politics* 34:319–26.

Conover, Pamela Johnston. 1988. "Feminists and the Gender Gap." *Journal of Politics* 50:985–1010.

Conover, Pamela Johnston, and Virginia Gray. 1983. *Feminism and the New Right.* New York: Praeger.

Conover, Pamela Johnston, and Virginia Sapiro. 1993. "Gender, Feminist Consciousness, and War." *American Journal of Political Science* 37:1079–99.

Considine, Mark, and Iva Ellen Deutchman. 1996. "Instituting Gender: State Legislators in Australia and the United States." *Women & Politics* 16:1–19.

Constantini, Edmond. 1990. "Political Women and Political Ambition: Closing the Gender Gap." *American Journal of Political Science* 34:741–70.

Conway, M. Margaret, Gertrude A. Steuernagel, and David W. Ahern. 1997. *Women and Political Participation.* Washington, DC: CQ Press.

Cook, Elizabeth Adell. 1989. "Measuring Feminist Consciousness." *Women & Politics* 9:71–88.

Cook, Elizabeth Adell. 1994. "Voter Responses to Women Senate Candidates." In *The Year of the Woman: Myths and Realities,* ed. Elizabeth Adell Cook, Sue Thomas, and Clyde Wilcox. Boulder, CO: Westview Press, pp. 217–36.

Cook, Elizabeth Adell, and Clyde Wilcox. 1991. "Feminism and the Gender Gap – A Second Look." *Journal of Politics* 53:1111–22.

Cook, Elizabeth Adell, and Clyde Wilcox. 1995. "Women Voters in the Year of the Woman." In *Democracy's Feast: Elections in America,* ed. Herbert Weisberg. Chatham House, NJ: Chatham House, pp. 195–219.

Cooperman, Rosalyn, and Bruce I. Oppenheimer. 2001. "The Gender Gap in the House of Representatives." In *Congress Reconsidered,* ed. Lawrence C. Dodd and Bruce I. Oppenheimer. 7th ed. Washington, DC: CQ Press, pp. 125–40.

Cornwall, Andrea, and Anne Marie Goetz. 2005. "Democratizing Democracy: Feminist Perspectives." *Democratization* 12:783–800.

Costa, Paul, Jr., Antonio Terracciano, and Robert R. McCrae. 2001. "Gender Differences in Personality Traits across Cultures: Robust and Surprising Findings." *Journal of Personality and Social Psychology* 81:322–31.

Costain, Anne N. 1992. *Inviting Women's Rebellion: A Political Process Interpretation of the Women's Movement.* Baltimore: Johns Hopkins University Press.

Costain, Anne N. 2000. "Women's Movements and Nonviolence." *PS: Political Science and Politics* 33(2):175–80.

Costain, Anne N., and W. Douglas Costain. 1987. "Strategy and Tactics of the Women's Movement in the United States: The Role of Political Parties." In *The Women's Movements of the United States and Western Europe: Consciousness, Political Opportunity, and Public Policy,* ed. Mary Fainsod Katzenstein and Carol McClurg Mueller. Philadelphia: Temple University Press, pp.196–214.

Cott, Nancy F. 1977. *The Bonds of Womanhood.* New Haven, CT: Yale University Press.

Cott, Nancy F. 1987. *The Grounding of Modern Feminism*. New Haven, CT: Yale University Press.

Cott, Nancy F. 1990. "Across the Great Divide: Women in Politics before and after 1920." In *Women, Politics, and Change*, ed. Louise Tilly and Patricia Gurin. New York: Russell Sage Foundation, pp. 43–68.

Cott, Nancy. 2000. *Public Vows: A History of Marriage and the Nation*. Cambridge, MA: Harvard University Press.

Cox, Gary W., and Mathew D. McCubbins. 1993. *Legislative Leviathan: Party Government in the House*. Berkeley: University of California Press.

Cox, Gary W., and Mathew D. McCubbins. 2005. *Setting the Agenda: Responsible Party Government in the U.S. House of Representatives*. New York: Cambridge University Press.

Crawford, Vicki. 2001. "African American Women in the Mississippi Freedom Democratic Party." In *Sisters in the Struggle: African American Women in the Civil Rights-Black Power Movement*, ed. Bettye Collier-Thomas and V. P. Franklin. New York: New York University Press, pp. 121–38.

Crenshaw, Kimberle. 1989. "Demarginalizing the Intersection of Race and Sex: A Black Feminist Critique of Anti-Discrimination Doctrine, Feminist Theory and Antiracist Politics." *University of Chicago Legal Forum* 129:139–67.

Crenshaw, Kimberle. 1991. "Mapping the Margins: Intersectionality, Identity Politics, and Violence against Women of Color." *Stanford Law Review* 43(July):1241–99.

Crenshaw, Kimberle. 1998. "Demarginalizing the Intersection of Race and Sex: A Black Feminist Critique of Antidiscrimination Doctrine, Feminist Theory, and Antiracist Politics." In *Feminism and Politics*, ed. Anne Phillips. New York: Oxford University Press, pp. 314–43.

Crenshaw, Kimberle. 2000. "The Intersectionality of Race and Gender Discrimination." Unpublished manuscript.

Cress, Daniel, and David Snow. 1998. "Mobilization at the Margins: Organizing by the Homeless." In *Social Movements and American Political Institutions*, ed. Anne Costain and Andrew McFarland. Boulder, CO: Rowman and Littlefield, pp. 73–98.

Crowley, Jocelyn Elise. 2004. "When Tokens Matter." *Legislative Studies Quarterly* 29:109–36.

Curran, Laura. 2005. "Social Work's Revised Maternalism: Mothers, Workers, and Welfare in Early Cold War America, 1946–1963." *Journal of Women's History* 17:112–36.

Dabelko, Kristin, and Paul Herrnson. 1997. "Women's and Men's Campaigns for the U.S. House of Representatives." *Political Research Quarterly* 50:121–35.

Dahl, Robert A. 2002. *How Democratic Is the American Constitution?* New Haven, CT: Yale University Press.

Dahlerup, Drude. 2003. "Quotas as a 'Fast Track' to Equal Political Representation for Women." Paper presented at the American Political Science Association Annual Meeting, Philadelphia.

Dahlerup, Drude. 2006a. "The Story of the Theory of Critical Mass." *Politics & Gender* 2:511–22.

Dahlerup, Drude, ed. 2006b. *Women, Quotas and Politics*. London: Routledge, Taylor and Francis Group.

Daley, Caroline, and Melanie Nolan, eds. 1995. *Suffrage and Beyond: International Feminist Perspectives*. New York: New York University Press.

Darcy, R., Susan Welch, and Janet Clark. 1994. *Women, Elections, and Representation*. 2nd ed. Lincoln: University of Nebraska Press.

Darling, Marsha J. 1998. "African American Women in State Elective Office in the South." In *Women and Elective Office: Past, Present, and Future*, ed. Sue Thomas and Clyde Wilcox. New York: Oxford University Press, pp. 150–62.

Davies, Michelle. 2004. "Correlates of Negative Attitudes toward Gay Men: Sexism, Male Role Norms, and Male Sexuality." *Journal of Sex Research* 41:259–66.

Davis, Angela Y. 1981. *Women, Race and Class*. New York: Vintage Books.

Davis, Nancy J., and Robert V. Robinson. 1991. "Men's and Women's Consciousness of Gender Inequality: Austria, West Germany, Great Britain, and the United States." *American Sociological Review* 56:72–84.

Dawson, Michael. 1994. *Behind the Mule: Race and Class in African-American Politics*. Princeton, NJ: Princeton University Press.

Dawson, Michael. 2001. *Black Visions: The Roots of Contemporary African-American Political Ideologies*. Chicago: University of Chicago Press.

Day, Christine L. 1994. "State Legislative Voting Patterns on Abortion Restrictions in Louisiana." *Women & Politics* 14:45–64.

Day, Christine L., and Charles D. Hadley. 1997. "The Importance of Attitudes toward Women's Equality: Policy Preferences among Southern Party Elite." *Social Science Quarterly* 78:672–87.

Day, Christine L., and Charles D. Hadley. 2005. *Women's PACs: Abortion and Elections*. Upper Saddle River, NJ: Pearson Prentice Hall.

Day, Christine, Charles Hadley, and Megan Brown. 2001. "Gender, Feminism, and Partisanship among Women's PAC Contributors." *Social Science Quarterly* 82:687–700.

De Beauvoir, Simone. 1952. *The Second Sex*. New York: Knopf.

Delli Carpini, Michael X., and Scott Keeter. 1993. "Measuring Political Knowledge: Putting First Things First." *American Journal of Political Science* 37:1179–206.

Delli Carpini, Michael X., and Scott Keeter. 1996. *What Americans Know about Politics and Why It Matters*. New Haven, CT: Yale University Press.

Diamond, Irene. 1977. *Sex Roles in the State House*. New Haven, CT: Yale University Press.

Diamond, Irene, and Nancy Hartstock. 1981. "Beyond Interests in Politics: A Comment on Virginia Sapiro's 'When Are Interests Interesting? The Problem of Political Representation of Women.'" *American Political Science Review* 75:717–21.

Diani, Mario. 1992. "The Concept of Social Movement." *Sociological Review* 40:1–25.

di Stefano, Christine. 1997. "Integrating Gender into the Political Science Curriculum: Challenges, Pitfalls, and Opportunities." *PS: Political Science and Politics* 30:204–6.

Dodson, Debra L. 1998. "Representing Women's Interests in the U.S. House of Representatives." In *Women and Elective Office: Past, Present, and Future*, ed. Sue Thomas and Clyde Wilcox. New York: Oxford University Press, pp. 130–49.

Dodson, Debra L. 2001. "Acting for Women: Is What Legislators Say, What They Do?" In *The Impact of Women in Public Office*, ed. Susan J. Carroll. Bloomington: Indiana University Press, pp. 225–42.

Dodson, Debra L. 2005. "Making a Difference: Behind the Scenes." In *Women and Elective Office: Past, Present, and Future*, ed. Sue Thomas and Clyde Wilcox. 2nd ed. New York: Oxford University Press, pp. 130–49.

Dodson, Debra L. 2006. *The Impact of Women in Congress*. New York: Oxford University Press.

Dodson, Debra L., and Susan J. Carroll. 1991. *Reshaping the Agenda: Women in State Legislatures*. New Brunswick, NJ: Center for American Women and Politics.

Dolan, Julie. 1997. "Support for Women's Interests in the 103rd Congress: The Distinct Impact of Congressional Women." *Women & Politics* 18:81–92.

Dolan, Julie, and Jonathan S. Kropf. 2004. "Credit Claiming from the U.S. House: Gendered Communication Styles?" *Harvard International Journal of Press/Politics* 9:41–59.

Dolan, Kathleen. 1998. "Voting for Women in 'The Year of the Woman.'" *American Journal of Political Science* 42:272–93.

Dolan, Kathleen. 2004. *Voting for Women: How the Public Evaluates Women Candidates*. Boulder, CO: Westview Press.

Dolan, Kathleen. 2005. "Do Women Candidates Play to Stereotypes? Do Men Candidates Play to Women? Candidate Sex and Issue Priorities on Campaign Websites." *Political Research Quarterly* 58:31–44.

Dolan, Kathleen. 2006. "Symbolic Mobilization? The Impact of Candidate Sex in American Elections." *American Politics Research* 34(November): 687–704.

Dolan, Kathleen, and Lynne E. Ford. 1995. "Women in the State Legislatures: Feminist Identity and Legislative Behavior." *American Politics Quarterly* 23:96–108.

Dolan, Kathleen, and Lynne E. Ford. 1998. "Are All Women State Legislators Alike?" In *Women and Elective Office: Past, Present, and Future*, ed. Sue Thomas and Clyde Wilcox. New York: Oxford University Press, pp. 73–86.

Donahue, Jesse. 1997. "It Doesn't Matter: Some Cautionary Findings about Sex and Representation from School Committee Conversations." *Policy Studies Journal* 25:630–47.

Dovi, Suzanne. 2002. "Preferable Descriptive Representatives: Or Will Just Any Woman, Black, or Latino Do?" *American Political Science Review* 96:745–54.

Dovi, Suzanne. 2006. "Making Democracy Work for Women." Paper presented at the Conference on Political Women and American Democracy, University of Notre Dame, South Bend, IN.

Dovi, Suzanne. 2007. *The Good Representative*. New York: Blackwell.

Downs, Anthony. 1957. *An Economic Theory of Democracy*. New York: Harper and Row.

Driscoll, Amanda, and Kristin Kanthak. n.d. "Patterns of Colleague Support in the U.S. House: Why Democrats Have an 'Old Girls Network,' but Republican Women Want to Be 'Just One of the Boys.'" Unpublished manuscript, University of Arizona, Tucson, AZ.

Dryzek, John. 1996. "Political Inclusion and the Dynamics of Democratization." *American Political Science Review* 90:475–87.

DuBois, Ellen Carol. 1998. *Woman Suffrage and Women's Rights*. New York: New York University Press.

Dudziak, Mary. 2000. *Cold War, Civil Rights*. Princeton, NJ: Princeton University Press.

Duerst-Lahti, Georgia. 2002. "Knowing Congress as a Gendered Institution: Manliness and the Implications of Women in Congress." In *Women Transforming Congress*, ed. Cindy Simon Rosenthal. Norman: University of Oklahoma Press, pp. 20–49.

Duerst-Lahti, Georgia. 2005. "Institutional Gendering: Theoretical Insights into the Environment of Women Officeholders." In *Women and Elective Office: Past, Present, and Future*, ed. Sue Thomas and Clyde Wilcox. 2nd ed. New York: Oxford University Press, pp. 230–43.

Duerst-Lahti, Georgia, and Rita Mae Kelly. 1995a. "On Governance, Leadership, and Gender." In *Gender Power, Leadership, and Governance*, ed. Georgia Duerst-Lahti and Rita Mae Kelly. Ann Arbor: University of Michigan Press, pp. 11–38.

Duerst-Lahti, Georgia, and Rita Mae Kelly, eds. 1995b. *Gender Power, Leadership and Governance*. Ann Arbor: University of Michigan Press.

Duverger, Maurice. 1955. *The Political Role of Women*. Paris: UNESCO.

Eagly, Alice H. 1987. *Sex Differences in Social Behavior: A Social-Role Interpretation*. Mahwah, NJ: Lawrence Erlbaum.

Eagly, Alice H., and Maureen Crowley. 1986. "Gender and Helping Behavior: A Meta-Analytic Review of the Social Psychological Literature." *Psychological Bulletin* 100:283–308.

Eagly, Alice H., Amanda B. Diekman, Mary C. Johannesen-Schmidt, and Anne M. Koenig. 2004. "Gender Gaps in Sociopolitical Attitudes: A Social Psychological Analysis." *Journal of Personality and Social Psychology* 87:796–816.

Eagly, A. H., and V. J. Steffen. 1984. "Gender Stereotypes Stem from the Distribution of Women and Men into Social Roles." *Journal of Personality and Social Psychology* 46:735–54.

Edwards, Rebecca. 1997. *Angels in the Machinery: Gender in American Party Politics from the Civil War to the Progressive Era*. New York: Oxford University Press.

Einhorn, Barbara. 1993. *Cinderella Goes to Market*. London: Verso.

Einhorn, Barbara, and Charlotte Sever. 2003. "Gender and Civil Society in East Central Europe." *International Feminist Journal of Politics* 5:163–90.

Eisenberg, N., and R. Lennon. 1983. "Sex-Differences in Empathy and Related Capacities." *Psychological Bulletin* 94:100–31.

Elazar, Daniel J. 1984. *American Federalism: A View from the States*. Boston: Addison-Wesley.

Ellickson, Mark C., and Donald E. Whistler. 2000. "A Path Analysis of Legislative Success in Professional and Citizen State Legislatures: A Gender Comparison." *Women & Politics* 21:77–103.

Elman, R. Amy. 1996. *Sexual Subordination and State Intervention: Comparing Sweden and the United States*. Providence, RI: Berghahn Books.

Elman, R. Amy. 2003. "Refuge in Reconfigured States: Shelter Movements in the United States, Britain and Sweden." In *Women's Movements Facing the*

Reconfigured State, ed. Lee Ann Banaszak, Karen Beckwith, and Dieter Rucht. Cambridge: Cambridge University Press, pp. 94–113.

Elshtain, Jean Bethke. 1981. *Public Man, Private Woman: Women in Social and Political Thought*. Princeton, NJ: Princeton University Press.

Elson, Diane. 2004. "Engendering Government Budgets in the Context of Globalization(s)." *International Feminist Journal of Politics* 6(December):623–42.

Elster, Jon. 1985. *Making Sense of Marx*. Cambridge: Cambridge University Press.

Enloe, Cynthia. 1989. *Bananas, Beaches, and Bases: Making Feminist Sense of International Politics*. Berkeley: University of California Press.

Epstein, Cynthia Fuchs. 1988. *Deceptive Distinctions: Sex, Gender, and the Social Order*. New Haven, CT: Yale University Press.

Epstein, Leon D. 1986. *Political Parties in the American Mold*. Madison: University of Wisconsin Press.

Epstein, Michael J., Richard G. Niemi, and Lynda W. Powell. 2005. "Do Women and Men State Legislators Differ?" In *Women and Elective Office: Past, Present, and Future*, ed. Sue Thomas and Clyde Wilcox. 2nd ed. New York: Oxford University Press, pp. 94–109.

Erie, Steven P., and Martin Rein. 1988. "Women and the Welfare State." In *The Politics of the Gender Gap: The Social Construction of Political Influence*, ed. Carol M. Mueller. Newbury Park, CA: Sage, pp. 173–91.

Escobar-Lemmon, Maria, and Michelle M. Taylor-Robinson. 2005. "Women Ministers in Latin American Government: When, Where, and Why?" *American Journal of Political Science* 49:829–44.

Esping-Andersen, Gøsta. 1990. *The Three Worlds of Welfare Capitalism*. Princeton, NJ: Princeton University Press.

European Union. 1997. "Treaty of Amsterdam." Accessed July 28, 2006. http://eur-lex.europa.eu/en/treaties/dat/11997D/htm/11997D.html.

Evans, Jocelyn Jones. 2005. *Women, Partisanship, and the Congress*. New York: Palgrave Macmillan.

Evans, Peter B., Dietrich Rueschemeyer, and Theda Skocpol, eds. 1985. *Bringing the State Back In*. Cambridge: Cambridge University Press.

Faderman, Lillian. 1991. *Odd Girls and Twilight Lovers*. New York: Columbia University Press.

Fausto-Sterling, Anne. 1985. *Myths of Gender*. New York: Basic Books.

Feather, N. T. 1984. "Masculinity, Femininity, Psychological Androgyny, and the Structure of Values." *Journal of Personality and Social Psychology* 47:604–20.

Feldman, Stanley, and Marco R. Steenbergen. 2001. "The Humanitarian Foundation of Public Support for Social Welfare." *American Journal of Political Science* 45:658–77.

Fenno, Richard F., Jr. 1973. *Congressmen in Committees*. Boston: Little, Brown.

Fenno, Richard F., Jr. 1978. *Home Style: House Members in Their Districts*. Boston: Little, Brown.

Ferguson, Kathy. 1984. *The Feminist Case against Bureaucracy*. Philadelphia: Temple University Press.

Fernandes, Leela. 2004. *Transforming Feminist Practice: Non-violence, Social Justice and the Possibilities of a Spiritualized Feminism*. San Francisco: Aunt Lute Books.

Fernandes, Sujatha. 2005. "Transnationalism and Feminist Activism in Cuba: The Case of Magín." *Politics & Gender* 1:431–52.

Ferraro, Kenneth F. 1996. "Women's Fear of Victimization: Shadow of Sexual Assault?" *Social Forces* 75:667–90.

Ferree, Myra Marx. 2003. "Resonance and Radicalism: Feminist Framing in the Abortion Debates of the United States and Germany." *American Journal of Sociology* 109:304–44.

Ferree, Myra Marx. 2004. "Soft Repression: Ridicule, Stigma, and Silencing in Gender-Based Movements." In *Research in Social Movements, Conflicts and Change* 25, ed. Daniel J. Myers and Daniel M. Cress. San Diego: Elsevier, pp. 85–101.

Ferree, Myra Marx, William Gamson, Juergen Gerhards, and Dieter Rucht. 2002. *Shaping Abortion Discourse: Democracy and the Public Sphere in Germany and the United States*. Cambridge: Cambridge University Press.

Ferree, Myra Marx, and Beth B. Hess. 1985. *Controversy and Coalition: The New Feminist Movement*. Boston: Twayne.

Ferree, Myra Marx, and Carol McClurg Mueller. 2004. "Feminism and the Women's Movement: A Global Perspective." In *The Blackwell Companion to Social Movements*, ed. David Snow, Sarah Soule, and Hanspeter Kriesi. Oxford: Blackwell, pp. 576–607.

Fiber, Pamela. 2004. "Chances for Success: Examining Differences in Women's Congressional Candidacies." Paper presented at the Midwest Political Science Association Annual Meeting, Chicago, IL.

Fiorina, Morris P. 2002. "Parties, Participation, and Representation in America: Old Theories Face New Realities." In *Political Science: The State of the Discipline*, ed. Ira Katznelson and Helen V. Milner. New York: W. W. Norton, pp. 511–41.

Fiorina, Morris P. 2005. *Culture Wars? The Myth of a Polarized America*. New York: Pearson Longman.

Fite, David, Marc Genest, and Clyde Wilcox. 1990. "Gender Differences in Foreign Policy Attitudes: A Longitudinal Analysis." *American Politics Quarterly* 18:492–513.

Flammang, Janet A. 1985. "Female Officials in the Feminist Capital: The Case of Santa Clara County." *Western Political Quarterly* 38:94–118.

Flexner, Eleanor. 1975. *Century of Struggle: The Woman's Rights Movement in the United States*. Cambridge, MA: Belknap Press.

Fogg-Davis, Hawley. 2005. "Theorizing Black Lesbians within Black Feminism: A Critique of Same-Race Street Harassment." *Politics & Gender* 2(1):57–76.

Fonow, Mary Margaret. 2003. *Union Women: Forging Feminism in the United Steelworkers of America*. Minneapolis: University of Minnesota Press.

Ford, Lynne E., and Kathleen Dolan. 1995. "The Politics of Women State Legislators: A South/Non-South Comparison." *Southeastern Political Review* 23:333–48.

Foucault, Michel. 1990. *The History of Sexuality*. Vol. 1. New York: Vintage Books.

Fowlkes, Diane L. 1984. "Ambitious Political Woman: Countersocialization and Political Party Context." *Women & Politics* 4:5–32.

Fowlkes, Diane, Jerry Perkins, and Sue Tolleson-Rinehart. 1979. "Gender Roles and Party Roles." *American Political Science Review* 73:772–80.

Fox, Richard L. 1997. *Gender Dynamics in Congressional Elections.* Thousand Oaks, CA: Sage.

Fox, Richard L. 2006. "Congressional Elections: Where Are We on the Road to Gender Parity?" In *Gender and Elections: Shaping the Future of American Politics,* ed. Susan Carroll and Richard Fox. New York: Cambridge University Press, pp. 97–116.

Fox, Richard L., and Zoe Oxley. 2003. "Gender Stereotyping in State Executive Elections: Candidate Selection and Success." *Journal of Politics* 65:833–50.

Fox, Richard L., and Robert A. Schuhmann. 1999. "Gender and Local Government: A Comparison of Women and Men City Managers." *Public Administration Review* 59:231–42.

Frable, Deborrah E., and Sandra L. Bem. 1985. "If You Are Gender Schematic, All Members of the Opposite Sex Look Alike." *Journal of Personality and Social Psychology* 49:459–68.

Fraga, Luis Ricardo, Valerie Martinez-Ebers, Linda Lopez, and Ricardo Ramirez. 2005. "Strategic Intersectionality: Gender, Ethnicity, and Political Incorporation." Paper presented at the Western Political Science Association Annual Meeting, Oakland, CA.

Franceschet, Susan. 2003. "'State Feminism' and Women's Movements: The Impact of Chile's Servicio Nacional de la Mujer on Women's Activism." *Latin American Research Review* 38:9–40.

Frankovic, Kathleen. 1977. "Sex and Voting in the U.S. House of Representatives: 1961–1975." *American Politics Quarterly* 5:315–30.

Frankovic, K. A. 1982. "Sex and Politics – New Alignments, Old Issues." *PS: Political Science and Politics* 15:439–48.

Fraser, Nancy, and Linda Gordon. 1994. "Civil Citizenship against Social Citizenship?" In *The Condition of Citizenship,* ed. Bart Van Steenbergen. London: Sage, pp. 90–107.

Fraser, Nancy, and Linda Gordon. 1995. "A Genealogy of *Dependency*: Tracing a Keyword of the U. S. Welfare State." In *Rethinking the Political: Gender, Resistance and the State,* ed. Barbara Laslett, Johanna Brenner, and Yesim Arat. Chicago: University of Chicago Press, pp. 33–60

Frechette, Guillaume, Francois Maniquet, and Massimo Morelli. 2006. "Incumbents' Interests, Voters' Bias, and Gender Quotas." Unpublished manuscript, Ohio State University, Columbus.

Freedman, Paul. 1999. *Framing the Abortion Debate: Public Opinion and the Manipulation of Ambivalence.* Unpublished Ph.D. dissertation, University of Michigan, Ann Arbor.

Freeman, Jo. 1972. "The Tyranny of Structurelessness." *Berkeley Journal of Sociology* 17:118–49.

Freeman, Jo. 1975. *The Politics of Women's Liberation: A Case Study of an Emerging Social Movement and Its Relation to the Policy Process.* New York: David McKay.

Freeman, Jo. 1986. "The Political Culture of the Democratic and Republican Parties." *Political Science Quarterly* 101:327–56.

Freeman, Jo. 1987. "Who You Know versus Who You Represent: Feminist Influence in the Democratic and Republican Parties." In *The Women's Movements of the United States and Western Europe*, ed. Mary Katzenstein and Carol Mueller. Philadelphia: Temple University Press, pp. 215–44.

Freeman, Jo. 1989. "Feminist Activities at the 1988 Republican Convention." *PS: Political Science and Politics* 22:39–47.

Freeman, Jo. 1993. "Feminism vs. Family Values: Women at the 1992 Democratic and Republican Conventions." *PS: Political Science and Politics* (March):2–3, 10–17.

Freeman, Jo. 1999. "Sex, Race, Religion, and Partisan Realignment." In *"We Get What We Vote For . . . or Do We?" The Impact of Elections on Governing*, ed. Paul E. Scheele. Westport, CT: Praeger, pp. 167–90.

Freeman, Jo. 2000. *A Room at a Time: How Women Entered Party Politics*. Lanham, MD: Rowman and Littlefield.

Freeman, Jo. 2006. "The Search for Political Woman." Accessed September 28, 2006. http://www.jofreeman.com/academicwomen/polwoman.htm.

Fridkin, Kim, and Patrick Kenney. 2004. "Examining the Gender Gap in Children's Attitudes about Politics." Paper presented at the American Political Science Association Annual Meeting, Chicago, IL.

Fridkin, Kim L., and Gina Serignese Woodall. 2005. "Different Portraits, Different Leaders? Gender Differences in U.S. Senators' Presentation of Self." In *Women and Elective Office: Past, Present, and Future*, ed. Sue Thomas and Clyde Wilcox. 2nd ed. New York: Oxford University Press, pp. 81–93.

Friedman, Elisabeth J. 1998. "Paradoxes of Gendered Political Opportunity in the Venezuelan Transition to Democracy." *Latin American Research Review* 33:87–136.

Friedman, Elisabeth J. 2000. *Unfinished Transitions: Women and the Gendered Development of Democracy in Venezuela, 1936–1996*. University Park: Pennsylvania State University Press.

Friedman, Elisabeth J. 2005. "The Reality of Virtual Reality: The Internet and Gender Equality Advocacy in Latin America." *Latin American Politics and Society* 47:1–43.

Friedman, Elisabeth J., Kathryn Hochstetler, and Ann Marie Clark. 2005. *Sovereignty, Democracy, and Global Civil Society: State-Society Relations at UN World Conferences*. Albany, NY: SUNY Press.

Frymer, Paul. 1999. *Uneasy Alliances: Race and Party Competition in America*. Princeton, NJ: Princeton University Press.

Frymer, Paul. 2005. "Race, Parties, and Democratic Inclusion." In *The Politics of Democratic Inclusion*, ed. Christina Wolbrecht and Rodney E. Hero. Philadelphia: Temple University Press, pp. 122–42.

Funk, Nanette, and Magda Mueller, eds. 1993. *Gender Politics and Post-Communism: Reflections from Eastern Europe and the Former Soviet Union*. New York: Routledge.

Fuss, Diana. 1989. *Essentially Speaking: Feminism, Nature & Difference*. New York: Routledge Press.

Gaddie, Keith, and Charles Bullock. 1995. "Congressional Elections and the Year of the Woman: Structural and Elite Influences on Female Candidacies." *Social Science* 76:749–62.

Gamson, William, and David S. Meyer. 1996. "Framing Political Opportunity." In *Comparative Perspectives on Social Movements*, ed. Doug McAdam, John D.

McCarthy, and Mayer N. Zald. New York: Cambridge University Press, pp. 275–90.

Gamson, William, and Andre Modigliani. 1987. "The Changing Culture of Affirmative Action." *Research in Political Sociology* 3:137–77.

Garcia Bedolla, Lisa, Katherine Tate, and Janelle Wong. 2005. "Indelible Effects: The Impact of Women of Color in the U.S. Congress." In *Women and Elective Office: Past, Present, and Future*, ed. Sue Thomas and Clyde Wilcox. 2nd ed. New York: Oxford University Press, pp. 152–75.

Gaventa, John. 1982. *Power and Powerlessness: Quiescence and Rebellion in an Appalachian Valley.* Champaign: University of Illinois Press.

Gay, Claudine. 2002. "Spirals of Trust? The Effect of Descriptive Representation on the Relationship between Citizens and Their Government." *American Journal of Political Science* 46:717–32.

Gehlen, Frieda L. 1977. "Women Members of Congress: A Distinctive Role." In *Portrait of Marginality: The Political Behavior of the American Woman*, ed. Marianne Githens and Jewell Prestage. New York: Longman, pp. 304–19.

Gelb, Joyce. 1989. *Feminism and Politics: A Comparative Perspective.* Berkeley: University of California Press.

Gelb, Joyce. 2004. *Gender Politics in Japan and the United States: Comparing Women's Movements, Rights and Politics.* New York: Palgrave Macmillan.

Gerhards, Jurgen, and Dieter Rucht. 1992. "Mesomobilization: Organizing and Framing in Two Protest Campaigns in West Germany." *American Journal of Sociology* 98:555–96.

Gertzog, Irwin N. 2004. *Women and Power on Capitol Hill: Reconstructing the Congressional Women's Caucus.* Boulder, CO: Lynne Rienner.

Gibson, James L., Cornelius P. Cotter, John F. Bibby, and Robert J. Huckshorn. 1983. "Assessing Party Organizational Strength." *American Journal of Political Science* 27:193–222.

Giddings, Paula. 1984. *When and Where I Enter: The Impact of Black Women on Race and Sex in America.* New York: William Morrow.

Gilens, Martin. 1988. "Gender and Support for Reagan: A Comprehensive Model of Presidential Approval." *American Journal of Political Science* 32:19–49.

Gilligan, Carol. 1982. *In a Different Voice: Psychological Theory and Women's Development.* Cambridge, MA: Harvard University Press.

Githens, Marianne. 1977. "Spectators, Agitators or Lawmakers: Women in State Legislatures." In *A Portrait of Marginality: The Political Behavior of the American Woman*, ed. Marianne Githens and Jewel Prestage. New York: McKay, pp. 196–209.

Glazer, Sarah. 2004. "Lost in Translation." *New York Times*, August 22.

Goffman, Erving. 1977. "The Arrangement between the Sexes." *Theory and Society* 4:301–31.

Goldstein, Joshua. 2001. *War and Gender: How Gender Shapes the War System and Vice Versa.* New York: Cambridge University Press.

Goodin, Robert E. 2005. "The Philosophical Foundation of Party Democracy." Unpublished manuscript, Research School of Social Sciences, Australian National University, Canberra.

Goodwin, Robin, Michelle Willson, and Stanley Gaines Jr. 2005. "Terror Threat Perception and Its Consequences in Contemporary Britain." *British Journal of Psychology* 96:389–406.

Gordon, Linda. 1994. *Pitied but Not Entitled: Single Mothers and the History of Welfare, 1890–1935.* New York: Free Press.

Gould, Carol. 1996. "Diversity and Democracy: Representing Differences." In *Democracy and Difference: Contesting the Boundaries of the Political,* ed. Seyla Benhabib. Princeton, NJ: Princeton University, pp. 171–86.

Grant, Jacquelyn. 1979. "Black Theology and the Black Woman," *Black Theology: A Documentary History, 1966–1979,* ed. S. Welmore and J. Cone. Maryknoll, NY: Orbis, pp. 418–33.

Grant, Ruth, and Robert O. Keohane. 2005. "Accountability and Abuses of Power in World Politics." *American Political Science Review* 99:29–44.

Green, Joanne Connor. 2003. "The Times . . . Are They a-Changing? An Examination of the Impact of the Value of Campaign Resources for Women and Men Candidates for the US House of Representatives." *Women & Politics* 25:1–29.

Greenberg, Anna. 2001. "Race, Religiosity, and the Women's Vote." *Women & Politics* 22:59–82.

Guinier, Lani. 1994. *Tyranny of the Majority: Fundamental Fairness in Representative.* New York: Free Press.

Gurin, Patricia. 1985. "Women's Gender Consciousness." *Public Opinion Quarterly* 49:143–63.

Gustafson, Melanie Susan. 2001. *Women and the Republican Party, 1854–1924.* Urbana: University of Illinois Press.

Gustafson, Melanie, Kristie Miller, and Elisabeth Israels Perry, eds. 1999. *We Have Come to Stay: American Women and Political Parties, 1880–1960.* Albuquerque: University of New Mexico Press.

Guy-Sheftall, Beverly, ed. 1995. *Words of Fire: An Anthology of African-American Feminist Thought.* New York: New Press.

Gwartney-Gibbs, Patricia A., and Denise H. Lach. 1991. "Sex Differences in Attitudes toward Nuclear War." *Journal of Peace Research* 28:161–74.

Hale, Mary M., and Rita Mae Kelly, eds. 1989. *Gender, Bureaucracy, and Democracy: Careers and Equal Opportunity in the Public Sector.* New York: Greenwood Press.

Halim, Shaheen, and Beverly L. Stiles. 2001. "Differential Support for Police Use of Force, the Death Penalty, and Perceived Harshness of the Courts: Effects of Race, Gender, and Region." *Criminal Justice and Behavior* 28:3–23.

Hall, Richard L. 1996. *Participation in Congress.* New Haven, CT: Yale University Press.

Hampton, Dream. 1999. "Bad Boy." In *The Vibe History of Hip Hop,* ed. Alan Light. New York: Three Rivers Press, pp. 339–43.

Hancock, Ange-Marie. 2007. "When Multiplication Doesn't Equal Quick Addition: Examining Intersectionality as a Research Paradigm." *Perspectives on Politics* 5:63–79.

Handler, Joel, and Lucie White. 1999. *Hard Labor: Women and Work in the Post-Welfare Era.* Armonk, NY: M. E. Sharpe.

Haney, Lynne A. 2004. "Gender, Welfare, and States of Punishment." *Social Politics: International Studies in Gender, State and Society* 11:333–62.

Hansen, Susan. 1997. "Talking about Politics: Gender and Contextual Effects on Political Proselytizing." *Journal of Politics* 59:73–103.

Hansen, Susan B., Linda M. Franz, and Margaret Netemeyer-Mays. 1976. "Women's Political Participation and Policy Preferences." *Social Science Quarterly* 54:576–90.

Harris, Frederick C. 1994 "Something Within: Religion as a Mobilizer of African-American Political Activism." *Journal of Politics* 56:42–68.

Harris, Frederick C. 1999. *Something Within: Religion in African-American Political Activism.* New York: Oxford University Press.

Harris-Lacewell, Melissa. 2003. "The Heart of the Politics of Race: Centering Black People in the Study of White Racial Attitudes." *Journal of Black Studies* 34(November):222–49.

Harrison, Cynthia. 1988. *On Account of Sex: The Politics of Women's Issues, 1945–1968.* Berkeley: University of California Press.

Harvey, Anna L. 1998. *Votes without Leverage: Women in American Electoral Politics, 1920–1970.* Cambridge: Cambridge University Press.

Hassim, Shireen. 2006. *Women's Organizations and Democracy in South Africa: Contesting Authority.* Madison: University of Wisconsin Press.

Haussman, Melissa, and Birgit Sauer, eds. 2006. *Gendering the State in the Age of Globalization. Women's Movements and State Feminism in Post Industrial Democracies.* New York: Rowman and Littlefield.

Hawkesworth, Mary. 1997. "Confounding Gender." *Signs* 22(Spring):649–85.

Hawkesworth, Mary. 2003. "Congressional Enactments of Race-Gender: Toward a Theory of Race-Gendered Institutions." *American Political Science Review* 97(November):529–50.

Hawkesworth, Mary. 2005. "Engendering Political Science: An Immodest Proposal." *Politics & Gender* 1(1):141–56.

Hawkesworth, Mary. 2006. *Globalization and Feminist Activism.* Lanham, MD: Rowman and Littlefield.

Hawkesworth, Mary, Kathleen J. Casey, Krista Jenkins, and Katherine E. Kleeman. 2001. *Legislating by and for Women: A Comparison of the 103rd and 104th Congresses.* New Brunswick, NJ: Center for American Women and Politics.

Hayes, Bernadette C., Ian McAllister, and Donley T. Studlar. 2000. "Gender, Postmaterialism, and Feminism in Comparative Perspective." *International Political Science Review* 21:425–39.

Hayward, Clarissa. 2000. *De-Facing Power.* Cambridge: Cambridge University Press.

Heldman, Caroline, Sue Carroll, and Stephanie Olson. 2005. "She Brought Only a Skirt: Print Media Coverage of Elizabeth Dole's Bid for the Republican Presidential Nomination." *Political Communication* 22:315–35.

Herek, Gregory M. 2002. "Gender Gaps in Public Opinion about Lesbians and Gay Men." *Public Opinion Quarterly* 66:40–66.

Herrnson, Paul S. 1988. *Party Campaigning in the 1980s.* Cambridge, MA: Harvard University Press.

Herrnson, Paul, J. Celeste Lay, and Atiya Stokes. 2003. "Women Running as 'Women': Candidate Gender, Campaign Issues, and Voter-Targeting Strategies." *Journal of Politics* 65:244–55.

Hibbing, John R., and Sue Thomas. 1990. "The Modern United State Senate: What Is Accorded Respect?" *Journal of Politics* 52:126–45.

Higginbotham, Evelyn Brooks. 1990. "In Politics to Stay: Black Women Leaders and Party Politics During the 1920s." In *Women, Politics, and Change*, ed. Louise Tilly and Patricia Gurin. New York: Russell Sage, pp. 199–220.

Hill, David B. 1983. "Women State Legislators and Party Voting on the ERA." *Social Science Quarterly* 64:318–26.

Hine, Darlene Clark. 1988. "Rape and the Inner Lives of Black Women in the Middle West: Preliminary Thoughts on the Culture of Dissemblance." *Signs* 14(August):912–20.

Hinojosa, Magdalena. 2005. "The Paradox of Primaries: Candidate Selection Processes and Women's Representation in Chilean Municipalities." Paper presented at the American Political Science Association Annual Meeting, Washington, DC.

Hoffman, Kim, Carrie Palmer, and Ronald Keith Gaddie. 2001. "Candidate Sex and Congressional Elections: Open Seats before, during and after the Year of the Woman." *Women & Politics* 23:37–58.

hooks, bell. 1981. *Ain't I a Woman: Black Women and Feminism*. London: Pluto Press.

hooks, bell. 1984. *Feminist Theory: From Margin to Center*. Boston: South End Press.

Horton, Carol. 2005. *Race and the Making of American Liberalism*. Oxford: Oxford University Press.

Howell, Jude. 2003. "Women's Organizations and Civil Society in China Making a Difference." *International Feminist Journal of Politics* 5:191–215.

Howell, Susan E., and Christine L. Day. 2000. "Complexities of the Gender Gap." *Journal of Politics* 62:858–74.

Htun, Mala. 2003. *Sex and the State: Abortion, Divorce, and the Family under Latin American Dictatorships and Democracies*. New York: Cambridge University Press.

Htun, Mala. 2004. "Is Gender Like Ethnicity? The Political Representation of Identity Groups." *Perspectives on Politics* 2:439–58.

Htun, Mala, and Mark P. Jones. 2002. "Engendering the Right to Participate in Decision-Making: Electoral Quotas and Women's Leadership in Latin America." In *Gender, Rights and Justice in Latin America*, ed. Nikki Craske and Maxine Molyneux. London: Palgrave, pp. 69–93.

Huddy, Leonie, and Teresa Capelos. 2002. "Gender Stereotyping and Candidate Evaluation: Good News and Bad News for Women Politicians." In *The Social Psychology of Politics*, ed. Victor Ottati et al. New York: Kluwer Academic Press, pp. 29–54.

Huddy, Leonie, Erin Cassese, and Mary-Kate Lizotte. 2008. "Sources of Political Unity and Disunity among Women: Placing the Gender Gap in Perspective." In *The Gender Gap: Voting and the Sexes*, ed. L. D. Whittaker. Champaign: University of Illinois Press.

Huddy, Leonie, Stanley Feldman, and Erin Cassese. 2007. "On the Distinct Political Effects of Anxiety and Anger." In *The Affect Effect: Dynamics of Emotion in Political Thinking and Behavior*, ed. W. Russell Neuman, George E. Marcus, Tim Crigler, and Michael MacKuen. Chicago: University of Chicago Press, pp. 202–30.

Huddy, Leonie, Stanley Feldman, and Erin Cassese. In press. "Gender Differences in Response to Terrorism and War." In *Terrorism and Torture: An Interdisciplinary Perspective*, ed. Werner Stritzker. New York: Cambridge University Press.

Huddy, Leonie, Stanley Feldman, and Sarah Dutton. 2005. "Not So Simple: The Role of Religion in the 2004 Presidential Election." *Public Opinion Pros*. Accessed July 26, 2007. http://www.publicopinionpros.com/features/2006/jan/huddyns.asp.

Huddy, L., S. Feldman, C. Taber, and G. Lahav. 2005. "Threat, Anxiety, and Support of Antiterrorism Policies." *American Journal of Political Science* 49:593–608.

Huddy, L., F. K. Neely, and M. R. Lafay. 2000. "The Polls – Trends: Support for the Women's Movement." *Public Opinion Quarterly* 64:309–50.

Huddy, Leonie, and Nayda Terkildsen. 1993a. "Gender Stereotypes and the Perception of Male and Female Candidates." *American Journal of Political Science* 37 :119–47.

Huddy, Leonie, and Nayda Terkildsen. 1993b. "The Consequences of Gender Stereotypes for Women Candidates at Different Levels and Types of Offices." *Political Research Quarterly* 46:503–25.

Hughes, Melanie M., and Pamela Paxton. 2007. "Familiar Theories from a New Perspective: The Implications of a Longitudinal Approach to Women in Politics Research." *Politics & Gender* 3(September):307–77.

Hughes, Michael, and Steven A. Tuch. 2003. "Gender Differences in Whites' Racial Attitudes: Are Women's Attitudes Really More Favorable?" *Social Psychology Quarterly* 66(4, Special Issue: Race, Racism, and Discrimination):384–401.

Huntington, Samuel P. 1968. *Political Order in Changing Societies*. New Haven, CT: Yale University Press.

Hurley, Patricia A. 1989. "Partisan Representation and the Failure of Realignment in the 1980s." *American Journal of Political Science* 33:240–61.

Hurwitz, Jon, and Shannon Smithey. 1998. "Gender Differences on Crime and Punishment." *Political Research Quarterly* 51:89–115.

Iannocone, Lawrence R. 1991. "Religious Practice: A Human Capital Approach." *Journal for the Scientific Study of Religion* 29:297–314.

Inglehart, Ronald, and Pippa Norris. 2000. "The Developmental Theory of the Gender Gap: Women's and Men's Voting Behavior in Global Perspective." *International Political Science Review* 21:441–63.

Inglehart, Ronald, and Pippa Norris. 2003. *Rising Tide: Gender Equality and Cultural Change around the World*. New York: Cambridge University Press.

International Feminist Journal of Politics. 2005. "Special Issue: Gender Mainstreaming." *International Feminist Journal of Politics* 7.

International IDEA. 2006. "Global Database of Quotas for Women." International IDEA and Stockholm University. Accessed April 26, 2006. http://www.quotaproject.org.

Inter-Parliamentary Union. 2006. "Women in National Parliaments." Accessed September 11, 2006. http://www.ipu.org/wmn-e/classif.htm.

Inter-Parliamentary Union. 2007. "Women in National Parliaments." Accessed June 15, 2007. http://www.ipu.org/wmn-e/classif.htm.

Iversen, Torben, and Frances Rosenbluth. 2006. "The Political Economy of Gender: Explaining Cross-National Variation in the Gender Division of Labor and the Gender Voting Gap." *American Journal of Political Science* 50:1–19.

Jackman, Mary R. 1994. *The Velvet Glove: Paternalism and Conflict in Gender, Class, and Race Relations*. Berkeley: University of California Press.

Jaffee, Sara, and Janet Shibley Hyde. 2000. "Gender Differences in Moral Orientation: A Meta-Analysis." *Psychological Bulletin* 126:703–26.

Jaquette, Jane S., ed. 1994. *The Women's Movement in Latin America: Participation and Democracy*, 2nd ed. Boulder, CO: Westview Press.

Jaquette, Jane S., and Sharon L. Wolchik, eds. 1998. *Women and Democracy*. Baltimore: Johns Hopkins University Press.

Jelen, Ted, Sue Thomas, and Clyde Wilcox. 1994. "The Gender Gap in Comparative Perspective." *European Journal of Political Research* 25:171–86.

Jelín, Elizabeth. 1991. *Family, Household and Gender Relations in Latin America*. London: Kegan Paul International, in association with UNESCO.

Jennings, Kent. 1983. "Gender Roles and Inequalities in Political Participation: Results from an Eight-Nation Study." *Western Political Quarterly* 36:364–85.

Jennings, M. Kent. 1990. "Women in Party Politics." In *Women, Politics, and Change*, ed. Louise A. Tilly and Patricia Gurin. New York: Russell Sage Foundation, pp. 221–48.

Jennings, M. Kent, and Barbara G. Farah. 1981. "Social Roles and Political Resources: An Over-Time Study of Men and Women in Party Elites." *American Journal of Political Science* 25:462–82.

Jennings, M. Kent, and Richard G. Niemi. 1981. *Generations and Politics*. Princeton, NJ: Princeton University Press.

Jenson, Jane. 1987. "Changing Discourse, Changing Agendas: Political Rights and Reproductive Policies in France." In *The Women's Movements of the United States and Western Europe*, ed. Mary Katzenstein and Carol Mueller. Philadelphia: Temple University Press, pp. 64–88.

Jewell, Malcolm E., and Marcia Lynn Whicker. 1994. *Legislative Leadership in the American States*. Ann Arbor: University of Michigan Press.

Jeydel, Alana S. 2004. *Political Women: The Women's Movement, Political Institutions, the Battle for Women's Suffrage and the ERA*. New York: Routledge.

Jeydel, Alana, and Andrew J. Taylor. 2003. "Are Women Legislators Less Effective? Evidence from the U.S. House in the 103rd–105th Congress." *Political Research Quarterly* 56:19–27.

Johnson, Cathy Marie, Georgia Duerst-Lahti, and Noelle H. Norton. 2007. *Creating Gender: The Sexual Politics of Welfare Policy*. Boulder, CO: Lynne Rienner.

Johnson, Marilyn, and Susan Carroll. 1978. "Statistical Report: Profile of Women Holding Office, 1977." In *Women in Public Office: A Biographical Directory and Statistical Analysis*, compiled by the Center for the American Woman and Politics, Eagleton Institute, Rutgers University. Metuchen, NJ: Scarecrow, pp. 1A–64A.

Johnston, Hank, and Bert Klandermans, eds. 1995. *Social Movements and Culture*. Minneapolis: University of Minnesota Press.

Jónasdóttir, Anna G. 1989. "On the Concept of Interest, Women's Interests, and the Limitations of Interest Theory." In *The Political Interests of Gender: Developing Theory and Research with a Feminist Face*, ed. Anna G. Jónasdóttir and Kathleen B. Jones. New York: Sage, pp. 33–65.

Jones, John Paul, III, ed. 1997. *Thresholds in Feminist Geography: Difference, Methodology, Representation*. New York: Rowman and Littlefield.

Jones, Lisa. 1994. *Bulletproof Diva: Tales of Race, Sex, and Hair.* Anchor Books: Doubleday.

Jones, Mark P. 1996. "Increasing Women's Representation via Gender Quotas: The Argentine Ley de Cupos." *Women & Politics* 16:75–97.

Jones, Mark P. 1998. "Gender Quotas, Electoral Laws, and the Election of Women: Lessons from the Argentine Provinces." *Comparative Political Studies* 31:3–21.

Jones, Mark P. 2004. "Quota Legislation and the Election of Women: Learning from the Costa Rican Experience." *Journal of Politics* 66:1203–23.

Jones, Mark P. 2005. "The Desirability of Gender Quotas: Considering Context and Design." *Politics & Gender* 1(4):645–52.

Jones, Mark P., and Patricio Navia. 1999. "Gender Quotas, Electoral Laws, and the Election of Women: Assessing the Effectiveness of Quotas in Open List Proportional Electoral Systems." *Social Science Quarterly* 80:341–55.

Jones, Tamara. 2000. "Building Effective Black Feminist Organizations." *Souls* 2(4):55–60.

Jordan, June. 1992. "A New Politics of Sexuality." In *Technical Difficulties.* New York: Pantheon, pp. 181–93.

Jordan-Zachery, Julia S. 2007. "Am I a Black Woman or a Woman Who Is Black? A Few Thoughts on the Meaning of Intersectionality." *Politics & Gender* 3(2):26–35.

Judd, Ellen R. 2002. *The Chinese Women's Movement between State and Market.* Stanford, CA: Stanford University Press.

Junn, Jane. 2007. "Square Pegs and Round Holes: Challenges of Fitting Individual-Level Analyses to a Theory of Politicized Context of Gender." *Politics & Gender* 3(1):124–34.

Junn, Jane, and Kerry Haynie, eds. Forthcoming. *New Race Politics: Understanding Minority and Immigrant Politics.* Cambridge: Cambridge University Press.

Kahn, Kim Fridkin. 1992. "Does Being Male Help? An Investigation of the Effects of Candidate Gender and Campaign Coverage on Evaluations of U.S. Senate Candidates." *Journal of Politics* 54:497–517.

Kahn, Kim Fridkin. 1994a. "The Distorted Mirror: Press Coverage of Women Candidates for Statewide Office." *Journal of Politics* 56:154–73.

Kahn, Kim Fridkin. 1994b. "Does Gender Make a Difference? An Experimental Examination of Sex Stereotypes and Press Patterns in Statewide Campaigns." *American Journal of Political Science* 38:162–95.

Kahn, Kim Fridkin. 1996. *The Political Consequences of Being a Woman: How Stereotypes Influence the Conduct and Consequences of Political Campaigns.* New York: Columbia University Press.

Kahn, Kim Fridkin. 2003. "Assessing the Media's Impact on the Political Fortunes of Women." In *Women and American Politics: New Questions, New Directions,* ed. Susan Carroll. New York: Oxford University Press, pp. 73–89.

Kalmuss, D., P. Gurin, and A. L. Townsend. 1981. "Feminist and Sympathetic Feminist Consciousness." *European Journal of Social Psychology* 11:131–47.

Kampwirth, Karen. 2002. *Women and Guerrilla Movements: Nicaragua, El Salvador, Chiapas, Cuba.* University Park: Pennsylvania State University Press.

Kampwirth, Karen. 2004. *Feminism and the Legacy of Revolution: Nicaragua, El Salvador, Chiapas.* Athens: Ohio University Press.

Kampwirth, Karen, and Victoria Gonzalez, eds. 2001. *Radical Women in Latin America: Right and Left*. University Park: Pennsylvania State University Press.

Kann, Mark. 1991. *On the Man Question: Gender and Civic Virtue in America*. Philadelphia: Temple University Press.

Kanter, Rosabeth M. 1977. "Some Effects of Proportions on Group Life: Skewed Sex Ratios and Responses to Token Women." *American Journal of Sociology* 82:965–91.

Kaplan, Temma. 1997. *Crazy for Democracy: Women in Grassroots Movements*. New York: Routledge.

Kathlene, Lyn. 1994. "Power and Influence in State Legislative Policy-Making: The Interaction of Gender and Position in Committee Hearing Debates." *American Political Science Review* 88:560–76.

Kathlene, Lyn. 1995. "Alternative Views of Crime: Legislative Policymaking in Gendered Terms." *Journal of Politics* 57:696–723.

Katzenstein, Mary Fainsod. 1987. "Comparing the Feminist Movements of the United States and Western Europe: An Overview." In *The Women's Movements of the United States and Western Europe: Consciousness, Political Opportunity, and Public Policy*, ed. Mary Fainsod Katzenstein and Carol McClurg Mueller. Philadelphia: Temple University Press, pp. 3–20.

Katzenstein, Mary Fainsod. 1998. *Faithful and Fearless: Moving Feminist Protest inside the Church and Military*. Princeton, NJ: Princeton University Press.

Katzenstein, Mary Fainsod, and Carol McClurg Mueller, eds. 1987. *The Women's Movements of the United States and Western Europe*. Philadelphia: Temple University Press.

Katznelson, Ira. 2005. *When Affirmative Action Was White*. New York: W. W. Norton.

Kaufmann, Karen M., and John R. Petrocik. 1999. "The Changing Politics of American Men: Understanding the Sources of the Gender Gap." *American Journal of Political Science* 43:864–87.

Keck, Margaret, and Kathryn Sikkink. 1998. *Activists beyond Borders: Advocacy Networks in International Politics*. Ithaca: Cornell University Press.

Kelley, J., and N. D. DeGraaf. 1997. "National Context, Parental Socialization, and Religious Belief: Results from 15 Nations." *American Sociological Review* 62:639–59.

Kelly, Rita Mae, and Kimberly Fisher. 1993. "An Assessment of Articles about Women in the 'Top 15' Political Science Journals." *PS: Political Science and Politics* 26(September):544–58.

Kenney, Sally J. 1996. "New Research on Gendered Political Institutions." *Political Research Quarterly* 49(June):445–66.

Kenney, Sally. 2002. "Breaking the Silence: Gender Mainstreaming and the European Judiciary." *Feminist Legal Studies* 10:257–70.

Kenney, Sally J. 2004. "Equal Employment Opportunity and Representation: Extending the Frame to Courts." *Social Politics* 11:86–116.

Kenski, Henry C. 1988. "The Gender Factor in a Changing Electorate." In *The Politics of the Gender Gap: The Social Construction of Political Influence*, ed. Carol M. Mueller. Newbury Park, CA: Sage, pp. 38–59.

Kerber, Linda K. 1980. *Women of the Republic: Intellect and Ideology in Revolutionary America*. Chapel Hill: University of North Carolina Press.

Kerber, Linda K. 1998. *No Constitutional Right to Be Ladies: Women and the Obligations of Citizenship*. New York: Hill and Wang.

Kessler-Harris, Alice. 1995. "Designing Women and Old Fools." In *US History as Women's History: New Feminist Essays*, ed. Linda Kerber et al. Chapel Hill: University of North Carolina Press, pp. 87–106.

Kessler-Harris, Alice. 2001. *In Pursuit of Equity: Women, Men, and the Quest for Economic Citizenship in 20th Century America*. New York: Oxford University Press.

Kessler-Harris, Alice. 2004. "Reframing the History of Women's Wage Labor: Challenges of a Global Perspective." *Journal of Women's History* 15:186–206.

Kinder, Donald R., and Lynn Sanders. 1990. "Mimicking Political Debate with Survey Questions: The Case of White Opinion on Affirmative Action for Blacks." *Social Cognition* 8:73–103.

Kinder, Donald R., and Lynn Sanders. 1996. *Divided by Color: Racial Politics and Democratic Ideals*. Chicago: University of Chicago Press.

King, Brayden, Marie Cornwall, and Eric Dahlin. 2005. "Winning Woman Suffrage One Step at a Time: Social Movements and the Logic of the Legislative Process." *Social Forces* 83:1211–34.

King, David, and Richard Matland. 2003. "Sex and the Grand Old Party: An Experimental Investigation of the Effect of Candidate Sex on Support for a Republican Candidate." *American Politics Research* 31:595–612.

King, Deborah K. 1988. "Multiple Jeopardy, Multiple Consciousness: The Context of a Black Feminist Ideology." *Signs* 14:42–72.

King, Desmond, Robert C. Lieberman, Gretchen Ritter, and Laurence Whitehead, eds. Forthcoming. *Democratization in America: American Political Development as a Process of Democratization*. Baltimore: Johns Hopkins University Press.

King, Desmond, and Rogers Smith. 2005. "Racial Orders in American Political Development." *American Political Science Review* 99:75–92.

Kirkpatrick, Jeane J. 1974. *Political Woman*. New York: Basic Books.

Kite, M. E., and B. E. Whitley. 1996. "Sex Differences in Attitudes towards Homosexual Persons, Behaviour, and Civil Rights: A Meta-Analysis." *Personality and Social Psychology Bulletin* 22:336–53.

Kitschelt, Herbert. 1986. "Political Opportunity Structures and Political Protest: Anti-Nuclear Movements in Four Democracies." *British Journal of Political Science* 16:57–85.

Kittilson, Miki Caul. 2005. "In Support of Gender Quotas: Setting New Standards, Bringing Visible Gains." *Politics & Gender* 1(4):638–45.

Kittilson, Miki Caul. 2006. *Challenging Parties, Changing Parliaments: Women and Elected Office in Contemporary Western Europe*. Columbus: Ohio State University Press.

Klatch, Rebecca. 1987. *Women of the New Right*. Philadelphia: Temple University Press.

Klatch, Rebecca. 2002. "The Development of Individual Identity and Consciousness among Movements of the Left and Right." In *Social Movements: Identity, Culture, and the State*, ed. David S. Meyer, Nancy Whittier, and Belinda Robnett. Oxford: Oxford University Press, pp. 185–204.

Klein, Ethel. 1984. *Gender Politics: From Consciousness to Mass Politics*. Cambridge, MA: Harvard University Press.

Klinker, Philip, and Rogers Smith. 1999. *The Unsteady March*. Chicago: University of Chicago Press.

Koch, Jeffrey. 1997. "Candidate Gender and Women's Psychological Engagement in Politics." *American Politics Quarterly* 25:118–33.

Koch, Jeffrey. 1999. "Candidate Gender and Assessments of Senate Candidates." *Social Science Quarterly* 80:84–96.

Koch, Jeffrey. 2002. "Gender Stereotypes and Citizens Impression of House Candidates Ideological Orientations." *American Journal of Political Science* 46:453–62.

Kollman, Ken. 1998. *Outside Lobbying: Public Opinion and Interest Group Strategies*. Princeton, NJ: Princeton University Press.

Kriesi, Hanspeter, Ruud Koopmans, Jan Willem Duyvendak, and Marco G. Guigni. 1995. *New Social Movements in Western Europe*. Minneapolis: University of Minnesota Press.

Kropf, Martha, and John Boiney. 2001. "The Electoral Glass Ceiling? Gender, Viability, and the News in U.S. Campaigns." *Women & Politics* 23:79–101.

Kryder, Daniel. 2000. *Divided Arsenal: Race and the American State during World War II*. New York: Cambridge University Press.

Kunovich, Sheri, and Pamela Paxton. 2005. "Pathways to Power: The Role of Political Parties in Women's National Political Representation." *American Journal of Sociology* 111:505–52.

LaMar, L. M., and M. E. Kite. 1998. "Sex Differences in Attitudes towards Gay Men and Lesbians: A Multi-Dimensional Perspective." *Journal of Sex Research* 35:189–96.

Landes, Joan. 1988. *Women and the Public Sphere in the Age of the French Revolution*. Ithaca, NY: Cornell University Press.

Lang, Sabine. 1997. "The NGOization of Feminism." In *Transitions, Environments, Translations*, ed. Joan Wallach Scott, Cora Kaplan, and Debra Keates. New York: Routledge, pp. 290–304.

Lawless, Jennifer. 2004. "Politics of Presence? Congresswomen and Symbolic Representation." *Political Research Quarterly* 57:81–99.

Lawless, Jennifer, and Richard Fox. 2005. *It Takes a Candidate: Why Women Don't Run for Political Office*. New York: Cambridge University Press.

Lazarsfeld, Paul F., Bernard Berelson, and Hazel Gaudet. 1944. *The People's Choice: How the Voter Makes Up His Mind in a Presidential Campaign*. New York: Columbia University Press.

Leader, Shelah Gilbert. 1977. "The Policy Impact of Elected Women Officials." In *The Impact of the Electoral Process*, ed. Louis Maisel and Joseph Cooper. Beverly Hills, CA: Sage, pp. 265–84.

LeDuc, Lawrence, Richard Niemi, and Pippa Norris. 1996. *Comparing Democracies: Elections and Voting in Global Perspectives*. Thousand Oaks, CA: Sage.

Lee, Taeku. 2002. *Mobilizing Public Opinion: Black Insurgency and Racial Attitudes in the Civil Rights Era*. Chicago: University of Chicago Press.

Leeper, Mark. 1991. "The Impact of Prejudice on Female Candidates: An Experimental Look at Voter Inference." *American Politics Quarterly* 19:248–61.

Lerner, Gerda. 1979. *The Majority Finds Its Past: Placing Women in History*. New York: Oxford University Press.

Lewis, Carolyn. 1999. "Are Women for Women? Feminist and Traditional Values in the Female Electorate." *Women & Politics* 20:1–28.

Lien, Pei-Te, M. Margaret Conway, and Janelle Wong. 2004. *The Politics of Asian Americans: Diversity and Community*. New York: Routledge.

Lijphart, Arend. 1984. *Democracies: Patterns of Majoritarian and Consensus Government in Twenty-one Countries*. New Haven, CT: Yale University Press.

Lipman-Blumen, Jean. 1984. *Gender Roles and Power*. Englewood Cliffs, NJ: Prentice-Hall.

Lipset, Seymour Martin, and Stein Rokkan. 1967. *Party Systems and Voter Alignments: Cross-National Perspectives*. New York: Free Press.

Lorde, Audre. 1984. "Age, Race, Class, and Sex: Women Redefining Difference." In *Sister Outsider*. Trumansburg, NY: Crossing Press, pp. 114–123.

Lovenduski, Joni. 1998. "Gendering Research in Political Science." *Annual Review of Politics* 1:333–56.

Lovenduski, Joni, ed. 2005. *State Feminism and Political Representation*. New York: Cambridge University Press.

Lovenduski, Joni, and Pippa Norris, eds. 1993. *Gender and Party Politics*. London: Sage.

Lovenduski, Joni, and Pippa Norris, eds. 1996. *Women and Party Politics*. New York: Oxford University Press.

Lovenduski, Joni and Pippa Norris. 2003. "Westminster Women: The Politics of Presence." *Political Studies* 51:84–102.

Lublin, David. 1997. *The Paradox of Representation: Racial Gerrymandering and Minority Interests in Congress*. Princeton, NJ: Princeton University Press.

Lublin, David, and Sarah Brewer. 2003. "The Continuing Dominance of Traditional Gender Roles in Southern Elections." *Social Science Quarterly* 84:379–96.

Luciak, Ilja A. 2001. *After the Revolution: Gender and Democracy in El Salvador, Nicaragua and Guatemala*. Baltimore: Johns Hopkins University Press.

Luker, Kristin. 1984. *Abortion and the Politics of Motherhood*. Berkeley: University of California Press.

Lynn, Susan. 1992. *Progressive Women in Conservative Times: Racial Justice, Peace, and Feminism, 1945 to the 1960s*. New Brunswick, NJ: Rutgers University Press.

MacKinnon, Catharine. 1987. "Difference and Dominance." In *Feminism Unmodified*. Cambridge, MA: Harvard University Press, pp. 32–45.

MacKinnon, Catharine. 1988. *Feminism Unmodified*. Cambridge, MA: Harvard University Press.

MacManus, Susan A. 2006. "Voter Participation and Turnout: It's a New Game." In *Gender and Elections: Shaping the Future of American Politics*, ed. Susan J. Carroll and Richard L. Fox. New York: Cambridge University Press, pp. 43–73.

Maestas, Cheri, L. Sandy Maisel, and Walter Stone. 2005. "National Party Efforts to Recruit State Legislators." *Legislative Studies Quarterly* 30:277–300.

Mann, Patricia. 1997. "Musing as a Feminist in a Postfeminist Era." *Feminism and the New Democracy: Resisting the Political*, ed. Joni Dean. London: Sage, pp. 222–42.

Mansbridge, Jane J. 1980. *Beyond Adversary Democracy*. Chicago: University of Chicago Press.

Mansbridge, Jane J. 1985. "Myth and Reality: The ERA and the Gender Gap in the 1980 Election." *Public Opinion Quarterly* 49:164–78.

Mansbridge, Jane J. 1986. *Why We Lost the ERA*. Chicago: University of Chicago Press.

Mansbridge, Jane. 1999. "Should Blacks Represent Blacks and Women Represent Women? A Contingent 'Yes'." *Journal of Politics* 61:628–57.

Mansbridge, Jane. 2003. "Rethinking Representation." *American Political Science Review* 97(4):515–28.

Manza, Jeff, and Clem Brooks. 1998. "The Gender Gap in U.S. Presidential Elections: When? Why? Implications?" *American Journal of Sociology* 103:1235–66.

Marable, Manning. 1983. *How Capitalism Underdeveloped Black America*. Boston: South End Press.

Marilley, Suzanne M. 1996. *Woman Suffrage and the Origins of Liberal Feminism in the United States, 1820–1920*. Cambridge, MA: Harvard University Press.

Mathews, Donald, and Jane Sherron DeHart. 1992. *Sex, Gender and the Politics of the ERA*. New York: Oxford University Press.

Mathews-Gardner, A. Lanathea. 2003. *From Woman's Club to NGO: The Changing Terrain of Women's Civil Engagement in the Mid-Twentieth-Century United States.* Unpublished Ph.D. dissertation, Syracuse University, New York.

Matland, Richard E. 1993. "Institutional Variables Affecting Female Representation in National Legislatures: The Case of Norway." *Journal of Politics* 55:737–55.

Matland, Richard E. 1998. "Women's Representation in National Legislatures: Developed and Developing Countries." *Legislative Studies Quarterly* 23:109–30.

Matland, Richard E., and Deborah D. Brown. 1992. "District Magnitude's Effect on Female Representation in State Legislatures." *Legislative Studies Quarterly* 17:469–92.

Matland, Richard E., and Katheen A. Montgomery. 2003. "Recruiting Women to National Legislatures: A General Framework with Applications to Post-Communist Democracies." In *Women's Access to Political Power in Post-Communist Europe*, ed. Richard E. Matland and Kathleen A. Montgomery. Oxford: Oxford University Press, pp. 19–42.

Matland, Richard E., and Donley T. Studlar. 1996. "The Contagion of Women Candidates in Single-Member District and Proportional Representation Electoral Systems: Canada and Norway." *Journal of Politics* 58:707–33.

Matland, Richard E., and Michelle Taylor. 1997. "Electoral and Representation: Theoretical Arguments and Evidence from Costa Rica." *Comparative Political Studies* 2:186–210.

Mazur, Amy, ed. 2001. *State Feminism, Women's Movements, and Job Training: Making Democracies Work in the Global Economy*. New York: Routledge.

Mazur, Amy. 2002. *Theorizing Feminist Policy*. Oxford: Oxford University Press.

McAdam, Doug. 1982. *Political Process and the Development of Black Insurgency, 1930–1970*. Chicago: University of Chicago Press.

McAdam, Doug, John McCarthy, and Mayer Zald, eds. 1996. *Comparative Perspectives on Social Movements*. Cambridge: Cambridge University Press.

McCall, Leslie. 2005. "The Complexity of Intersectionality." *Signs* 30:1771–800.

McCammon, Holly. 2001. "Stirring Up Suffrage Sentiment: The Emergence of the State Woman Suffrage Movements, 1866–1914." *Social Forces* 80:449–80.

McCammon, Holly. 2003. "'Out of the Parlors and into the Streets': The Changing Tactical Repertoire of the U.S. Women's Suffrage Movements." *Social Forces* 81:787–818.

McCammon, Holly J., Karen E. Campbell, Ellen M. Granberg, and Christine Mowery. 2001. "How Movements Win: Gendered Opportunity Structures and the State Women's Suffrage Movements, 1866–1919." *American Sociological Review* 66:49–70.

McCarthy, John, and Mayer Zald. 1977. "Resource Mobilization and Social Movements: A Partial Theory." *American Journal of Sociology* 82:1212–41.

McConnaughy, Corrine M. 2004. *The Politics of Suffrage Extension in the American States: Party, Race, and the Pursuit of Women's Voting Rights*. Unpublished Ph.D. dissertation, University of Michigan, Ann Arbor.

McConnaughy, Corrine. 2005. "Bringing Politics Back In: How Politicians Decided the Fate of Woman Suffrage in the American States." Paper presented at the American Political Science Association Annual Meeting, Washington, DC.

McDermott, Monika L. 1997. "Voting Cues in Low-Information Elections: Candidate Gender as a Social Information Variable in Contemporary United States Elections." *American Journal of Political Science* 41:270–83.

McDonagh, Eileen. 2002. "Political Citizenship and Democratization: The Gender Paradox." *American Political Science Review* 96:535–52.

McGerr, Michael. 1990. "Political Style and Women's Power, 1830–1930." *Journal of American History* 77:864–85.

Merritt, Sharyne. 1980. "Sex Differences in Role Behavior and Policy Orientations of Suburban Officeholders: The Effect of Women's Employment." In *Women in Local Politics*, ed. Debra Stewart. Metuchen, NJ: Scarecrow Press, pp. 115–29.

Mettler, Suzanne. 1998. *Divided Citizens: Gender and Federalism in New Deal Policy*. Ithaca, NY: Cornell University Press.

Mettler, Suzanne. 2005. *From Soldiers to Citizens: The G.I. Bill and the Making of the Greatest Generation*. New York: Oxford University Press.

Mettler, Suzanne. Forthcoming. "The Development of Democratic Citizenship: A New Research Agenda." In *Democratization in America: American Political Development as a Process of Democratization*, ed. Desmond King et al. Baltimore: Johns Hopkins University Press.

Mettler, Suzanne, and Joe Soss. 2004. "The Consequences of Public Policy for Democratic Citizenship: Bridging Policy Studies and Mass Politics." *Perspectives on Politics* 2:55–73.

Meyer, David S., and Debra Minkoff. 2004. "Conceptualizing Political Opportunity." *Social Forces* 82:1457–92.

Mezey, Susan Gluck. 1978a. "Support for Women's Rights Policy: An Analysis of Local Politicians." *American Politics Quarterly* 6:485–97.

Mezey, Susan Gluck. 1978b. "Women and Representation: The Case of Hawaii." *Journal of Politics* 40:369–85.

Mezey, Susan Gluck. 1978c. "Does Sex Make a Difference? A Case Study of Women in Politics." *Western Political Quarterly* 31:492–501.

Miller, Arthur H., Patricia Gurin, Gerald Gurin, and Oksana Malanchuk. 1981. "Group Consciousness and Political Participation." *American Journal of Political Science* 25:494–511.

Miller, Joanne, and Wendy Rahn. 2002. "Identity-based Thoughts, Feelings and Actions: How Being Influences Doing." Unpublished manuscript, University of Minnesota, Minneapolis.

Mink, Gwendolyn. 1990. "The Lady and the Tramp: Gender, Race and the Origins of the American Welfare State." In *Women, the State and Welfare*, ed. Linda Gordon. Madison: University of Wisconsin Press, pp. 92–122.

Mink, Gwendolyn. 1995. *The Wages of Motherhood: Inequality in the Welfare State, 1917–1942*. Ithaca, NY: Cornell University Press.

Minkoff, Debra. 1995. *Organizing for Equality: The Evolution of Women's and Racial-Ethnic Organizations in America, 1955–1985*. ASA Rose Book Series. New Brunswick, NJ: Rutgers University Press.

Minkoff, Debra. 1997. "Innovating at the Margins: Comparing the Organizations of White Women and Women of Color." In *Women Transforming Politics*, ed. Cathy Cohen, Kathleen Jones, and Joan Tronto. New York: New York University Press, pp. 477–96.

Minkoff, Debra. 1999. "Bending with the Wind: Organizational Change in American Women's and Minority Organizations." *American Journal of Sociology* 104:1666–703.

Mittelstadt, Jennifer. 2005. *From Welfare to Workfare: The Unintended Consequences of Liberal Reform, 1945–1965*. Chapel Hill: University of North Carolina Press.

Moghadam, Valentine M. 1993. *Modernizing Women: Gender and Social Change in the Middle East*. Boulder, CO: Lynne Rienner.

Moghadam, Valentine M. 2005. *Globalizing Women: Transnational Feminist Networks*. Baltimore: Johns Hopkins University Press.

Mohanty, Chandra Talpade. 1991. "Introduction. Cartographies of Struggle: Third World Women and the Politics of Feminism." In *Third World Women and the Politics of Feminism*, ed. Chandra T. Mohanty, Ann Russo, and Lourdes Torres. Bloomington: Indiana University Press, pp. 1–47.

Moi, Toril. 2002a. "While We Wait: The English Translation of 'The Second Sex'." *Signs* 27(Summer):1005–35.

Moi, Toril. 2002b. *Sexual/Textual Politics: Feminist Literary Theory*, 2nd ed. New York: Taylor and Francis.

Momsen, Janet, and Vivian Kinnaird, eds. 1993. *Different Places, Different Voices: Gender and Development in Africa, Asia and Latin America*. New York: Routledge.

Mondak, Jeffery J., and Belinda Creel Davis. 2001. "Asked and Answered: Knowledge Levels When We Will Not Take 'Don't Know' for an Answer." *Political Behavior* 23:199–224.

Moon, Katharine. 1997. *Sex among Allies: Military Prostitution in US-Korea Relations*. New York: Columbia University Press.

Moraga, Cherrie. 1981. "La Güera" In *This Bridge Called My Back: Writings by Radical Women of Color*, ed. Cherrie Moraga and Gloria Anzaldúa. New York: Kitchen Table Press, pp. 27–34.

Morgan, Joan. 1999. *When Chickenheads Come Home to Roost: A Hip-Hop Feminist Breaks It Down*. New York: Touchstone.

Morgen, Sandra. 2002. *Into Our Own Hands: The Women's Health Movement in the United States, 1969–1990*. New Brunswick, NJ: Rutgers University Press.

Mouffe, Chantal. 1992. *Dimensions of Radical Democracy: Pluralism, Citizenship, Community*. New York: Verso.

Mueller, Carol M. 1988a. "The Empowerment of Women: Polling and the Women's Voting Bloc." In *The Politics of the Gender Gap: The Social Construction of Political Influence*, ed. Carol M. Mueller. Newbury Park, CA: Sage, pp. 17–36.

Mueller, Carol McClurg, ed. 1988b. *The Politics of the Gender Gap: The Social Construction of Political Influence*. Newbury Park, CA: Sage.

Mulvad, Eva. 2007. "NOW Transcript: Show 309 (March 2)." Accessed May 4, 2007. http://www.pbs.org/now/transcript/309.html.

Muncy, Robyn. 1991. *Creating a Female Dominion in American Reform, 1890–1935*. New York: Oxford University Press.

Naples, Nancy, ed. 1998. *Community Activism and Feminist Politic: Organizing across Race, Class, and Gender*. New York: Routledge.

Naples, Nancy A., and Manisha Desai, eds. 2002. *Women's Activism and Globalization: Linking Local Struggles and Transnational Politics*. New York: Routledge.

Nechemias, Carol. 1985. "Geographic Mobility and Women's Access to State Legislatures." *Western Political Quarterly* 38(1):119–31.

Nelson, Barbara. 1990. "The Origins of the Two Channel Welfare State: Workmen's Compensation and Mothers' Aid." In *Women, the State and Welfare*, ed. Linda Gordon. Madison: University of Wisconsin Press, pp. 123–52.

Nelson, Barbara J., and Najma Chowdhury. 1994. *Women and Politics Worldwide*. New Haven, CT: Yale University Press.

Newman, Jody. 1994. "Perception and Reality: A Study Comparing the Success of Men and Women Candidates." A Report for the National Women's Political Caucus.

Nicholson, Linda. 1994. "Interpreting Gender." *Signs* 20(Autumn):79–105.

Nie, Norman, Jane Junn, and Kenneth Stehlik-Barry. 1996. *Education and Democratic Citizenship in America*. Chicago: University of Chicago Press.

Nieman, Donald. 1991. *Promises to Keep: African Americans and the Constitutional Order, 1776 to the Present*. New York: Oxford University Press.

Nincic, Miroslav, and Donna J. Nincic. 2002. "Race, Gender, and War." *Journal of Peace Research* 39:547–68.

Niven, David. 1998a. *The Missing Majority: The Recruitment of Women as State Legislative Candidates*. Westport, CT: Praeger.

Niven, David. 1998b. "Party Elites and Women Candidates: The Shape of Bias." *Women & Politics* 19:57–80.

Niven, David, and Jeremy Zilber. 2001. "How Does She Have Time for Kids and Congress? Views on Gender and Media Coverage from House Offices." *Women & Politics* 23:147–66.

Norrander, Barbara. 1997. "The Independence Gap and the Gender Gap." *Public Opinion Quarterly* 61:464–76.

Norrander, Barbara, and Clyde Wilcox. 1998. "The Geography of Gender Power: Women in State Legislatures." In *Women and Elective Office: Past, Present, and Future*, ed. Sue Thomas and Clyde Wilcox. New York: Oxford University Press, pp. 103–17.

Norris, Pippa. 1993. "Conclusions: Comparing Legislative Recruitment." In *Gender and Party Politics*, ed. Joni Lovenduski and Pippa Norris. London: Sage, pp. 309–30.

Norris, Pippa. 1995. *Political Recruitment: Gender, Race and Class in the British Parliament*. Cambridge: Cambridge University Press.

Norris, Pippa. 2000. "Women's Representation and Electoral Systems." In *The International Encyclopedia of Elections*, ed. Richard Rose. Washington, DC: Congressional Quarterly Press, pp. 348–51.

Norris, Pippa, and Ronald Inglehart. 2005. "Women as Political Leaders Worldwide: Cultural Barriers and Opportunities." In *Women and Elective Office: Past, Present, and Future*, ed. Sue Thomas and Clyde Wilcox. 2nd ed. New York: Oxford University Press, pp. 244–63.

Norris, Pippa, and Joni Lovenduski. 1989. "Women Candidates for Parliament: Transforming the Agenda?" *British Journal of Political Science* 19(1):106–15.

Norton, Noelle H. 1995. "Women, It's Not Enough to Be Elected: Committee Position Makes a Difference." In *Gender, Power, Leadership, and Governance*, ed. Georgia Duerst-Lahti and Rita Mae Kelly. Ann Arbor: University of Michigan Press, pp. 115–40.

Norton, Noelle H. 2002. "Transforming Policy from the Inside: Participation in Committee." In *Women Transforming Congress*, ed. Cindy Simon Rosenthal. Norman: University of Oklahoma Press, pp. 316–40.

Novkov, Julie. 2001. *Constituting Workers, Protecting Women: Gender, Law and Labor in the Progressive Era and New Deal Years*. Ann Arbor: University of Michigan Press.

Novkov, Julie. Forthcoming. *Racial Union: Law, Intimacy, and the White State in Alabama, 1865–1954*. Ann Arbor: University of Michigan Press.

Oberschall, Anthony. 1973. *Social Conflicts and Social Movements*. Englewood Cliffs, NJ: Prentice Hall.

Okeke-Ihejirika, P. E., and Susan Franceschet. 2002. "Democratization and State Feminism: Gender Politics in Africa and Latin America." *Development and Change* 33:439–66.

Okin, Susan Moller. 1989. *Justice, Gender and the Family*. New York: Basic Books.

Oliver, Melvin, and Thomas Shapiro. 2006. *Black Wealth/White Wealth: A New Perspective on Racial Inequality*, 2nd ed. New York: Routledge.

Omolade, Barbara. 1983. "Hearts of Darkness." In *Powers of Desire: The Politics of Sexuality*, ed. Ann Snitow, Christine Stansell, and Sharon Thompson. New York: Monthly Review Press, pp. 350–67.

Ondercin, Heather. 2007. *The Changing Social Definitions of Men and Women and Their Effect on the Partisan Gender Gap, 1953–2003*. Unpublished Ph.D. dissertation, Pennsylvania State University, University Park.

Ondercin, Heather, and Susan Welch. 2005. "Women Candidates for Congress." In *Women and Elective Office: Past, Present, and Future*, ed. Sue Thomas and Clyde Wilcox. 2nd ed. New York: Oxford University Press, pp. 60–80.

O'Neal, S. J. 2000. *Shattering Silence: Expressions of Resistance in the Poetry and Hip Hop and Negritude*. Unpublished master's thesis, University of California, Los Angeles.

O'Regan, Valerie. 2000. *Gender Matters: Female Policymakers' Influence in Industrialized Nations*. Westport, CT: Praeger.

Orloff, Ann Shola. 1988. "The Political Origins of America's Belated Welfare State." In *The Politics of Social Policy in the United States*, ed. Margaret Weir, Ann Shola Orloff, and Theda Skocpol. Princeton, NJ: Princeton University Press, pp. 37–80.

Orren, Karen. 1991. *Belated Feudalism: Labor, the Law and Liberal Development in the United States*. New York: Cambridge University Press.

Orren, Karen, and Stephen Skowronek. 2004. *The Search for American Political Development*. New York: Cambridge University Press.

Osborn, Tracy. 2003. "Institutional Context and Support for a Women's Agenda in the State Legislatures." Paper presented at the American Political Science Association Annual Meeting, Philadelphia.

Outshoorn, Joyce, ed. 2004. *The Politics of Prostitution: Women's Movements, Democratic States, and the Globalization of Sex Commerce*. New York: Cambridge University Press.

Oxley, Zoe, and Richard Fox. 2004. "Women in Executive Office: Variation across American States." *Political Research Quarterly* 57:113–20.

Paddock, Joel, and Elizabeth Paddock. 1997. "Differences in Partisan Style and Ideology between Female and Male State Party Committee Members." *Women & Politics* 18:41–56.

Palmer, Barbara, and Dennis Simon. 2001. "The Political Glass Ceiling: Gender, Strategy, and Incumbency in U.S. Elections, 1978–1998." *Women & Politics* 23:59–78.

Palmer, Barbara, and Dennis Simon. 2003. "Political Ambition and Women in the US House of Representatives." *Political Research Quarterly* 56:127–38.

Palmer, Barbara, and Dennis Simon. 2005. "When Women Run against Women: The Hidden Influence of Female Incumbents in Elections to the U.S. House of Representatives, 1956–2002." *Politics & Gender* 1(1):39–63.

Palmer, Barbara, and Dennis Simon. 2006. *Breaking the Political Glass Ceiling: Women and Congressional Elections*. New York: Routledge.

Paolino, Phillip. 1995. "Group-Salient Issues and Group Representation: Support for Women Candidates in the 1992 Senate Elections." *American Journal of Political Science* 39:294–313.

Pateman, Carole. 1970. *Participation and Democratic Theory*. Cambridge: Cambridge University Press.

Pateman, Carole. 1988. *The Sexual Contract*. Palo Alto, CA: Stanford University Press.

Pateman, Carole. 1994. "Three Questions about Womanhood Suffrage." In *Suffrage and Beyond: International Feminist Perspectives*, ed. Caroline Daley and Melanie Nolan. Washington Square: New York University Press, pp. 331–48.

Paxton, Pamela. 1997. "Women in National Legislatures: A Cross-National Analysis." *Social Science Research* 26:442.

Paxton, Pamela, and Melanie M. Hughes. 2007. *Women, Politics and Power: A Global Perspective*. Thousand Oaks, CA: Pine Forge Press.

Paxton, Pamela, and Sheri Kunovich. 2003. "Women's Political Representation: The Importance of Ideology." *Social Forces* 82:87–114.

Payne, Charles M. 1995. *I've Got the Light of Freedom: The Organizing Tradition and the Mississippi Freedom Struggle.* Berkeley: University of California Press.

Pearson, Kathryn, and Jennifer Lawless. Forthcoming. "The Primary Reason for Women's Under-Representation? Reevaluating the Conventional Wisdom." *Journal of Politics.*

Peek, Charles, George D. Lowe, and Jon P. Alston. 1981. "Race and Attitudes toward Local Police: Another Look." *Journal of Black Studies* 11:361–74.

Peterson, V. Spike. 1992. *Gendered States: Feminist (Re)visionings of International Relations Theory.* Boulder, CO: Lynne Reinner.

Peterson, V. Spike, and Anne Sisson Runyan. 1999. *Global Gender Issues,* 2nd ed. Boulder, CO: Westview Press.

Phillips, Anne. 1991. *Engendering Democracy.* New York: Polity Press.

Phillips, Anne. 1995. *The Politics of Presence.* New York: Oxford University Press.

Phillips, Anne. 1998. "Democracy and Representation: Or, Why Should It Matter Who Our Representatives Are?" *Feminism and Politics.* Oxford: Oxford University, pp. 224–40.

Pierson, Paul. 2004. *Politics in Time: History, Institutions, and Social Analysis.* Princeton, NJ: Princeton University Press.

Piscopo, Jennifer M. 2005. "Engineering Quotas in Latin America." Paper presented at the Latin American Studies Association Annual Meeting, San Juan, Puerto Rico.

Pitkin, Hanna. 1967. *The Concept of Representation.* Berkeley: University of California Press.

Piven, Frances F. 1985. "Women and the State: Ideology, Power and the Welfare State." In *Gender and the Life Course,* ed. Alice S. Rossi. New York: Aldine, pp. 265–87.

Plotke, David. 1997. "Representation is Democracy." *Constellations* 4:19–34.

Plutzer, Eric. 1988. "Work Life, Family Life, and Women's Support of Feminism." *American Sociological Review* 53:640–9.

Plutzer, Eric, and John Zipp. 1996. "Identity Politics, Partisanship, and Voting for Women Candidates." *Public Opinion Quarterly* 60:30–57.

Pomper, Gerald M. 2001. "The Presidential Election." In *The Election of 2000,* ed. Gerald M. Pomper. New York: Chatham House, pp. 125–54.

Poole, Keith T., and L. Harmon Zeigler. 1985. *Women, Public Opinion, and Politics.* New York: Longman.

Pough, Gwendolyn D. 2002. "Love Feminism but Where's My Hip Hop? Shaping a Black Feminist Identity." In *COLONIZE THIS!: Young Women of Color on Today's Feminism,* ed. Daisy Hernandez and Bushra Rechman. New York: Seal Press, pp. 85–98.

Pough, Gwendolyn D. 2003. "Do the Ladies Run This...? Some Thoughts on Hip-Hop Feminism." In *Catching a Wave: Reclaiming Feminism for the 21st Century,* ed. Rory Dicker and Alison Piepmier. Boston: Northeastern University Press, pp. 232–43.

Prince-Gibson, Eeta, and Shalom H. Schwartz. 1998. "Value Priorities and Gender." *Social Psychology Quarterly* 61:49–67.

Putnam, Robert. 2000. *Bowling Alone: The Collapse and Revival of American Community.* New York: Simon and Schuster.

Raeburn, Nicole. 2004. *Changing Corporate America from Inside Out*. Minneapolis: University of Minnesota.

Rahn, Wendy M. 1993. "The Role of Partisan Stereotypes in Information Processing about Political Candidates." *American Journal of Political Science* 37:472–96.

Randall, Vicki. 2002. "Feminism." In *Theory and Methods in Political Science*, eds. D. Marsh and G. Stoker. Basingstoke: Palgrave, pp. 109–30.

Rapoport, Ronald B. 1982. "Sex Differences in Attitude Expression: A Generational Explanation." *Public Opinion Quarterly* 46:86–96

Rapoport, Ronald B. 1985. "Like Mother, Like Daughter: Intergenerational Transmission of DK Response Rates." *Public Opinion Quarterly* 49:198–208.

Reed, Adolph, Jr. 1986. *Race, Politics and Culture*. New York: Greenwood Press.

Reger, Jo. 2002. "More Than One Feminism: Organizational Structure, Ideology and the Construction of Collective Identity." In *Social Movements: Identity, Culture and the State*, ed. David. S. Meyer, Nancy Whittier, and Belinda Robnett. New York: Oxford University Press, pp. 171–84.

Reger, Jo, ed. 2005. *Different Wavelengths: Studies of the Contemporary Women's Movement*. New York: Routledge.

Reger, Jo, and Suzanne Staggenborg. 2005. "Grassroots Organizing in a Federated Structure: NOW Chapters in Four Local Fields." In *The US Women's Movement in a Global Perspective*, ed. Lee Ann Banaszak. Lanham, MD: Rowman and Littlefield, pp. 95–116.

Rehfeld, Andrew. 2006. "Toward a General Theory of Political Representation." *Journal of Politics* 68:1–21.

Reingold, Beth. 2000. *Representing Women: Sex, Gender, and Legislative Behavior in Arizona and California*. Chapel Hill: University of North Carolina Press.

Reingold, Beth, and Paige Schneider. 2001. "Sex, Gender, and the Status of 'Women's Issue' Legislation in the States." Paper presented at the American Political Science Association Annual Meeting, San Francisco.

Reskin, Barbara F., Debra B. McBrier, and Julie A. Kmec. 1999. "The Determinants and Consequences of Workplace Sex and Race Composition." *Annual Review of Sociology* 25:335–61.

Research Network on Gender Politics and the State. 2007. Accessed July 26, 2007. http://libarts.wsu.edu/polisci/rngs/index.html.

Reynolds, Andrew. 1999. "Women in Legislatures and Executives of the World: Knocking at the Highest Glass Ceiling." *World Politics* 51:547–72.

Rhodebeck, Laurie A. 1989. *Maternal Thinking: Towards a Politics of Peace*. Boston: Beacon Press.

Rhodebeck, Laurie A. 1996. "The Structure of Men's and Women's Feminist Orientations: Feminist Identity and Feminist Opinion." *Gender & Society* 10:386–403.

Richardson, Lilliard E., and Patricia K. Freeman. 1995. "Gender Differences in Constituency Service among State Legislators." *Political Research Quarterly* 48:169–79.

Riker, William H., and Peter C. Ordeshook. 1968. "A Theory of the Calculus of Voting." *American Political Science Review* 62(March):25–42.

Ríos Tobar, Marcela. 2003. "Chilean Feminisms in the 1990s: Paradoxes of an Unfinished Transition." *International Feminist Journal of Politics* 5:256–80.

Ritter, Gretchen. 2000. "Gender and Citizenship after the Nineteenth Amendment." *Polity* 32:301–31.

Ritter, Gretchen. 2002. "Jury Service and Women's Citizenship before and after the Nineteenth Amendment." *Law and History Review* 20:479–515.

Ritter, Gretchen. 2003. "US Gender Politics in Transatlantic Dialogue: Internationalism and the Debate over Women's Rights in the US in the 1940s." Paper presented at the American Political Science Association Annual Meeting, Philadelphia, PA.

Ritter, Gretchen. 2006. *The Constitution as Social Design: Gender and Civic Membership in the American Constitutional Order*. Palo Alto, CA: Stanford University Press.

Ritter, Gretchen, and Nicole Mellow. 2000. "The State of Gender in Political Science." *Annals of the American Academy of Political and Social Science* 571:121–34.

Roberts, Tara. 2006. *What Your Mama Never Told You: True Stories about Sex and Love*. Boston: Graphia.

Robnett, Belinda. 1996. "African American Women in the Civil Rights Movement, 1954–1965: Gender, Leadership, and Micromobilization." *American Journal of Sociology* 101:1661–93.

Robnett, Belinda. 2000. *How Long? How Long?: African-American Women in the Struggle for Civil Rights*. Oxford, UK: Oxford University Press.

Robnett, Belinda. 2006. "Political Mobilization: African American Gendered Repertoires." In *U.S. Women's Movements in a Global Perspective*, ed. Lee Ann Banaszak. Lanham, MD: Rowman and Littlefield, pp. 117–31.

Rodgers, Thomas Earl. 2005. "Billy Yank and G. I. Joe: An Exploratory Essay on the Sociopolitical Dimensions of Soldier Motivation." *Journal of Military History* 69:93–121.

Rohde, David W. 1991. *Parties and Leaders in the Postreform House*. Chicago: University of Chicago Press.

Rohlinger, Deana, and David S. Meyer. 2005. "Transnational Framing of Access to Abortion in the United States, England, and Ireland." In *The US Women's Movement in a Global Perspective*, ed. Lee Ann Banaszak. Lanham, MD: Rowman and Littlefield, pp. 197–214.

Rosenstone, Steven J., and John Mark Hansen. 1993. *Mobilization, Participation, and Democracy in America*. New York: Macmillan.

Rosenthal, Cindy Simon. 1995. "The Role of Gender in Descriptive Representation." *Political Research Quarterly* 48:599–611.

Rosenthal, Cindy Simon. 1998. *When Women Lead: Integrative Leadership in State Legislatures*. New York: Oxford University Press.

Rosenthal, Cindy, ed. 2002. *Women Transforming Congress*. Norman: University of Oklahoma Press.

Rosenthal, Cindy Simon. 2005. "Women Leading Legislatures: Getting There and Getting Things Done." In *Women and Elective Office: Past, Present, and Future*, ed. Sue Thomas and Clyde Wilcox. 2nd ed. New York: Oxford University Press, pp. 197–212.

Roth, Benita. 2004. *Separate Roads to Feminism: Black, Chicana, and White Feminist Movements in America's Second Wave*. Cambridge: Cambridge University Press.

Rubin, Gayle. 1984. "Thinking Sex: Toward a Radical Theory of the Politics of Sexuality." In *Pleasure and Danger: Exploring Female Sexuality*, ed. Carole Vance. New York: Routledge, pp. 267–319.

Rubin, Marilyn Marks, and John R. Bartle. 2005. "Integrating Gender into Government Budgets: A New Perspective." *Public Administration Review* 65(May):259–72.

Ruddick, Sara. 1989. *Maternal Thinking: Towards a Politics of Peace*. Boston: Beacon Press.

Rule, Wilma. 1981. "Why Women Don't Run: The Critical Contextual Factors in Women's Legislative Recruitment." *Western Political Quarterly* 34(1):60–77.

Rule, Wilma, and Joseph F. Zimmerman, eds. 1994. *Electoral Systems in Comparative Perspective: Their Impact on Women and Minorities*. Westport, CT: Greenwood Press.

Rupp, Leila. 1997. *Worlds of Women: The Making of an International Women's Movement*. Princeton, NJ: Princeton University Press.

Rupp, Leila, and Verta Taylor. 1987. *Survival in the Doldrums: The American Women's Rights Movement, 1945 to the 1960s*. New York: Oxford University Press.

Ryan, Barbara. 1992. *Feminism and the Women's Movement*. New York: Routledge.

Ryan, Mary P. 1990. *Women in Public: Between Banners and Ballots, 1825–1880*. Baltimore: Johns Hopkins University Press.

Ryan, Mary P. 1997. *Civic Wars: Democracy and Public Life in the American City During the Nineteenth Century*. Berkeley: University of California Press.

Rymph, Catherine E. 2006. *Republican Women: Feminism and Conservatism from Suffrage through the Rise of the New Right*. Chapel Hill: University of North Carolina Press.

Saint-Germain, Michelle A. 1989. "Does Their Difference Make a Difference? The Impact of Women on Public Policy in the Arizona Legislature." *Social Science Quarterly* 70:956–68.

Saltzstein, Grace Hall. 1986. "Female Mayors and Women in Municipal Jobs." *American Journal of Political Science* 30:140–64.

Sanbonmatsu, Kira. 2002a. "Gender Stereotypes and Vote Choice." *American Journal of Political Science* 46:20–34.

Sanbonmatsu, Kira. 2002b. "Political Parties and the Recruitment of Women to State Legislatures." *Journal of Politics* 64:791–809.

Sanbonmatsu, Kira. 2004. *Democrats, Republicans, and the Politics of Women's Place*. Ann Arbor: University of Michigan Press.

Sanbonmatsu, Kira. 2005. "Do Parties Know That Women Win? Party Leader Beliefs about Women's Electability." Paper presented at the American Political Science Association Annual Meeting, Washington, DC.

Sanbonmatsu, Kira. 2006. *Where Women Run: Gender and Party in the American States*. Ann Arbor: University of Michigan Press.

Sapiro, Virginia. 1979. "Women's Studies and Political Conflict." In *The Prism of Sex: Essays in the Sociology of Knowledge*, ed. J. Sherman and E. Beck. Madison: University of Wisconsin Press, pp. 253–66.

Sapiro, Virginia. 1981. "Research Frontier Essay: When Are Interests Interesting? The Problem of Political Representation of Women." *American Political Science Review* 75:701–16.

Sapiro, Virginia. 1982. "Private Costs of Public Commitments or Public Costs of Private Commitments? Family Roles versus Political Ambition." *American Journal of Political Science* 26:265–79.

Sapiro, Virginia. 1983. *The Political Integration of Women*. Urbana: University of Illinois Press.

Sapiro, Virginia. 1987. "What Research on the Political Socialization of Women Can Tell Us about the Political Socialization of People." In *The Impact of Feminist Research in the Academy*, ed. C. Farnham. Bloomington: Indiana University Press: pp. 148–73.

Sapiro, Virginia. 1991a. "Gender Politics, Gendered Politics: The State of the Field." In *Political Science: Looking to the Future*. Evanston, IL: Northwestern University Press, pp. 165–87.

Sapiro, Virginia. 1991b. "Feminism: A Generation Later." *Annals of the American Academy of Political and Social Science* 515:10–22.

Sapiro, Virginia. 2003. "Theorizing Gender in Political Psychology Research." In *Oxford Handbook of Political Psychology*, ed. David O. Sears, Leonie Huddy, and Robert Jervis. New York: Oxford University Press, pp. 601–36.

Sapiro, Virginia, and Pamela Johnston Conover. 1997. "The Variable Gender Basis of Electoral Politics: Gender and Context in the 1992 US Election." *British Journal of Political Science* 27:497–523.

Sapiro, Virginia, and Katherine Cramer Walsh. 2002. "Doing Gender in Congressional Campaign Advertisements." Paper presented at the International Society for Political Psychology Annual Meeting, Berlin.

Sarkees, Meredith Reid, and Nancy E. McGlen. 1999. "Misdirected Backlash: The Evolving Nature of Academia and the Status of Women in Political Science." *PS: Political Science and Politics* 32:100–8.

Schafer, Joseph A., Beth M. Huebner, and Timothy S. Bynum. 2006. "Fear of Crime and Criminal Victimization: Gender-Based Contrasts." *Journal of Criminal Justice* 34:285–301.

Schattschneider, E. E. 1942. *Party Government*. New York: Rinehart.

Schlesinger, Joseph A. 1975. "The Primary Goals of Political Parties: A Clarification of Positive Theory." *American Political Science Review* 69:840–9.

Schlesinger, Mark, and Caroline Heldman. 2001. "Gender Gap or Gender Gaps? New Perspectives on Support for Government Action and Policies." *Journal of Politics* 63:59–92.

Schlozman, Kay Lehman, and Sidney Verba. 1979. *Injury to Insult: Unemployment, Class, and Political Response*. Cambridge: Harvard University Press

Schmidt, Gregory D., and Kyle L. Saunders. 2004. "Effective Quotas, Relative Party Magnitude, and the Success of Female Candidates: Peruvian Municipal Elections in Comparative Perspective." *Comparative Political Studies* 37:704–34.

Schreiber, Ronnee. 2002a. "Playing 'Femball': Conservative Women's Organizations and Political Representation in the United States." In *Right Wing Women: From Conservatives to Extremists around the World*, ed. Paola Bacchetta and Margaret Power. New York: Routledge, pp. 211–24.

Schreiber, Ronnee. 2002b. "Injecting a Woman's Voice: Conservative Women's Organizations, Gender Consciousness, and the Expression of Women's Policy Preferences." *Sex Roles* 47:331–42.

Schroedel, Jean Reith, and Marcia L. Godwin. 2005. "Prospects for Cracking the
Political Glass Ceiling: The Future of Women Officeholders in the Twenty-first
Century." In *Women and Elective Office: Past, Present, and Future*, ed. Sue Thomas
and Clyde Wilcox. 2nd ed. New York: Oxford University Press, pp. 264–80.

Schumaker, Paul, and Nancy Elizabeth Burns. 1988. "Gender Cleavages and the
Resolution of Local Policy Issues." *American Journal of Political Science* 32:1070–
95.

Schumpeter, Joseph. 1976. *Capitalism, Socialism, and Democracy.* London: Allen
and Unwin.

Schwartz, Shalom H., and Tammy Rubel. 2005. "Sex Differences in Value Priorities:
Cross-Cultural and Multimethod Studies." *Journal of Personality and Social
Psychology* 89:1010–28.

Schwindt-Bayer, Leslie A., and Renato Corbetta. 2004. "Gender Turnover and Roll-
Call Voting in the U.S. House of Representatives." *Legislative Studies Quarterly*
29:215–29.

Schwindt-Bayer, Leslie A., and William Mishler. 2005. "An Integrated Model of
Women's Representation." *Journal of Politics* 67:407–28.

Scott, Anne Firor. 1984. *Making the Invisible Woman Visible.* Urbana: University of
Illinois Press.

Scott, James. 1979. *Weapons of the Weak: Everyday Forms of Peasant Resistance.*
New Haven, CT: Yale University Press.

Scott, Joan W. 1986. "Gender: A Useful Category of Historical Analysis." *American
Historical Review* 91(December):1053–75.

Scott, Joan. 1988. *Gender and the Politics of History.* New York: Columbia University Press.

Scott, Joan Wallach. 2005. *Parité!: Sexual Equality and the Crisis of French Universalism.* Chicago: University of Chicago Press.

Sears, David O., and Leonie Huddy. 1990. "On the Origins of the Political Disunity
of Women." In *Women, Politics, and Change*, ed. Patricia Gurin and Louise Tilly.
New York: Russell Sage, pp. 249–77.

Seltzer, Richard A., Jody Newman, and Melissa Vorhees Leighton. 1997. *Sex as a
Political Variable: Women as Candidates and Voters in U.S. Elections.* Boulder,
CO: Lynne Rienner.

Shafer, Byron E. 1983. *Quiet Revolution: The Struggle for the Democratic Party and
the Shaping of Post-Reform Politics.* New York: Russell Sage Foundation.

Shange, Ntozake. 1975. *for colored girls who have considered suicide / when the
rainbow is enuf.* New York: Macmillian.

Shapiro, Robert Y., and Harpreet Mahajan. 1986. "Gender Differences in Policy
Preferences: A Summary of Trends from the 1960s to the 1980s." *Public Opinion
Quarterly* 50:42–61.

Sharp, Rhonda, and Ray Broomhill. 2002. "Budgeting for Equality: The Australian
Experience." *Feminist Economics* 8(March):25–47.

Shklar, Judith N. 1991. *American Citizenship: The Quest for Inclusion.* Cambridge,
MA: Harvard University Press.

Sidanius, J., and F. Pratto. 1999. *Social Dominance: An Intergroup Theory of Social Hierarchy and Oppression*. New York: Cambridge University Press.

Sidanius, Jim, Felicia Pratto, Colette van Laar, and Shana Levin. 2004. "Social Dominance Theory: Its Agenda and Method." *Political Psychology* 25(6): 845–80.

Siegel, Reva. 1994. "The Modernization of Marital Status Law: Adjudicating Wives's Rights to Earnings, 1860–1930." *Georgetown Law Journal* 82:2127–211.

Sigel, Roberta S. 1996. *Ambition and Accommodation: How Women View Gender Relations*. Chicago: University of Chicago Press.

Sigelman, Lee, and Susan Welch. 1984. "Race, Gender, and Opinion toward Black and Female Candidates." *Public Opinion Quarterly* 48:467–75.

Silver, Roxanne C., Alison E Holman, Daniel N. McIntosh, Michael Poulin, and Virginia Gil-Rivas. 2002. "Nationwide Longitudinal Study of Psychological Responses to September 11." *Journal of the American Medical Association* 288:1235–44.

Simien, Evelyn M. 2006. *Black Feminist Voices in Politics*. Albany, NY: SUNY Press.

Simien, Evelyn M. 2007. "Doing Intersectionality Research: From Conceptual Issues to Practical Examples." *Politics & Gender* 3(2):36–43.

Simien, Evelyn M., and Rosalee A. Clawson. 2004. "The Intersection of Race and Gender: An Examination of Black Feminist Consciousness, Race Consciousness, and Policy Attitudes." *Social Science Quarterly* 85(3):793–810.

Simon, R. J., and J. M. Landis. 1989. "Women's and Men's Attitudes about a Woman's Place and Role." *Public Opinion Quarterly* 53:265–76.

Skocpol, Theda. 1992. *Protecting Soldiers and Mothers: The Political Origins of Social Policy in the United States*. Cambridge, MA: Harvard University Press.

Skocpol, Theda. 2004. *Diminished Democracy: From Membership to Management in American Civic Life*. Norman: University of Oklahoma Press.

Skocpol, Theda, and Morris P. Fiorina, eds. 1999. *Civic Engagement in American Democracy*. Washington, DC: Brookings Institution.

Skocpol, Theda, and Gretchen Ritter. 1991. "Gender and the Origins of Modern Social Policies in Britain and the United States." *Studies in American Political Development* 5:36–93.

Slater, Robert Bruce. 1997. "In Higher Education Black Women Are Far Outpacing Black Men." *Journal of Blacks in Higher Education* (Autumn):84–6.

Sloat, Amanda. 2005. "The Rebirth of Civil Society: The Growth of Women's NGOs in Central and Eastern Europe." *European Journal of Women's Studies* 12:437–52.

Smith, Barbara. 1985. "Some Home Truths on the Contemporary Black Feminist Movement," *Black Scholar* 16(March/April):4–13.

Smith, Eric R. A. N., and Richard Fox. 2001. "The Electoral Fortunes of Women Candidates for Congress." *Political Research Quarterly* 54:205–21.

Smith, Kevin. 1997. "When All's Fair: Signs of Parity in Media Coverage of Female Candidates." *Political Communication* 14:71–82.

Smith, Tom W. 1984. "The Polls: Gender and Attitudes toward Violence." *Public Opinion Quarterly* 48:384–96.

Smooth, Wendy G. 2001. *African American Women State Legislators: The Impact of Gender and Race on Legislative Influence*. Unpublished Ph.D. dissertation, University of Maryland, College Park.

Smooth, Wendy. 2006. "Intersectionality in Electoral Politics: A Mess Worth Making," *Politics & Gender* 2(3):400–13.

Snow, David, and Robert Benford. 1988. "Ideology, Frame Resonance, and Participant Mobilization." *International Social Movement Research* 1:197–217.

Snow, David, and Robert Benford. 1992. "Master Frames and Cycles of Protest." In *Frontiers of Social Movement Theory*, ed. Aldon D. Morris and Carol McClurg Mueller. New Haven, CT: Yale University Press, pp. 133–55.

Snow, David, E. Burke Rochford Jr., Steven Worden, and Robert Benford. 1986. "Frame Alignment Processes, Micromobilization, and Movement Participation." *American Sociological Review* 51:464–81.

Solomon, Zahava, Marc Gelkopf, and Avraham Bleich. 2005. "Is Terror Gender-Blind? Gender Differences in Reaction to Terror Events." *Social Psychiatry and Psychiatric Epidemiology* 40:947–54.

Somers, Margaret. 1994. "The Narrative Constitution of Identity: A Relational and Network Approach." *Theory and Society* 23:605–49.

Soss, Joe. 1999. "Lessons of Welfare: Policy Design, Political Learning, and Political Action." *American Political Science Review* 93:363–80.

Soss, Joe. 2000. *Unwanted Claims: The Politics of Participation in the US Welfare System*. Ann Arbor: University of Michigan Press.

Soule, John W., and Wilma E. McGrath. 1977. "A Comparative Study of Male-Female Political Attitudes at Citizen and Elite Levels." In *A Portrait of Marginality*, ed. Marianne Githens and Jewel L. Prestage. New York: McKay, pp. 178–95.

Sperling, Valerie. 1999. *Organizing Women in Contemporary Russia: Engendering Transition*. New York: Cambridge University Press.

Springer, Kimberly. 2005. *Living for the Revolution*. Durham, NC: Duke University Press.

Squires, Judith. 1999. *Gender in Political Theory*. Cambridge, UK: Polity Press.

Squires, Judith. 2005. "Rethinking Substantive Representation." Paper presented at the General Conference of the European Consortium for Political Research, Budapest.

Stack, Steven. 2000. "Support for the Death Penalty: A Gender Specific Model." *Sex Roles* 43:163–79.

Staeheli, Lynne A., Eleonore Kofman, and Linda J. Peake, eds. 2004. *Mapping Women, Making Politics: Feminist Perspectives on Political Geography*. New York: Routledge.

Staggenborg, Suzanne. 1989. "Organizational and Environmental Influences on the Development of the Pro-Choice Movement." *Social Forces* 68:204–40.

Staggenborg, Suzanne. 1991. *The Pro-Choice Movement: Organization and Activism in the Abortion Conflict*. New York: Oxford University Press.

Staggenborg, Suzanne. 2001. "Beyond Culture vs. Politics: A Case Study of a Local Women's Movement." *Gender & Society* 15:507–30.

Staggenborg, Suzanne. 2002. "The 'Meso' in Social Movement Research." In *Social Movements: Identity, Culture, and the State*, ed. David S. Meyer, Nancy Whittier, and Belinda Robnett. Oxford: Oxford University Press, pp. 124–39.

Staggenborg, Suzanne, and David S. Meyer. 1996. "Movements, Countermovements, and the Structure of Political Opportunity." *American Journal of Sociology* 10:1628–60.

Staggenborg, Suzanne, and Verta Taylor. 2005. "Whatever Happened to the Women's Movement?" *Mobilization* 10:37–52.

Stark, Steven. 1996. "Gap Politics." *Atlantic Monthly* 278:70–80.

Stenner, Karen. 2001. "Betsy, Beverly and Monica: The Impact of Female Candidates and Role Models on Women's and Men's Political Engagement." Unpublished manuscript, Princeton University.

Stephen, Lynn. 1997. *Women and Social Movements in Latin America: Power from Below*. Austin: University of Texas Press.

Stetson, Dorothy McBride, ed. 2001. *Abortion Politics, Women's Movements and the Democratic State: A Comparative Study of State Feminism*. Oxford: Oxford University Press.

Stetson, Dorothy M., and Amy Mazur. 1995. *Comparative State Feminism*. Thousand Oaks, CA: Sage.

Stewart, Abigail J., and Christa McDermott. 2004. "Gender in Psychology." *Annual Review of Psychology* 55:519–44.

Stivers, Camilla. 1992. *Gender Images in Public Administration: Legitimacy and the Administrative State*. Newbury Park, CA: Sage Publications.

Strach, Patricia. 2007. *All in the Family: The Private Roots of American Public Policy*. Palo Alto, CA: Stanford University Press.

Strickler, Jennifer, and Nicholas L. Danigelis. 2002. "Changing Frameworks in Attitudes toward Abortion." *Sociological Forum* 17:187–201.

Strolovitch, Dara. 2007. *Affirmative Advocacy: Race, Class, and Gender in Interest Group Politics*. Chicago: University of Chicago Press.

Studlar, Donley T., Ian McAllister, and Bernadette C. Hayes. 1998. "Explaining the Gender Gap in Voting: A Cross-National Analysis." *Social Science Quarterly* 79:779–98.

Swain, Carol M. 1995. *Black Faces, Black Interests: The Representation of African Americans in Congress, Enlarged Edition*. Cambridge, MA: Harvard University Press.

Swers, Michele L. 2002. *The Difference Women Make: The Policy Impact of Women in Congress*. Chicago: University of Chicago Press.

Swers, Michele L., and Carin Larson. 2005. "Women in Congress: Do They Act as Advocates for Women' Issues?" In *Women and Elective Office: Past, Present, and Future*, ed. Sue Thomas and Clyde Wilcox. 2nd ed. New York: Oxford University Press, pp. 110–28.

Swidler, Ann. 1986. "Culture in Action: Symbols and Strategies." *American Sociological Review* 51:273–86.

Szymanski, Ann-Marie. 2003. *Pathways to Prohibition: Radicals, Moderates and Social Movement Outcomes*. Durham, NC: Duke University Press.

Tamerius, Karin L. 1995. "Sex, Gender, and Leadership in the Representation of Women." In *Gender Power, Leadership, and Governance*, ed. Georgia Duerst-Lahti and Rita Mae Kelly. Ann Arbor: University of Michigan Press, pp. 93–112.

Tarrow, Sidney. 1995. "States and Opportunities: The Political Structuring of Social Movements." In *Comparative Perspectives in Social Movments: Political Opportunities, Mobilizing Structures and Cultural Framings*, ed. Doug McAdam, John D. McCarthy, and Mayer Zald. New York: Cambridge University Press, pp. 41–61.

Tarrow, Sidney. 1998. *Power in Movement*, 2nd ed. Cambridge: Cambridge University Press.

Tate, Katherine. 1991. "Black Political Participation in the 1984 and 1988 Presidential Elections." *American Political Science Review* 85:1159–76.

Tate, Katherine. 1994. *From Protest to Politics: The New Black Voters in American Elections*. Cambridge, MA: Harvard University Press.

Tatur, Melanie. 1992. "Why Is There No Women's Movement in Eastern Europe?" In *Democracy and Civil Society in Eastern Europe*, ed. Paul G. Lewis. New York: St. Martin's Press, pp. 61–75.

Taylor, Verta. 1996. *Rock-a-Bye Baby: Feminism, Self-Help and Post-Partum Depression*. New York: Routledge.

Taylor, Verta, and Nancy Whittier. 1992. "Collective Identity in Social Movement communities: Lesbian Feminist Mobilization." In *Frontiers of Social Movement Theory*, ed. Aldon Morris and Carol McClurg Mueller. New Haven, CT: Yale University Press, pp. 104–30.

Taylor-Robinson, Michelle M., and Roseanna Michelle Heath. 2003. "Do Women Legislators Have Different Policy Priorities Than Their Male Colleagues? A Critical Case Test." *Women & Politics* 24:77–101.

Tétreault, Mary Ann, ed. 1994. *Women and Revolution in Africa, Asia, and the New World*. Columbia: University of South Carolina Press.

Thomas, Sue. 1989. "Voting Patterns in the California Assembly: The Role of Gender." *Women & Politics* 9:43–56.

Thomas, Sue. 1992. "The Effects of Race and Gender on Constituency Service." *Western Political Quarterly* 45:161–80.

Thomas, Sue. 1994. *How Women Legislate*. New York: Oxford University Press.

Thomas, Sue. 2005. "Introduction." In *Women and Elective Office: Past, Present and Future* (2nd ed.), ed. Sue Thomas and Clyde Wilcox. Oxford: Oxford University Press, pp. 3–25.

Thomas, Sue, and Susan Welch. 1991. "The Impact of Gender on Activities and Priorities of State Legislators." *Western Political Quarterly* 44:445–56.

Thompson, Edward H. 1991. "Beneath the Status Characteristic: Gender Variations in Religiousness." *Journal for the Scientific Study of Religion* 30:381–94.

Threlfall, Monica. 1996. *Mapping the Women's Movement: Feminist Politics and Social Transformation in the North*. London: Verso.

Tickner, J. Ann. 1992. *Gender in International Relations: Feminist Perspectives on Achieving Global Security*. New York: Columbia University Press.

Tickner, J. Ann. 2001. *Gendering World Politics: Issues and Approaches in the Post–Cold War Era*. New York: Columbia University Press.

Tickner, J. Ann. 2005. "Gendering a Discipline: Some Feminist Methodological Contributions to International Relations." *Signs* 30:2173–89.

Tilly, Charles. 1999. *Durable Inequality*. Berkeley: University of California Press.

Tingsten, Herbert Lars Gustaf, and Vilgot Hammarling. 1937. *Political Behavior*. London: P. S. King.

Tolbert, Caroline J., and Gertrude A. Steuernagel. 2001. "Women Lawmakers, State Mandates and Women's Health." *Women & Politics* 22:1–39.

Tolleson-Rinehart, Sue. 1991. "Do Women Leaders Make a Difference? Substance, Style, and Perceptions." In *Gender and Policymaking: Studies of Women in Office*, ed. Debra L. Dodson. New Brunswick, NJ: Center for American Women and Politics.

Tolleson-Rinehart, Sue. 1992. *Gender Consciousness and Politics*. New York: Routledge.

Tolleson-Rinehart, Sue, and Susan J. Carroll. 2006. "'Far from Ideal': The Gender Politics of Political Science." *American Political Science Review* 100(November):507–13.

Tolleson-Rinehart, Sue, and Jerry Perkins. 1989. "The Intersection of Gender Politics and Religious Beliefs." *Political Behavior* 11:33–55.

Tolleson-Rinehart, Sue, and Jeanie R. Stanley. 1994. *Claytie and the Lady: Ann Richards, Gender, and Politics in Texas*. Austin: University of Texas Press.

Towns, Ann E. 2003. "Women Governing for Modernity: International Hierarchy and Legislature Sex Quotas." Paper presented at the American Political Science Association Annual Meeting, Philadelphia.

Tripp, Aili Mari. 2003. "Transformations in African Political Landscapes." *International Feminist Journal of Politics* 5:233–55.

Tripp, Aili Mari. 2006. "Why So Slow? The Challenges of Gendering Comparative Politics." *Politics & Gender* 2(2):249–63.

Tripp, Aili Mari, and Alice Kang. Forthcoming. "The Global Impact of Quotas: On the Fast Track to Increased Female Legislative Representation." *Comparative Political Studies*.

True, Jacqui. 2003. "Mainstreaming Gender in Global Public Policy." *International Feminist Journal of Politics* 5:368–96.

van Assendelft, Laura, and Karen O'Connor. 1994. "Backgrounds, Motivations, and Interests: A Comparison of Male and Female Local Party Activists." *Women & Politics* 14:77–92.

Van de Vleuten, Anna. 2005. "Pincers and Prestige: Explaining the Implementation of EU Gender Equality Policy." *Comparative European Politics* 3:464–88.

Van Dyke, Nella, Sarah Soule, and Verta Taylor. 2004. "The Targets of Social Movements: Beyond a Focus on the State." *Research in Social Movements, Conflict and Change* 25:27–51.

Vega, Arturo, and Juanita M. Firestone. 1995. "The Effects of Gender on Congressional Behavior and the Substantive Representation of Women." *Legislative Studies Quarterly* 20:213–22.

Verba, Sidney, Nancy Burns, and Kay Lehman Schlozman. 1997. "Knowing and Caring about Politics: Gender and Political Engagement." *Journal of Politics* 59:1051–72.

Verba, Sidney, and Norman Nie. 1972. *Participation in America: Political Democracy and Social Equality*. New York: Harper and Row.

Verba, Sidney, Norman H. Nie, Jae-on Kim, and Goldie Shabad. 1978. "Men and Women: Sex-Related Differences in Political Activity." In *Participation and Political Equality*, ed. Sidney Verba, Norman H. Nie, and Jae-on Kim. Cambridge: Cambridge University Press, pp. 234–68.

Verba, Sidney, Kay Lehman Schlozman, and Henry Brady. 1995. *Voice and Equality: Civic Voluntarism in American Politics.* Cambridge, MA: Harvard University Press.

Walker, Alice. 1984. *In Search of Our Mothers' Gardens: Womanist Prose.* San Diego: Harcourt Brace Jovanovich.

Walker, L. J. 1984. "Sex Differences in the Development of Moral Reasoning: A Critical Review." *Child Development* 55:677–91.

Wallace, Michelle. 1978. *Black Macho and the Myth of the Superwoman.* New York: Dial Press.

Wallace, Michelle. 1990. *Invisibility Blues: From Pop to Theory.* London: Verso.

Walsh, Katherine Cramer. 2002. "Enlarging Representation: Women Bringing Marginalized Perspectives to Floor Debate in the House of Representatives." In *Women Transforming Congress,* ed. Cindy Simon Rosenthal. Norman: University of Oklahoma Press, pp. 370–98.

Walter, T., and G. Davie. 1998. "The Religiosity of Women in the Modern West." *British Journal of Sociology* 49:640–60.

Walton, Hanes, Jr. 1985. *Invisible Politics: Black Political Behavior.* Albany, NY: SUNY Press.

Walton, Hanes, Jr., and Robert C. Smith. 2000. *American Politics and the African American Quest for Universal Freedom.* New York: Addison-Wesley Longman.

Ware, Susan. 1981. *Beyond Suffrage: Women in the New Deal.* Cambridge, MA: Harvard University Press.

Warren, Mark, and Dario Castiglione. 2004. "The Transformation of Democratic Representation." *Democracy and Society* 2:5, 20–2.

Waylen, Georgina. 1993. "Women's Movements and Democratization in Latin America." *Third World Quarterly* 14:573–87.

Waylen, Georgina. 1994. "Women and Democratization." *World Politics* 43:327–54.

Weitzer. Ronald. 2000. "Racialized Policing: Residents' Perceptions in Three Neighborhoods" (in Symposium on Norms, Law, and Order in the City). *Law and Society Review* 34:129–55.

Welch, Susan. 1977. "Women as Political Animals? A Test of Some Explanations for Male-Female Political Participation Differences." *American Journal of Political Science* 21:711–30.

Welch, Susan. 1985. "Are Women More Liberal Than Men in the U.S. Congress?" *Legislative Studies Quarterly* 10:125–34.

Welch, Susan. 1989. "Congressional Nomination Procedures and the Representation of Women." *Congress & the Presidency* 16:121–35.

Welch, Susan, and John Hibbing. 1992. "Financial Conditions, Gender, and Voting in American National Elections." *Journal of Politics* 54:197–213.

Welch, Susan, and Donley T. Studlar. 1990. "Multimember Districts and the Representation of Women: Evidence from Britain and the United States." *Journal of Politics* 52:391–412.

Weldon, S. Laurel. 2002a. *Protest, Policy, and the Problem of Violence against Women: A Cross-National Comparison.* Pittsburgh, PA: University of Pittsburgh Press.

Weldon, S. Laurel. 2002b. "Beyond Bodies: Institutional Sources of Representation for Women in Democratic Policymaking." *Journal of Politics* 64(4):1153–74.

Weldon, S. Laurel. 2004. "The Dimensions and Policy Impact of Feminist Civil Society: Democratic Policymaking on Violence against Women in the Fifty U.S. States." *International Feminist Journal of Politics* 6:1–28.

Weldon, S. Laurel. 2006. "The Structure of Intersectionality: A Comparative Politics of Gender." *Politics & Gender* 2(2):235–48.

Welke, Barbara Young. 2001. *Recasting American Liberty: Gender, Race, Law and the Railroad Revolution, 1865–1920.* New York: Cambridge University Press.

Werner, Brian. 1998. "Financing the Campaigns of Women Candidates and Their Opponents: Evidence from Three States, 1982–1990." *Women & Politics* 18:81–97.

West, Lois A. 1997. *Feminist Nationalism.* New York: Routledge.

White, Deborah Gray. 1985. *Ar'nt I a Woman? Female Slaves in the Plantation South.* New York: W. W. Norton.

White, Deborah Gray. 1999. *Too Heavy a Load: Black Women in Defense of Themselves, 1894–1994.* New York: W. W. Norton.

White, Julie Anne. 2007. "The Hollow and the Ghetto: Space, Race, and the Politics of Poverty." *Politics & Gender* 3(2):43–52.

Whitehead, John T., and Michael B. Blankenship. 2000. "The Gender Gap in Capital Punishment Attitudes: An Analysis of Support and Opposition." *American Journal of Criminal Justice* 25:1–13.

Whittier, Nancy. 1995. *Feminist Generations: The Persistence of the Radical Women's Movement.* Philadelphia: Temple University Press.

Whittier, Nancy. 2005. "From the Second to the Third Wave: Continuity and Change in Grassroots Feminism." In *The U.S. Women's Movement in a Global Perspective,* ed. Lee Ann Banaszak. Lanham, MD: Rowman and Littlefield, pp. 45–68.

Wilcox, Clyde. 1990. "Black Women and Feminism." *Women & Politics* 10:65–84.

Wilcox, Clyde. 1997. "Racial and Gender Consciousness among African-American Women: Sources and Consequences." *Women & Politics* 17:73–94.

Wilcox, Clyde, Lara Hewitt, and Dee Allsop. 1996. "The Gender Gap in Attitudes toward the Gulf War: A Cross-National Perspective." *Journal of Peace Research* 33:67–82.

Williams, Melissa. 1998. *Voice, Trust, and Memory: Marginalized Groups and the Failings of Liberal Representation.* Princeton, NJ: Princeton University.

Wilson, William J. 1980. *The Declining Significance of Race,* 2nd ed. Chicago: University of Chicago Press.

Witt, Linda, Karen Paget, and Glenna Matthews. 1994. *Running as a Woman: Gender and Power in American Politics.* New York: Free Press.

Wolbrecht, Christina. 2000. *The Politics of Women's Rights: Parties, Positions, and Change.* Princeton, NJ: Princeton University Press.

Wolbrecht, Christina. 2002a. "Explaining Women's Rights Realignment: Convention Delegates, 1972–1992." *Political Behavior* 24:237–82.

Wolbrecht, Christina. 2002b. "Female Legislators and the Women's Rights Agenda: From Feminine Mystique to Feminist Era." In *Women Transforming Congress,* ed. Cindy Simon Rosenthal. Norman: University of Oklahoma Press, pp. 170–97.

Wolbrecht, Christina, and David E. Campbell. 2007. "Leading by Example: Female Members of Parliament as Political Role Models." *American Journal of Political Science* 51(October):921–39.

Wolfinger, Raymond E., and Steven J. Rosenstone. 1980. *Who Votes?* New Haven, CT: Yale University Press.

Wolpert, Robin M., and James G. Gimpel. 1998. "Self-Interest, Symbolic Politics, and Public Attitudes toward Gun Control." *Political Behavior* 20:241–62.

Wong, Cara. 1998. "Group Closeness." Pilot Study Report for the 1997 National Election Studies Pilot Study. Accessed July 26, 2007. http://www.umich.edu/~nes.

Woolf, Virginia. 1966. *Three Guineas*. Orlando, FL: Harcourt.

Yamin, Priscilla. 2005. *Nuptial Nation: Marriage and the Politics of Civic Membership in the United States*. Unpublished manuscript, University of Oregon, Eugene, OR.

Young, Brigitte. 1999. *Triumph of the Fatherland: German Unification and the Marginalization of Women*. Ann Arbor: University of Michigan Press.

Young, Iris Marion. 1986. "Deferring Group Representation." In *Nomos: Group Rights*, ed. Will Kymlicka and Ian Shapiro. New York: New York University Press, pp. 349–76.

Young, Iris Marion. 1990. *Justice and the Politics of Difference*. Princeton, NJ: Princeton University Press.

Young, Iris. 1994. "Gender as Seriality: Thinking about Women as a Social Collective." *Signs* 19:713–39.

Young, Iris Marion. 1997. *Intersecting Voices: Dilemmas of Gender, Political Philosophy, and Policy*. Princeton, NJ: Princeton University Press.

Young, Iris Marion. 2000. *Inclusion and Democracy*. Oxford: Oxford University Press.

Young, Lisa. 2000. *Feminists and Party Politics*. Vancouver: UBC Press.

Young, Lyndsey R. 2006. "The Impact of Gender on Legislative Campaign Committee Expenditures." Paper presented at the Southern Political Science Association Annual Meeting, Atlanta.

Yuval-Davis, Nira. 1997. *Gender and Nation*. London: Verso Press.

Zald, Mayer, and Roberta Ash. 1966. "Social Movement Organizations: Growth, Decay and Change." *Social Forces* 44:327–40.

Zaller, John. 1992. *The Nature and Origins of Mass Opinion*. New York: Cambridge University Press.

Zeiger, Susan. 2003. "The Schoolhouse vs. the Armory: U.S. Teachers and the Campaign Against Militarism in the Schools, 1914–1918." *Journal of Women's History* 15:150–79.

Zeigler, Sara L. 1996a. "Uniformity and Conformity: Regionalism and the Adjudication of the Married Women's Property Acts." *Polity* 28:467–95.

Zeigler, Sara L. 1996b. "Wifely Duties: Marriage, Labor and the Common Law in Nineteenth-Century America." *Social Science History* 20:63–96.

Zerilli, Linda. 1998. "Doing without Knowing: Feminism's Politics of the Ordinary." *Political Theory* 26:435–58.

Zerilli, Linda M. G. 2005. *Feminism and the Abyss of Freedom*. Chicago: University of Chicago Press.

Zipp, John F., and Eric Plutzer. 1985. "Gender Differences in Voting for Female Candidates: Evidence from the 1982 Election." *Public Opinion Quarterly* 49:179–97.

Zook, Kristal, Brent. 2006. *Black Women's Lives: Stories of Power and Pain*. New York: Nation Books.

Zwingel, Suzanne. 2005. "From Intergovernmental Negotiations to (Sub)National Change: A Transnational Perspective on the Impact of CEDAW." *International Feminist Journal of Politics* 7:400–24.

Index

Abramovitz, Mimi, 22

accountability, women's representatives and alternative forms of, 161

Acker, Joan, 6, 155

activism: and gender differences in support of social welfare, 39–41; of second wave feminism and women's movements, 86–7; of women's movements within institutions, 81. *See also* politics; social movements

Africa, and political influence of women's movements, 172

African Americans: and citizenship, 29n4; and higher education, 69; and linkage of race and gender in politics, 9; political parties and barriers to representation of, 109n8; and sexual stereotypes of women, 78n5. *See also* black feminism; race; racism

aggregate analysis, of gender differences in political action, 50–3, 59–62

aggression, and gender differences in public opinion, 42–3

Aid to Families with Dependent Children, 36

Aldrich, John, 196n11

ambition, and women as candidates in American politics, 113–15

Americanists, and comparative literature on political status of women, 167–8, 175–6

American National Election Studies (ANES), 38, 41, 45, 68

American Political Development (APD): gender as category of analysis in, 12–29; and women's movements, 82–6

American Political Science Review (*APSR*), 2, 10n3–4

Andersen, Kristi, 57, 85, 98, 197n15

Anthony, Susan B., 85

Anzaldua, Gloria, 75

Ards, Angela, 73

Arizona, and women's issues in state legislature, 131

Badu, Eryah, 74

Baer, Denise L., 101, 102, 108

Baker, Paula, 27

Baldez, Lisa, 3, 9, 89–90, 189, 190, 195

Banaszak, Lee Ann, 9, 144, 162, 172, 173, 181–2, 189, 190, 193

Barakso, Maryann, 86–7, 88, 89

Barrett, Edith, 138

Beck, Susan Abrams, 131, 134

Beckwith, Karen, 3, 4, 5, 32, 57, 65, 95n3, 189, 190, 193

Bederman, Gail, 14

Bedolla, Lisa Garcia, 76

Beijing Platform for Action, 176

Beltran, Cristina, 75, 76

Bem, Sandra L., 34

Bem Sex Role Inventory, 34

Berelson, Bernard, 53–4, 55

Bernardino, Minerva, 25

Bernstein, Mary, 88

black feminism: Combahee River Collective and origins of, 64; and intersectional theory, 71–8

Bleich, Avraham, 43

Bonk, Kathy, 61

Borris, Eileen, 22

Bositis, David A., 102
Bourque, Susan, 8
Box-Steffensmeier, Janet, 36–7
Brady, Henry, 196n3
Bratton, Kathleen, 121, 138, 141
Braun, Carol, 166n29
Brent-Zook, Kristal, 73
Brown, Nadia, 37, 162, 191
Brown, Wendy, 15
Brubaker, Rogers, 62
Burns, Nancy, 8, 10n5, 32, 67, 68, 132, 173, 178–9
Burrell, Barbara, 114
Bush, George W., 12, 18, 29n5, 48
Butler, Judith, 165n15
Byrd, Ayana, 73
Bystrom, Dianne, 118

California, and women's issues in state legislature, 131
Campbell, Angus, 54
campaigning, and women as political candidates, 117–19
Caraway, Teri L., 197n20
Carroll, Susan J., 37, 134–5, 137, 138
Carter, Jimmy, 176
Catholic Church, 61, 87
Catt, Carrie Chapman, 85–6
Center for American Women and Politics (CAWP), 1, 134, 137
Child Labor Amendment, 85
Childs, Sarah, 157, 161
Chowdhury, Najma, 185–6
citizenship, and U.S. Constitution, 29n4
civic membership, and gender, 16–18
Clark, Janet, 188
Clarke, Cheryl, 72, 73
class. *See* socioeconomic status
Clemens, Elisabeth, 83
Clinton, Bill, 45, 49n2
Clinton, Hillary, 2, 126, 156, 176
Cohen, Cathy, 74–5, 76, 159
Coker, Cheo, 74
Coleman, John J., 109n3
collective identity, and social movements, 82, 87, 88, 93–4
Collins, Patricia Hill, 72, 74
Colorado, and women's legislative caucus, 100
Combahee River Collective, 64, 72, 78n2
Commission for Human Rights, 24
communism, and women's movements, 171

comparative politics: and future research on political women, 195; review of literature on political status of women, 167–79
comparative state feminism, 176–8
compassion: and gender differences in support of social welfare, 39, 40; and stereotypes of women as political candidates, 116
Concerned Women for America, 80, 91
Congress (U.S.): and gender differences in behavior, 107; numbers of women representatives in current, 164n5, 167, 183, 197n15; political ideology and women's representation in, 136, 137; women and position power in, 139; women's issues and committees of, 100; women's issues and Republican control of, 131, 135, 142–3, 144
Congressional Caucus for Women's Issues (CCWI), 7, 142
Conover, Pamela Johnston, 36, 44, 57, 59
consciousness: and gender differences in political action, 58–9, 63n7; theoretical approaches to gender in politics and feminist, 35–6, 43–4
conservatives and conservatism: and future research on political women, 192; and women's groups, 80
constituent responsiveness, and research on women in political office, 133–5
Constitution (U.S.): and definition of citizenship, 29n4; electoral system and women's political representation, 197n16; gender and civic membership, 17, 18; and gender equality, 167. *See also* Equal Rights Amendment
context: and future research on political women, 193–4; and gender differences in political action, 59; and individual-level analysis of gender and politics, 67–9; and women as office holders, 143–5
Convention to End All Forms of Discrimination Against Women (CEDAW), 167, 176, 179
Converse, Philip, 54
Cook, Elizabeth Adell, 36
Cooper, Frederick, 62
Costa, Paul T., 33, 42
Costain, Anne N., 59, 98, 105, 183
Costain, W. Douglas, 98, 105

Cott, Nancy F., 17, 60
Crenshaw, Kimberle, 72
criminal justice system, and gender
    differences in opinions on use of force,
    41-2
critical mass, of women in elective office,
    140-1, 192-3
cross-national studies. *See* comparative
    politics
cultural feminism, and women's movements,
    89, 95n10
culture: and theoretical perspectives on social
    movements, 82, 95n5; women's
    movements and intersection of political
    opportunities, 89-90; and women's
    participation in political parties, 107,
    185

Dahl, Robert, 197n16
Dahlerup, Drude, 146n4
Darcy, R., 188
Darling, Marsha, 138-9
Davis, Angela Y., 72
Davis, Nancy J., 35
Dawson, Michael, 61
Day, Christine L., 40
De Beauvoir, Simone, 54, 63n4, 165n15
De Boef, Suzanna, 36-7
decentralized states, and political
    participation, 184
democracy and democratization: and current
    political status of women in U.S.,
    181-95; and gender analysis in
    American Political Development, 18-20;
    role of U.S. women's movements in
    American, 79-94
Democratic Party: and gender equality
    reforms, 99; and gender gap in electoral
    politics, 31, 45-6, 48, 104, 136; and
    gender quotas, 175; and political
    ideology, 136, 137; and representation of
    women's policy preferences, 102; and
    women as political candidates, 117, 121;
    and women's movements, 91; women's
    participation and culture of, 107, 185.
    See also political parties
Derthick, Martha, 22
descriptive representation: and alternate
    theoretical views of representation, 150,
    157-8, 166n29; and political parties, 96,
    99, 100, 102-103, 106-108, 135-6. *See
    also* representation

Diamond, Irene, 3, 109n5
Diekman, Amanda B., 34-5, 40, 44-5
Di Stefano, Christine, 164n6
district magnitude, and comparative
    literature on women in elective office,
    174
Dodson, Debra L., 6, 134, 136, 137, 142,
    144, 146n4, 165n16
Dolan, Kathleen, 5, 126, 136-7, 143, 159,
    182, 186, 193
Dole, Elizabeth, 119-20
Donahue, Jesse, 133
Dovi, Suzanne, 8, 146n1, 186, 191, 194-5
Dryzek, John, 160
Duerst-Lahti, Georgia, 6
Duverger, Maurice, 54, 168

Eagly, Alice H., 34-5, 40, 44-5
Eastern Europe, and women's movements,
    171
economic status, and gender gap in electoral
    politics, 48. *See also* financing;
    socioeconomic status
economic vulnerability hypothesis, 36-7
education, as explanatory variable for
    political action, 68-9
egalitarianism, and gender differences in
    support of social welfare, 39-41
electoral system, gender and structural issues
    in, 120-3, 188, 197n16
eligibility pool, for women as political
    candidates, 113-14
EMILY's List, 107, 121
empathy, and gender differences in support
    of social welfare, 39
Enloe, Cynthia, 23
Epstein, Leon D., 101
Equal Rights Amendment (ERA), 24, 25, 45,
    60, 84, 91
Escobar-Lemmon, Maria, 176
essentialism, and feminist approaches to
    women's representation, 153-4
Europe. *See* Eastern Europe; European
    Union Treaty; France
European Union Treaty, 177
Evans, Jocelyn Jones, 107, 147n10

federalism, and political participation, 184
Feldman, Stanley, 40
feminism and feminist theory: and
    comparative literature, 176-8;
    contributions to understanding of

feminism and feminist theory (*cont.*)
  women's representation, 152–8; and
  definition of women, 165n15; and future
  research on political women, 194–5;
  gender equality and women's
  identification as, 165n16; historical
  legacies of international, 85–6; meaning
  and importance of gender, 165n20; and
  research on influence of women's
  movements on democracy, 82–5; and
  theoretical approaches to gender in
  politics, 35–6, 43–4; and use of term
  "women's movement," 80. *See also*
  black feminism; cultural feminism;
  women's movements
Fenno, Richard F., Jr., 137
Ferguson, Kathy, 164n10
Fernandes, Leela, 66
Ferraro, Geraldine, 2
Ferree, Myra Marx, 89
financing, of political campaigns, 121
Fiorina, Morris P., 105
Fisher, Kimberley, 10n4
Flexner, Eleanor, 196n2
Fogg-Davis, Hawley, 72
Ford, Lynne E., 136–7, 143
formalistic view, of representation, 150
Fox, Richard, 113–14, 115, 122, 146n5
Fraga, Luis Ricardo, 138
France, and gender quotas, 109n7, 174,
  180n6
Fraser, Nancy, 15–16, 22–3
Frechette, Guillaume, 109n7
Frederick, Brian, 114
Freedman, Paul, 61
"freedom of contract" doctrine, 17
Freeman, Jo, 2, 60, 91, 101, 102, 105
Fridkin, Kim. *See* Kahn, Kim Fridkin
Friedman, Elisabeth J., 175

Gaudet, Hazel, 53–4, 55
Geventa, John, 70
gay rights: and analysis of social movements
  and identity, 87, 88; gender differences
  in opinions on, 44; and marriage, 17
Gelkopf, Marc, 43
gender: aggregate and individual approaches
  to analysis of political action, 50–62;
  broad theoretical approaches to, 32–8;
  as category of analysis in American
  Political Development, 12–29; and civic
  membership, 16–18; and

democratization, 18–20; and differences
  in public opinion, 38–45; as dynamic
  category of analysis, 65; and electoral
  system, 188; as feature of state
  institutions, 20–1; feminism and
  meaning and importance of, 165n20;
  future research on political processes
  and, 194–5; and global context of
  political science research, 23–6; and
  ideology of inequality in U.S. political
  system, 66; and incumbency, 188–9; and
  intersectionality in political science
  research, 64–78; and liberalism, 15–16;
  as opposed to sex difference in political
  science research, 5–6, 10–11n7–8, 155;
  as political identity, 14–15; and political
  party system, 187–8; as property of
  groups and systems, 50, 51; and public
  policy, 21–3; and review of scholarship
  on political parties, 96–108; role of in
  politics as theme, 5–10; and use of
  terminology, 32, 109n1; and women as
  political candidates, 110–27. *See also*
  gender gap; gender quotas; sex
  differences; women
gender gap: and comparative political
  literature, 169–70; and Democratic
  Party, 31, 45–6, 48, 136; in electorial
  politics, 45–8; and growing political
  awareness of women, 34–5; and public
  opinion on social welfare, 38–41; use of
  term, 11n8
gender quotas: and candidates of major
  political parties, 99; and comparative
  literature on women in elective office,
  174–5, 180n6; and party representation
  in France, 109n7; and shifting of
  gendered political structures, 189
General Social Survey, 38
generational effects, and patterns of change,
  192–3
Gertzog, Irwin N., 142
Giddings, Paula, 72
Gilligan, Carol, 39, 42
Ginsburg, Ruth Bader, 2
global context and globalism: and gender in
  American Political Development, 23–6;
  and historical legacies of international
  feminism, 85–6; and transnational
  women's movements, 172–3
Godwin, Marcia L., 196–7n12
Goffman, Erving, 63n8

Goldstein, Joshua, 23
Gordon, Linda, 16, 22–3
Grant, Jacquelyn, 72
Grant, Ruth, 161
Gray, Virginia, 59
Grossholtz, Jean, 8
group consciousness, and political gender
    differences, 35
Gulf War, 41, 44
Gurin, Patricia, 58
Guy-Sheftall, Beverly, 72
gyroscopic representation, alternative
    approaches to women's representation,
    152

Hampton, Dream, 73
Hancock, Ange-Marie, 76
Hansen, Mark, 58, 59
Harris-Lacewell, Melissa, 70
Hartsock, Nancy, 109n5
Harvey, Anna L., 59, 61, 98, 104
Hawkesworth, Mary, 6, 71, 138–9
Haynie, Kerry, 138
Herrnson, Paul S., 118
heterosexism, and models of
    intersectionality, 72
Hine, Darlene Clark, 72
hip-hop music, and intersectional analysis,
    73–4
Hobby, Oveta Culp, 101
homophobia. *See* heterosexism
hooks, bell, 72, 74
Howell, Susan E., 40
Huddy, Leonie, 57
Hughes, Michael, 38–9
humanitarianism, and gender differences in
    support of social welfare, 39–41

ideational elements, and social movements,
    81, 82
identity: gender as form of political, 14–15;
    intersectionality and multiple locations
    of, 74–7; women's movements and
    multiple, 87–8. *See also* collective
    identity
ideology: and gender analysis in American
    Political Development, 28–9; of gender
    inequality in U.S. political system, 66;
    political parties, 136–7; political party
    leader perceptions about women's,
    107–108; role of gender in nationalist,
    14–15

inclusion problem, in research on women's
    representation, 150, 158–60
individual analysis: and current state of
    knowledge in participation literature,
    70–1; of gender differences in political
    action, 50–3, 59–62; and politicized
    context of gender, 67–9
Inglehart, Ronald, 35, 169
institutions: and analysis of gender-related
    public policy, 178; and gender analysis
    in American Political Development,
    20–1, 27–8; and women in elective
    office, 139–43; and women's movement
    activism, 81. *See also* organizations
interests argument, and women's
    representation in U.S., 157
International Council of Women, 85
International Woman Suffrage Alliance, 85
International Year of the Woman (1975), 172
internet, and women's advocacy groups,
    172–3
intersectionality and intersectional analysis:
    and gender gap in electoral politics, 47;
    and influence of women's movements on
    American democracy, 88–90; and
    partisan differences in ideology, 137–8;
    and political science research on role of
    women in American politics, 64–78
Iraq War, 41, 43
Iversen, Torben, 169–70

Jackson, Andrew, 27
Jones, Lisa, 73
Jones, Mark P., 189
Jones, Tamara, 73
Jordan, June, 72
Jordan-Zachery, Julia S., 76
Joya, Malalai, 166n30
Junn, Jane, 37, 78n4, 162, 191
justice argument, and female representation
    in U.S., 156

Kahn, Kim Fridkin, 58, 115, 120, 133
Kanter, Rosabeth Moss, 140, 141
Kathlene, Lyn, 133, 140
Katzenstein, Mary Fainsod, 61, 87, 193
Katznelson, Ira, 11n9, 59
Kelly, Rita Mae, 6, 10n4
Kenney, Patrick, 115
Kenney, Sally J., 6, 176
Keohane, Robert, 161
Kerber, Linda K., 14

Kessler-Harris, Alice, 22
Kinder, Donald, 58
King, Brayden, 95n9
King, Deborah K., 72
King, Desmond, 18, 29n3
Kirk, Celeste Montoya, 89–90
Kirkpatrick, Jeane J., 1, 2, 6, 9, 64, 181
Kitschelt, Herbert P., 183, 184
Kittilson, Miki Caul, 173–4, 175, 188,
    197n13
Klein, Ethel, 59
Kollman, Ken, 59, 61
Korean War, 41
Kriesi, Hanspeter, 184
Krook, Mona Lena, 161

labor, division of: and comparative research
    on the gender gap, 170; and studies of
    gender and political action, 56
Landrieu, Mary, 126
Larson, Carin, 137
Latin America, and women's movements,
    171
Latinas: and linkage of race and gender in
    American politics, 9; race and multiple
    locations of identity, 75; and state
    legislatures, 138, 198n23. *See also* race
law(s), and gender quotas, 174–5
Lawless, Jennifer, 113–14, 115, 126
Lay, J. Celeste, 118
Lazarsfeld, Paul F., 53–4, 55
Leader, Shelah Gilbert, 130
leadership: and legislative styles of women,
    132–3; and policy preferences of women
    as officeholders, 130–1; of political
    parties, 108
League of Nations, 24–5, 86
legislative service organizations (LSOs),
    142
legislature. *See* Congress; states and state
    legislative
legitimacy argument, and women's
    representation in U.S., 156–7,
    165–6n21, 166n26
Leighton, Melissa Vorhees, 5
liberalism: and gender in American Political
    Development, 15–16; and partisan
    stereotypes of women candidates, 116;
    and policy preferences of women as
    officeholders, 129
Lieberman, Robert, 18
Lijphart, Arend, 197n17

Lil' Kim (musician/artist), 73–4
Lin, Tse-Min, 36–7
Lipman-Blumen, Jean, 154
lobbying, and women's movements, 85
Lorde, Audre, 72

MacKinnon, Catharine, 155, 158
macro analysis. *See* aggregate analysis
Mann, Patricia, 165n15
Mansbridge, Jane J., 19, 60, 125, 151–2,
    157–8, 166n29
marginalization, and inclusion problem in
    women's representation, 159–60
marriage, and civic membership, 17
Matthews, Donald, 60
Mazur, Amy, 177
McCall, Leslie, 76
McCammon, Holly, 84, 89, 95n6
McConnaughy, Corrine M., 58, 59,
    103
McCrae, Robert R., 33
McDermott, Monika L., 57
McDonagh, Eileen, 16, 19–20
McGovern, George, 57
McPhee, William, 54
media coverage, of women as political
    candidates, 119–20
Mendelberg, Tali, 29n5
Mettler, Suzanne, 18–20, 22, 23, 58
Meyer, David S., 87, 91
Michigan Election Studies, 54, 57
micro analysis. *See* individual analysis
Middle East, and women's movements,
    172
military: and gender differences in attitudes
    toward use of governmental force, 41–4;
    and gender gap in electoral politics,
    47–8
Miller, Arthur H., 35
Miller, Warren, 54
Mink, Gwendolyn, 22
Minkoff, Debra, 93
Mishler, William, 174
mobilizing structures, and social movements,
    81–2
Moon, Katharine, 23
Moraga, Cherrie, 75
morality, and gender differences in public
    opinion, 44–5, 49
Morgan, Joan, 73
morselization, and role of gender in political
    action, 52–3

Mueller, Carol McClurg, 59
music. *See* hip-hop music

National Election Study, 123
nationalism, central role of gender in
    ideology of, 14–15
National Organization for Women (NOW),
    61, 86–7, 88, 99, 197n14. *See also*
    EMILY's List
National Women's Party, 24, 92
National Women's Political Caucus, 7
Nelson, Barbara, 22, 23, 185–6
Nepal, and gender quotas, 174
neutrality, and individual agency in current
    state of knowledge in literature on
    political participation, 70–1
Newman, Jody, 5
Nie, Norman, 78n4
Nincic, Donna J. & Miroslav, 41
Niven, David, 114
non-governmental organizations (NGOs),
    and transnational women's movements,
    173
Norrander, Barbara, 143
Norris, Pippa, 35, 164n5, 169
Norton, Anne, 29n3
Norton, Noelle H., 139, 160
Novkov, Julie, 17

O'Connor, Sandra Day, 1–2
Omolade, Barbara, 72
O'Neal, Shani Jamila, 73
Ordeshook, Peter C., 53
organizations, and gender differences in
    political action, 60. *See also* institutions;
    non-governmental organizations
Orloff, Ann Shola, 22, 23
Orren, Karen, 14, 28
Oxley, Zoe, 122

pacifism, and feminist consciousness, 43
Palmer, Barbara, 113, 122, 197n18
Pan American Union, 25
participation, political: average gender
    differences in, 196n3; culture of political
    parties and women's, 107; early history
    of study of gender and, 53–5; neutrality
    and individual agency in current state of
    knowledge on, 70–1; representation and
    components of democracy, 182–3; and
    women's movements, 183–5. *See also*
    politics

partisanship. *See* political parties
Pateman, Carole, 15, 185
patterns of change, and future research on
    political women, 192–3
Paul, Alice, 85–6
Pelosi, Nancy, 1, 101, 156
Perkins, Frances, 101n1
Perot, Ross, 49n2
personality, and theoretical approaches to
    gender differences in politics, 33–5,
    42–3
Peterson, V. Spike, 23
Phillips, Anne, 153, 156, 165–6n21, 166n32,
    185
Pitkin, Hanna, 150–1, 165n11
Plotze, David, 165n13
Plutzer, Eric, 118
policy, public: and comparative literature on
    women, 176–8; and gender analysis in
    American Political Development, 21–3;
    and influence of women's movements on
    American democracy, 85; racialization
    of, 11n9; and stereotypes of women as
    political candidates, 116; and women as
    officeholders, 129–32
political opportunities, and social
    movements, 81, 82
political opportunity model, and patterns of
    change, 192–3
political parties: control of and dominant
    factions, 142–3; and emergence of
    women as political candidates, 114–15;
    and gender quotas, 175; and ideology,
    136–7; organizational strength of,
    196n11; and representation of women,
    96–108; and stereotypes of women
    candidates, 116–17; and structure of
    elections, 121; system of as gendered,
    187–8. *See also* Democratic Party;
    National Women's Party; Republican
    Party
Political Role of Women, The (Duverger
    1955), 168
political science: aggregate and individual
    approaches to analysis of gender in
    political action, 50–62; current status of
    literature on women in American
    politics, 1–10, 181–95; gender as
    category of analysis, 12–29; and
    intersectionality in analysis of political
    roles of women, 64–78; political parties
    and representation of women, 96–108;

political science (*cont.*)
     and research on accomplishments of
         women in elective office, 128–46; and
         research on women in comparative
         democracies, 167–79; and role of U.S.
         women's movements in American
         democracy, 79–94; and theoretical
         approaches to gender, public opinion,
         and political reasoning, 31–49; and
         theories on women's representation in
         U.S., 148–64; and third parties, 197n14;
         and women as candidates in American
         politics, 110–27. *See also* politics
political space, and context, 193–4
political women, use of term, 2
Political Woman (Kirkpatrick 1974), 2, 64,
     181
politics: and comparative literature on
         women in elective office, 173–6; and
         concept of women as political actors as
         theme, 4, 5; current political science
         literature and status of women in
         American, 1–2; gender gap in electoral,
         45–8; redefinition of nature and content
         of as theme, 4; and role of gender as
         theme, 5–10. *See also* activism;
         conservatives and conservatism; gender
         gap; liberalism; participation; policy,
         public; political parties; political science;
         representation
Politics & Gender (journal), 75–6
Politics of Women's Liberation, The
     (Freeman 1975), 2
Pough, Gwendolyn D., 73, 74
power, of women in institutions, 141–2
primaries, and access of women to political
         candidacy, 120–1
promissory representation, and alternative
         views of representation, 151–2
proportional representation (PR) systems,
         and comparative literature on political
         status of women, 168, 174, 175
psychology: and gender differences in
         political action, 55, 57; and gender
         differences in vulnerability, 42–3;
         suffrage and racialization in U.S.
         political system, 66
public opinion: gender differences in, 38–45;
         impact of women as political
         candidates on, 125–6; and voting
         behavior in comparative politics,
         168–70

public policy. *See* policy
punctuated equilibrium, and patterns of
         change, 192–3

Quota Project, 175
quotas. *See* gender quotas

race: aggregate and individual analyses of
         gender in political action and, 51–2; and
         citizenship, 29n4; and gender differences
         in political action, 61; and gender
         equality movements, 8–9; and gender
         gap in electoral politics, 48; and partisan
         differences in ideology, 137–9; and
         public policy, 11n9; and representation
         in political parties, 109n2; and response
         of political parties to gender, 108; and
         women's movements, 80–1. *See also*
         African Americans; Latinas
racism, and women of color in elective office,
         138–9
rap music. *See* hip-hop music
Reagan, Ronald, 45, 47, 48
recruitment pool, for political candidates,
         114
Reed, Adolph, Jr., 152
Reger, Jo, 86, 87–8
regionalism, and women as political
         candidates, 122. *See also* South
Reingold, Beth, 5, 131, 134, 138, 155, 157,
         169, 194
religion and religiosity: and gender
         differences in morality, 44; and gender
         gap in electoral politics, 48; institutions
         and gender differences in political
         action, 60. *See also* Catholic Church
representation: gender analysis and forms of,
         19; participation and political women in
         U.S. democracy, 182–3, 185–90; theories
         of women's in U.S., 148–64. *See also*
         descriptive representation; substantive
         representation; symbolic representation
Republican Party: and gender quotas, 175;
         gender and partisan stereotypes, 100,
         117; and influence of women's
         movements, 102; and political ideology,
         136, 137; and women as political
         candidates, 117, 121; women's issues
         and control of Congress, 131, 135,
         142–3, 144; women's participation and
         culture of, 107, 185. *See also* political
         parties

Research Network on Gender Politics
(RNGS), 177
reserved seats, and gender quotas, 174
revolution: and concept of women as
political actors, 4; and current status of
women in American politics, 1, 9–10,
64–7, 181, 195
Richards, Ann, 57
Riker, William H., 53
Ritter, Gretchen, 6, 7, 17, 155, 167, 172,
173, 190, 191, 195
Roberts, Tara, 73
Robinson, Robert V., 35
Rohlinger, Deana, 87
role-model argument, and female
representation in U.S., 156
Roosevelt, Eleanor, 24
Rosenbluth, Frances, 169–70
Rosenstone, Steven J., 58, 59
Rosenthal, Cindy Simon, 140–1, 142
Rubel, Tammy, 40
Rucht, Dieter, 189
Ruddick, Sara, 42
Runyon, Anne Sisson, 23

Saltzstein, Grace Hall, 132, 146n7
Sanbonmatsu, Kira, 8, 90–1, 104, 114, 122,
124, 175, 186, 187, 190, 197n14
Sander, Lynn, 29n5, 58
Sapiro, Virginia, 22, 44, 57, 109n5, 118
Schaffner, Margaret A., 10n3
Schattschneider, E. E., 98, 186
Schlafly, Phyllis, 91
Schlozman, Kay Lehman, 196n3
Schroedel, Jean Reith, 196–7n12
Schroeder, Pat, 117
Schuhmann, Robert A., 146n5
Schumaker, Paul, 132
Schumpeter, Joseph, 156, 165n18
Schwartz, Shalom H., 40
Schwindt-Bayer, Leslie A., 174
Scott, James, 70
self-interest, and theoretical approaches to
gender in politics, 36–8, 40
Seltzer, Richard A., 5
Senate, representation of women in, 183
sex, and use of term "gender," 32, 181–2
sex difference: in legislative and leadership
styles, 133; as opposed to gender in
political science research, 5–6,
10–11n7–8, 155; in policy leadership,
131; in policy preferences of

officeholders, 129–30; and structural
forms of discrimination, 165n19; and
study of gender and political action, 54
sexism, and women of color in elective office,
138–9
Sex Roles in the Statehouse (Diamond 1977),
3
sexual assault, and gender differences in
attitudes toward violence, 43
Sexual Contract, The (Pateman 1988), 15
sexuality: and intersectional analysis, 72–4;
and stereotypes of black women, 78n5.
See also gay rights; heterosexism
Shange, Ntozoke, 74
Shepard-Towner Act, 85
Sherron De Hart, Jane, 60
Siegel, Reva, 28
Sigel, Roberta S., 59, 109n1
Simien, Evelyn M., 76
Simon, Dennis, 113, 122, 197n18
Skocpol, Theda, 14, 18, 22, 23, 84, 85
Skowronek, Stephen, 14
Smith, Barbara, 72, 73
Smooth, Wendy G., 66, 76, 138–9
social change, relationship of women's
movements to large-scale, 90–2
socialization: and literature on gender and
political action, 55, 63n6; and
theoretical approaches to gender
differences in politics, 33–5, 115
social movements: definition of, 79–80; and
elite party realignment, 105; and gender
differences in political action, 61–2;
theoretical perspectives on, 81–2, 95n5.
See also women's movements
Social Security Act, 22
social welfare: and gender analysis in
American Political Development, 22–3,
28; gender and differences in public
opinion on, 38–41, 48
socioeconomic status (SES): and education as
explanatory variable for political action,
68–9; and future research on political
women, 191–2. *See also* economic status
sociology, and scholarly analyses of gender
and political activity, 55
Solomon, Zahava, 43
South: and women as political candidates,
122; and women in state legislatures,
143
Soviet Union, and women's movements, 171
Springer, Kimberley, 87–8

Squires, Judith, 161
Staggenborg, Suzanne, 83, 86–7, 89, 91
standards problem, and research on women's
    representation, 8, 150, 158–60
Stanley, Jeanie, 57
Stanton, Elizabeth Cady, 85
states and state legislature: representation of
    women in, 183; and sex differences in
    legislative styles, 133; and sex
    differences in policy leadership, 131; and
    studies of women of color, 138; women
    and southern political culture, 143
Steenbergen, Marco R., 40
Stehlik-Barry, Kenneth, 78n4
Stenner, Karen, 57–8
stereotypes: black women and sexual, 78n5;
    of women as candidates for elective
    office, 115–20, 124–5
Stokes, Atiya Brown, 118
Stokes, Donald, 54
substantive representation: and alternative
    theoretical views of representation,
    150–1; and political parties, 100, 102,
    103–108, 135–6; and women as political
    candidates, 125. *See also* representation
suffrage. *See* race; Voting Rights Act;
    woman's suffrage movement
surrogate representation, and alternative
    forms of democratic representation, 19,
    165n12
Swers, Michele L., 107, 131, 137, 139,
    144
symbolic representation: and alternative
    theoretical views of representation, 150;
    and political parties, 125–6

Tamerius, Karin L., 155
Tarrow, Sidney, 184, 185, 189
Taylor, Verta, 83
Taylor-Robinson, Michelle M., 176
Terkildsen, Nayda, 57
Terracciano, Antonio, 33
terrorism: gender differences in response to,
    43; and gender gap in electoral politics,
    48
Tharps, Lori, 73
Thomas, Sue, 130, 142
Thorson, Stuart, 197n15
Tickner, J. Ann, 23, 24
tokenism, and critical mass of women in
    institutions, 141
Tolleson-Rinehart, Sue, 57, 58

transformative argument, and female
    representation in U.S., 157
trust argument, and women's representation
    in U.S., 156, 165–6n21, 166n26
Tubman, Harriet, 64
Tuch, Steven A., 38–9

Unifem, 176
United Nations (UN): and history of
    women's rights, 25, 86; and
    transnational women's movements, 172.
    See also Convention to End All Forms of
    Discrimination Against Women
    (CEDAW); Universal Declaration of
    Human Rights; World Conferences on
    Women
United States: and current political status of
    women, 1–2, 181–92; and political
    status of women in comparative
    democracies, 167–79, 196n6–8. *See also*
    Congress; democracy; politics;
    representation; Senate; South; states and
    state legislatures
Universal Declaration of Human Rights, 24

values, and gender differences in support of
    social welfare, 40
Verba, Sidney, 196n3
Vermont, and lesbian-gay movements, 87, 88
Vietnam War, 41
violence, and gender differences in attitudes
    toward governmental use of force, 42–4
visibility, and effects of integration and
    intimacy on gender, 52
voluntary quotas, and gender quota laws,
    174
vote choice: and gender gap in electoral
    politics, 45–8; and public opinion in
    comparative politics, 168–70; and
    women as political candidates, 123–5
Voting Rights Act (1965), 18, 66

Walker, Alice, 78n1
Wallace, Michele, 69, 72
Walsh, Katherine Cramer, 118
war, and gender differences in public
    opinion, 43, 44
Welch, Susan, 188
Weldon, S. Laurel, 76, 144–5, 151, 177
Welke, Barbara Young, 28
West Coast Hotel v. Parrish (1937), 17
White, Julie Anne, 76

Whittier, Nancy, 87
Wilcox, Clyde, 36, 143
Williams, Melissa, 162
Wolbrecht, Christina, 3, 91, 131, 193, 195
Womanism. *See* black feminism
woman's suffrage movement, 83–4, 95n9,
    103–104
women: as candidates in American politics,
    110–27; comparative literature on
    political status of, 167–79; current
    political status of in U.S., 1–2, 181–95;
    feminist theory and definition of,
    165n15; review of research on
    accomplishments of in elective office,
    128–46; revolution and concept of as
    political actors, 4, 5; and theories of
    representation of in U.S., 148–64. *See
    also* gender
women's movements: and comparative
    politics, 170–3; and gender differences
    in political action, 60; influence of on
    American democracy, 79–94; influence
    of within political parties, 104–105; as

key actors in political change, 189–90;
    and political participation, 183–5; and
    transnational cooperation among
    organizations, 24–5. *See also* feminism
    and feminist theory
Women's Trade Union League (WTUL), 83
Wong, Cara, 58
Woodall, Gina, 133
Woolf, Virginia, 164n9
World Conferences on Women (UN), 172,
    176
World War II, 41

Yamin, Priscilla, 17
"Year of the Woman" (1992), 135
Young, Iris Marion, 15, 50, 149, 154–5,
    159
Young, Lisa, 91, 98–9, 104, 107

zero-sum dynamic, between women's
    political influence and strength of
    political parties, 98–9
Zipp, John F., 118